Caste and Kinship in a Modern Hindu Society

BIBLIOTHECA HIMALAYICA
SERIES III
VOLUME 18

ART – ARCHAEOLOGY – ARCHITECTURE – RELIGION – ETHNOLOGY

THE PURPOSE OF
BIBLIOTHECA HIMALAYICA
IS TO MAKE AVAILABLE WORKS
ON THE CIVILIZATIONS AND NATURAL
HISTORY OF CENTRAL ASIA AND THE HIMALAYA

Caste and Kinship in a Modern Hindu Society

The Newar City of Lalitpur, Nepal

Mark Pickett

Orchid Press

Mark Pickett
CASTE AND KINSHIP IN A MODERN HINDU SOCIETY:
The Newar City of Lalitpur, Nepal

ORCHID PRESS
P.O. Box 1046,
Silom Post Office,
Bangkok 10504, Thailand
www.orchidbooks.com

BIBLIOTHECA HIMALAYICA

Front cover image: During the Mohani festival, a priest carries the image of Taleju Bhavani and the sword of Sri Nivas; Lalitpur, Kathmandu.

Back cover image: Children dressed up for Krishna Pujā; Lalitpur, Kathmandu.

ISBN 978-974-524-136-7

For Becky,

for my parents,

and for Philip, Sarah, Lydia, Katie and Beth

Acknowledgements

In the course of my research I have accumulated a lot of debts. My advisor at Tribhuvan University, Prem Kumar Khatry, was the first to suggest what to me was the wild idea of working on a doctorate. I am grateful that, in turn, he accepted the challenge to be my guide through the convoluted corridors of studentdom in Nepal. I am thankful to Tulasi Ram Vaidya and Dilli Ram Dahal of the research committee, to Tri Ratna Manandhar, the Dean of the Faculty of Humanities and Social Sciences, and Mukunda Aryal, the Head of the Central Department of Culture who patiently kept me on track throughout the course of my research.

I have a great deal of respect and thanks for the people of Haugaḥ, Mangaḥ, Kuti Saugaḥ, Ikhā, Cāka Bahi, Yānamugaḥ and Yāngu Bāhāḥ who bore my incessant inquisitions with the patience of Job. They were always ready to sit and chat and never gave me the impression that they felt I was intruding. Those who deserve special mention are Dil Mohan Tamrakar, Hem Lal Tamrakar, Surendra Silpakar, Madan Lal Tamrakar, Dharma Krishna Sikahmi, Nem Krishna Tamrakar and Binod Rajkarnikar of Lalitpur, and Hiraman Kaji Tamrakar and his sons Govinda and Gopal of Bhaktapur. To their wives and daughters who selflessly plied me with sustaining tea, and often much more, through those long sessions, I am indeed most grateful. Kashinath Tamot and Hemraj Shakya gave some very helpful advice on historical and linguistic matters.

David Gellner, Declan Quigley and Bruce Owens answered numerous questions about their writings. Prem Kumar Khatry, Tulasi Ram Vaidya, Dilli Ram Dahal, Mary Morgan, David Gellner, Richard Hivner and John Locke read the manuscript and suggested many helpful corrections. Don Messerschmidt provided important editorial assistance on behalf of the publisher, Orchid Press. Mahesh Man Singh of Lalitpur Sub-Municipality furnished me with maps of the city that I could use as base maps for my own. Craig Drown of Sustainable Solutions rescued me from many a slough of despond encountered during word processing.

It was Ravi and Nirmala Rajkarnikar of 'House' who introduced me to the complexities of Newar life. They welcomed my wife and me into their home and have helped us in a great many ways. Nirmala was my Nepali teacher for two years and helped me get started on Newar. Together they acted as *thākāli* and *thākāli nakī* for the First Rice-Feeding of our daughter Lydia, and Ravi kept watch by my bedside when I was seriously ill.

My father, John Malcolm Pickett died while I was in the midst of research. He and my mother Sylvia Doris Pickett always supported me in my work though I know it has often been difficult for them with me being so far from home. Finally, my wife Becky and children Philip, Sarah, Lydia, Catherine and Elizabeth have put up with a great deal of inconvenience as I have gone about my work. Becky has pressed on through many difficulties with utmost patience and steadfast resilience.

> A wife of noble character who can find? She is worth far more than rubies.
>
> Her husband has full confidence in her and lacks nothing of value.
>
> She brings him good, not harm, all the days of her life.
>
> (Proverbs 31: 10-12)

Contents

Illustrations

Plates

Tables

Figures

Maps

Preface

'Like heaven, in every way it is delightful.' So wrote the 17th century poet Kunu Sharma of the glorious City of Lalitpur in what today sounds like tourist-brochure excess (1961: 26 and 57, *sloka* 93). The pandit had, of course, a particular purpose in writing. My purpose is different. I am not out to wax lyrical on the majesty of the city. But, like my predecessor, with whom I feel a certain affinity, I have come to love the city all the same. Pandit Sharma would not have felt any compulsion to claim objectivity about his writing. Neither do I. The city has changed me, just as, in some minute way, I have changed the city.

Having said that, I approach my study under the assumption that it is actually possible and, moreover, worthwhile to come to what at first sight (to the outsider) is an overwhelming tangle of cultural facts that constitute Newar culture, and begin to make sense of them. I am well aware of the inadequacies of my work. There are loose ends, questions unanswered, and interpretations that may be proved to be untenable. So be it. In that sense the work is incomplete. Such a realization should never prevent the presentation of such a work, however. So as I present this I beg, in the good Asian tradition, the learned reader's forgiveness for any errors that may have crept in. They are all my own.

In transliterating Newar into English I have chosen to take the route that produces the most readable text while ensuring that the reader can make a pretty decent attempt at pronunciation. Newar is a Tibeto-Burman language that has a number of sounds that are not found in the national language, Nepali. Having said that, the influence of Sanskrit is huge and most Newars only read their mother tongue in Devanagari script. In keeping with Nepali and other Sanskrit-derived languages, a vowel may be long or short. In most cases this makes little difference to the way the word is pronounced. The exception to this is that of 'a'. I differentiate the two sounds by the use of the macron over the long 'a', thus: ā. It is also helpful in pronunciation to be alerted to the nasalization of a vowel. Although there are two ways to nasalize a vowel—the *candrabindu* (ँ) and the *anusvara* (ं)—I have simplified this by using only the tilde (˜), thus: 'ã', as it makes no difference in pronunciation. As with other Sanskrit influenced languages, Newar uses three sibilants. 'स' is shown as 's' but the other two, 'श' and 'ष' are not distinguished, both being written as 'sh' as the pronunciation is unaffected. (The one exception to this spelling is in the word 'Sri', which simply looks awkward when it is written 'Shri' and is rarely pronounced with the English 'sh' anyway.)

The *visarga*, that lengthens the preceding vowel, is not shown as the colon as it creates too much confusion, but as 'ḥ'. The non-aspirated fricative 'च' is shown as 'c' in keeping with standard convention and the aspirated 'छ' as 'ch'. *C* then is pronounced like the first 'ch' of 'church' and never as 'k'; *ch* is pronounced with aspiration. I have made no attempt to distinguish between either the retroflex or dental 't', 'th', 'd' or 'dh' as it makes much less difference in Newar than it does in Nepali. Likewise the three varieties of 'n' are not distinguished. *V* is pronounced like 'w' in combination with other consonants (e.g., Sarasvati) but closer to 'b' in other situations (e.g., Vajrācārya).

The letter 'y' is used to express a sound not found in Nepali. The sound 'ay' at the end of the word *kay* (meaning 'son') then should be pronounced like 'care'. The combined sound 'ri' is left as it is rather than complicate things by introducing a diacritic. Finally, the last letter of the alphabet 'ज्ञ' is transliterated, in keeping with convention, as 'jñ' but is to be pronounced 'gyan'.

Generally, I have followed the spelling in Thakur Lal Manandhar's *Newari-English Dictionary* (1986) and where I have used Nepali this is according to the *Nepāli Brihat Shabdakosh* published by the Royal Nepal Academy (Pokharel *et al.* 1983). The exceptions to Manandhar (after Gellner 1992: 37-8) are the use of 'aḥ' instead of the more traditional 'o' and the use of Sanskrit *tatsamas* (words in the same form as in Sanskrit) instead of *tadbhavas* (words deriving from Sanskrit, but taking a different form). Also after Gellner, I have usually only included the Sanskrit inherent 'a' at the end of a word when it is normally pronounced by Newars themselves. Diacritics have been omitted from personal names and well-known place names as well as from capitals. Sanskritic, rather than colloquial, names of gods have been employed to make it easier to compare with other South Asian ethnographies.

Italicized words are Newar unless otherwise indicated. I have also adopted the South Asianist convention of writing a particular caste name with a capital letter. So 'Blacksmith' is a member of a caste, many of which practice smithery, but 'blacksmith' is a person so engaged regardless of his caste. I have used the term 'Nepalese' to refer to the people of Nepal as well as an adjective in keeping with Nepalese writers, reserving 'Nepali' for the language. Similarly, 'Newar' is both a noun and an adjective, but, per current usage, 'Newar' refers also to the language.

This book is based upon Mark Pickett's 2005 PhD dissertation, *Caste and Kingship in the Newar City of Lalitpur* (Kathmandu, Tribhuvan University, Faculty of Humanities and Social Sciences, Central Department of Culture). Dr Pickett is currently lecturing at the Wales Evangelical School of Theology.

Abbreviations

CE	Common Era or Christian era (*Anno Domini*, AD)
CNRS	Centre National de Recherche Scientifique, Paris
cf.	compare
CUP	Cambridge University Press
EJS	*European Journal of Sociology*
f./ff.	and following pages
H.	Hindi
IJHS	*International Journal of Hindu Studies*
Np.	Nepali
NS	*Nepal Samvat*, the era traditionally used by Newars, which began in November 879 CE
Nw.	Newar (*Nepal Bhāshā*)
OUP	Oxford University Press
SV	under the word (Latin *sub verbo*)
Skt.	Sanskrit
VS	*Vikram Samvat*, the official Nepalese era, which began in 57 BCE

1. Introduction

> An attempt to disentangle an incomprehensible conglomeration, and to show the system behind a mass of seemingly disjunct facts, might help experts to realize that very good reasons usually lie behind what are, apparently, queer and peculiar patterns of behaviour.
> Gutschow and Kölver (1975: 6)

1.1. Purpose of and approach to the study

This is intended as a contribution to the anthropology of caste, and of Hindu society more generally. Specifically, it sets out to examine the relationship of caste to both kinship and kingship in the society of the Newars of the Kathmandu Valley in the hope that it will shed light on both Newar society in particular and South Asian societies in general.

The institution of caste, though modified and transformed by South Asia's contact with modernity, is far from dead. Caste-based societies are invariably looked upon as essentially a system of hierarchy, with Brahman Priest at the top and Untouchable Sweeper at the bottom.[1] This position, championed by Louis Dumont in his magnum opus, *Homo Hierarchicus* (1980 [1972]), is the dominant approach both of foreign observers and of many South Asians themselves. This long-standing viewpoint was challenged, however, half a century ago by Arthur Maurice Hocart, whose important work, *Caste: A Comparative Study* (1950), argued for a sacrificial theory of caste with the notion of kingship at its centre. Hocart's position was taken up and expounded by Declan Quigley in his *The Interpretation of Caste* (1993). The caste system, assert Hocart and Quigley, is produced by the tension that exists between the forces of kinship and kingship. To test this theory I have looked at one South Asian community, the Newar City of Lalitpur in the Kathmandu Valley. More specifically I have observed a little-known caste of artisans who call themselves the *Pengu Daḥ* (lit. 'Four Groups') in order to see the structure and functioning of kinship, and have examined their relations to the city as a whole, and in particular to the institution of kingship as it is expressed, no longer personally but symbolically, in space and time during the festivals of the city.

The Pengu Daḥ consists of the following four groups:

Colloquial	Honorific	English
Tamvaḥ	Tāmrakār, Tamot	Coppersmiths
Sikaḥmi	Bārāhi, Sthāpit, Kāsthakār, Shilpakār, Sikaḥmi	Carpenters
Lwahākaḥmi	Shilpakār, Shilākār	Stonemasons
Marikaḥmi	Rājkarnikār, Halawāi, Haluwāi	Sweetmakers

The central problem of this study of the Pengu Daḥ is threefold:

1. What makes the Pengu Daḥ a caste, and what differentiates it from the other castes around it?
2. How does the institution of kingship express itself in the life of the city?
3. How may we characterize the relationship between the two?

In asking these questions, however, we are assuming that it is possible, even beneficial, to answer them with some kind of coherence. But how near can we get to really 'knowing' who the Pengu Daḥ, for instance, actually are? Any degree of understanding will come only as the observer participates in the life of the observed. This I have attempted to do. An exhaustive study of Lalitpur's social system would include a detailed study of each caste as I have attempted here for the Pengu Daḥ. This is, however, beyond the resources of the present writer and, moreover, is unnecessary; others have written extensively on various castes of Lalitpur. Foremost of these other studies is Gellner's work (1984–97) on the Shākya/Vajrācārya combine.[2] Gellner and Pradhan (1995) have introduced us to the Maharjans of the city, as has Gellner (1995c) to the low castes of Lalitpur. Others have written extensively on analogous castes of other cities such as Quigley (1984–95) on the Shresthas of Dhulikhel, Lewis on the Urāy of Kathmandu (1984–96), Toffin (1977–95) on various castes of Bhaktapur, Panauti and Pyangaon, and Levy (1990) on Bhaktapur. I have learned much from these works and interact freely with them in the discussion below.

Plate 1. Some of my Tāmrakār informants in front of their shops, Cāka Bahi.

In order to observe the culture of Lalitpur, I lived with my family for several years just outside the old boundaries of the city in Puco (Pulchok, Np.). It proved impossible to rent a house that was big enough for a large family in the middle of the old city itself, rentable properties being found, almost exclusively, in the newer 'suburbs'. The compact character of Newar settlements is such, however, that I could get into the centre of the city in five minutes on my bicycle. Though not fluent in Newar I was able, after a couple of years, to engage on most topics in that language and when I felt out of my depth my interlocutors were kind enough to switch to Nepali, in which I am more able (Plate 1). Over the course of the years of my research I was able to observe nearly all the festivals of the city and several more than once. Certain neighbourhoods of the city became very familiar to me as I also became familiar to their inhabitants. I established a rapport with many families and was able to sit frequently with the men in their shops to pump them with what must have seemed relentless questions. With one exception, I was invited to attend all the life-cycle rituals that a Newar goes through and did so repeatedly during the course of the study.[3]

Living outside the actual confines of the old city, however, occasionally put me at a disadvantage. This was most pronounced in my total inability to observe the cremation of a member of the Pengu Daḥ. No matter how often I informed my friends of my desire to be present at a funeral I was never called. Had I lived in the locality I would have heard immediately when someone died. It is a measure, perhaps, of the desire for privacy at such a time that I always found out after the initial death rites had all been completed. For those initial death rites, and a few other events in which it was not possible for me to be in attendance, I have had to rely on the descriptions of my informants. Furthermore, at the performance of certain rites I was told, as others have been before me that, as a foreigner, I was not welcome (e.g., see Gellner 1992: 308). One such occasion was the divinizing rite of a Tāmrakār man at his Old-Age Initiation. His son was most embarrassed by the insistence on my exclusion by the Brahman priest.

It is often impossible to both participate in and observe many festivals at the same time. As Gellner says, 'Newar culture is so complicated that, taken literally, participant observation sometimes seems like a contradiction in terms: either one observes or one participates, but to do both is impossible' (1992: 7). In a number of rites so much is going on at one time that a platoon of observers is required to really get an overall picture. I employed no research assistants but tried to get around this difficulty by observing the same rite several times and by carefully interviewing the participants after the event. As a Christian there were certain ritual acts that I felt I could not participate in without violating my conscience: I could not join my friends in the worship of other deities, though I often observed such rituals. Clearly, then, I was often more of an observer than I was a participant.

In one arena I took every opportunity I could to participate in the life of my host community—that of feasts! Newars, by their own admission, eat a lot of feasts. The Nepali saying, '*Parbati bigrincha mojle, Newār bigrincha bhojle*' (Parbatiyā [Nepalese of the hills] destroy themselves with pleasures, Newars destroy themselves with feasting) is frequently recited, more often than not by Newars themselves.

Evans-Pritchard argues that anthropologists should not take their wives into the field because they form an emotionally self-sufficient island (in Srinivas 1998: 217). I contend, however, that by having my wife and children with me I gained a great deal. Three of my children were born in the same maternity ward where many Lalitpurians have entered the world. I would not have had any sense of how the Newar approaches pregnancy and childbirth had I not sat with my wife through a host of advice sessions by well-meaning friends. Furthermore, in giving our daughter, Lydia, a somewhat attenuated First Rice-Feeding ceremony we were able to experience first-hand something of the significance of such life-cycle rituals and their attendant feasts.

The need for reflexivity in the ethnographic process is clear. The process of reflexive thinking seeks to make explicit the interaction between observer and observed in the ethnographic encounter. Over recent decades, however, there has been a growing introversion in ethnographic writing in which the author talks more about himself than about the people he is ostensibly describing. In reaction to the study of the 'Other' many ethnographers have turned inward and produced, in the end, a study of the self as researcher, author and theorist. For this reason Steven Parish asks the pertinent question whether reflexivity has finally been anything more than a reprivileging of Western voices (1997a: x). I trust the present study has avoided such a pitfall.

Is it meaningful to compare societies? Some would argue that as there is not, in their view, any real unity in human experience, it is nonsense to even attempt such a project. I argue on the contrary that there *is* an indivisible unity to the human species. The diversity of human cultures is vast. But there are certain phenomena that are common to all men.[4] All men create; all communicate. The reason I can have some understanding of Newar culture is that there is a basic ability to communicate across the cultural chasm that is not present in the relationship between myself and, say, the amoeba that has taken up residence in my digestive tract.

In my research, many long hours of observation were always followed up by many more long hours of discussion with key informants. The most helpful informants I discovered were mostly senior men. Not only were they usually able to tell me what was going on but they also, in their capacity as shopkeepers, sometimes had long periods of relative quietude to engage in friendly discourse with their importunate visitor. Asking the 'right' person for his (or her) interpretation of a local custom is a tricky business. Mikesell (1993: 233) accuses Levy of relying much too heavily on the collaboration of two Brahmans and a western-educated Vajrācārya Sanskrit scholar in his study of Bhaktapur (Levy 1990), thereby making his analysis essentially biased toward the perspective of the literati. I would not pretend that my informants, or myself for that matter, were in any way objective in their perspective on Lalitpur's culture. My study largely lacks the angle that a woman would give the subject. My interaction with women was, though not heavily restricted, definitely constrained by my maleness. Furthermore I had little interaction with Untouchable caste members of Lalitpur's society. For the most part, then, my information came in personal observation and in interviews with Pengu Daḥ men in their shops and out on the streets.

Any description of Newar culture in a foreign language inevitably demands the translation of local categories of thought and action. Without such translation the description would be meaningless to the reader and any cross-cultural value of the study would be lost. Fuller (1992) criticizes Marriott and Inden (1985) for their insistence that any structural analysis of Hindu religion and society is dependent on the categories of western thought. There is, they say, no such separation made by the Hindus themselves. Fuller says that actually the social science of India has not developed from thought about Western as opposed to Indian cultural realities, but from thought about their interaction. Thus, he concludes, 'when we look closely at 'Indian categories'—as we must—we have to do so through a comparative, cross-cultural lens' (Fuller 1992: 10).

In describing the culture of Lalitpur I have tried to avoid the temptation to write in terms of how 'different' the Newars are. After Said (1994 [1979]), Inden criticizes the 'Orientalist' approach that holds, or simply assumes, that the essence of Indian civilization is just the opposite of the West's, which is portrayed as rational and scientific (1986: 402). Indological discourse, he asserts, gave the West a pretext for colonization with the rationale that, if they can't rule themselves properly we had better do it for them.

In contrast to Inden (1986: 414) and Steven Parish (1997a: 98) I have approached this work under the assumption that there is a certain coherence to culture. Parish roundly criticizes Dumont for his belief in a unity of Indian culture. For Parish an important aspect of the way that Newars view caste is that those views are often contradictory. It is not just that there are different ways of viewing caste from within caste society, but individuals within that society may have conflicting and even contradictory views. For this reason Parish does not attempt to come up with any one overall theory or model of caste to explain the system as a whole. His analysis intentionally leaves this question open. 'Dumont's project,' as Parish puts it, 'was to isolate an ideology and show how it constituted the structure for social life' (1997a: 12). Parish, on the other hand, attempts to isolate the critique of ideology in everyday consciousness. In this he is consciously exploring an area of inquiry that was defined by a dialogue between Hans Georg Gadamer and Jürgen Habermas.

Parish writes: 'We have little basis for assuming that any ideology or discourse, dominant or subversive, entirely determines what social actors think and feel: as if actors did not have lives, minds, interpretive powers' (1997a: 64). On this basis, Parish indicts *Homo Hierarchicus* with the charge that it is the product of Western minds, 'an apparition that mirrors the way the West has imagined India' (ibid.: 66). 'In making hierarchy the central principle of Indian life, the principle that gives an identity to India,' he says, 'I think Dumont's paradigm has substituted a part... for the whole...' (ibid.: 78). It is not, argues Parish, that the principle of hierarchy is central but that '... hierarchy and equality entail and presuppose each other' (ibid.: 85). But Parish overstates his point. Just because hierarchy entails equality it does not follow that one society cannot be more hierarchical than another. Dumont was right to emphasize India's value of hierarchy. Where he went wrong was in his attempt to explain everything in Indian culture in terms of that single value.

In positing the significance of constructions of order to an understanding of Newar culture, Parish sees in it an invitation to counter-constructions 'in a kind of dialectic of rhetorics' (ibid.: 151). He refuses to bring any closure to the interpretive process since, he asserts, no such closure is evident in the culture itself. Robert Levy, Parish's mentor, seems to disagree. In his monumental study of Bhaktapur, *Mesocosm,* Levy writes that he is aware of the potential criticism of his work as 'liable to appear regressive, ideological, Orientalist, and various other unpleasant things...' (1990: 9). He goes on to defend his approach, however, as that of describing a normative order, an ideal order. The book is in part, he explains, a presentation of the order of the elite informants he interviewed. 'For Bhaktapur, that conception is not just the wishful ideological thinking and propaganda of precarious elites but a powerful force that in itself helps to create order.'

> This coherent symbolic order is a peculiar attempt to order a community. It is not in itself adequate to represent 'the life of the community.' That life has many aspects, levels, and kinds of order and disorder. To try to make one aspect the 'real' one is to engage in ideological polemics or, worse, tendentious and covert use of the exotic. However, to neglect order where it does exist is another and peculiarly postmodern move in itself. (Ibid.: 10)

Parish employs Hegelian terminology to describe the relation of the religion of power and the religion of purity in Levy's work. '*Mesocosm* suggests how Tantric power and Brahmanical purity achieved a synthesis in the role of the Rājopādhyāya Brahmans whose religious power and mastery of sacred mysteries are certainly as critical to their place in society as their purity' (Parish 1997b: 457). In positing a synthesis of conflictual meanings, says Parish, Levy is suggesting that the citizens of Bhaktapur are actively avoiding the rational imperative to follow one or other position to its logical conclusion. Levy argues that Newars often resolve their ambivalences about animal sacrifice by resorting to a sort of Kirkegaardian 'leap of faith', affirming the religious truth of the act in the face of its apparent contradiction of the moral order (ibid.: 456).[5]

Gellner points out that in the debate over the unity of culture Levy and Parish are on opposite sides (1997c: 556). Since Émile Durkheim it has been one of the ambitions of social and cultural anthropologists to produce a coherent account of the people they study (ibid.: 541). It has become recognized, however, that such coherence is not a static phenomenon but has to be continually policed and created. Gellner then asks whether such cultures as have been described are not just imagined but essentially imaginary? He goes on to assert that to produce a systematic account of a culture is not wrong so long as the researcher remains alert to conflict, polysemy, etc. The postmodern presupposition that all societies are equally and inherently chaotic cannot be sustained. Just because modern societies are chaotic it doesn't follow that all societies at all times have been so. It is valid, Gellner asserts, to ask the question why is this so? What are the antecedents of coherence and structure? Man is always out to create an ordered culture. That he does not completely succeed does not mean that such a value does not exist at all. There is coherence in cultures. That coherence is forever compromised but it does not, for this reason, cease to exist altogether.[6] In this study, therefore, I presuppose that, though it is not the whole story, a unified account of the culture of Lalitpur is a worthwhile and noble goal for the writer.

1.2. Historical background and contemporary context

The modern state of Nepal is a landlocked country of over 28 million inhabitants (2007 estimate) sandwiched between the giants of India to the south and China (Tibet) to the north (Map 1). The three main geographical

Map 1. The modern state of Nepal.

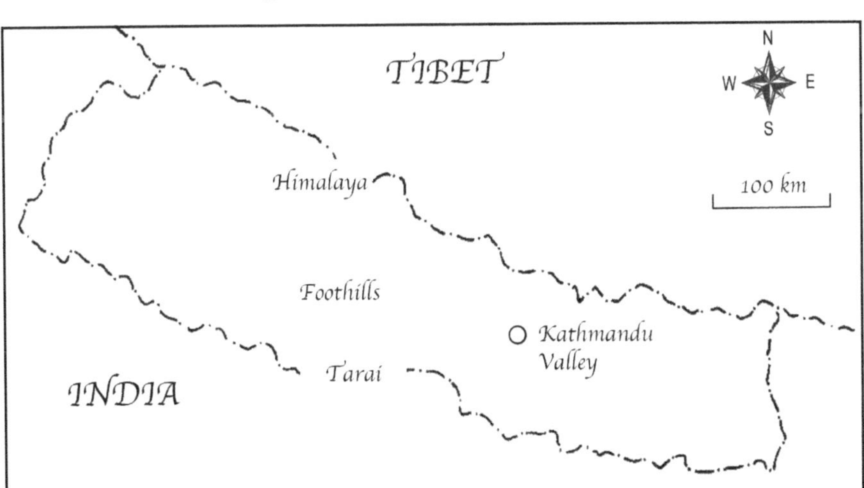

zones, extending roughly north-west to south-east along the length of the country divide the population into three general types: Mountain, Hill and Plains. Most of the Tarai (plains) communities are socially and linguistically one with those of the major north Indian groups, speaking such languages as Maithili, Bhojpuri, Awadhi and Urdu. Similarly, the Mountain peoples have a close affinity with those of the Tibetan plateau. The peoples of the middle hills where the majority of the population lives, however, constitute an agglomeration of Parbatiya who originated from the south, generally espousing Shaivite, Vaishnavite or Shakti ideals, and various ethnic groups from the north having a Buddhist or shamanistic orientation. Some of these communities, however, having migrated from the east are not unambiguously aligned with either of the great traditions but are generally labelled 'animist'.

The history of the Kathmandu Valley goes back many centuries and can be divided neatly into five dynastic eras. The first period, about which little is known except from traditional chronicles, is that of the Gopāla, Ahir (or Mahisapāla) and Kirāta dynasties. These are followed by the Licchavi period, the oldest extant artefact of which is that of a life-size sandstone sculpture of King Jaya Varma stumbled on by workers digging a foundation ditch in 1992 and dating to 184/5 CE (Tamot and Alsop 1996).[7]

Much has been learned of the Licchavi period from the examination of around 200 extant inscriptions. Much less is known of the Thakuri period that follows, beginning around the ninth century. Political fragmentation and the rise of Tantrism as a powerful religious movement are certainly features. The Malla period, beginning in the thirteenth century, is much better known as there is a large body of documentary evidence including not only stone inscriptions but also copper plate inscriptions, personal diary entries called *thyasaphu*s and palm leaf manuscripts. The Malla era saw the emergence of a 'Golden Age' of Newar art and culture. The cities of Kathmandu, Lalitpur and Bhaktapur thrived on trade and industry and much of what we see today in the palace squares of these urban centres was built at this time.

After a long period of internecine unrest in the eighteenth century the Malla period came to an end with the 1768/69 conquest of the Kathmandu Valley by Prithvi Narayan Shah (founder of the Shah dynasty). From the mid-nineteenth century the Shah kings were confined largely to their palace by an oligarchy of Rana Prime Ministers that, under its illustrious founder, Jang Bahadur, had wrested control of the country. European-style palaces were built on confiscated farm land and the country was secluded from all but minimal outside influence until 1950/51 when late King Tribhuvan led a movement against the Ranas and ushered in a period of relative openness and experimentation with democracy. Political freedom was short-lived, however. King Tribhuvan's son, Mahendra, dissolved parliament in 1963 and instituted direct rule through the Pancāyat system, which was itself subsequently overthrown as a result of the 1990 'People's Movement for Democracy'.

The dominant group of modern Nepal, the 'nation' that is of the Parbatiyā, make up 38 per cent of the total population (Gellner 1997a: 8; CBS 2002; Dahal 2003).[8] Socially the Parbatiyā are divided into a simple system, with many lineages claiming Chetri (Kshatriya) or Bāhun (Brahman) pedigree, alongside the underprivileged or Dalit castes (formerly known as 'Untouchable') of Tailors (Damai), Cobblers (Sarki), Blacksmiths (Kāmi), Goldsmiths (Sunār), and others. The groups of the Tarai are divided into many more castes than the Parbatiyā, reflecting their kinship with groups over the border in India with whom they continue to maintain marriage relations.

The Tibeto-Burman language speaking ethnic groups of the middle hills, however, do not have a developed hierarchical system. Social relations among these tribes tend to be less hierarchical than do those of the Parbatiyā. Nevertheless, these groups, such as the Magar, Gurung, Tamang, Rai and Limbu have been influenced by their close contact with the Parbatiyā over the last few centuries. This has led, as Harka Gurung observes, to cleavages within some ethnic groups in which some sections have adopted caste tenets and even invented genealogies to claim southern Indic (*kāshyap-gotra*) Aryan ancestry as against that of northern Bodic (*lhāsā-gotra*) ancestry (1997: 506).[9]

Newars occupy a unique place in the ethnic matrix of the country. According to the 2001 census the Newars total 1,245,232 or 5.6 per cent of the population of the country (CBS 2002; Dahal 2003). Looking at ethnic identity in general, however, it is important to note here that ethnicity is essentially subjective. That is, it is conceived of as such even though it may not have any objective 'reality'. It is, moreover, relational in that 'it is the outcome of an interplay between self-assessment and outside-assessment' (Höfer 1979: 47). Newar culture is clearly of South Asian affinity (Gellner 1986: 115). Having said this, however, it must be admitted that Newar culture does have some features that connect it with the north rather than the south. Apart from the obvious feature of the language some have seen the use of the carrying pole and baskets as reminiscent of China (D.R. Regmi 1960: 13). How much the Newars perceive themselves as an ethnic group is a moot question. Quigley contends that for the Newar population as a whole the sense of Newar ethnicity has always been relatively weak (1987: 152). It is apparent that, far from being a throwback to some primordial self-assessment, Newar ethnic identity is one that has grown with the impact of modernity.

In the study of Nepal's ethnic matrix, communities have traditionally been distinguished by means of an opposition between caste and tribe. Prayag Raj Sharma (1978), however, prefers to see the caste-tribe as a spectrum and Dilli Ram Dahal (1979) protests the use of the word tribe at all. There has been a tendency to regard Parbatiyā Hinduism as orthodox in contrast to Newars and tribes. Gellner (1991) proposes, for analytical purposes, a trichotomy of Tribal-Newar-north Indian Brahmanic, which represent three points of a triangle. Such a trichotomous typology, however, obfuscates more than it clarifies. The Newar social system is basically one with that of north India with the element of centralization at its heart (Quigley 1995b). Any differences between Newar culture and north Indian Brahmanic culture are not sufficient to make the Newars a unique case— a reality parallel to many groups within the Hindu world.

This issue is not merely of academic interest. It takes on huge significance when one asks whether the Newars count as one of Nepal's 'Indigenous' peoples or not. The whole category of Indigenous has in Nepal, as it has across much of the world (championed in part by the United Nations Organization) taken on great political importance. The 'Indigenous Peoples' movement of Nepal, organized under the umbrella of the Nepal Janajāti Mahāsangh (Nepal Federation of Nationalities) has had great difficulty defining its boundaries. Some wish to define the movement socially and religiously, excluding all those that have placed a high value on hierarchy. By this token, Dalits ('Oppressed'—Parbatiyā 'Untouchables'; by all accounts an underprivileged community) and Newars are excluded.[10] Those wishing to define the movement linguistically—those communities that speak a Tibeto-Burman language—have to defend a rationale that excludes the Dalits while including the Newars. It is true that Newars often feel themselves to be left out and disadvantaged in comparison with other groups in the country, especially with Bāhuns. They see their own numbers ever dwindling in proportion to the massive numbers of migrants who have come to settle in the Valley over the past few decades. But in the recent, highly sophisticated statistical analysis of data from the 1991 census the Newars come out as the group with the highest quality of life in the entire country (Gellner 1999: 5). Clearly there is a gap between the Newars' own perception of their lot and the perspective of others towards them. Hence, there is antipathy by some to including the Newars within the Indigenous Peoples movement, as the whole purpose of such a confederation for them is to press for affirmative action, hardly convincing when one of the communities represented seems to be doing so well.

The question of how to define a Newar is a pressing one as there is no distinctive religion. Furthermore, neither festivals nor rituals are universally observed by Newars. The criterion that is usually invoked is that of language but that proves problematic, as so many no longer speak Newar. It is estimated that about one third of all Newars have adopted Nepali and given up speaking Newar (ibid.: 3). This is not, however, as high a language loss as that of the Magar, Gurung and Thākāli.[11] The biggest single factor in language loss in Nepal is surely that of education. Throughout the Pancāyat era all state-run educational institutions were Nepali-medium. It was hoped, and to some extent one might say realized, that through Nepali-medium education and radio the very diverse communities of the country would grow to accept a strong sense of national identity. This all changed with the People's Movement for Democracy in 1990 and the subsequent reintroduction of a party-based democratic political system. Political discourse was thrown wide open to the hitherto suppressed voices of dissent and heterogeneity. Ethnic and linguistic movements emerged that later coalesced to form the Nepal Janajāti Mahāsangh.

Not only did national identity begin to lose ground to the competing claims of ethnic communities but some of those groups, till now seen as monolithic, began to express just how little sense of community they really felt. Among the Newars, as in India (Fuller 1996), while inter-caste relations have declined, intra-caste solidarity has increased (Ishii 1987). Among the Newars there are, so far, organized bodies representing the Brahmans, Vajrācāryas, Kamsakārs, Maharjans, Nakaḥmis, Mānandhars, Citrakārs, Tandukārs, Khadgis, and Kāpālis (Gellner 1999: 16). There is also an *ad hoc* committee to represent the wider Urāy community though no rules or aims of the committee have yet been published. No such group has yet been created among the Pengu Daḥ, although the Tāmrakārs and Rājkarnikārs have formed their own societies.

Since the reintroduction of parliamentary democracy in 1990, various communist parties have dominated political life in the Kathmandu Valley (Gellner 1997b). The General Election of May 1999 resulted in all three Lalitpur District wards going to Communist Party of Nepal (Unified Marxist-Leninist), Ward No.2, which includes the City of Lalitpur being won by Krishna Lal Maharjan. Many Newars have supported the various communist-leaning parties as they have championed the cause of land reform. Their slogan 'Land to the tiller' resonates deeply with the large numbers of Maharjans even though many are now no longer tenants but landlords themselves.

Since 1990 there has been a succession of governments with almost as many Prime Ministers as there have been years. Accusations of government nepotism and greed reached a new low when the members of the lower house of parliament under the then Prime Minister, Sher Bahadur Deuba, voted to award themselves generous tax breaks on the import of luxury four-wheel-drive vehicles. The 'Pajero Culture' that this situation engendered led in 1996 to the exit from the political arena of the Communist Party of Nepal (Maoist). The subsequent death and destruction left in the wake of the Maoist 'People's Liberation Army' resulted, in 2001, in the imposition of a state of emergency by the government, to deal with the insurgency. The same year also witnessed the bizarre palace massacre of the entire royal family of King Birendra by the then Crown Prince that shocked the nation and led to a profound outpouring of collective grief and anger. Curiously, the publicity following this event was poorly handled by the Palace and government. To this day most of my informants (and the majority of the populace?) believe some or other conspiracy theory.[12]

The economy of the country was badly hit by the Maoist insurgency. Villages typically became homes to only the elderly and children, a whole generation having fled to the city (or out of the country) to escape forced conscription by the Maoists or abuse by the security forces in retaliation for the Maoists' attacks. Tourism, Nepal's main source of much-needed foreign exchange, went into a steep decline with fewer and fewer foreigners willing to visit what was generally perceived as a country locked in civil war. Hundreds of thousands of young men migrated to the Arabian peninsular or elsewhere for work and, increasingly, many have little incentive to return. The sad refrain one often heard during the height of the insurgency was: '*Nepal khatam jula*' ('Nepal is finished'). In April 2006 a 'Democracy Movement' led to the return of the Maoists to conventional politics and eventually to the abdication of the king and the formation of the Federal Democratic Republic of Nepal. The political scene has subsequently continued to be characterized by instability.

1.3. The arena of the study

The Kathmandu Valley is a large fertile bowl situated at an altitude of 1,350 metres (4,400 feet) in the middle hills of Nepal (Map 2). The name Nepal, in

Map 2. The Kathmandu Valley

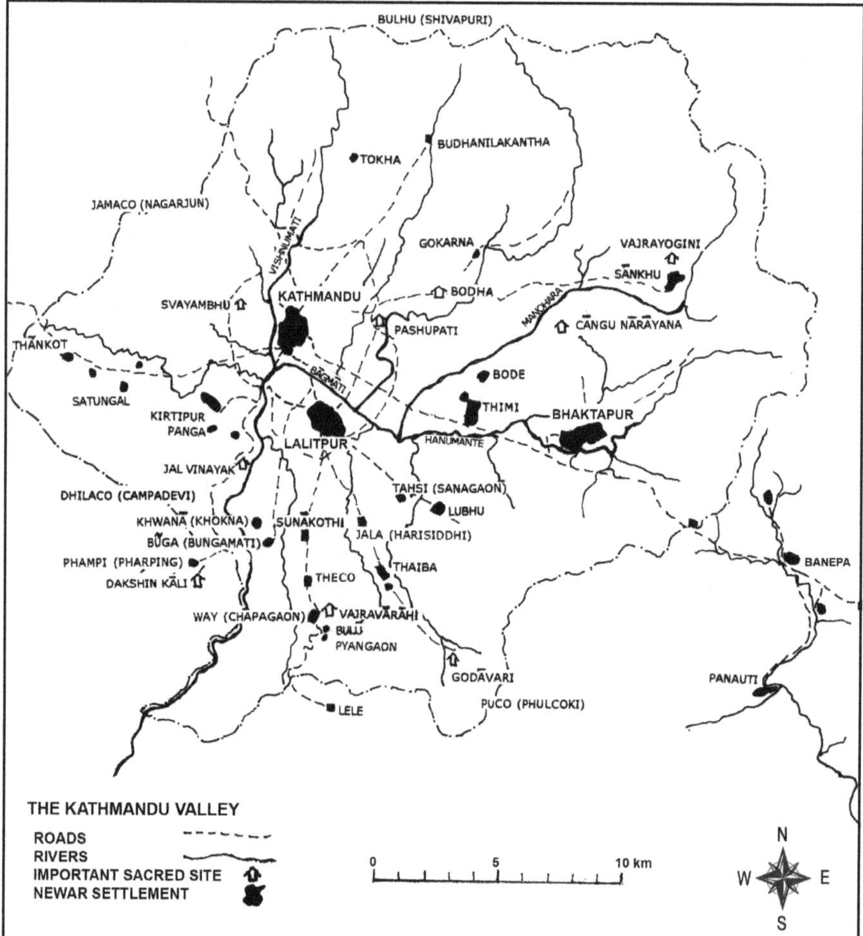

fact, at one time applied only to the Valley. Even today, people on the trails around the Valley often say that they are 'going to Nepal'. The cities of the Valley gained wealth and prestige by their strategic location on the ancient trade routes between the north Indian plains and the Tibetan plateau. This led to the early flowering of an artistic, urban culture with a complex social system.

The old cities of the Kathmandu Valley are models of compact settlement. As with all Newar settlements, though the cities are home to many farmers, they live characteristically in close proximity to each other and some distance from their fields. This is in marked contrast to the villages of the Parbatiyā that are scattered over a wider area, farmers preferring to live among their fields and at a distance from their neighbours. Newar cities, then, are densely populated.[13]

The modern cities of Kathmandu and Lalitpur (Patan) have, in recent decades, merged into a sizeable conurbation, the encirclement by a Chinese-built ring road in the mid-1970s giving it the feel of one large city. The conurbation of Lalitpur south of the Bāgmati River is now recognized as a sub-metropolitan city with an elected mayor and seat of power in an incongruous modern building at Puco (Pulcok) (the scene of a Maoist bomb attack on the morning I first wrote this). The sub-metropolitan area, which covers a much wider area than the medieval city, is divided into twenty-two wards that bear no relation to the localities (*twaḥ*) of old Lalitpur.

The old city of Lalitpur (Yala, as it is called in colloquial Newar) is a most heterogeneous community of around 80,000 inhabitants (Map 3, p. 14). Although a part of the modern nation state of Nepal, it still maintains many rituals that hark back to the days of the Malla kings and earlier, when the city was the centre of its own thriving kingdom. The traditional localities are, as Levy succinctly puts it, 'the village in the city' (1990: 182).

The traditional Newar house is a three or four storey brick house with wooden doors and windows. The apex of the house runs parallel with the street (*galli*), adjacent houses abutting directly onto one another. The ground floor is unpaved but above the level of the road making a continuous raised threshold along the street protecting the house from monsoon flooding. Those houses that do not front onto the street are arranged around courtyards (*nani* or *cuka*) set back from the street and often only accessible by narrow ways through the ground floor of a street-front house. Courtyards are often only a few metres square offering very little in the way of light or breeze. A well might be the means of procuring water for household use although an intermittent mains water supply is now available across most of the urban area.

On the death of an elderly father, brothers will usually divide the house vertically ensuring equity of value by putting up dividing walls at exactly the correct spacing. This is so even when it is most inconvenient, causing, for

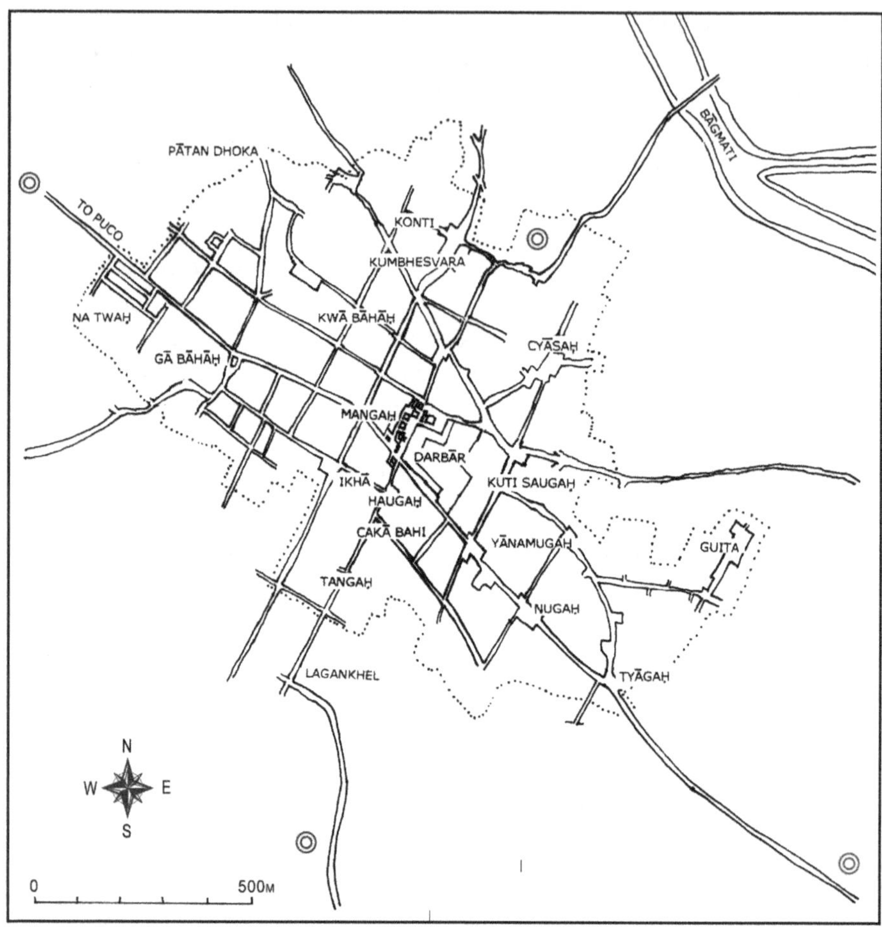

Map 3. The City of Lalitpur.

City walls are inferred from archaeological and ethnographic evidence. The city is now almost surrounded by new residential neighbourhoods and shopping districts but the lanes and courtyards of the city are pretty much as they were in Malla times (after Gutschow 1982: 149).

instance, new walls to be built right in the middle of a window or doorway. Often these days it is not practical to further divide the house vertically because the resulting space would be very narrow. In this case one brother may decide to move out of the old city and build a concrete house in one of the new 'suburbs' such as Sātdobāto or Lagankhel. In such a case his portion of the ancestral house is then bought by one of the remaining brothers.

Over the last few decades there has been a huge increase in the value of land in the city. The value of a house outside of the main business district in Kuti Saugaḥ, Lalitpur, for instance, is now worth one thousand times what it was thirty years ago. This pressure on land can be seen in the increasing narrowness and height of Newar houses. Five and six storey houses are no longer unusual. The narrowest house I have come across belongs to a Sthāpit family in Bā̃gemura, Kathmandu. The three brothers had just divided the 5.5m wide property between them. There was still a common entrance on the ground floor but when I entered the house I was presented with three separate wooden staircases each leading to a separate dwelling of less than two metres' width!

New houses on the main thoroughfares around Mangaḥ—the old city centre—have to meet certain aesthetic specifications that have been drawn up in conjunction with the development of the area as a UNESCO World Heritage Site. Residents may build a new concrete house as long as pillars and cement are not visible from the street. Thus a 'pillar-system' house (with the desired strength to withstand a moderately serious earthquake) has a façade of high-quality brick, and doors and windows of carved wood. The door and window frames are often reused from the old house that has been demolished. In at least one case the doorways have been widened and lengthened by adding matching pieces of carved wood in the middle of the lintel and at the bottom of each jamb. In the same house one set of three windows has been duplicated and matched by a new set on the same level. A separate smaller window, positioned in between the two sets of three windows, gives the new façade balance and brings the number of windows on that floor to the requisite odd number.

Space in the Newar houses is used to express notions of hierarchy. The ground floor (*cheli*) is outside the normal ordered space of the house just as cremation grounds are outside the ordinary ordered space of the city (Levy 1990: 767, n.54). Anyone, regardless of considerations of purity and pollution, may enter the ground floor of the house and indeed the space is often quite a public one. On the ground floor also, artisans have their workshop and traders display their wares. The workshop is often set back in a small courtyard behind the house where also, since modern plumbing and sewerage were introduced, is located a small bathroom and latrine. Access to higher floors is gained by means of steep wooden staircases that are oriented so that the user never has to face the inauspicious direction south (ibid.: 189). The next floor up (*mātā̃*) usually has bedrooms as well as a reception room, looking incomplete these days without a carefully covered 'sofa set' and carpets. The second floor (*cwatā̃*, third floor in US English), is open plan with a large room for eating feasts on long straw mats. It is on this floor that the large, outward-leaning, ornately carved windows of the wealthy give residents an almost uninterrupted view of the street. Here also (or sometimes on the floor above) auspicious life-cycle rituals such as the First Rice-Feeding ceremony are celebrated. The topmost level (*baigaḥ*) is where daily meals are eaten and worship of the household gods is offered. In traditional brick houses the *baigaḥ* is roofed with clay tiles. Part, however, is kept as an open space (*kaḥsi*). This space is where kites are flown during the autumn festival of Mohani and is sometimes important ritually such as when the menarche or pre-menarche girl is brought out of temporary Confinement to view the sun. Certain castes are permitted to certain levels, the topmost being accessible only to one's relatives and the domestic priest (*purohit*). In the house, therefore, purity is emphasized in the same way that it is demonstrated in the human body with the head being considered pure and the feet polluted.

A carved stone (*pikhā lakhu*) marks the ritual entrance to the house. The *pikhā lakhu* is regarded as Kumar and is worshipped first before Ganesh (being regarded as Ganesh's elder brother). At the close of certain festivals and life-cycle rituals, left over sacred items are often deposited at the *pikhā lakhu* as an alternative to being thrown in the river.

The basic social unit of the Newars is the household or family. The household is defined as the group of people who share a common hearth (*bhutu*). Traditionally, Newars have had a preference for joint families—that is, often multigenerational households with a plurality of nuclear families living together and, ideally, sharing income and resources. The Newar community has been going through a huge demographic transition over the last two generations. The population of the country at large is also going through a demographic transition but one that, with a baby boom between about 1980–86, is a generation behind that of the Valley. It was not uncommon for a Newar mother two generations ago to have eight to ten children. With the arrival of modern medicine to the Valley in the 1950s the vast majority of these survived to adulthood, something unthinkable to a previous generation.[14] Today, the present child-bearing generation of the Valley, with easy access to family planning is producing, almost without exception, just two children per couple. One Shrestha man with three children quite apologetically and without prompting told me that 'the family planning failed'! With five children I am repeatedly teased by my Newar friends with such quips as 'Don't you know about family planning?'

When asked why they want to limit their family to two children, Newars, as others who have migrated to the Valley, almost invariably reply in economic terms, particularly citing the cost of schooling. The widespread adoption of the two children 'Happy Family' (*sukhi parivar,* Np.) policy, in the city, is not so much a product of government campaigns but of widespread disaffection with government schools. This has led to a mass migration to the private sector with its burgeoning plethora of expensive 'English-medium boarding' schools.[15]

In the joint family, though there are always adults present to discipline children, no one adult is permanently on guard to check their child's behaviour. Child minding, then, is shared broadly with rules of behaviour more implicit than explicit. Cultural transmission within families is very strong. Levy states that the relationship between father and children is characterized by a 'certain restraint' (1990: 112). It is said that any sentimental affection might weaken his authority to discipline his children. The relationship of the mother's brother with his sisters' children is seen, in contrast, as one in which he gives treats and does not expect to exercise discipline. He is, however, expected to give assistance in later life.

Rules of deference in the household are clear. Formally, a man must bow before his father, mother, elder brothers, grandparents, and elder sisters' husbands. The married woman must defer to her husband's elder brothers and sisters, his mother and father, father's brothers and all household gods as well as to her own father and mother and father's brothers by touching her head to their feet. In practice few would allow her to bow so low. To her husband's father's brothers' wives, his elder sisters' husbands, her father's brothers' wives, and mother's brothers a simple bow is sufficient. Generation always takes precedence over age (ibid.: 118) so that an individual will bow even to an uncle who is younger than himself.

The position of women in Newar society is best seen in contrast to other groups that live nearby. In general, women in Hindu society are carefully protected and governed by a succession of male relatives—father, husband, and son (Fuller 1992: 20-24). Though it is not uniform, women in Newar society are, to a greater or lesser extent, freer than those of plains Hindu societies. Women from castes strongly influenced by north Indian ideals experience less freedom than those of castes that are less influenced. Newars agree, at least those of middle and higher castes, that Maharjan women are the freest of all. A Tāmrakār shopkeeper will joke and chat with Maharjan women in his shop and remark that, of all the Newar women, those of the Maharjan caste are the most friendly and least shy. B. Pradhan (1981) argues that Maharjan women (and Newar women in general) are more highly valued than are Parbatiyā women because they play an important economic role in the fields, making such matters as ritual impurity less important (a situation that has also been observed among other hill-peoples such as the Pahāri in Garhwal [Berreman 1972: 76]). Gellner, however, questions this deduction, as Parbatiyā women are also necessary for agricultural labour.[16]

Women of other castes, such as the Pengu Daḥ, are aware that their lot is better than that of Parbatiyā women. They will point out that their men folk are often happy to help out in household chores for instance—something that a Bāhun or Chetri woman would not expect. Although the Newar woman might not be a partner in the family business she has a strong role to play in the home and is not afraid to voice her opinions. Older and unmarried women (in short those not encumbered by small children) are, moreover, often free to work in the family business. Unlike their Parbatiyā neighbours many Newars de-emphasize menstrual pollution (Lewis 1984: 163). Women in their period do not need to sleep separately and may continue to cook at the hearth. They may not, however, be allowed to continue ritual activities such as carrying pure water and may not touch *pujā* trays (ibid.: 204).

The Newar girl is constantly reminded, however, whether explicitly or implicitly, that she does not belong to the family of her birth. She will one day leave home and go to live with the family of her husband. The tears that are shed by the bride and her parents on leaving her natal home are very real. She may return, for months at a time even, during the first couple of years but she will never belong there any more and feels that deeply.

There is no doubt that women often get the short straw when it comes to disputes. Adultery, for instance, is seen, as it is by Nepalis more generally, as being the fault of the woman rather than the man. Illness is often thought to be the consequence of witchcraft, an older known woman invariably being suspected as the malicious offender. Recent studies of possession in the Kathmandu Valley have also highlighted the exclusion of women from orthodox religious power (Dougherty 1986; Coon 1989; Gellner and Shrestha 1993).

Whether or not, as Sharma suggests (1983), the greater freedom of women in Newar society is a product of a non-Hindu tribal past—a notion opposed by Gellner (1991)—it is clear that Newar kings, with their undoubted connections to the south, placed greater kudos on Hindu orthopraxy. The wives of Bhupalendra Malla of Kathmandu committed *sati* (self-immolation on ones husband's funeral pyre) in 1701 CE, as did the thirty-two wives of Yog Narendra Malla of Lalitpur four years later (D.R. Regmi 1965-66: II,331; Burleigh 1976: 48).

Newars have a keen sense of the value of privacy. The terms 'public' (*manka*) and 'private' (*yakaḥti*), however, are relative terms depending on the context in which they are used. A shrine, for instance, that is public for a family may not be so for the entire lineage. One that is public to the lineage may not be so for the entire *thar.* Again, it may be public for the *thar* but not for others. Relative privacy, therefore, not only reflects but reinforces social closure, demonstrating that Evans-Pritchard's observation (1940) for a very different community that the society is characterized by nested units, is true of the Newars as well.

Newar religion is, for the most part, starkly social. Excepting they whose job it is to know what they believe the priests—most Newars do not see their religion as something to be understood so much as something to be done. Indeed, when asked why they do a certain ritual, Newars are more than likely to reply that 'This is what we have always done.' Broadly speaking, Newars can be divided into two main streams according to the orientation of their domestic priest (*purohit*). Those who call the Buddhist Vajrācārya priest to perform life-cycle rituals are termed *buddhamārgi* (<*mārg,* Skt., 'way') while those who call a Brahman priest are *shivamārgi* (Gellner 1992: 71). For most Newars this distinction has little import. It is relevant neither to marriage nor to commensality, nor does it bar anyone from participating in any festival. Although many researchers would translate these terms as 'Hindu' (*shivamārgi*) and 'Buddhist' (*buddhamārgi*), I believe these terms obfuscate rather than clarify. Most Newars would identify themselves as Hindu even though they retain a Buddhist domestic priest (*purohit*). Indeed, many Newars are stumped by the question 'Are you Hindu or Buddhist?'. For this reason Gellner refers to the majority of Newars as neither Hindu nor Buddhist but 'Ordinary Newar' (ibid.).

I would rather refer to all Newars as Hindu in the sense that they all fall well within the ambit of the great South Asian tradition.[17] Those who self-consciously follow the path of Buddha we may call Buddhist. This does not make them any less Hindu in the sense that I have defined it but marks them out as having a particularity that the others do not have. Furthermore, one might have a Brahman domestic priest (and so socially be *shivamārgi*) while following Buddhist doctrine in his personal, soteriological religion.

It is true as Gellner writes that 'almost every expression of soteriological piety has social implications...' (ibid.: 70). But these rarely translate into anything of major significance. The bottom line for most Newars seems to be that it matters not what an individual may believe so long as he keeps the traditions of the fathers. Though such a situation is socially acceptable, however, the vast majority of Newars do not take advantage of it. The designation 'Hindu', then, as I hope to demonstrate later, is more useful as a *structural,* not a philosophical or 'religious' term.

Newars distinguish three different basic types of food (Gellner 1992: 30-31; Löwdin 1998). The twice-daily staple meal based on boiled rice (*jā*) is eaten around nine or ten o'clock in the morning and again at seven or eight o'clock at night. This food is considered highly susceptible to pollution. As such it is eaten hurriedly, in the home, with or without other members of the family, and uninterrupted by conversation. In the afternoon a different type of food, based on beaten rice (*baji*), is consumed.[18] This food is less susceptible to pollution and is eaten in a more relaxed atmosphere. Moreover it is the food that may be consumed out in the fields by farmers and can be eaten in full view of others. Feast food is somewhat like the latter in that it is based on beaten rice. It is distinguished from a simple *baji* meal, however, by the great variety of dishes and the elaboration of courses, as well as by the formality of the occasion.

Dumont and Pocock report that in some cases food has to be desacralized before it can be eaten, by a part of it being offered in the fire of the hearth or in some other way (1959: 37). Newars achieve this by placing a small amount of food next to the plate—an action variously interpreted but usually seen as an offering to the gods and deceased ancestors. Another way to desacralize food, in order to make it palatable to members of other castes, for instance, is to add a spoonful of clarified butter (*ghyaḥ*). The addition of *ghyaḥ* to boiled rice makes it, in effect, a completely different order of food—*pukka* rather than *kacha* (Dumont 1980: 84-85).

Various foodstuffs are banned as unclean. Generally all *buddhamārgi*s and all that have taken initiation (*dekhā*) avoid chicken meat and eggs. Again, this is variously interpreted, either because chickens eat dung or by reference to Gautama Buddha, as this from Kirti Kumar Tamrakar:

> Buddha had a sore on his ankle. He slept under a tree and a chicken came along, pecked at the sore and ate a worm from it causing the sore to heal. From that time on Buddha said, 'We will not eat chicken'. Furthermore, certain groups, that would not in the ordinary course of things have any prohibition against certain foods, restrict their diet on special occasions. The Bārāhi, for instance, may not eat chicken, or garlic, during the annual Jātrā of Bũgadyaḥ because to do so would be to compromise their purity and thus their fitness to work on the chariots.

With the exception of Brahmans (whose identity as Newar is, in any event, ambiguous), Newars have no ban on the eating of buffalo meat, which is, in fact, an essential ingredient in a number of feast dishes. Until very recently, however, no Newar, except those belonging to the Untouchable castes, would eat pork. Various sanctions were imposed on those who did, such as seven days of purification rites before being permitted to re-enter the house. After one Tāmrakār man ate pork he was barred from access into the temple of Vishvakarma in Tichu Galli, a temple that theoretically unites all Lalitpur Tāmrakārs, and above which the Nāyaḥ lineage Tantric shrine is located. His descendants are not considered to have lost their place in either lineage or caste although the shame of the event still haunts the family concerned.

Newars have a strong sense that their culture is rapidly changing. In a familiar way, older generations see these changes largely in negative terms. Ravi Rajkarnikar put it like this:

> Newar culture is breaking up. People are not interested in religion anymore. People are more self-centred than they used to be. There is no longer any fear. Before when someone wanted to do something bad they would think twice and would fear that something bad would happen to them because of their sin. But now people have no fear of God. It is because of television. They shoot each other and do bad things on the films and people copy that.

However tempting it is to contrast tradition with modernity, however, it must be understood that the latter is merely the latest of many cultural movements to impact the Newars. This study will not focus on these changes so much as what Newars themselves perceive to be their traditional culture. By piecing together both well-known and explicit cultural and historical phenomena, as well as the more subjective interpretation of much that is taken for granted, we will take a look back and see what we can learn about the development of Lalitpur's social system.

2. Newar Kinship

> In the world of caste, virtually every aspect of behaviour is regulated by kin—not only major decisions such as marriage, occupation, and place of residence, but everyday activities such as what one eats and who with, or forms of address one employs for different categories of people.
>
> Declan Quigley (1993: 87)

2.1. The word 'caste'

In the analysis of caste we must begin by carefully choosing our terms. The English word caste comes from the Portuguese for 'species'—*castas*. It has been argued, by some, that the use of such a foreign term prejudices the inquiry before we begin. They have called, therefore, for an abandonment of the word in favour of indigenous terms such as *jāti* and *varna.* But there is a major obstacle here: resorting to native terminology throws up its own problems because definitions of *jāti* and *varna* are not universally accepted. What profit can we get from an analysis of these terms? Taking the term *jāti* it is apparent that people use the word in different ways in different contexts. Nepalese, for instance, will use the term not only in reference to people but also in reference to animals and plants. They will distinguish, then, between two different *jāti*s of banana. Again, I was often told by informants, who were perhaps somewhat irritated with my constant interrogation, that 'There are only two *jāti*s—men and women'. The broad usage of the word, then, does not permit us to define it too narrowly. Béteille approaches the apparent ambiguity of the term *jāti* by viewing the caste system as segmentary (1964: 131); analogous to the membership of various nested units among the Nuer of Africa (Evans-Pritchard 1940). 'The fact that caste is a segmentary system means (and has always meant) that people view themselves as belonging to units of different orders in different contexts' (Béteille 1964: 133).

Quigley deals with this at length to clear the ground before going on with his argument. 'The sense of *jāti* is of those people who are in some fundamental way alike because of their common origins, and fundamentally different from those who do not share those origins' (1993: 4). 'The sense of *varna* is quite different. The basic idea is not of birth but of function, and not simply any function, but one which is necessary to ensure that social harmony and cosmic stability are maintained' (ibid.: 5). We will come back to this later (§3.2).

Robert Levy prefers not to use the word 'caste' at all opting for the neologism 'macro-status levels' instead (1990: 70). In his opinion, the use of caste terminology would be to try to force Bhaktapur's status system into a 'procrustean bed of generalizing analytic terms' (ibid.: 74). But this begs the question whether Bhaktapur's social system is so different from that of other South Asian cities that it cannot be compared with them? In trying to fit Bhaktapur's social system into a general South Asian scheme does one end up lopping off its communal arms and legs? I think not. Bhaktapur's social system is not unique. Shall we invent neologisms for each Newar city? Parish points out that the reason Levy does this is that the actual units of a caste system are usually more fluid and dynamic and contextually determined than is usually assumed (1997b: 449). But if that is the case, as it surely is with all caste systems, why not say so instead of introducing yet another terminology to confuse? Levy's problem is that he does not recognize that Bhaktapur's social organization is structurally one and the same as those that have been called caste in India.[1] In this work, therefore, I have kept the older term in the hope that not only will it be helpful for comparison, but that a better understanding of the system it purports to represent will result from the analysis.

Now it is necessary to locate the ethnographic data that follow in the context of the theoretical discussion of caste in general. To do this we will take as our starting point the work of Louis Dumont.

2.2. Dumont's theory of caste

Dumont's works, culminating in the monumental *Homo Hierarchicus* (1980 [1972]), have been very widely read in the field of South Asian studies and have had a profound impact on the Western understanding of caste. Dumont's own starting point is the definition of caste by Bouglé (1908):

> [T]he caste system divides the whole of society into a large number of hereditary groups, distinguished from one another and connected together by three characteristics: *separation* in matters of marriage and contact, whether direct or indirect (food); *division* of labour, each group having, in theory or tradition, a profession from which their members can depart only within certain limits; and finally *hierarchy*, which ranks the groups as relatively superior or inferior to one another.

Bouglé based all three of these together on the opposition between the pure and impure (Dumont 1980: 21,30).

> Dumont is concerned that we not impose our modern, individualistic perspective on Hindu society and thus reduce caste to just one form of social stratification as in Europe. Because we (moderns) are individualistic, he suggests, we always perceive hierarchy in terms of inequality. Traditional society, in contrast, perceives hierarchy in terms of holism. And in order to do proper comparative sociology (anthropology) we need to first understand caste holistically.

Dumont's position, simply put, is that the caste system is a hierarchy based on the opposition of purity and impurity with the Brahman on the top and the

Untouchable on the bottom: 'superiority and superior purity are identical: it is in this sense that, ideologically, distinction of purity is the foundation of status' (ibid.: 56). Dumont defines hierarchy as the '*principle by which the elements of a whole are ranked in relation to the whole...*' (ibid.: 66). He goes on, 'The principle of hierarchy is the *attribution* of a rank to each element *in relation to the whole*' (ibid.: 91, original emphasis). This Dumont calls *holism*. One of the foundational elements of Dumont's theory is that ritual purity and power are divided at the top between the *brahmans* and the *kshatriyas*. In this way, argues Dumont, Hindu society is unique. The king, as a *kshatriya*, Dumont asserts, is 'deprived of any sacerdotal function' as only the Brahman may perform the sacrifice (ibid.: 68). It is this assertion that enables Dumont to state that 'In theory, power is ultimately subordinate to priesthood...' (ibid.: 71).

Dumont's work has the effect of reducing the ethnographic data to the level of ideology. For him the issue of whether castes are actual, discrete, substantial groups is not significant. But it is my contention that this is an important issue. If discrete caste groups are no more than a product of the sociological imagination then the caste system, as Dumont asserts, may rightly be reduced to an ideology. But if there are substantial, discrete groups that we can label castes, it calls into question his whole approach. It does not deny the involvement of ideology, but it does suggest that ideology is not the whole story. Dumont's theory, then, according to Quigley (1993: Ch. 4), is not powerful enough to explain how one can be a Brahman (i.e., a member of a particular kinship group) and yet not be a *brahman*, (i.e., a practising priest). Dumont's work leads one to assume that the two words represent coextensive semantic fields. But is the recognition of discrete caste groups, with carefully defined boundaries and identities, merely a 'substantialist fallacy'? A careful look at the internal structure of the Pengu Daḥ will help us to answer this. But before we do this we have to clarify the use of kinship terminology among the Newars.

2.3. Kinship terminology

Several scholars have discussed Newar kinship terminology in the course of their studies (e.g., Sresthacarya 1977, Toffin 1984: 168-73, and Levy 1990: 630-634). I suggest that the word *phuki* is used solely as a relational term for kinsman (after Ishii 1995: 141, Nepali 1965: 194 and Toffin 1984: 168, 647; cf. *phukijyā*, Tamot n.d.: sv).[2] Gellner categorizes kin by three distinct terms: distant kin (*tāpā phuki*), kin (*phuki*), and close kin (*syāḥ phuki*) (1992: 24f.). It is my experience, however, that these are not so much three distinct categories of kin but rather a cluster of terms used quite loosely with *phuki* being a more general term than either *syāḥ* or *tāpā phuki.*

Traditionally, but decreasingly, the lineage observes both Lineage Deity Worship (§9.23) and Mohani (*Dashaĩ*, Np.; §8.8) together. On this basis they refer to each other as *syāḥ phuki.* Thirteen days of impurity are observed on the death of a *syāḥ phuki. Tāpā phuki* are those that have discontinued observing Lineage Deity Worship together. When a *tāpā phuki* dies, one is obliged to observe only the minimal period of impurity by bathing and changing ones clothes (Appendix 9, p.314).

The Pengu Daḥ usually use the term '*khalaḥ*' to denote a lineage. Marriage is never permissible between those who observe any kind of ritual kinship. In the case of the Bārāhi and the two other Sikaḥmi lineages this is strictly extended to everyone who belongs to the named lineage whether or not this is any longer expressed ritually. This is usually true as well for the Tamvaḥ and Lwahākaḥmi. In a few instances, however, Tamvaḥ have invoked the more general rule of marriage being permissible between relatives seven generations distant even though the couple are known to be from the same maximal lineage. The Marikaḥmi, who for the most part do not have named lineages, usually abide by the seven-generation rule. These days, however, some are ready to consider a proposal from someone five generations distant. Others are not yet ready to intermarry even though they are seven generations distant because of a known patrilineal relationship.

Some lineages split up into largely unnamed, but clearly defined, sub-groups termed *kawaḥ.* In these cases, such as that of the Tamvaḥ Itāchẽ lineage, the ritually relevant group of *syāḥ phuki* is the *kawaḥ*, those of the wider lineage being *tāpā phuki.*[3] In the analysis below, I follow Ishii's (1978: 514) use of the term maximal lineage rather than clan for the wider named kin group.[4]

2.4. The Newar *thar*

When one asks a Newar what his *thar* is (use of *jāt* runs the risk of offending) his answer is always in terms of kinship. (The reason for this is that it may be perceived as an attempt to expose a person's status, which especially for members of underprivileged groups may be painful or embarrassing.) A Coppersmith, then, would immediately reply that he is a Tāmrakār even though he no longer works copper himself and, moreover, not all those who work copper are entitled to that name. Neither would a Coppersmith reply that he is a member of the Pengu Daḥ (for reasons explained below). The very lack of an encompassing name for the group speaks volumes about its significance for a person's identity. What the person is asserting is his identity as a member of a particular lineage or group of lineages.

How may one translate the term *thar*? Gellner makes an analytic distinction between sub-castes, and caste sub-groups. On the one hand sub-castes, he says, are meant to be and thought of as being wholly endogamous. Caste sub-groups, on the other hand, are often thought of (usually erroneously) as exogamous groups within a larger caste or sub-caste (1992: 65). The gloss sub-caste for *thar* or *jāti*, as Quigley points out, is extremely misleading as it implies that a number of sub-castes somehow join together to make up a caste (1993: 128). Any relationship between so-called sub-castes is always highly contested with one group claiming inclusion (into the wider Shrestha caste for instance) and the others denying it. The term ‘caste sub-group’, however, may be useful to translate the word *thar* in situations where a number of such groups join together to make a caste. Table 1 shows as complete a list as I can come up with of the castes that belong to Lalitpur.

The periphrasis ‘Pengu Daḥ’ (lit. ‘Four Groups’) is used to identify collectively a complex community of four separate Lalitpur *thar*s or sub-groups, each with a traditional craft and, again traditionally, with multiple roles in the larger city community.[5] By and large, Newars will use the colloquial identifier in reference to a member of a particular *thar*—e.g., Jyāpu of a Farmer, but prefer to use the Sanskritic title in address—in this case Maharjan or Dãgol. In the case of the Pengu Daḥ, the members of any one *thar* may have any of three or four different surnames making it difficult to identify them definitively. For the purposes of analysis, therefore, I have resorted, for the most part, to the colloquial appellation in each case.

Table 1. Castes at Lahtpur.

<u>Key</u>: *Thar* titles are <u>underlined</u>. Traditional marriage circles are in **bold type**. English equivalents are capitalized in keeping with South Asianist protocol.

<u>Note</u>: The castes are listed according to the English alphabet at this point because to do otherwise would be to accept certain and, I believe, false, presuppositions about the caste system.

<u>Bhatta</u> – Brahman Priests at Shankamul temple.

<u>Carmakār (Kulu/Kul)</u> – Drum-makers.

<u>Citrakār (Pũ)</u> – Painters.

<u>Cyāmkhalaḥ (Cyāme)</u> – Sweepers.

<u>Dyaḥlā (Pwaḥ/Pwarya; Pode, Np.)</u> – Sweepers, Fishermen.

Kāpāli/Darsandhari (Jogi; Kusle, Np.) – Musicians, death specialists.

- <u>Kāpāli/Darsandhari (Jogi; Kusle, Np.)</u> – Tailors/*muhāli* (shawm) players, death specialists.
- <u>Vādyakār/Bādikār (Dom/Dwã)</u> – Drummers, vegetable and curio sellers.

<u>Karamjit (Bhāḥ)</u> – Mahābrāhman death specialists.

<u>Khadgi/Shāhi (Nay; Kasai, Np.)</u> – Butchers and milk sellers, drummers.

Maharjan (Jyāpu) – (Like the Shresthas this, the largest caste, is not uniform).

- <u>Awāle (Kumhah)</u> – Potters and Farmers.
- <u>Dãgol (Jyāpu)</u> – Farmers.
- <u>Maharjan (Jyāpu)</u> – Farmers.

<u>Māli/Mālākār (Gathu)</u> – Gardeners.

<u>Mishra</u> – Brahman temple Priests.

<u>Nakaḥmi/Lohakār (Kau)</u> – Blacksmiths.

Table 1 (continued).

Nāpit (Nau) – Barbers.

Pengu Daḥ (here I list the colloquial title first to avoid confusion)

- Lwahākaḥmi (Shilpakār/Shilākār) – Stonemasons, now mostly wood carvers.
- Marikaḥmi (Rājkarnikār/Halawāi/Haluwāi) – Sweetmakers.
- Sikaḥmi (Bārāhi/Sthāpit/Kāsthakār/Shilpakār/Sikaḥmi) – Carpenters; builders of *ratha* (Bārāhi).
- Tamvaḥ (Tāmrakār/Tamot) – Coppersmiths.

Rajaka (Dhubya/Dhobi) – Washermen.

Rājopādhyāya (Bramhu/Dyaḥbhāju) – Brahman domestic and temple Priests.

Ranjitkār (Chipa) – Dyers.

Shrestha (Shesyaḥ) – Landowners, government ministers, civil servants and merchants.

- Amātya (Mahāju) – Ministers.
- Joshi – Astrologers.
- Karmācārya (Acāḥju) – Shaivite Tantric priests; some internal division.
- Malla – descendants of Malla kings.
- Pradhān (Paḥmay) – Ministers.
- Rājbhandāri (Bhani) – Royal Storekeepers.
- Shrestha (Shesyaḥ) – Landowners, businessmen.
- Vaidya – Ayurvedic physicians.

Tandukār (Khusaḥ) – Farmers, musicians.

Vajrācārya/Shākya

- Shākya (Bare) – Goldsmiths.
- Vajrācārya (Gubhāju) – Buddhist Priests.

Vyanjankār (Tepay) – Market Gardeners, farmers.

When a member of the Pengu Daḥ is asked to enumerate the *thar*s that make up their marriage circle he is often at a loss. A Marikaḥmi, for instance, might easily identify Rājkarnikār, Tāmrakār and Shilpakār but have difficulty naming a fourth, all the while maintaining that four is indeed the proper number. There is no theoretical bar against marriage between two people of the same thar. That bar is set, as I shall explain, at the level of maximal lineage (and certain other related lineages, §2.7). We will take the marriage circle defined by an elderly Tamvaḥ woman as our starting point: 'We can intermarry with anyone from the Pengu Daḥ—Tamvaḥ, Sikaḥmi, Lwahākaḥmi and Marikaḥmi'. This immediately begs the question, What about the Bārāhi? The Bārāhi are often omitted in a list of the Pengu Daḥ.[6] If asked, an informant might reply that they are Sikaḥmi—an assertion that the Bārāhi are willing to accept so long as it is understood that they are a special kind of Sikaḥmi in their relation to the building of the Bũgadyaḥ chariot.[7]

The marriage circle is often seen as wider than it actually is in normal practice. Though disputed by the Tulādhars of Kathmandu, members of the

Pengu Daḥ will often assert that the Tulādhar *thar* is one of the four. The geographical limits of the marriage circle are hotly disputed. Some will assert the right to intermarry with analogous groups in other towns while others deny it. A careful comparison with analogous castes in other towns leads one to conclude that, until recently, town-endogamy was the rule and not the exception.[8] Communities of *five* different groups of artisans are not uncommon in South Asia. Pocock reports that artisan groups in north and south India are often known by a collective name suggesting some nominal grouping of five (1962: 85). These groups are usually said to claim an origin from Brahmans and to have some myth of common descent from Vishvakarma. It would seem, however, that the five-fold grouping was not dominant in Nepal.

2.5. Criteria for identifying the Pengu Daḥ

It is possible, by eliciting the right information from an individual, to ascertain exactly whether they belong to a certain group or not. These criteria are based on the access to various shrines and temples that belong to the groups involved. Lineage names are often a good way to establish an individual's identity. Such names as Pwāḥsyāḥ (Stomachache), Kwaḥ (Crow), and Khica (Dog) are specific and easily verifiable. Membership of certain *guthi*s (the most important being the death and Lineage Deity *guthi*s) seems to have been more important as an indicator of one's identity in the past than it is today (Quigley 1985b). In some castes, notably that of the Shresthas, it seems to have been almost definitive in the establishment of the eligibility of a prospective spouse.

Every Newar has a Lineage Deity (*digu dyaḥ*) and, whether they worship it or not, this deity establishes a certain belonging. Some Lineage Deities, however, are worshipped by groups who make no claim to any patrilineal relation.[9] Tamkadyaḥ (the Lineage Deity of all the Tāmrakārs of Lalitpur) is a prime example.[10] Furthermore, certain Lineage Deities (that of Siddhilakshmi Purnacandi is the prime example) are worshipped not only by a multiplicity of lineages of the same *thar* but by lineages belonging to a variety of castes, so it is not possible on this ground alone to be sure of an individual's pedigree. Quigley finds it bizarre that those who are not agnatic kin should worship the same Lineage Deity (1985b: 49).[11] To understand this phenomenon we must appreciate that opportunity has existed in the past for certain Lineage Deities to be adopted. In so doing, groups that were alike by occupation could achieve ritually what was not actually possible physically—express a kind of mock agnatic relationship. It is precisely because the cult of the Lineage Deity is so cohesive that similar groups fused in this way. The result is that persons who may be considered agnatically related by outsiders have the opportunity to intermarry as Gellner has observed among the Shākyas of Kwā Bāhāḥ (1992: 241).

Access to the Tantric shrine (*āgã chẽ*) is more informative.[12] Only bona fide members of the lineage in question are allowed such access. This criterion, however, is oftentimes too narrow to ascertain the boundaries of a lineage. Certain individuals, for one reason and another, may forego the required initiation and thereby be denied access. Their agnatic kinsmen, nevertheless, will all agree that the individual is a member of the lineage. The acceptance or otherwise of an individual or family as members of a caste group is a matter of the establishment of their descent. If a Tāmrakār, for instance, wants to gain membership in the Ugracandimai Sewā Samiti (a community organization, §6.4.2) he has to establish his pedigree as the descendant of a Lalitpur Tāmrakār of known identity. This is, as far as I have ascertained, never a very difficult process, as nearly everyone who claims identity as a Lalitpur Tāmrakār is already known by several others, whose credentials have already been established. Though they may not know the name of their lineage, it will be known by one of their caste fellows. In Table 2 the composition of the Pengu Daḥ is displayed *in toto.*

2.6. The four *thar*s

2.6.1. Tamvaḥ

The Tamvaḥ of Lalitpur usually use the *thar* label Tāmrakār though some, especially those of Bhojpur (Taksār) in eastern Nepal, call themselves Tamot.[13] The Tamvaḥ constitute the largest *thar* of the Pengu Daḥ and are still today, for the most part, workers and traders of copperware. I have recorded 305 households, around eighty of which live outside Lalitpur, mostly in Panauti and Bhaktapur (Appendix 1, p. 288).[14]

There is much confusion in the artificial lists drawn up by foreign observers as to the identity, rank, and religious affiliation of Newar Coppersmiths. Petech (1958: 185) bases his system on the foundational principle that the basic division within Newar society is that between *shivamārgi*s and *buddhamārgi*s. (As will be seen in the ongoing discussion, this is by no means a basic division at all.)

Oldfield (1981[1880]: 180ff), Petech (ibid.: 182) and Lienhard (1995: 44,n.116) each state that 'Thambat' are among the Buddhist castes. This is, of course, a reference to the Urāy Tavaḥ of Kathmandu who are all *buddhamārgi* but only account for perhaps 10 per cent of Coppersmiths in the Valley.[15]

Tāmrakārs have no myth of origin but seem to have been present in Lalitpur since Licchavi times. When a Tamvaḥ is asked where his ancestors came from he will invariably reply, 'We have always been here'.[16] The origins of the Newar hollow metal craft technique are disputed. In the early nineteenth century Hamilton suggested that most of the arts of Nepal had been derived from Tibet (1971 [1819]: 29). Chattopadhyay (1980: 19) disagrees, arguing for the immigration of metallurgists from India, which seems most likely considering the high degree of cultural influence from the south by Licchavi times.

Table 2. The Composition of the Pengu Daḥ.

4th branch lineage	3rd branch lineage	2nd branch lineage	1st branch lineage	Maximal lineage	ãgã chẽ	alternat-ive ãgã chẽ	digu dyaḥ	thar	
								honor-ific	collo-quial
				Bhyā			Tamka-dyaḥ	Tāmrakār	Tamvaḥ
				Hãchu	Hãchu Galli				
				Haugaḥ					
			Dhasi Hãe						
			Kwakhā						
			Manaḥ						
			Mulasi						
				Itāchẽ	I Bāhāḥ Bahi				
			Bāgaḥ						
			Dhusi						
			Dhyākwa						
				Jyoti					
			Gwārā						
				Kothu-jhvaḥchẽ	Kothu-jhvaḥchẽ				
				Kũḥchẽ	Kũḥchẽ Vishva karma				
			Talachẽ						
				Kwaḥ	Kwā Bāhāḥ				
			Lā Manaḥ						
				Lachica					
			Naḥ Bāhāḥ		Naḥ Bāhāḥ				
		Jhvaḥchẽ							
	Cabāḥchẽ								
Twānāḥ									
		Pwāḥsyāḥ							
				Nāyaḥ	Vishva-karma				
			Nwa Mawāḥ						
			Dune	Sukuḥ					
			Pine						
				Panauti	Panauti	Bhaktapur	Panauti & Bhaktapur		
				Hukā Bāgaḥ	Cibhāḥ Nani	Tu Nani	Mani Dwā	Shilpakār	Lwahākaḥmi
				Katilāḥ					
				Khica					
				Yākami					
				Gãyrā simga					
				Khwapa					

Table 2 (continued).

4th branch lineage	3rd branch lineage	2nd branch lineage	1st branch lineage	Maximal lineage	āgā̃ chē̃	alternative āgā̃ chē̃	digu dyaḥ	thar	
								honorific	colloquial
				Kāji					
				Vishvakarma	Bega Nani		Cākupat	Sthāpit	Sikaḥmi
				Paḥmā	Kuti Saugaḥ		Thāpahiti		
				Bārāhi	Yāngu Bāhāḥ		Siddhilakshmi–Purnacandi	Bārāhi	
				Palmā	Haugaḥ Bāhāḥ		Iti	Rājkarnikār	Marikaḥmi

The earliest historical evidence for the existence of copper workers in Nepal is found in Licchavi inscriptions. In Licchavi times copper was being exported from Nepal to India (Slusser 1998[1982]: I,5). The Naxal Narayanchaur inscription dating from the reign of Jayadeva (713-33 CE) reports the existence of copper pounders (*tāmrakuttaka*) and copper smithies (*tāmrakuttashālā*) (Vajracarya 1973: 565, Inscription 149). These proto-Tamvaḥ, as we might call them, lived in the ancient Licchavi capital that was located at Mānesvara (Harigaon) to the north of the present royal palace. The inscription refers to *tāmrakuttashālā* as a *dranga*—that is that it had a higher status than a mere village. P.R. Sharma writes that the Licchavi kings took seriously their patronage of the crafts, even gifting land to several different groups of artisans (1983: 34).

It is likely that these early workers of copper migrated to Lalitpur after a fire destroyed the capital (Lewis 1995: 55; Slusser 1998 [1982]: I, 364; Vajracarya 1973). Present Tamvaḥ have no oral historical accounts of this migration. If, however, this awful conflagration was the epochal event that began the Nepal Era, as some have suggested, then their migration can be tentatively placed at November 879 CE. The location of the old Lineage Deity of the Tamvaḥ (that is, shared with four Urāy lineages—two lineages of Kathmandu Coppersmiths, 'Tavaḥ', one lineage of Baniya and the single lineage of Sindhurakār) is also indicative of a previous residence at Mānesvara. The Lineage Deity at Dhobichaur to the north of the Nārāyanhiti royal palace is not ordinarily worshipped by Lalitpur Tamvaḥ any more, but older Tamvaḥ agree that it used to be worshipped regularly in the past. The Lineage Deity worshipped today as Tamkadyaḥ, and also known as Ugracandimai, is located in Jawalakhel near to what is now the St. Xavier school. Tamvaḥ say that the deity was 'transferred' ('sālāḥ taye') from Dhobichaur some four hundred years ago to be nearer their present settlement (Map 4). Malla era inscriptions that mention the Tamvaḥ include one on a *cibhāḥ* (Buddhist shrine) at Tangaḥ, dated 787 NS (1667 CE), that was established by an ancestor of the Sukuḥ lineage (Tamrakar with Tamot 1994: 3).[17]

Though several lineages worship the same Lineage Deity, it seems highly unlikely that the Tamvaḥ have a common origin at all. A number of cultural artefacts point to a multifarious origin for the several lineages.[18] One of these is the plurality of Tantric Deities that are worshipped by Tamvaḥ (Map 5). Some lineages of Tamvaḥ have no Tantric Deity though it is not clear whether they once had one or not. Those who have no extant Tantric Deity often lay claim to the shrine above the Vishvakarma temple, although they are denied access into the innermost shrine by the Nāyaḥ lineage members who have exclusive ownership.

Hãchu lineage has a Tantric shrine in a house in Hãchu Galli, Ikhā and, until it was stolen some years ago, Kothujhvaḥchẽ lineage worshipped a separate Tantric Deity in their courtyard. Kwaḥ lineage worships at the Tantric shrine in Kwā Bāhāḥ on a certain day each year and Naḥ Bāhāḥ lineage (including Jhvaḥchẽ, Pwāḥsyāḥ and Cabāchẽ) worships the Tantric Deity at Naḥ Bāhāḥ (Cakravarna Mijālā Pucha).[19] Kũḥchẽ lineage recognizes the Vishvakarma temple located immediately behind the Kũḥchẽ shelter (*phālca*) as their Tantric shrine. The elders of Itāchẽ lineage likewise remember a time when the Tantric Deity at I Bāhāḥ Bahi, contiguous with their courtyard, was

Map 4. Lineage Deity sites of the Pengu Daḥ.

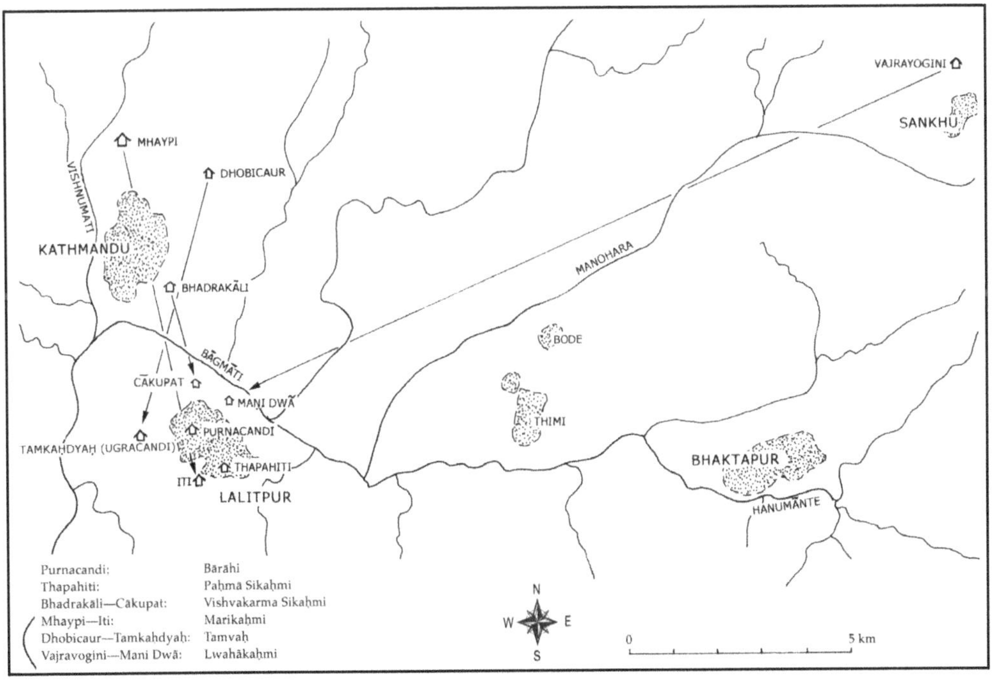

worshipped as their own. Separate Tamvaḥ Tantric shrines are also found at Bhaktapur and Panauti. Not a lot can be concluded from the use of these Tantric shrines, except that, today, these lineages have a separate identity. It is not possible on the basis of this evidence to conclude anything about common ancestry or otherwise.

The set of Tamvaḥ that falls within the acceptable marriage circle of the Pengu Daḥ is not limited to those who have access to the Tamvaḥ Lineage Deity at Jawalakhel. Intermarriage with Tamvaḥ of Bhojpur is accepted, as these are known to have migrated from Lalitpur. The Tamvaḥ of Panauti and Bhaktapur are also accepted within the marriage circle, even though they worship at a different Lineage Deity shrine in close proximity to their towns. Panauti and Bhaktapur Tamvaḥ assert that the Lineage Deity at Panauti was transferred from Lalitpur many generations ago and that of the Tamvaḥ of Bhaktapur transferred from Panauti around five generations ago. The Ugracandimai Sewā Samiti, however, does not accept this claim and therefore bars these Tamvaḥ from membership.[20] The Tamvaḥ of Taksār (Bhojpur), who have mostly migrated again to other towns on the Tarai or back to Lalitpur or Kathmandu, also have a Lineage Deity at Taksār.[21] This is, however, considered a copy of the one at Jawalakhel in a way that those of Bhaktapur and Panauti are not. Therefore, it is argued, the Taksār Tamvaḥ are permitted to become members of the Ugracandimai Sewā Samiti (§6.3.2).

Furthermore, there are, immediately behind Tamkadyaḥ, two smaller shrines that belong to the descendants of Tamvaḥ men who married Maharjan women several generations ago. These people are considered Maharjan and are barred from Ugracandimai Sewā Samiti membership. The descendants of a Tāmrakār man who married a Mānandhar woman in the early decades of the twentieth century are permitted to worship Tamkadyaḥ but are, nevertheless, also barred from Ugracandimai Sewā Samiti membership.

Newar civilization dominated a territory extending beyond its 'immediate hearth zone' for at least 1,500 years (Lewis and Shakya 1988: 25). The Himalaya mountain range to the north and malarial Tarai to the south insured the Valley's continuing autonomy for a long time. Not much is known about pre-Shah migration and settlement, though Dolakha certainly was an outlying town. Towards the end of the Malla era, or soon after the conquest of the Valley by the Shahs, members of at least one lineage of Tamvaḥ would seem to have migrated to Panauti, the small Newar town situated in the adjacent Banepa valley to the east.[22]

Some generations later, some of these Panauti Tamvaḥ further migrated to Bhaktapur. The Tamvaḥ of Bhaktapur and Panauti intermarry with those of Lalitpur and claim common descent. At the turn of the twenty-first century there were forty Tamvaḥ households in Panauti and twenty-seven in Bhaktapur.[23]

Map 5. Tamvaḥ lineages in their localities.
(Lineages in italics; small lineages omitted.)

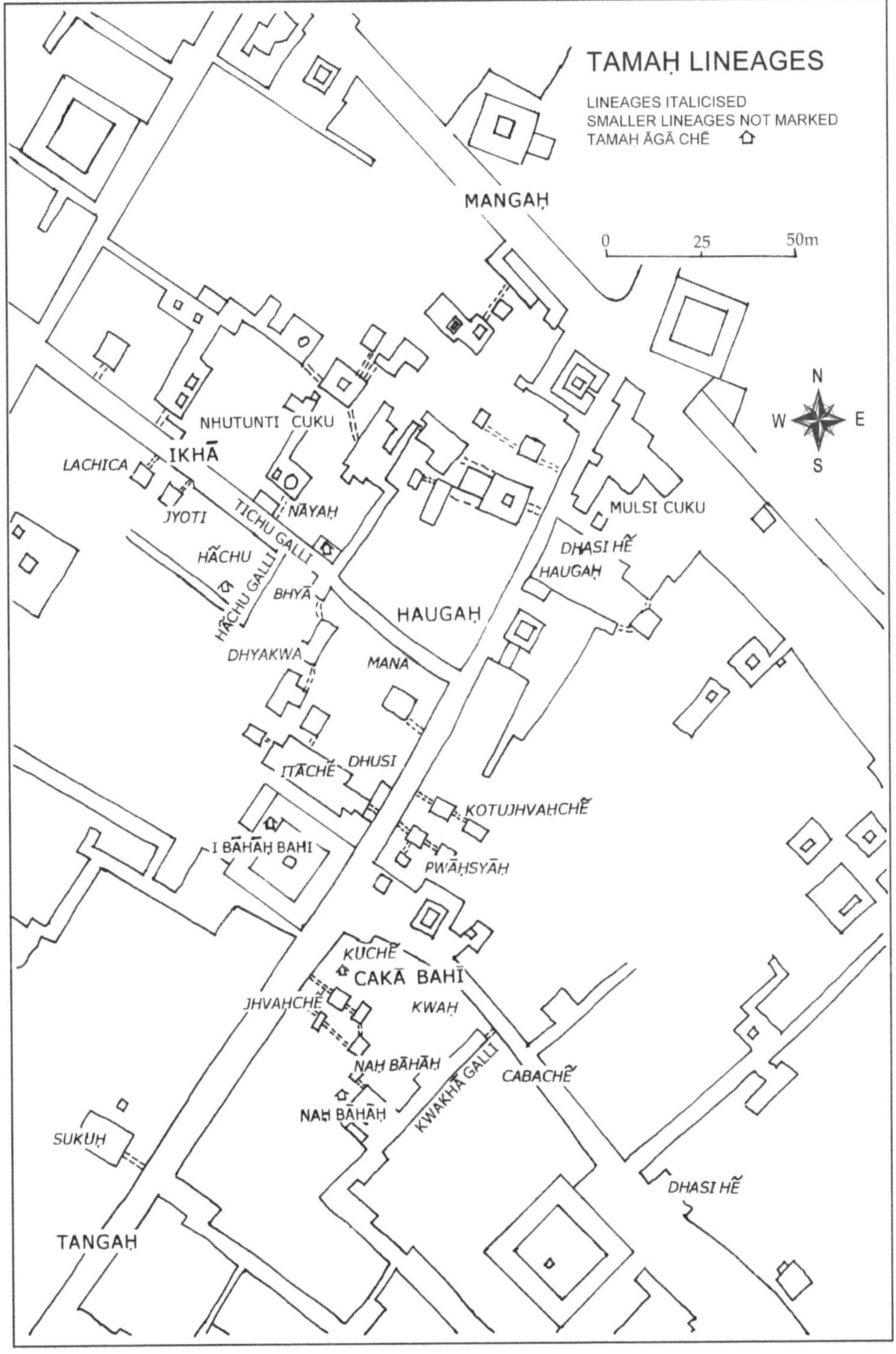

By Shah times the rulers recruited Newars to perform tasks that they deemed necessary for national integration. As with other Newar artisans and merchants, migration took place along 'migration corridors' (Lewis and Shakya 1988: 25). In 1815, the Office of Mines was opened at Bhojpur (Taksār) in east Nepal (K.Tamot 1981, 1992). Among the Shākyas and Tamvaḥ who went there from Lalitpur was Harsha Narayan Tamot of Sukuḥ lineage who was titled as the *taksāri* (Official of the Royal Mint).[24] Bhyā and Hãchu lineages were also represented. Inscriptions at Bhojpur mention Tamvaḥ frequently.[25] Unlike for others, however, this migration did not result in the dissolution of alliances with the Valley.

Mikesell (1993), writing about Bhaktapur, argues that the demise of the palace must have had a huge impact on the commercial life of the city. The dissolution of the palace of Lalitpur with all the activities of the court—the provisioning of the palace and barracks and the large group of retainers and merchants sustained by it—must likewise have had a significant impact on this city. Oldfield, writing as he did a century or so after the Gorkha conquest, describes a city that was in a state of decay. Estimating the population of the city as 60,000 he observes: 'The city looks too large for its inhabitants; its streets as well as its buildings appear to be half empty; there is none of the bustle and activity and palpable prosperity which are visible throughout Kathmandu and Bhatgaon' (1981 [1880]: 116-7).

Writing nearly half a century later, Landon was of a different opinion. The city he says, 'remains a populous and busy centre; and though her streets are not so rich in colour as those of the capital, and her standard of living is more primitive—Patan needs no sympathy' (1976 [1928]: 206). It would seem then that, though Lalitpur underwent considerable negative changes with the transfer of power to Kathmandu, it might have fared better under the patronage of the Ranas.

Migration of at least some citizens to other settlements in the new polity was almost inevitable and must also have been made more attractive with the new security and stability brought by the Gorkha regime. Many Newars, however, also tell of a terrible plague of smallpox that befell the Valley. Acyut Krishna Tamrakar offered this account to me:

> During the reign of Rana Bahadur Shah there was a severe smallpox epidemic.[26] Many had died. Those who had survived were permanently scarred but at least would never get the disease again. The king was desperate to save his family from the fatal disease and so decreed that all those not yet affected should leave the Valley.[27]

When the mines were closed after the relocation of the mints to Kathmandu only metal-work and trade continued. Today Bhojpur (Taksār) is two or three days rigorous walk from the nearest roadhead (Chatara, Sunsāri district) or one hour flight from Kathmandu. This and the impact of industrialization have resulted in the out-migration of many Tamvaḥ from Bhojpur to other towns in the region and even back to Lalitpur.

Circumstantial evidence leads one to question whether the Tamvaḥ have, as they would claim, 'always been' *shivamārgi*—i.e., followers of Shiva. One writer who has voiced such a doubt is Lienhard:

> It lies close to hand to assume that, after the establishment of the Krishna cult, the Tāmrakārs, who live in the quarter of the coppersmiths, broke away from the Urāyas and became Hindus; a conversion in which economic considerations and the attainment of a new social status were the main motivations. (1995: 44)

There is evidence that at least some Tamvaḥ used to be *buddhamārgi*: the strong attachment of Naḥ Bāhāḥ lineage to the Buddhist monastery from which it derives its name; the existence of the Naḥ Bāhāḥ Gũlā Pāru *guthi* which sings *bhajan*s throughout the Buddhist holy month of Gũlā; the apparently vestigial attachment to other monasteries of Kwaḥ and Itāchẽ lineages; the contiguity of Tamvaḥ residences to the principal Buddhist monastery of Panauti (Toffin 1984: 275, n.27); the strong representation of Tamvaḥ in the Nasantya Dāphā Guthi for worship of the Buddhist deity Karunāmaya (§6.2.6); the Tamvaḥ custom of welcoming the initiate into the house via the first floor window upon their receiving the third Old-Age Initiation (Appendix 9, p. 314); the playing of the *dhāḥ* drum in Nyaku Jātrā (§7.18.3); and, finally, the strongly Buddhist orientation of the Tavaḥ of Kathmandu. Having delineated these points, however, evidence still remains that at least some Tamvaḥ have been *shivamārgi* for a long time. The association of the Tamvaḥ Lineage Deity with Mahādyaḥ (Shiva) since ancient times suggests that some lineages of Tamvaḥ may have always been *shivamārgi.*

Most Tamvaḥ are not aware of any dissonance between their customs and their soteriological orientation.[28] They will simply say that they 'have always been *shivamārgi*'. Some, however, do admit that some of their customs do point to a possible Buddhist origin and will tell stories that attempt to account for their apparent 'conversion'. Kalyan Tamrakar recounted a story that a Shākya had told him thus:

> At the time of Juddha Shamsher (or some other Rana) a Tāmrakār woman and a Jyāpuni were fasting at Kwā Bāhāḥ. There was a dispute over precedence with the Tāmrakār asserting her higher caste status and the Maharjan her higher age. The priest decided in favour of the Maharjan. This so incensed the Tāmrakārs that they became Hindu.

Kalyan was quick to add, however, that 'we don't believe it—it gives us a headache'.

Laxmi Rajkarnikar told me a different version of what seems to be the same story:

> Around 100–150 years ago a Tāmrakār daughter married to a Rājkarnikār man was doing an Observance (*vrata*) at Kwā Bāhāḥ for one whole

> month. On completion her husband failed to collect her. The Tāmrakārs were so upset that they decided to become *shivamārgi* from that time on.

Octogenarian Mahila Shilpakar confirmed that the incident took place but denied that the Tāmrakārs became *shivamārgi* as a result.

Tentatively I conclude, therefore, that the early Tamvaḥ, who may have migrated from India during the Licchavi period, were *shivamārgi.* These early lineages migrated from the Licchavi capital after the great fire of 879 CE and settled in Lalitpur in the vicinity of Ikhā constituting the four Ikhā lineages. Other lineages of Tamvaḥ may have been created as members of Lalitpur's monastic communities, such as those of Naḥ Bāhāḥ, Kwā Bāhāḥ and I Bāhāḥ Bahi, married Tamvaḥ women, adopted their trade and Lineage Deity, and gave up their monastic status.[29] These lineages, Naḥ Bāhāḥ, Kwaḥ, Itāchẽ and probably others, gave up employing Buddhist priests and took on Newar Brahman priests instead.

2.6.2. Marikaḥmi

The second largest *thar* of the Pengu Daḥ is that of the Marikaḥmi. The Marikaḥmi have largely retained their traditional occupation and dominate the sweetmaking business of the Valley. One hundred and thirty-five households are registered with the Rājkarnikār Samāj (Society). I have records of 101 households, forty-three of which live in the old city of Lalitpur, the rest mostly scattered around Kathmandu and its suburbs[30] The Marikaḥmi almost invariably go by the surname Rājkarnikār though others usually refer to them as Haluwāi or Marikaḥmi.[31] All Rājkarnikārs trace their ancestry back to Haugaḥ Bāhāḥ (Hasnapur/Hastināgal Mahāvihāra) in Lalitpur where they still return for *guthi* celebrations. Rājkarnikār Sweetmakers are to be found in many parts of the modern city of Kathmandu as well as in and around Haugaḥ.

Older Marikaḥmi are quick to retell their legend of origin. According to the story, a Brahman (or sometimes two, three or four Brahman brothers) was invited by Sthiti Malla from Kanauj (India) to be the royal sweetmaker. On arrival in the Valley he was given quarters by the king in Haugaḥ Bāhāḥ.[32]

Nanda Govinda Rajkarnikar put it like this:

> When King Jayasthiti Malla[33] was ruling he was designating everyone's caste. But he found no one to be Haluwai so a Brahman from Kanauj came up and settled here. He had four sons who married Tāmrakārs and Shilpakārs; and that is how the Rājkarnikār group began. They took on the religion of Buddha because that is what everyone was here.

This begs the question whether, if they came up at the invitation of Sthiti Malla, they would have been housed at Haugaḥ, when his court was at Bhaktapur. But, since the Pramānas recognized Sthiti Malla as overlord and gave him full royal titles, they must have ruled, at least nominally, in the name of the king. Thus they may well have been dubbed Royal Sweetmakers. The techniques and ingredients for sweetmaking that are employed by the

Marikaḥmi do point clearly to an Indian origin. There is, moreover, a parallel claim brought by the Rājopādhyāya Brahmans of a migration from Kanauj (Toffin 1995a: 188).

Kashinath Tamot argues, however, that, since some Rājopādhyāyas were in the Valley in Licchavi times, their claim to have come from Kanauj during the reign of Sthiti Malla is spurious.[34] The Kanauj connection seems to have come from the nineteenth century chronicle, the *Bhāshā Vamshāvali* (published by Paudel and Lamshal 1963), which attributed an Indic ancestry to several such *thar*s. This must cast some doubt, then, on the parallel claim of the Rājkarnikārs as well. Sthiti Malla is credited in the chronicles with the construction of the caste system in Nepal—a claim widely believed by Newars. It is accepted that Sthiti did order the translation of the *Naradasmriti*, the second oldest book in Newar, in 1380. To credit the illustrious king with the single-handed creation of Nepal's caste system, however, is to attribute a greater weight to the evidence than it deserves.

Foreign observers frequently make mention of the Marikaḥmi.[35] The earliest written evidence for Rājkarnikārs is found in a copper plate at Haugaḥ Bāhāḥ bearing the names of a certain Rājkarnikār and his wife, the date 728 NS (1607 CE), and signature in Ranjana script. So they were definitely in residence before Siddhi Narasimha Malla became king of Lalitpur. The proximity of Haugaḥ

Map 6. Marikaḥmi homes and shops in and around Haugaḥ today.

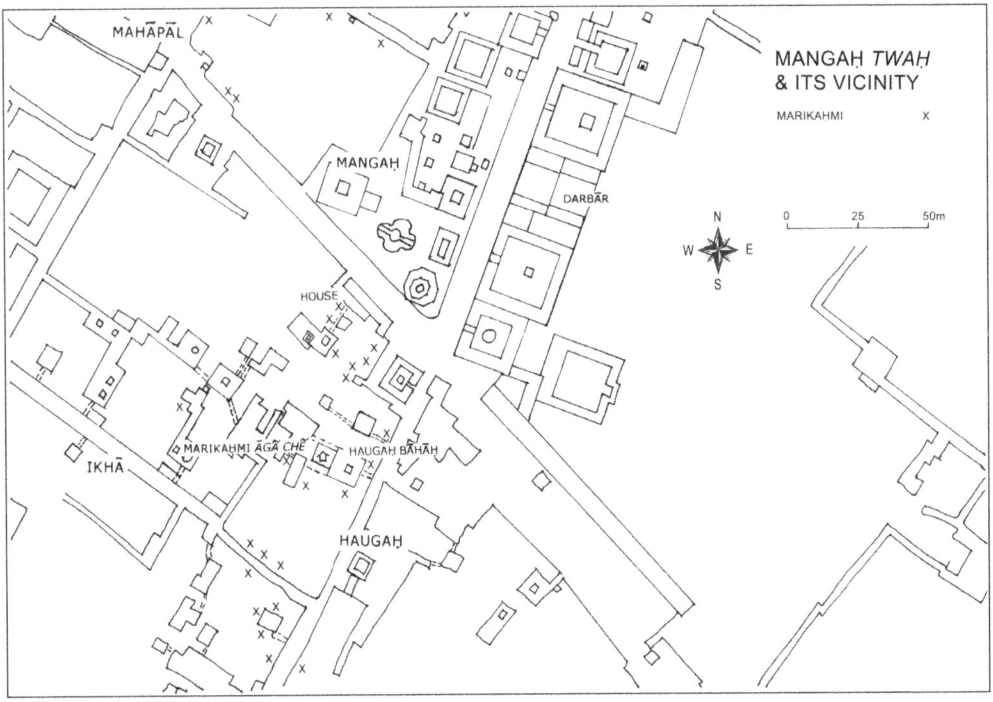

Bāhāḥ (indisputably the ancestral locality of the Rājkarnikārs) to the palace (it is only 50m or so from Sundāri Cok) does present strong evidence for their claim. The Rājkarnikār Lineage Deity worshipped today is at Iti immediately outside what was the Malla city wall, hard by the Butchers' quarters (Map 4). The original Marikaḥmi Lineage Deity, however, was at Mhaypi, west of the ancient Licchavi capital at Mānesvara.[36]

It remains to be explained why, if the Marikaḥmi migrated from Kanauj and settled in Haugaḥ, they placed their Lineage Deity so far away. Lineage Deities were always placed at a convenient distance away, just outside the boundary of the settlement.

Today, Rājkarnikārs reside invariably either very close to the palaces of the Malla kings of Lalitpur and Kathmandu, or in pockets directly in front of old Rana palaces (see Map 6). It is clear that a migration took place in the nineteenth and early twentieth centuries as aspiring rulers graced their dining tables with delicacies freshly prepared by their own tenured Sweetmaker. The present royal palace at Nārāyanhiti still today has quarters for a Rājkarnikār and his family who have that very role.

The balance of evidence, then, points to a three-phase migration: from India to the Valley during the Licchavi period at which time they settled at the capital; a second migration to Haugaḥ in Lalitpur, most likely as part of the diaspora that fled the capital with its destruction by fire in 879 CE; and finally a dispersion to all parts of the cities of Lalitpur and Kathmandu under the Shahs and Ranas.[37]

2.6.3. Lwahãkaḥmi

The Lwahãkaḥmi (Stonemason) usually go by the surname Shilpakār—'sculptor' (<*silpa*, Skt., 'sculpture' + *kārya*, 'work'; Manandhar 1986: sv)—a fact reported also by Lévi (in Chattopadhyay 1980: 107). Two families use the more specific Shilākār—'stonemason' (<*sila*, Skt., 'stone' + *kārya*, 'work'; Manandhar 1986: sv). The Lwahãkaḥmi have entirely abandoned their traditional occupation of stonemasonry and are now engaged largely in carving wood. Almost all of the fifty-four households of Lwahãkaḥmi live in their ancestral locality of Ikhā in both Jom Bāhāḥ and Tichu Galli. Most lineages are based around one or two courtyards each (Map 7). Only four households have migrated outside Lalitpur.

The leading claim to fame of the Lwahãkaḥmi is as the builders of the superb stone temple to Krishna that stands in the palace square at Mangaḥ. In 1630 Siddhi Narasimha Malla gave orders to construct the Krishna temple after having a vision of Rādhā and Krishna. It was dedicated in Phāgun 757 NS (1637 CE). According to Lwahãkaḥmi tradition, the temple was built by five clans of Lwahãkaḥmi—the original four lineages plus a fifth, Khwapa, that was brought from Bhaktapur specifically for this purpose.[38] The Lwahãkaḥmi are also the builders of the intricately carved gate of Kwā Bāhāḥ (Hiranyavarna

Mahāvihāra) which was completed during the reign of Rana Bahadur Shah (1777–1799).[39]

The Lwahãkaḥmi are divided into seven lineages (Appendix 2, p.292). The original Lineage Deity of the Lwahãkaḥmi, worshipped by all seven lineages, is located at Vajrāyogini near Sankhu, though this is rarely, if ever, visited anymore. Lineage Deity Worship is performed today at a shrine at Mani Dwã, north of Bagalāmukhi, the deity having been 'pulled' from Sankhu beyond living memory (Map 4). Gellner reports that many Shākyas and Vajrācāryas of Kathmandu also worship Lineage Deities that have been brought from Sankhu (1992: 240). He suggests an historical and ritual link with the Licchavi period when one of the biggest monasteries of the Valley, Gum Vihāra, was at the site of Vajrāyogini. It does strongly suggest that the original Lwahãkaḥmi were monks from that monastery, an opinion supported by Locke (1986).

There are two Tantric Deities worshipped by the Lwahãkaḥmi, both of which are located at Jom Bāhāḥ, Ikhā (Map 7). Of the seven lineages only four are eligible for access to the Cibhāḥ Nani Tantric shrine. Of the three lineages that are denied access to this shrine, one is the Khwapa lineage which was brought from Bhaktapur for the building of the Krishna temple, another (Kāji) is the lineage descended from a member of the Kāji Shrestha lineage of Mahāpā who married a Lwahãkaḥmi woman. The last is the Gãyrāsimga (Rhino horn) or Sukuḥ (Lean and Thin) lineage, the members of which have no recollection of their origins. The latter lineage lives exclusively outside Jom Bāhāḥ in the contiguous Tichu Galli. The only surviving household of Khwapa lineage lives along the lane in Ikhā Lakhu. The three households of Kāji lineage also, though not living in Tichu Galli, are somewhat outside the core of Jom Bāhāḥ in the adjacent Bega Nani.

The Tantric Deity at Tu Nani is more inclusive than that behind Cibhāḥ Nani being worshipped not only by all Lwahãkaḥmi but also by the Vishvakarma Sikaḥmi. It is this fact that gives the two *thar*s a measure of a single identity that is also expressed in the appellation Shilpakār, shared by both groups.

Jom Bāhāḥ is not really a *bāhāḥ* in the architectural sense or in the sense that it has a monastic community (*samgha*). Locke (1985) reports that the Tantric shrine at Jom Bāhāḥ (Tu Nani) was built by the Sthāpits (i.e., Vishvakarma Sikaḥmi) from Lagan, Kathmandu. I was informed that there is a copper inscription about this indicating that the shrine dates from the seventeenth century.[40] The Vishvakarma Sthāpit Shilpakārs perform Sixteen [Day] Ancestor Worship (*sohra shrāddha*) by offering boiled rice, a custom that is followed in Kathmandu but not normally in Lalitpur. Locke says that the lineage deity was 'brought' from Kāmi Nani attached to Lagan Bāhāḥ in Kathmandu. Vajrācāryas of Ta Bāhāḥ do Daily Worship (*nitya pujā*) there and receive a stipend for doing so.

Jom Bāhāḥ belongs to a type of monastery called a lineage monastery. Though lineage monasteries are the most common type of monastery (there being over 130 in Lalitpur alone) they are the least conspicuous. Most are very small and are often included in the house of the founder. 'The [lineage] monastery provides a focus for, and defines the unity of, a group of lineages, in the same way that main monasteries do for Shākyas and Vajrācāryas' (Gellner 1987b: 403). In the case of Jom Bāhāḥ it belongs to the Shilpakārs as a whole and unites two otherwise different and differentiated groups.

2.6.4. Sikaḥmi

The Sikaḥmi are divided into three exogamous lineages, Vishvakarma, Paḥmā, and Bārāhi, that have little relation to each other apart from the fact that they are permitted to intermarry. They are no closer to each other, then, than they are to any of the other lineages of the Pengu Daḥ. The twenty-eight households of the Paḥmā Sikaḥmi usually go by the surname Sthāpit (< *sthapati*, Skt., 'architect')[41] or Kāsthakār (< *kāsthakāra*, Skt., 'wood worker'), though one has recently adopted the Newar 'Sikaḥmi' itself as his surname as a statement of Newar identity.[42] Ten of the eleven households of Vishvakarma Sikaḥmi usually go by the name Shilpakār, reflecting their proximity to, and identification with, the Lwahãkaḥmi. To distinguish them from the Lwahãkaḥmi, however, they add Vishvakarma Sthāpit. The other household of this lineage goes by Tulādhar indicating perhaps an attempt at social advancement. Very few Sikaḥmi have migrated out of Lalitpur and most are still engaged in carpentry.

By the Vishvakarma Sikaḥmi's own account their ancestors were brought to Lalitpur to build the temple to Taleju in the palace complex in the seventeenth century.[43] Mahila Shilpakar, one of the elders of the lineage, recounted that the great Malla brother kings Siddhi Narasimha of Lalitpur and Lakshmi Narasimha of Kathmandu swapped craftsmen from their cities. A lineage of Lwahãkaḥmi from Lalitpur was exchanged for a lineage of Sikaḥmi from Kathmandu.[44] The descendants of that lineage of Lwahãkaḥmi from Lalitpur live today in Makhan, Kathmandu, not far from the Taleju temple of that city but have lost all recollection of their ancestry. Their houses are contiguous to those of Kathmandu's Sikaḥmi just as the houses of the Vishvakarma Sikaḥmi of Lalitpur are contiguous to those of the Lwahãkaḥmi in Tichu Galli, Ikhā—very strong support for the oral historical account.

The Vishvakarma Sikaḥmi Tantric shrine is located at Bega Nani, Jom Bāhāḥ, tucked away in a very small courtyard accessible only by way of the private courtyard of a family of Lwahãkaḥmi (Map 7). Access is restricted to initiated members of the lineage.[44] Their Lineage Deity is located in a field in Cākupat having been 'pulled' from Bhadrakāli in Kathmandu (Map 4).[45]

The Paḥmā Sikaḥmi are the descendants of a Paḥmā Shrestha man from Saugaḥ who married, against the wishes of family, a Sikaḥmi woman. They are one exogamous lineage but have two separate Tantric shrines ('because of a fight') located around the courtyard at Kuti Saugaḥ where many of the lineage live (Map 8).[46] Their Lineage Deity is still shared with the original Shrestha lineage from which they split (Map 4). The location of the Lineage Deity (Thāpahiti) attests to some antiquity for the original lineage as these shrines are (almost without exception) established outside the boundaries of the settlement.

The Bārāhi are a single exogamous lineage of Carpenters who are well known as the builders of the chariots of Bũgadyaḥ and Cākwāḥdyaḥ.[47] They comprise twenty-nine households, only one of which lives outside Lalitpur.

The Sanskrit title Bārāhi is used over much of India and often figures in Indian ethnographies. Carpenter-masons from neighbouring villages to Sirkanda are called *'BaRhai'* and intermarry with other Dom Untouchables (Berreman 1972). The Bārāhi of Lalitpur, however, assert that they are descended from the son and daughter of Bũgadyaḥ who married and had three boys. The Bārāhi also say they are the kinsmen of Bũgadyaḥ having originally come to Nepal from Kāmarup following shortly after Karunāmaya himself. An important Bārāhi tradition recounts that, when they first settled in Nepal they had to send their young men back to India to find brides but they often would not return. This was a problem which was resolved when, at the Phaila Bhu feast (§10.7.1), Bũgadyaḥ himself spoke to them telling them not to send their young men to India any more but to intermarry with the Pengu Daḥ, which they have done ever since.

Map 7. Shilpakār lineages and tantric shrines.

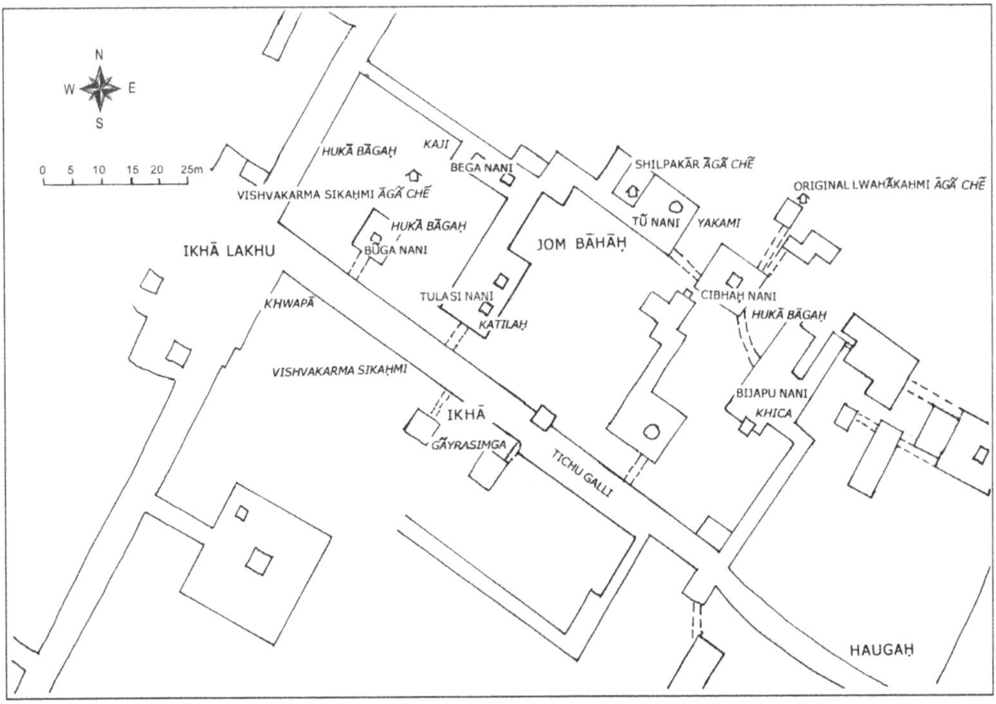

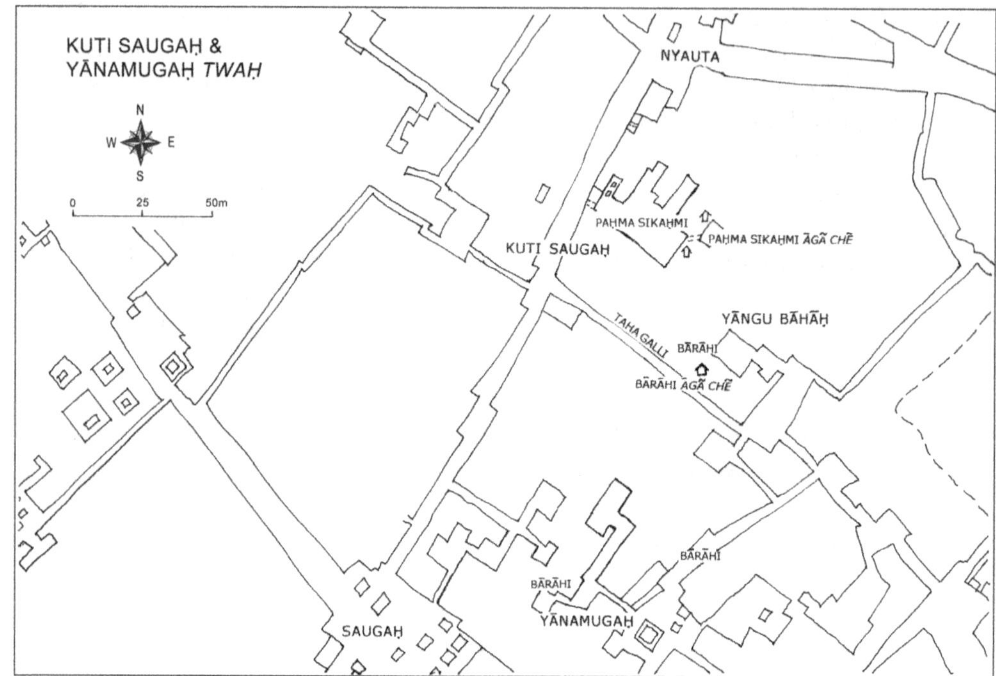

Map 8. Paḥmā Sikaḥmi and Bārāhi localities.

The Bārāhi also claim a former status as Pānjus. According to Owens, they claim that the priest who sits on the deity's left in the chariot (the 'Khal' Pānju) used to be a Bārāhi (1989: 164).[48] One year, they say, the Bārāhi 'Khal' Pānju went to an outlying village (Kamani) to marry and stayed there with his wife compelling the other Pānjus to supply one of their own for the position. In support of this claim they cite a number of traditions: the Bārāhi have rights to a half of all the offerings brought to Bũgadyaḥ though this has since been fixed at a low amount. They are also entitled to one half of the banners (*patāḥ*), once the Jātrā has ended. The restrictions that the Bārāhi observe during the Jātrā are also very similar to those observed by the Pānjus (ibid.). Further evidence is suggested in the *Buddhist Vamshāvali*, which reports the following:

> Seeing that there were not enough carpenters enough in the town, [King Siddhi Narasimha Malla] made Bandyas take up the trade, and assigned *guthis* to the Nāïkyās, to give them a feast on a certain day of every year. (Wright 1993: 234)[49]

The Bārāhi have the most extensive ritual and feasting responsibilities of any of those involved in the Jātrā after the Pānjus (Owens 2000: 713). The Bārāhi traditionally shave their head the day after the image is placed in the chariot, though, unlike the Pānjus they leave a top-knot indicating that they are householders, not monks.

Another piece of evidence the Bārāhi cite for their former status is that they go through an elaborate *thākāli luyegu* initiation. The Bārāhi contend that, after taking the *thākāli* initiation they are entitled to touch the Bũgadyaḥ image which is deemed to be necessary when the chariot falls over.[50]

The Bārāhi title is accounted for in a myth that the Bārāhi tell. The account reported by Owens (ibid.) is as representative as any other so I will reproduce that here:

> It is because of the boar's snout (*bārāha twāḥ*) that we have our name, Bārāhi. Once when they had to build a wheel, they went into the forest to cut a tree. In those days trees could hear, so when the tree heard them discussing which kind of tree would be strong and deciding which one would be suitable, the tree [intended for cutting] hid in the mud. They could not find the tree anywhere. They were afraid, for they had received the strictest orders to come back with the wood under threat of *jiu dhan sārkār* (impounding of all property). So they wandered about the forest crying. *Ban devi* (goddess of the forest) [having heard their cries] told them to make a boar's snout and use it to dig up the hiding tree. The Bārāhi did a *pujā* to *ban devi*, made the *bārāha twāḥ*, and found the tree. The *bārāha twāḥ* is still worshipped at the place it used to hang on the wall at I Bahi. It has been stolen and could not be re-placed for even ten *lakh*s of rupees. It was 1,400 years old.

The Bārāhi's relationship to Bhairava seems to be of even greater concern to them than that with Bũgadyaḥ. The image that is handed down from one Bārāhi *thākāli* to another is of Bhairava. It is to him that blood sacrifices are frequently to be made.

Non-Newars and even some Newars often refer to the Bārāhi as 'Badhai' believing that their name comes from the Nepali for 'congratulations'. Non-Bārāhis, including many that belong to the Pengu Daḥ, often subsume the group under the category of Sikaḥmi.[51] This the Bārāhis accept so long as there is a recognition of what, for them, is *the* peculiar identifier of the group, namely that they and they alone are the builders of the Bũgadyaḥ chariot.

Historical evidence for the Bārāhi does indeed go back a few centuries. Locke gives a synopsis of a long inscription put up by Sri Nivas Malla in 793 NS (16 February 1673 CE) at Ta Bāhāḥ. In it the king gives a list of regulations for the cult including a mention that 'The carpenters... must be notified on time. [They] are bound to contribute their services; they may not refuse to come, and they must not delay' (1980: 309).[52]

Oldfield also mentions the Bārāhi. He divides what he calls the third class into six groups of 'Jaffus' above and twenty-four of others that are below them including 'Balhaiji, men who make the wheels for the car of Machendra; they occasionally do a little other carpentering' (1981: 186). Hodgson's list adds that the 'Barhi or Yang Karmi—wheel wrights and makers of spinning wheels' are 'Brahman or Bandya according to creed' (in Chattopadhyay 1980: 114).

The Bārāhi Tantric shrine is situated at Yāngu Bāhāḥ, a short distance from Yānamugaḥ where most of the Bārāhi reside (Map 8). Only those initiated by the Supervisor (Nāyaḥ) can enter. At the time of research only ten, including the Nāyaḥ and his younger brother, the Bhai Nāyaḥ are initiated.

The Bārāhi Lineage Deity is Siddhilakshmi Purnacandi at Ga Bāhāḥ (Map 4). Interestingly this Lineage Deity is also shared by lineages of Rājopādhyāya Brahmans, Rājbhandāris and Maharjans. Not only so, but Limbus and Rais also gather at the temple on a specific day during Dewāli to do *pujā* to *their* tutelary deity (Vergati 1995: 154,n.28). Rājopādhyāya men, who live opposite, serve as Temple Priests (*pujāri*) while local Maharjans act as god guardian (*dyaḥ pālā*). These disparate groups make no claim to kinship so at least some of them must have adopted (*nala kayegu*) this god as their Lineage Deity some time after its establishment.

2.7. Lineage exogamy

Restrictions on marriage among the Newars are based on kinship proximity: all members of one's parents and grandparents lineages are proscribed. Practically speaking, one may not marry into either one's own lineage, the lineage of one's mother's brother (*pāju khalaḥ*), that of either parent's mother's brother (also referred to as *pāju khalaḥ*), or that of any grandparent's mother's brother.[53] Theoretically, then, this rule proscribes eight separate lineages. Clearly this would make it very difficult to find suitable marriage partners if there were few lineages in a caste (as, in fact, it has become in that of the Rājopādhyāyas). As we can see above, the Pengu Daḥ have no such problem.

In theory everyone up to fifth cousins is excluded, counting through women as well as men. Gellner reports that for the Vajrācāryas and Shākyas, 'In practice *any* remembered patrilineal relation is forbidden' (1995b: 227). This is not quite true for the Pengu Daḥ, as members of certain lineages are quite conscious of their patrilineal relation and yet are open to intermarriage as long as the required number of generations has passed. Although there is no pressure for intra-lineage marriage, Dune Sukuḥ and Pine Sukuḥ branch lineages have contracted a total of four marriages between them.[54] With one exception (Palmā lineage) the Marikaḥmi are *not* divided into named exogamous lineages. The only apparent reason for this is that all recognize that they are patrilineally related and therefore have little motivation to name branches. This is strong evidence that the oral historical account of their origins has a high degree of credibility.

Gellner (1995b: 218-20) has shown how, though Vajrācāryas and Shākyas constitute a single endogamous caste, they nevertheless have a tendency to marry within the *thar* rather than between the *thar*s. I do not have the data to demonstrate such preferences within the Pengu Daḥ. My informants insisted, rather, that no such preference exists. Instead, other criteria come into play when exploring eligibility for marriage. Among these are character (or behaviour, *pahaḥ*), financial security (especially for the bride), education, and physical appearance (with disabled girls particularly disadvantaged).

It is generally accepted that the couple should be closely matched in the level of education attained. As for the personal character of the prospective spouse, Nirmala Rajkarnikar was of the opinion that attitudes had changed, with the younger generation counting character more important than do their parents:

> In our case we consider whether they are able to work on their own or not but the older generation it is quite different. They look on wealth and possessions. Though the boy is good or bad the girl's parents see the boy's family background or possessions and whether their daughter will get happiness in that house. They don't care much about the job and appearance of the boy, but rather see the status or prestige of the boy's home.

2.8. Kinship and caste

Kinship, as I have attempted to show in the argument above, is the most significant identifier for a Newar. It is not the building of the Bũgadyaḥ chariot, therefore, that makes a person a Bārāhi—it is his identity as one of the kinship group that builds the chariot. Occupation is not the central issue—it is relation. 'It is not so much that everyone has (or ever had) a caste-specific occupation in the first instance. Rather, everyone belongs to kin groups whose traditional function it is (or was) to provide certain functionaries for certain occasions' (Quigley 1993: 91). It is kinship then, and no other criterion, that establishes whether a person belongs to a particular caste.[55]

Kinship is often expressed ritually in the cults of the Lineage Deity and Tantric Deity. Toffin states that 'the cult of tutelary divinities is a decisive element: it gives substance to kin groups, attaches them to mythic times, and maintains their spirit of solidarity' (1984: 81, translated and quoted by Owens 1989: 65). It is clear from the above data that it is not so much the worship of the Lineage Deity that establishes one's kin qualifications as that of the worship of the Tantric Deity. Access to some Lineage Deities was at one time open within limits, it seems, to all who shared the craft. Access to the Tantric deity, however, is strictly on the basis of kinship. As both Toffin (1984: 555) and Gellner (1992: 308) point out, Tantra is used to maintain social closure.[56] The new bride must be introduced to the deity before she becomes, formally, a member of the lineage. Married-out women belong to a different lineage and therefore may not enter the innermost room of their natal Tantric shrine. Kinship, then, is of utmost importance in the assessment of caste status. It is only by knowing what a person's lineage is that one can assess his caste credentials. '...Caste', asserts Quigley, 'is inextricably tied to kinship' (ibid.: 87). The data I have adduced above demonstrate the soundness of such an assertion. It is vitally important to belong to a recognized lineage if one wants to retain any status within traditional caste social structure.

3. Intercaste Relations

> ...Newar castes form a system–in the highest sense–and this system is profoundly Indian.
>
> Gérard Toffin (1984: 222; my translation)

3.1. Contested hierarchies

In order to properly understand the caste system it is necessary to examine in detail the relations between castes. Transactions between castes tell us about perceived attitudes to hierarchy and subordination. An interesting fact of caste systems, however, is that not all castes have ritual relations with all others. Indeed, because of this, an attempt to determine the relative status between such groups may be an artificial exercise.

One of the phenomena that characterizes the caste system of the Newars (and all caste systems) is that the hierarchy of relations is essentially *contested* (Gellner and Quigley 1995). The relations between castes are viewed variously from different angles. For example, consider Toffin's discussion about the complex attitudes of caste that exist between Pyangaon and other nearby villages.

> It is particularly difficult... to appreciate objectively and completely the position of two groups involved in a quarrel.... By giving a static picture of the Newar caste system, the fact that these quarrels play an important, if not essential part in this system, is ignored. (1978: 469)

This is clearly demonstrated in the relations of the Pengu Daḥ. The way members of the Pengu Daḥ view their relations with those of other castes is not the way those others would see the relationship.

Many authors have attempted to delineate a pan-Newar ranking of castes.[1] Basing his research on a household census of the entire Newar community in the Valley (except for Kathmandu and Lalitpur, whose constitution was estimated from various reports and informants), Rosser (1966: 83) concludes that Newar society as a whole comprises twenty-six castes ('*jāt*'). The attempt to delineate a pan-Newar caste system, however, is flawed for one basic reason—there was never a pan-Newar society. It is true that at the time of Sthiti Malla the entire Valley was unified under a single ruler. But the three cities and their satellite villages and towns remained discrete settlements with their own social organization. For this reason it is specious to create a pan-Newar table of castes as if these all related to one another in any meaningful way.

Synthesizing the work of Toffin (1978) and Gellner (1992) we may delineate seven criteria for situating oneself in relation to others. These are:

1. sharing of cooked food (commensality),
2. sharing of the hookah (water pipe),

3. sharing of water,
4. access to the services of certain ritual specialists,
5. touch,
6. access to different floors of the house, and
7. marriage (connubium or consexuality).

Toffin considers the sharing of cooked food as the most important criterion of all. Generally speaking, one may eat cooked food prepared by anyone from one's own caste and any other considered higher. This is also true for the sharing of the hookah though there are some concessions made for lower castes (§3.4.1). Few men now use the hookah so this is hardly a live issue. Gellner emphasizes the significance of the 'Water line'. Those belonging to 'clean' castes will not accept water from those below them. Those above the line are called 'laḥ calay ju' (lit. 'water goes'), and they refer to those below the line as 'laḥ calay maju' (lit. 'water does not go'). Gellner also points out the significance of access to the services of certain ritual specialists, such as Brahman or Vajrācārya domestic priest and Nāpit Barber for purification.

Traditionally the criterion of touch was the most basic division of the caste system. For older persons this continues to be very important. By comparison, access to different floors in the house is also not as strictly controlled as it once was. The criterion of marriage, however, seems today to be almost as strong as it was in times past, although, without precise historical data it is impossible to tell how strictly the rules used to be enforced.[2] Dumont (1964: 98), working on the preliminary ethnographic reports of Fürer-Haimendorf (1956, 1957, 1962) concludes that Nepal is characterized by a 'systematic use of the disjunction of commensality and connubium'.[3] He then deduces from this that Newar society is not a caste society, a position affirmed by Doherty (1978: 442).[4] This conclusion, as Gellner (1995a: 21) points out, has been criticized by most anthropologists on the Newars. '...Newar society is a paradigm of caste society, not a peripheral, half-tribal exception' (ibid.: 32). Again, 'Caste is, even today, the single most important determinant of a persons attitudes...' (Gellner 1992: 43).

Stephen Greenwold defines Newar castes as 'local, kinship-delimited, preferentially endogamous, commensally restricted groups arranged in a hierarchy' (1978: 484). He also disagrees with Dumont asserting that, in fact, the Newar system 'conforms most stringently to Dumont's definition' of a caste based society (ibid.: 487):

> The Newars, however, do possess a true caste structure; one that contains the essential properties outlined by Dumont. At the heart of caste lies the peculiar and unique relationship between priest and ruler, between Brahman and Kshatriya. In part this relationship is governed by the opposition of purity and impurity. The Brahman is the embodiment of ritual status and his purity is separate from and superior

> to the Kshatriya's embodiment of physical force and political power. (Greenwold 1975: 50)

To assess the rules that govern intercaste relations we need to take a detailed look at the ethnographic data. But before that we shall take a short excursus to examine the meaning of the term *varna.*

3.2. *Varna*

There has been much argument over the relation of the terms *jāt/jāti* with *varna* (§2.1). It is clear that the terms are not synonymous. Furthermore, there are no substantive caste groups that can be properly categorized as *varna.* To Dumont this does not seem to be a problem as neither *jāti* nor *varna*, in his scheme, need represent actual discrete groups. Dumont's theory, however, does not take seriously the difference between the way these two terms are used. There may, for instance, be two or three types of Brahman in any given locality. Such is the case in Lalitpur. If these castes have no commensal or marriage relations, however, there is no reason to group them together. By calling all such groups Brahman we are accepting their self-designation even though they may not accept one another as such. Rather, then, *varna* is an ideal, a notion, to which various groups, in the mind of the local person, belong. It is meaningless to try to fit substantive caste groups into some definitive *varna* frame. This will always be a contentious issue. *Varna*, then, is more a function of self- and other-consciousness reflecting and, to a certain extent enforcing, certain patterns of behaviour that are thought to be suitable to such a person. As Quigley argues (1993: 139), those from a single *jāti* could belong to any *varna* in the sense that they may take on the roles that traditionally belong to those *varna.* This then makes sense of the wealthy female Tāmrakār informant who insisted most strongly that Tāmrakārs are *kshatriya.* The Tāmrakār can become a *kshatriya* by gaining dominance over other groups and emulating the 'true' *kshatriya*, he may be a *shudra* if he simply provides copper pots for the other *jāti*s, or he may be *vaishya* by emulating the role of the *kshatriya* without having gained any real dominance. In such case the Tāmrakār shopkeeper is the paradigmatic *vaishya.* This explains how Tāmrakārs can see themselves in such different status positions and yet belong to one acknowledged marriage circle.

Newar society demonstrates many of the features found in other caste Hindu societies throughout South Asia. These include mutually endogamous castes and an interdependence of the castes on one another for ritual and economic services. The centrality of the king and the dominant caste (now not a political reality, but still an economically and ritually important one) is another important feature to which we will return in due course.

The Pengu Daḥ constitutes a non-dominant artisan caste in traditional Newar society. Its members provide no ritual services to other castes but are important for the crafts for which they are justly famous.

3.3. General relations of Pengu Daḥ with other castes and ethnic groups

3.3.1. Relations with Maharjans

In no relationship is the contested nature of caste more clearly seen than in that of the Pengu Daḥ with the Maharjan. Gellner (1992: 44) places the Pengu Daḥ alongside the Maharjans in his summary diagram of the castes of Lalitpur. This is the only way it can be demonstrated on a ladder-like diagram, as there is no agreement on the relative ranking of these two large and important groups. In general each will claim the higher ground in any dispute about status. So, for instance, Dil Mohan Tamrakar gave a clear hierarchy of castes in his locality (Cāka Bahi): of the four castes represented, Shrestha are at the top, followed in descending order by Shākya, Tamvaḥ and Jyāpu (Maharjan).[5]

Maharjans will invariably refer to the artisanship of the Pengu Daḥ as evidence for the lower status of the Pengu Daḥ. Certain Newar artisan castes, such as the Citrakār, Manandhar and Nakaḥmi, are less contentiously below the Maharjans. The Maharjan, however, will often make no distinction between these castes and those of the Pengu Daḥ. As artisans they are all tarred with the same brush.

This seems to be the case in other ethnographic settings as well. In the north Indian village of Sherupur, Goldsmiths (now working iron), Ironsmiths, Tailors and Water Carriers ranked slightly lower than common agriculturists (Gould 1964: 19).

The Pengu Daḥ, however, argue that this is a false association. For them, their higher status vis-à-vis the Maharjans, is clearly demonstrated in four ways: by their access to Tantric Initiation,[6] by reference to the Civil Code (*Muluki Ain*), by the fact that Maharjan tenants have traditionally had subservient *jajmāni* relations with their Pengu Daḥ landlords (§3.4.3), and by the fact that the Pengu Daḥ are seen increasingly as one with the Urāy of Kathmandu, who are indisputably higher than the Maharjans (§3.3.2). The status differential has been expressed in a number of different ways. One was in the language of deference with the tenant farmer expected to address the landlord as father (§3.4.3). Another was in eating arrangements, as Dil Mohan Tamrakar put it: 'In the past, when we had a feast (*bhway*) the Jyāpus would sit in a row by themselves and clear up their own place afterwards. Nowadays they leave it for us to clear up.'

Mahila Shilpakar contends that the old Civil Code listed the Maharjans as *shudra*, with a right to Rs. 60 as *biharpati*,[7] but that the Pengu Daḥ were considered in the same document as *vaishya*, those who have a right to Rs. 120 for the same.[8]

Both Gellner (1992: 52) and Vaidya (1986: 135) report the story of a dispute over precedence between 'two women, one Maharjan, one Tāmrakār *et al.*'. The fact of the dispute and its cause is not in doubt but the details of these reports are not accurate. During the rule of Bhim Shamsher Rana (1929-1932), three Tāmrakār and at least two Maharjan women were taking part in the Observance (*uposhadha vrata*) at Kwā Bāhāḥ. There arose a dispute over precedence that was eventually decided in favour of the Maharjans on the basis that Tamvaḥ eat chicken but these Maharjan women (having taken Tantric Initiation) did not.[9] Mahila Shilpakar was most emphatic that this was a mistake. One cannot, he insisted, compare whole castes on the basis of the Tantric Initiation of a few.[10]

One indicator of relative ritual status is that of commensality. In the dispute over relative ranking of the Pengu Daḥ and Maharjans, however, this also is not definitive. One Tāmrakār informant insisted that he could not eat boiled rice prepared by a Maharjan but that the Maharjan could eat rice prepared by a Tāmrakār. From the Maharjan perspective, however, it is the other way around. In actual fact Maharjans and members of the Pengu Daḥ never eat together in the normal run of things so such an argument is purely hypothetical.

Another aspect of commensality is the sharing of the hookah. Men of equal status as those of the Pengu Daḥ can share the entire hookah. Beyond that, however, there does not seem to be agreement on how much of the hookah (which comprises four parts) could be shared by those of other castes. Some Pengu Daḥ men say that lower castes including Maharjan and Khadgi (but not Dyaḥlā) could smoke from the top bowl (*cilā*) but others say that they might only smoke from half a coconut shell and are not to use any part of the hookah.

The Shilpakārs of Bhaktapur present yet another twist in the relations of the Pengu Daḥ with other castes. Fürer-Haimendorf asserts that there is no ban on the intermarriage of lineages of identical name that are found in more than one town (1956: 30). This is not wholly true of the Pengu Daḥ and analogous groups in other cities. The Pengu Daḥ of Lalitpur, and especially the related Tamvaḥ of Bhaktapur all agree, for instance, that the Shilpakārs of Bhaktapur are part of the Farmer caste (which are not called Maharjan in Bhaktapur but are considered of analogous status) and therefore not within the permissible marriage circle.[11] The consequence of this for the Tāmrakār families in Bhaktapur is that they usually have to contract marriages with families from Lalitpur or Panauti.

3.3.2. Relations with Urāy

The confusion that has often been evident in the literature over the relative identities of the Pengu Daḥ and Urāy is clearly a result of a tendency to assume one overall hierarchy within the entire Newar social field. A study of the relations of similar and analogous groups, across city boundaries demonstrates that this tendency is unfounded. The Urāy, or Tulādhar *et al.* (to use Gellner's terminology), are indeed analogous to the Pengu Daḥ in Kathmandu. The two groups have until relatively recently, however, barred intermarriage. Although there is a widespread understanding among members of the Pengu Daḥ that intermarriage is acceptable ('since democracy') this rarely takes place even today.[12] It is clear, however, that the rules have been relaxed in recent years. Kirti Kumar Tamrakar put it like this:

> They would say, 'We can't give you our daughters because you eat chicken'. But they gave their daughters anyway and said to them 'Just don't eat chicken when you are here at your natal home.'

Srinivas addresses this issue: 'Social relations tended to be confined within a chief's or Raja's territory.... One of the consequences of such a vertical division was that the horizontal spread of caste ties could not cross the political boundary' (Srinivas 1956, quoted in Pocock 1960: 67).

In a later essay he further states: 'The numerical strength of a caste influences the kind of relations which it has with the other castes, and this is one of the reasons why each multicaste village to some extent constitutes a unique hierarchy' (Srinivas 1998: 106).[13]

As many Rājkarnikārs live in Kathmandu and some have intermarried with Tulādhars, Lewis goes so far as to include the Rājkarnikār *thar* as a subgroup of the Urāy (1995: 47). In a discussion with Gellner, Lewis asserts that the Rājkarnikārs might be unique in breaking the normal town endogamy (ibid.: 76, n.20). It is only recently, however, that Rājkarnikārs have lived in Kathmandu.[14] The breaking of town endogamy must be seen as part of the impact of the 'unification' of Nepal with the ascendancy of the house of Shah and, even more, of the Ranas. The recently formed *ad hoc* committee of the Urāy has dealt with the vexing question of whether the Rājkarnikārs are part of the Urāy or not by saying that, for the time being, the organization is open only to those Urāy from Kathmandu (Gellner 1999: 17). This has effectively excluded the Rājkarnikārs until a national body is set up. Whether the Urāy will be inclined to form a national body with the Pengu Daḥ is yet to be seen. Doing so will certainly create a stronger political lobby but the boundaries that have been carefully policed for so long will inevitably be weaker and even indefensible. This is, as Gellner remarks, very much a modern conundrum. In the not-too-distant past there would have been no great felt need to define such neatly bounded units.

Many would place the Tulādhars and Pengu Daḥ on an equal footing in terms of ritual status but between the groups there is no consensus. One Rājkarnikār informant whose family have lived in Kathmandu for some generations was adamant that the Rājkarnikārs are a higher caste than the Tulādhars and should not intermarry with them. One Tulādhar man's father was a Rājkarnikār who did marry a Tulādhar woman. This was unacceptable to the Rājkarnikār community so he was excluded from his death *guthi.* The excommunicated Rājkarnikār's son now worships the Tulādhar Tantric Deity at Yetkha, Kathmandu, but also continues to worship the Rājkarnikār Lineage Deity at Iti *twaḥ*, Lalitpur. In this case lineal affiliation was not severed though membership in the caste *guthi* was. As Höfer writes of the Civil Code, 'While children belong to their father's descent group, they do not necessarily attain the latter's caste status' (1979: 81).

The Tāmrakārs living in Kathmandu belong to two distinct groups: those indigenous to Kathmandu and those who have recently migrated from Lalitpur, Bhaktapur or Panauti. The Tāmrakār of Kathmandu (referred to as Tavaḥ) are a sub-group of the Urāy and, unlike the Tavaḥ of Lalitpur, employ a Buddhist priest for life-cycle rituals. It seems that no intermarriage between the two groups has taken place.

Kathmandu also has its population of indigenous Lwahãkaḥmi. As with the Lwahãkaḥmi of Lalitpur (a few of whom have moved in recent generations to Kathmandu), Kathmandu's Lwahãkaḥmi are woodcarvers and stonemasons but do not belong to the same marriage circle. The Lwahãkaḥmi of Kathmandu, living in Yetkha, belong to different lineages from those of Lalitpur, worship a different Lineage Deity and intermarry with the other Urāy sub-groups.

The Sikaḥmi who live in Kathmandu, like the Tāmrakārs, are of two groups. The Pengu Daḥ will only intermarry with one lineage of Kathmandu Sikaḥmi, those considered *kāshyapgotra.* This clearly must be a lineage of Sikaḥmi who migrated from Lalitpur to Kathmandu not too long ago. Informants did not know of a time when they were not living in Kathmandu, so the migration has been forgotten, at least in the folklore of the average Pengu Daḥ member.

3.3.3. Relations with 'lower' castes in Lalitpur

Gellner's diagram of Lalitpur castes (1992: 44, Fig.6) clearly shows that the Pengu Daḥ are considered higher than such castes as the Citrakārs and Nāpits. This is expressed in the role of the Nāpit woman (Nauni) who, as she does for members of all castes higher than her own, pares the toenails of the Pengu Daḥ as part of their purification ritual.

For the most part members of the Pengu Daḥ have a clear view of which groups are below them in the caste hierarchy. These are groups with which they cannot eat boiled rice or share the hookah. As with other Newars, the Pengu Daḥ members express their attitude towards castes they consider lower than themselves by the use of space within the house. Such castes as Nāpit, Citrakār, Mānandhar, Ranjitkār, and Nakaḥmi were traditionally allowed up to the first floor (*mātã*) although the visiting Nāpit woman (Nauni) may today be invited up to the second floor (*cwata*) when she pares the toenails of her patrons. Below these castes are the 'water-unacceptable' (*laḥ calay maju*) groups such as the Khadgi butchers and the Kāpāli tailor-musicians and below them are the Dyaḥlā 'Untouchables', whose mere touch traditionally requires ritual purification. Traditionally (and still today but not so strictly) water-unacceptable castes are only allowed in to the ground floor (*cheli*) of the house. Marriage with one from any of these castes is strictly proscribed for the Pengu Daḥ. A generation ago a Tāmrakār man from Haugaḥ eloped with a Mānandhar woman and was immediately expelled from the death *guthi.* Their progeny have been forced to use the matronymic and in everyone's eyes belong to that caste.[15] Such intermarriage is not acceptable to the Pengu

Daḥ. Shepard also reports a marriage between a Lwahākaḥmi and a Citrakār that was not accepted by the caste (1985: 223).

3.3.4. Relations with 'higher' castes in Lalitpur

Though Jyāpu, being considered lower, are traditionally allowed only up to the second floor (*cwata*), members of other castes (Shrestha, Bramhu, Vajrācārya/Shākya) from whom a member of the Pengu Daḥ may take boiled rice are allowed right up to the top floor (*baigaḥ*). The Pengu Daḥ assert that they are free to intermarry with all such groups. Quigley (1995a) has demonstrated the extreme delicacy with which Shresthas have to carry out enquiries in looking for a suitable match for a son or a daughter. It is commonly known that any upwardly mobile Newars from the middle castes might change their name to Shrestha in order to give an appearance of higher status (Rosser 1966). I know of no instance in which a member of the Pengu Daḥ changed his name to Shrestha, though one family has adopted the title Tulādhar. The motivation, it seems to me, is purely the desire for greater prestige. There is a chance of intermarriage with Kathmandu Tulādhars but a simple change of name will certainly not enable that. It is easy to trace pedigree so I do not see this as an attempt to hoodwink more prestigious castes into contracting marriage alliances with them. Moreover, as pointed out earlier (§2.6.2), one Rājkarnikār goes by the name of Pradhān but likewise this does not seem to be an attempt at social climbing; his family was living for a long time in East Nepal where many Newars are called Pradhān.

Although small in proportion to the intracaste marriages contracted by the Pengu Daḥ a surprising number of Tāmrakār women have contracted marriages with Shresthas.[16] Furthermore, many Pengu Daḥ are relatively wealthy and seem to present an acceptable proposition to a Shrestha family seeking a secure and comfortable marriage for their daughter. Such acceptable intercaste marriages are invariably with Shresthas, rarely Shākyas, and unheard of with Vajrācāryas or Rājopādhyāyas.[17]

3.3.5. Relations with non-Newars

Traditionally, members of the Pengu Daḥ have not had much social interaction with non-Newars. Marriage with non-Newars is strongly taboo. The marriage of a Lwahākaḥmi with an Indian twenty years ago was strongly condemned by the caste (Shepard 1985: 223). One Tāmrakār who has settled with his family in New York recently brought each of his sons back to Nepal to marry women from the Pengu Daḥ. In recent years, however, with increased intercaste socialising a number of 'love marriages' have taken place with non-Newars. In one case, two daughters of one Rājkarnikār eloped with non-Newar men, one with a Rai and the other with a Gurung. While the women's grandfather was alive they were not even allowed in their natal house—they had become 'Untouchables'. After their grandfather's death they have been allowed in the home but are not allowed to touch the cooking hearth (*bhutu*).

3.3.6 Isogamy, hypergamy, introversion and endogamy

It will be clear from the foregoing discussion that the Pengu Daḥ constitute a prime example of an endogamous caste in which marriages are contracted isogamously (i.e., between equals). Other ethnographies demonstrate that this is the typical Newar pattern (e.g., Toffin 1984; Quigley 1986; Gellner and Quigley 1995). Moreover, there has been a strong felt need (one might even say a preoccupation) in the Newar community, with the policing of caste boundaries. Newar castes are, therefore, not only endogamous, but also introverted to a high degree. It is not that the Pengu Daḥ cannot countenance any intermarriage with other castes—as we have seen in the case of marriages contracted with Shresthas—but rather that there is a marked preference for marriage within the caste.

The distinction, then, is expressed in terms of purity and pollution. The crossing of the boundaries of ritual propriety can lead to the most dreadful consequences for the offender. Why this importance attached to issues of ritual purity? Is it, as Dumont would have us believe, because of the pervasion of notions of hierarchical ideology? Or is there some structural solution to this problem that holds even when the ideology is removed or transformed? As Quigley explains, the issues of pollution and caste separation are intimately related: 'The pervasiveness of notions of pollution and separation derives from the need to make kinship boundaries unambiguous as a way of creating stability in this political climate' (1993: 129). I will return to the 'political climate' in question later. For now we will be content to note this major theme of introversion and isogamy.

In spite of this strong tendency to isogamy there is, nevertheless, a minor theme of hypergamy (i.e., marrying women 'up') that begs for attention. It is notable that the majority of reported hypergamous unions of the Pengu Daḥ are with Shresthas. Hypergamy is a well-documented phenomenon among the Rājputs and Brahmans of north India (Parry 1979). The Rājputs of north India constitute the dominant caste in much the same way as the Shresthas of the Kathmandu Valley do but, unlike the Shresthas, strongly favour hypergamous unions. The remarkable fact that comes out of the ethnographies is that, in predominantly hypergamous contexts, lower castes are more eager to rise to the status of the *kshatriya* rather than of the *brahman*. This is borne out in the foregoing data as well. Although Newars are predominantly isogamous, members of castes such as the Pengu Daḥ, if considering a nonisogamous union, will very often prefer a hypergamous one with a member of the dominant Shrestha caste. This brings up a significant issue: 'In what sense, then' asks Quigley (1993: 101), 'are Brahmans the highest caste if there is no aspiration for social mobility into this group'? Before we can answer this question we must examine the place of *jajmāni* relations.

3.4. *Jajmāni* relations

3.4.1. The role of *jajmāni* relations in the caste system

The relation between a patron and client in South Asia has traditionally been labelled a *jajmāni* relation (<*jajmān*, Skt., 'patron'). Such patron-client relations have been observed in many varied ethnographic settings, being first described by Wiser in 1936. There has been much discussion in the literature over whether there is any justification for calling such relations a *jajmāni* system. The discussion hinges on whether the relation is purely economic or entails some element of ritual service. Beidelman criticizes Wiser and attempts to explain the '*jajmāni* system' in purely economic terms (Pocock 1962: 79). A number of authors distinguish between relations that are primarily economic, providing a commodity, and those that are ritual, providing a service (Harper 1959; Berreman 1972: 57-58; Mayer 1960: 63-72).

It is certainly too simplistic to view the patron-client relationship as purely exploitative in one direction only as Berreman does (1972: 60). Parry reports that the financial demands made by the Mahābrāhman death specialists of Banāras (equivalent to the Karamjit of the Kathmandu Valley) to his patron do not fit the usual presentation of *jajmāni* relations (1980: 102). These are one-off payments. There is no long-term stable relationship and there certainly does not seem to be exploitation by the patron. If anyone, it is the patrons who are being exploited by an unfair monopoly.

Pocock asserts that the test that divides religious specialists from those who are merely commercial is whether the caste survives when their secular activity is replaced. He gives the example of the continuity of the Barbers who have largely lost their work of shaving, and that of the Weavers who have, he asserts, been eliminated with the introduction of mill cloth (1962: 85). He reports that nowhere are artisan groups such as Carpenters, Ironsmiths, Potters and Stonemasons said to have tied, status-governed relationships that one associates with the religious *jajmāni* relationships (ibid.: 86). He concludes by arguing for the reservation of the term *jajmāni* for those relations with religious specialists such as Priests, Barbers and Washermen (ibid.: 92).

Others call for a complete abandonment of the notion of a *jajmāni* system citing that its misuse has led to much confusion (Parry 1980; Good 1982; Fuller 1989). Fuller argues that it was important for Dumont and others to project such institutions as the '*jajmāni* system' as characteristic of 'traditional' Indian society, in order to enhance their argument that it is fundamentally different from modern, Western society (1989: 33). He concludes, 'the concept of the *jajmāni* system... is predicated upon a combination of historical inaccuracy and the ahistorical premise of unchanging, "traditional" India' (ibid.: 57).

Nevertheless, as an analytic tool, the teasing out of relations between patron and clients can be most instructive. In this study I will keep the term *jajmāni* as an analytical tool while acknowledging that such a structure may not apply to all patron-client relations.

3.4.2. *Jajmāni* relations in Newar societies

Patron-client relations in Newar society persist to this day even though the economic interdependency that it represents is a shadow of its former self. In contrast to the form reported in some north Indian situations, Newar *jajmāni* relations seem to be rather less elaborate (Gellner 1992: 208). The most striking characteristic of *jajmāni* relations in Newar society is the marked difference between those of *shivamārgi* and those of *buddhamārgi* patrons: 'In the organization of priestly functions in the two religions there is a striking asymmetry. Whereas the Vajrācārya combines within himself the roles of teacher (*guru*) and priest of all kinds, the Shaivites have an extreme specialization of priestly functions' (ibid.: 60).

Why this extreme specialization of priestly functions among the Shaivites? Here the centrality of the king in Hindu society expresses itself very forcefully. It has always been true in Hindu society, as it was in the feudal society of medieval Europe, that the religious inclinations of the king and the ruling class have had a habit of replicating themselves within ever lower echelons of that society. It is well known that Hindu monarchs have had a penchant for multiplying the number and variety of specialists that serve them. In so doing the royal centre extended direct patronage to a maximum number of caste groups in the kingdom. A study of *jajmāni* relations in the Newar community seems to indicate that, over the centuries of Shaivite rule, an increasing proportion of Newars, especially those who think of themselves as *kshatriya*, have felt it advantageous to ape this greater specialization. Gellner puts it thus: 'High-caste Hindus are fulfilling the role of Kshatriyas, and to do that they have to have *jajmāni* links to as many specialists as possible' (1992: 61). In fact, however, it is not as simple as a case of high-caste Hindus attempting to fulfil the role of *kshatriya* as it is of Newars of *any* caste doing so.

Up to the recent past, payment for ritual services was almost always in kind (*bali*) (Toffin 1978: 475). Today payment is almost always in cash and can in some cases amount to considerable sums of money. Sambhu Raj Tamrakar voiced the sentiment of many a *jajmān* in relation to such inflationary costs: 'Before under the Rana regime the government had control. They would tell how much must be charged for a copper pot, for instance. Now there is no control.'

Pocock's (1962: 86) assertion that artisan groups have an internal hierarchy within which the higher one is he who is freer to trade competitively does not seem to be true of Newar artisans.

Newars traditionally have often used kinship terminology to express hierarchy in certain *jajmāni* relations. A Tāmrakār or *shivamārgi* Sikaḥmi, for instance, will address his Brahman domestic priest (*purohit*) as grandfather (*bājyā*). The same form of address was used, until recently, by the 'Untouchable' Dyaḥlā to any member of the middle and higher castes including the Pengu Daḥ.

3.4.3. *Jajmāni* relations common to all Pengu Daḥ

a. Maharjan

Many households of the Pengu Daḥ own some agricultural land, a few own a good deal of land including large acreage on the Tarai. As with the purchase of gold, wealthy Newars traditionally invested heavily in land that was considered to give a decent return for a low risk. Such land, if it was in the Valley, was almost always leased to Maharjan farmers. The relation of landlord (*taḥsī*) to tenant (*mhāy*), however, was always considered to be more than purely economic (Gellner and Pradhan 1995: 169). As the servant of the landlord the tenant would have a number of ritual functions to perform. Thus the relation of landlord to tenant, if not exactly like that to certain other castes, approximated to that of a *jajmāni* relationship. Furthermore, the relationship was virtually permanent—being passed on from generation to generation—and entailed moral responsibilities from both sides.

The head tenant (Mhāy Nāyaḥ) has the duty to ensure that the proper amount of grain from the land is brought to the landlord. In the past this was 50 per cent of the product, but the Land Reform Acts have fixed it at twenty-three *pāti*s of paddy per *ropani* of land, which, with increased yields from new varieties of rice has worked considerably in favour of the tenant. A common complaint from landlords is that the tenant hands over twenty-three *pāti*s of the worst quality rice from the yield. Land reform has also changed the way land can be bought and sold. In the past the tenants had no right to a share of the land. But since the 1960s the landlord has had to give, first 25 per cent, and now 50 per cent of the value of the land on its sale. Nowadays, landlords groan, the power of the tenant is so great that they can demand 'their' share at any time. Then if they continue to farm the remaining half of the land for the landlord, after three years they can claim a further 50 per cent. Dil Mohan Tamrakar, bemoaned this:

> Our fathers worked hard to buy land for their families. They bought land for farming, and built temples, dug wells. Now people just want to spend their money on televisions and videos. But our fathers had a lot of pain (*dukha*) to buy land. They worked hard with their hands and wore old clothes with holes in. In those days they only wore nice clothes when they were going to a feast. People would shout out 'Where are you going?' to them if they saw them in nice clothes. They didn't wear nice clothes like we do these days even when we sit in our shops or homes.

The new wealth and power of the tenant has also emboldened him to equalize the status relation between him and his landlord. Landlords, for their part, lament the current lack of deference shown by their tenants to them. In the past this was expressed in the language of a son to his father but such 'undemocratic' language is seldom heard today. Nevertheless, landlord-tenant relations live on if somewhat muted by modernity.

Traditional ritual duties continue to be fulfilled at certain festivals and life-cycle rites. With the ubiquitous use of the telephone, the old practice of sending the tenant to the house of married-out daughters to call them for a feast (*nakhaḥtyā*) is now defunct. He may, however, still be called to deliver the *lākha mari* sweet, which continues to act as a formal invitation to an upcoming wedding. Moreover, at the birth of a baby to a married-out daughter the Mhāy Nāyaḥ takes food and cloth to the woman on the day of Birth Purification (Macābu Bẽkegu).[18] On the marriage of the landlord's son it is the Mhāy Nāyaḥ who carries the pole and baskets (*khāmu*) in front of the procession. During the Mock Marriage (Ihi) ritual he is the one who carries the *khāmu* with *pujā* materials to the temple for the special worship ritual.

At the Old-Age Initiation (Bura Jãkwa) the Mhāy Nāyaḥ is given several fetching and carrying jobs. He is regarded as a faithful servant but never entrusted with more money that is necessary. During the procession he is the one who goes ahead of the palanquins to lay out the band of white cloth over which the initiated ones must pass.

b. Aji

The wife of the *mhāy nāyaḥ* often fulfils the role of the Midwife (Aji).[19] At the time of research the Aji's role as the traditional birth attendant is not required so much as mothers give birth largely in hospital. In spite of this, she is still considered important in her role in purification and appeasement of the malevolent goddess Ajimā (Hāriti). In this role the Pengu Daḥ call her for Birth Purification on the fourth, sixth, eighth or tenth day after birth. Interestingly she also acts as a sort of assistant to the Brahman priest at the House Purification rite (Ghaḥsu) after death though it is not clear whether any pure outsider to the lineage could have performed this role. One Tamvaḥ man was of the opinion that this relation goes back to when Tamvaḥ used Maharjan cremation specialists (Gwā) a practice that has been largely discontinued due to the rise in cost. As Gellner and Pradhan note it is interesting that Maharjan women are present at a birth while Maharjan men traditionally were present at death (1995: 173). The cremation specialists, associated with the fierce male god Bhairava, are feared as bogy figures, whereas the midwife is often resorted to as a folk healer with her special relationship to Ajimā, the goddess of smallpox.

c. Citrakār

All Pengu Daḥ call the Citrakār Painter at the auspicious life-cycle rites of Mock Marriage, Marriage (Ihipāḥ) and Old-Age Initiation. Their skill is considered essential for the painting of the auspicious symbols around the entrance to the house. In addition, depending on the occasion, there are often a number of other painted items that are required. At Mock Marriage, the Citrakār paints the clay pots for the *pujā* and pictures of deities on paper that are affixed to the girls' heads. For this he receives a formal proportion of the total ritual fee (*dakshina*). The Citrakār may also command a high additional fee for his services. For painting the house entrance and palanquin (*khaḥ*) at a Marikaḥmi Old-Age Initiation the Citrakār was paid Rs. 4,000—a very high fee for a morning's work reflecting the scarcity of capable Citrakārs in Lalitpur.[20]

d. Awāle

The Awāle (Potter) is called to make the pots (*kalĩca*) for the Flask Worship (*kalasha pujā*) that is performed at each of the auspicious life-cycle rites of Mock Marriage, Marriage and Old-Age Initiation. In Bhaktapur additionally the Tamvaḥ also call the Potter (Prajāpati) to make the *alindyaḥ*–a clay image for worship at Mock Marriage. The relation of patron to Potter is now not clearly one of permanence and mutual responsibility. Some Pengu Daḥ members purchase the necessary items with cash (*nyana hayegu*). It would seem, then, that the traditional *jajmāni* relationship has in a large measure broken down retaining its more traditional character in the more conservative city of Bhaktapur where the Potter continues to receive a share of the *dakshina.*

e. Kāpāli (Jogi)

All Pengu Daḥ call a female Kāpāli (Jogini) to be fed on the seventh day after a death in the household. From the Kāpāli's side this has a great stigma attached to it so, as many have other sources of income, most have given up the role altogether. I was told in 1999 that only one Kāpāli continues this tradition. She may charge up to Rs. 1,000 in addition to the large plate of food that she is presented.

In addition Kāpāli men would traditionally play the Medieval-style oboe or shawm (*muhāli*) at life-cycle processions and certain festivals, most importantly as part of the Nava Bājā group during the Nyaku Jātrā (§7.18.3). This has been largely abandoned altogether except at the important citywide festivals of Nava Bājā, Mohani (§8.8.2) and the Bũgadyaḥ Jātrā (§10.7.2). One Tamvaḥ man told me that this was purely economic—'If they can earn Rs. 300 or 400 by doing some other job they don't want to just get Rs. 100 for playing the *muhāli.* 'It would seem, however, that prestige is at stake here as well. The playing of the *muhāli* at processions clearly marks a man as a Kāpāli, whom most still consider to be unclean. Now, for city festivals, a group of three men of the Untouchable Parbatiyā caste, Damai, are called from nearby Jhāmsikhel to take their place. For weddings a larger group are usually hired. Interestingly the Damai have switched over entirely to what are considered more prestigious Western instruments, the leader on a Western oboe with the others playing trumpets, euphonia and drums—forming what is called a *ben bājā* (< Eng., 'band').

f. Nāpit (Nau/Nauni)

The relation between a *jajmān* and his Barber (Nāpit, Nau) continues to be strong. The Barber is called to shave the head of the *thākāli* (eldest male) for all major life-cycle rituals. He also has the role of shaving the head of Newar boys at their First Head-Shaving after the boy's maternal uncle has first shaved a token lock. In the past all men of the household and other close agnatic males would be shaved before all *samskāra*s. The vast majority of Newars no longer considers this necessary. Indeed many Nāpits have abandoned the trade altogether as other opportunities for employment have presented themselves in the modern economy. The paring of nails of the lineage by the Barber's wife or daughter (Nauni), however, is still considered an essential ritual of purification before all life-cycle rites. The day before the main ritual, or sometimes the morning of the ritual itself, the Nauni comes to cut, or touch (*lusi thiyegu*) the toenails and paint the toes of all the household members red. In the past this would also have been completed before Lineage Deity Worship (*digu dyaḥ pujā*; §9.23) but today is omitted by those, such as all the Lwahãkaḥmi, who do an attenuated form of this yearly ritual.

g. Dyaḥlā (Pwaḥ)

The relation of the Dyaḥlā 'Untouchable' Sweepers to the Pengu Daḥ seems never to have been that of a proper *jajmāni* relation, though they would address the Pengu Daḥ, as other middle and high caste Newars, as grandfather (*bājyā*) and grandmother (*aji*). Rather, the relation was more that of beggar to alms-giver. In the past when they would come to sweep the streets and clean latrines the householders would place rice or some other foodstuff into their bowl in exchange for their services. This highly precarious living on the part of the Dyaḥlā has been much improved by the forming of modern labour relations with the municipality that pays them a monthly salary for their work. Middle and high caste Newars expect no deference from the sweepers today and know they better watch out when a group of Dyaḥlā women wend their way down the street swinging their carrying poles with baskets full of dirt.

3.4.4. *Jajmāni* relations particular to *shivamārgi* Pengu Daḥ

a. Rājopādhyāya Brahman domestic priest (Brahmu *purohit*)

All Tamvaḥ (Figure 1), Pahmā Sikaḥmi and some Bārāhi call a Newar Brahman (Rājopādhyāya Brahmu) for the important *pujā*s associated with life-cycle rituals including all *samskāra*s except Birth Purification and all occasions of Ancestor Worship (*shraddha*). In addition, the Jhvaḥchẽ Tamvaḥ lineage calls the Brahmu priest to officiate at the full Lineage Deity Worship. They are, in fact, the last remaining lineage of Tamvaḥ to do this.

For most rituals only one Brahman priest is required. In recent years, however, when a Fire Sacrifice (*yajña*, *homa*) is required (such as at Mock Marriage, Marriage and Old-Age Initiation), Lalitpur's *shivamārgi*s have been forced to call on the services of two extra Brahmans. These take the place of the Joshi and Karmācārya who no longer fulfil their respective ritual services for their erstwhile *jajmān*s. The Brahmans receive a ritual fee (*dakshina*) for their services. Pengu Daḥ patrons often express resentment at the fact that they are dependent on the priests for their services. During the rituals attending the Old-Age Initiation of a Tamvaḥ man and his wife the *jajmān* expressed deep annoyance at the way the three Brahman priests were taking so long to complete the ritual keeping the rest of the proceedings on hold. With a shrug of the shoulders, he explained that at such times they are completely at the priests' mercy.

Sometimes the views of the priest are in direct contrast to those of his patron. During the preparatory discussions for the above-mentioned Old-Age Initiation the priest was most insistent that the chariots should not be welcomed to the house through the first-floor window after the procession. This custom, he argued, had no textual basis and had been adopted by the Tamvaḥ from their *buddhamārgi* affines. In the end a compromise was struck by which the priest got to do the ritual Welcome (*laskus*) at the door front and the couple were subsequently brought in through the window.

Apart from the standard ritual fee (*dakshina*), another type of prestation is also given to the Brahman priest from time to time. On the death of a family member, *shivamārgi* Pengu Daḥ give to their domestic priest (*purohit*) the inauspicious donation (*dān*). This is usually interpreted by the giver as a gift to the deceased though it is clear from studies of gift giving in India that such prestations have strongly impure connotations (Parry 1980, Raheja 1988a).

Buddhamārgi members of the Pengu Daḥ also, on occasion, employ a Brahman priest. The Marikaḥmi, for instance, call a Brahman if they want to sponsor the performance of a Satyanārāyana Pujā. Furthermore, on the occasion of a death in the family, they call the Brahman for the reading of the *Garuda Purāna* in the deceased's home. Pandit Madan Mohan Mishra sees these phenomena as evidence of their ostensible Brahman background.[21] To me, however, it seems more likely to be evidence of Brahmanization as a result of their relations with Rana rulers and relative economic prosperity over the last hundred years or so.[22] Interestingly, the family of former Tāmrakārs whose paternal grandfather married a Mānandhar (and was thence forced to adopt the matronymic, §3.4.3) still engages a Brahman domestic priest.

b. Joshi

Traditionally, and still today in Bhaktapur, the Joshi Astrologer had an important role as a kind of assistant to the Brahman domestic priest. In the joint celebration of Mock Marriage in the house of the host, Hiraman Kaji Tamrakar of Bhaktapur, the Joshi sat at the left hand of the Brahman as he conducted the Fire Sacrifice assisting him in many of the rituals. Today in Lalitpur, Joshis are no longer available to perform this service so, as I have already indicated, a second Brahman might take his place. In Lalitpur,

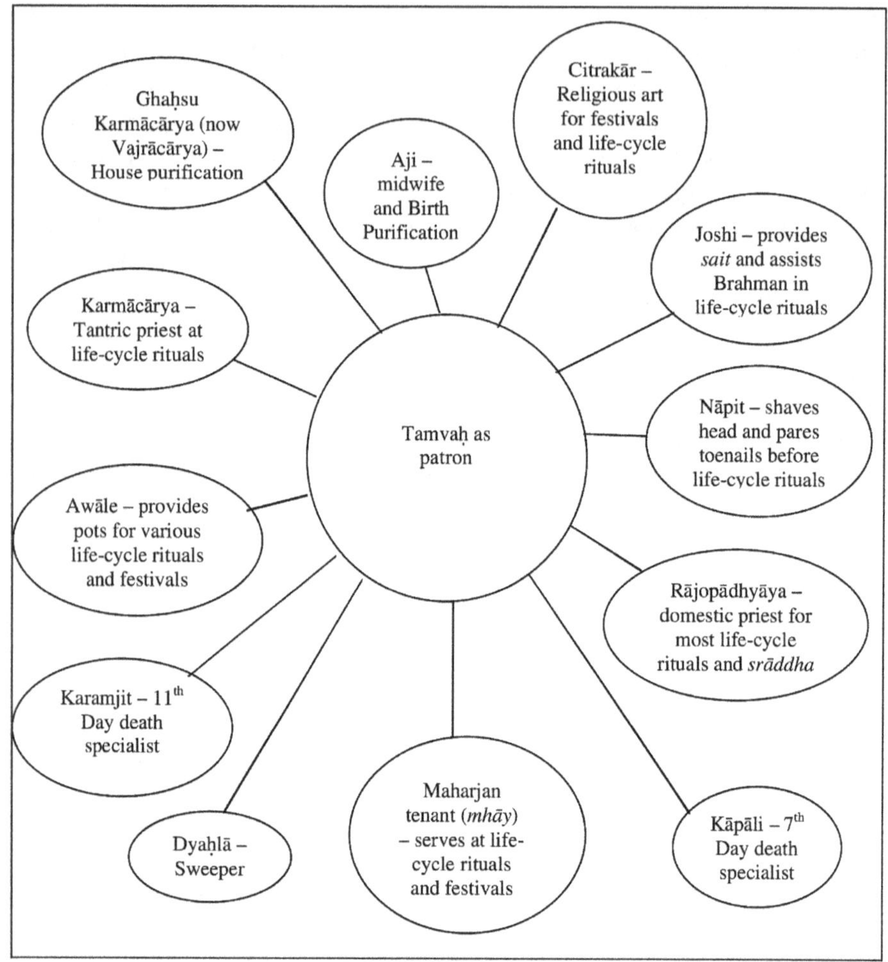

Figure 1. Traditional Tamvaḥ *jajmāni* relations.

nevertheless, the Joshi is consulted whenever someone needs to find out the auspicious time for the conducting of a life-cycle ritual or important *pujā.* Some Pengu Daḥ *jajmān*s, however, conscious of the high cost of such consultations today, skip it altogether, conducting the ritual at a time that is simply convenient.

c. Karmācārya (Acāḥju)

Until recently the Karmācārya Tantric priest was called by *shivamārgi jajmān*s on a number of occasions. This role is still performed by the Karmācārya at those occasions in the homes of Bhaktapur's Tamvaḥ *jajmān*s. During the Flask Worship and Fire Sacrifice conducted by the Brahman *purohit* and his Joshi assistant the Karmācārya performs a parallel *pujā* in which various Tantric deities are worshipped. His role also includes the sacrifice of a goat during the *pujā* at the Power-Place (*pitha*) outside the city. Bhaktapur's more conservative culture, then, probably retains such elements that would have been common to all three cities until fairly recently. Today in Lalitpur no Karmācārya is active in his traditional ritual role. Because of this, some Tamvaḥ have gone to the town of Thimi, near Bhaktapur, to call a Karmācārya to perform House Purification after a family member dies. The majority of *shivamārgi* Pengu Daḥ, however, have given up on Karmācārya altogether and begun hiring the services of a Vajrācārya priest to do this. A number of Pengu Daḥ men explained it purely in economic terms—the Karmācārya charges two or three times that of the Vajrācārya to perform House Purification.

A number of Pengu Daḥ men remarked to me that 'before' they only called Karmācārya but that at some time Brahmans gained ascendancy usurping their role. Surya Lal Barahi, whose household is self-consciously *shivamārgi*, insisted on this emphatically: 'In *satya yuga* we only had the Acāḥju.'[23]

d. Karamjit (Bhāḥ)

Till the recent past *shivamārgi* Pengu Daḥ called the Karamjit death specialist on the death of one of their household. The Karamjit, also called Mahābrāhman, constitute a small caste whose ritual role is most interesting. The main role of the Karamjit is to attend the house of the dead on the tenth or eleventh day and consume a plate of food that includes a pulverized piece of the deceased's skull (Gellner 1996a: 23; Toffin 1984: 291). In so doing the Karamjit becomes consubstantial with the dead. Today this practice has all but died out. Most Newars do not have any personal experience of this practice but see it as 'something that the royal family does'. And indeed, the royal family of Nepal does continue this practice. A Parbatiyā Jaisi Brahman, in their case, is fed the polluted food and traditionally banished from the kingdom having been laden with costly gifts. On the death of King Birendra in 2001 this was again practised, though the individual concerned was not banished.

Until recently, however, although it seems they had long since given up the practice of feeding pulverized skull to the Karamjit, *shivamārgi* Pengu Daḥ would, nevertheless, give the inauspicious gift (*dān*), consisting of food and cash, to the Karamjit on the seventh day. In Bhaktapur, as might be expected this custom lives on. The Karamjit (Bhã in Bhaktapur dialect) comes to the house to accept *dān* on the seventh, eleventh and thirteenth days after death. Moreover, whenever a Fire Sacrifice is performed at a Bhaktapur Tamvaḥ house, a portion of the ritual fee is given to the Karamjit. When this practice ceased in Lalitpur is not clear.

The difference between the traditional *jajmāni* relations of Tamvaḥ of Lalitpur and Bhaktapur demonstrate how contextual these relations are. Clearly one can only practically use the services of those castes that practice their role in the locality. The difficulty that Lalitpur's *shivamārgi* have had in securing the services of the Karmācārya show how each city could have developed its own unique variation on the *jajmāni* theme. Moreover, the existence (in Bhaktapur) of a locally unique caste, the Shivācārya (Tini), whose services the Tamvaḥ of that city are happy to employ, show how the aspiration to *kshatriya* status, locally expressed, leads to differences of religious practice that transcend the need for uniformity within any given caste.

3.4.5. *Jajmāni* relations particular to *buddhamārgi* Pengu Daḥ

The most glaring reality of the *jajmāni* relations of the *buddhamārgi*s is that, in marked contrast to the practice of the *shivamārgi*s, they use one priest for many of their various ritual needs. The Marikaḥmi (Figure 2), Lwahãkaḥmi and Vishvakarma Sikaḥmi all call a Vajrācārya domestic priest Lwahãkaḥmi exclusively. The same man is called for all life-cycle rituals, except Birth Purification (§3.5.3). He is also called for the performance of Ancestor Worship and Lineage Deity Worship. Moreover, the Vajrācārya *purohit* is the one individual to whom the inauspicious gift (*dān*) is given. In the case of the Marikaḥmi the Vajrācārya priest is presented with *dān* on the forty-fifth day after death and thereafter on the occasion of each monthly *shrāddha* up to and including the first year anniversary. This gift can often be quite substantial including not only cash but also items of furniture, cloth and food. One *jajmān* complained that his *purohit* had become bold and demanding presenting a list of what he wanted for *dān* each month before observing the Ancestor Worship. Over the course of the year it was estimated that the *jajmān* would give items with a total value in excess of Rs. 300,000—an enormous sum by Nepali standards.

3.4.6. The Bārāhi, a lineage in transition

The Bārāhi are unique among the Pengu Daḥ in that they cannot be simply categorized as *shivamārgi* or *buddhamārgi* according to their *jajmāni* relations.[24] Rather they fall into three groups that, we will see, demonstrate what seems to be a transition from *buddhamārgi* to *shivamārgi.* Of the sixteen households for which I have data eleven employ only a Vajrācārya priest for all life-cycle rituals (except, as usual, Birth Purification) and Ancestor Worship. Three households, however, employ only a Rājopādhyāya Brahman for all these rituals. Furthermore, two households, those of the Nāyaḥ and his younger brother, the Bhai Nāyaḥ, call a Rājopādhyāya for life-cycle rituals but a Vajrācārya for Ancestor Worship. Moreover, some Bārāhi boys take a Tantric initiation at their First Rice-Feeding which is performed by a Rājopādhyāya Brahman priest. In addition, some Bārāhi, irrespective of the religious orientation of their domestic priest would, until recently, engage the services of the Karamjit. What is most astonishing to me, however, is that some of the Bārāhi are not aware of this variation in *jajmāni* relations among them.

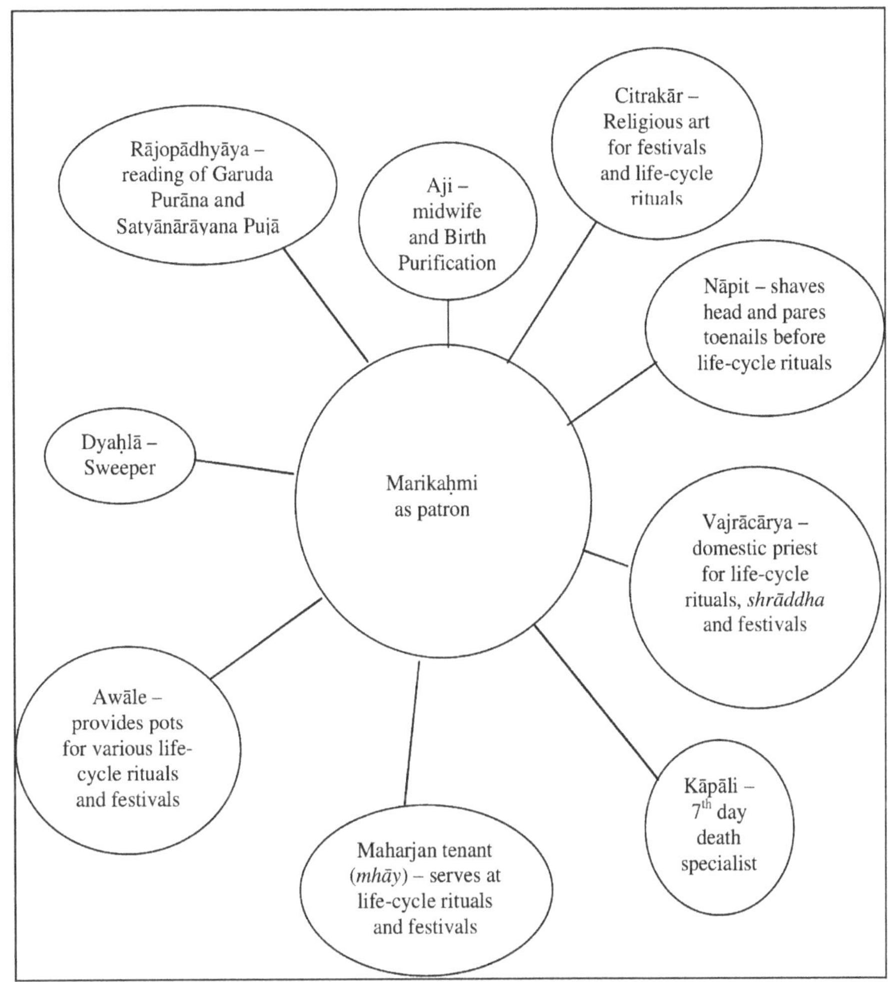

Figure 2. Traditional Marikaḥmi *jajmāni* relations.

This variation is not simply a modern phenomenon—earlier observers also reported the fact. Hodgson's list (in Chattopadhyay 1980: 114) includes 'Barhi or Yang Karmi—wheel wrights and makers of spinning-wheels, Brahman or Bāndya according to creed'. The question arises, then, whether, this variation has always been present, or whether it represents a transition from one path to another? When the Brahmanic initiation of the boys was first instituted is unknown. One Bārāhi, however, was of the opinion that it was somehow related to the Bũgadyaḥ Jātrā, which seems highly likely to me. If so, then it would seem probable that the initiation by a Rājopādhyāya began after, or concurrently with, the establishing of the practice of having two Rājopādhyāya Brahmans ride on the chariot as formal directors of the procession by King Siddhi Narasimha Malla in the mid-seventeenth century

(Locke 1980: 303). This act was surely an attempt by the king to bring the Jātrā, the most important festival of Lalitpur, under a more orthodox Brahmanic rubric (§8.4). If, as Owens reports, the Bārāhi were once Pānjus (1989: 164) then it is easy to see how, at least from the seventeenth century, there was an increasing Brahmanization of the group. Hodgson's report indicates that this transition was already underway in the nineteenth century. This conclusion is also attested by the continued practice of the Bārāhi to call two Vajrācārya priests to perform Lineage Deity Worship for them. Clearly it is easier for a household to switch from one priest to another than it is for an entire clan so this must be seen as representing an older orientation.

Several Bārāhi men agreed that the traditional *purohit* is the Vajrācārya. Kedar Barahi explained it this way: 'If a Gubhāju dies without a son, or the sons don't want to continue the work, then the *jajmān* can choose a new *purohit.* Gubhājus take more time and it needs two of them who both need to be fed. But Brahmans are simpler and you need only one.'[25]

3.4.7. Interpreting *jajmāni* relations

Jajmāni relations, as we have seen, are the relations of the patron, in his emulation of royal *kshatriya* status, to a number of ritual specialists. The ability to pass off as one of *kshatriya* status depends on an interplay of ritual and economic factors. It is not purely an economic issue as only those castes that are considered to be of a certain level of ritual purity have the option of calling the full complement of ritual specialists. The degree of specialization of *jajmāni* relations is not in itself an indicator of the purity, or otherwise, of a household. The religious orientation of the rulers did have an important part to play in influencing previously *buddhamārgi* Newars to switch their allegiance elsewhere. That this has not happened wholesale, however, could be a result of several factors: the deeply conservative nature of Newar society, the extremely small numbers of Rājopādhyāyas, the likelihood that the Malla Kings would not permit the Rājopādhyāyas to take on *jajmān*s too far down the social scale, and the high increase in cost for what is arguably a negligible increase in status that comes with the employment of a Rājopādhyāya domestic priest.

For the Pengu Daḥ, the calling of one or other domestic priest has very little to say about an individual's own religious path. The sentiments of one Tamvaḥ man are echoed by many others: 'I like Buddhist *dharma* even though we are *shivamārgi*'. So long as an individual continues to fulfil his traditional obligations to his family and caste he is free to take an interest in any religion. Furthermore, the precise characteristics of a household's *jajmāni* relations tell us nothing of the household's caste, as Toffin has also noted (1984: 230). The change from the hiring of a Vajrācārya domestic priest to that of a Brahman makes no difference to the marital prospects of that household's daughters or sons. This is an important point as the significance of ideology in the analysis of caste systems has, in my view, often been overrated.

In conclusion, this examination of the *jajmāni* relations of the Pengu Daḥ indicates that *jajmāni* relations, though they may reflect the desire to demonstrate a superior social status, actually make very little, if any, impact on the configuration of caste in Newar society. Rather, by replicating the role of the king—the *jajmān* par excellence—Pengu Daḥ and other *jajmān*s corroborate a key thesis of this work: that, as Quigley and Raheja have demonstrated and as I hope to expound further, the concept of centrality is an important theme of the caste system.

3.5. Intercaste relations and the problem with ladders

The above data on the relations of the Pengu Daḥ with other castes demonstrate that the construction of a ladder-like hierarchical diagram to explicate the caste system is fraught with difficulty. Hierarchy is contested. The ladder as it is perceived by one caste is different from that perceived by another. This is inevitable when such castes have no formal relations with each other.

> Externally, then, the orientation of castes is primarily to the dominant centre, not to each other. Potters and Tailors both know that they are inferior to dominant landholding castes because they have to serve them in various capacities. But if Potters and Tailors have neither economic nor ritual relations with each other, then *ipso facto* it will be impossible to decide who is higher and who is lower. (Quigley 1993: 166)

It is not that ladder diagrams have no place in the analysis of caste—they are one way that locals view the system themselves. A helpful adaptation of the ladder diagram is that of the two-dimensional diagrams of Gutschow (1982: 45) and Gellner (1992: 44). In these, castes such as the Pengu Daḥ and the Maharjan are placed side by side demonstrating the contested character of these hierarchical relations.[26] I have reproduced Gellner's diagram as Table 3.

Another way to diagram the caste system, which I will develop later, expresses visually the notions of centrality and kinship in much the same way that has been attempted above for the two *thar*s of Tamvaḥ and Marikaḥmi but with the entire system in view. This will be attempted later, once we have examined the role of kingship. Before we do that, however, we must take a careful look at the role of economics in the Newar social system. This is a tradition going back to Srinivas (1952) and Mayer (1966) in India.

Table 3. Gellner's Table of Lalitpur's Castes (Gellner 1992: 44).[27]

CLEAN CASTES

<table>
<tr><td colspan="2">RĀJOPĀDHYĀYA (Brahmū, Dyaḥbhāju)</td><td colspan="2" rowspan="2">VAJRĀCĀRYA (Gubhāju), Buddhist priests, and SHĀKYA (Bare), goldsmiths, artisans and shopkeepers</td></tr>
<tr><td colspan="2">SHREṢṬHA (Sheshyaḥ) including Joshī, astrologers, Kārmācarya (Ācāḥju): Shaivite Tantric priests; both of whom wear the sacred thread, and Rājbhaṇḍārī, Amātya and Shreṣṭhas, who do not</td></tr>
<tr><td colspan="4">Pãcthariya Shreṣṭhas</td></tr>
<tr><td colspan="2">MAHARJAN (Jyāpu), Dãgol (Dãgu, Jyāpu), and Āwāle (Kumhāḥ): farmers and potters; latterly masons, carpenters and many other trades</td><td colspan="2">TĀMRAKĀR (Tamaḥ, Tamot), copperworkers, Shilpakār (Lwahåkaḥmi), formerly stonemasons, now carpenters, Bārāhi. Kāṣṭhakār or Hastakār (Sikaḥmi), carpenters, Rājkarṇikār (Haluwāī, Marikaḥmi), sweetmakers</td></tr>
<tr><td>TAṆḌUKĀR (Khusaḥ), farmers, musicians</td><td colspan="2">VYAÑJANKĀR (Tepay), market gardeners</td><td>NĀPIT (Nau). barbers</td></tr>
</table>

<table>
<tr><td rowspan="2">WATER-UNACCEPTABLE CASTES</td><td>KHAḌGĪ/Shāhī (Nāy; Np. Kasāī), butchers, milk sellers, drummers</td></tr>
<tr><td>KĀPĀLĪ/Dashandhārī (Jogi; Np. Kusle), musicians, tailors, death specialists</td></tr>
<tr><td>Untouchables</td><td>DYAḤLĀ (Pwaḥ, Pwarhyā; Np. Poḍe), sweepers with rights at pīṭha and shmashāna, fishermen</td></tr>
</table>

Note: The broken line indicates the existence of formalized hierarchy within the caste.

4. The Economy of the Pengu Daḥ

> In order to protect this universe He, the most resplendent One, assigned different occupations and duties to those who originated from His mouth, arms, thighs and feet.
>
> *Manusmriti* I, 37

> The whole world came from the same parents. The mother told her sons, 'You work with wood, you work with iron and you work with stone'. And that is how it came about that there are different castes.
>
> Mahila Shilpakar

4.1. The household: The basic economic unit

4.1.1. The Newar joint family

The Newar household, as has already been stated, is usually a joint household—that is, it contains a plurality of nuclear families. The household, as I define it here, is the basic economic unit, the members sharing a common hearth (*bhutu*), though it is often seen as a somewhat wider group.[1] It has become commonplace to assert that modernization is leading to the break up of the joint family. Owens (1971: 223), however, discovered that the effects of industrialization in the city of Howrah, West Bengal, are more complex. Sometimes individuals and nuclear families consider it of economic value to remain in a joint family. Quigley (1985a) reports the same for the Shresthas of Dhulikhel.

Newar men usually explain the cause of division of a household as being largely due to the breakdown of relationships among the women. Married women in the Newar household, it will be remembered, join the family on marriage and have to adjust not only to their husband's family's ways of doing things but also to a position in the household that is subservient to the older women. The tension this causes is a frequent item of gossip and a popular theme for South Asian films and television programmes.

The results of a survey of 301 households of the Pengu Daḥ are set out in Table 4.[2] The average household size was found to be 6.7 persons.[3]

I have no data on the comparative wealth of Pengu Daḥ households. Quigley discovered in Dhulikhel that, in general, the greater the economic diversity of the household the greater the incentive to stay together as risk is spread better (1985a: 18). The richer per capita households are more often found to be the larger ones. Nevertheless, as in Howrah (Owens 1971: 248), if highly trained Newar professionals and entrepreneurs find themselves in a household situation in which their contribution to the running of the household is, in their view, unfair, they tend to split off because of the lack of

Table 4. Households of the Pengu Daḥ using Kolenda's typology (1968).[4]

Category No.	Category Name	Number of households	% of total	Average number of members
1	Nuclear	113	37.5	4.1
2	Supplemented Nuclear	52	17.3	6.1
3	Sub-nuclear	14	4.7	3.1
4	Single	3	1.0	1.0
5	Supplemented Sub-nuclear	2	0.7	6.0
6	Collateral Joint	6	2.0	8.5
7	Supplemented Collateral Joint	22	7.3	13.5
8	Lineal Joint	36	12.0	5.5
9	Supplemented Lineal Joint	4	1.3	8.5
10	Lineal-Collateral Joint	42	14.0	10.8
11	Suppemental Lineal-Collateral Joint	7	2.3	19.6
	Totals:	301	100	6.7

return on their investment. The vast majority of the Pengu Daḥ (with the notable exception of a large number of Marikaḥmi) still reside in their traditional localities in the old city of Lalitpur (Maps 5-8). Some have in recent decades moved out of the centre of the city to build a house in one of the 'suburbs' such as that of Sātdobāto to the south. Even with these, however, there is a strong tie to the ancestral home. There is nearly always a brother or cousin occupying the old house.

4.1.2. Household fission

The process of fission of a household is not straightforward. Two stages can be discerned, the first of which may be further sub-divided.[5]

- **Material division**
  - Division of kitchen. Nuclear family units set up separate kitchens—usually brothers from brothers, but it can also be brothers from their parents. This is usually now accomplished by the building of a new modern concrete house somewhere on the outskirts of the old city. At this stage the brothers' nuclear families begin to act as economically separate entities. Only at festivals and life-cycle rituals do they act together and share the financial burden. This can be done by mutual arrangement but often it falls to the brother or brothers who are doing better in business to carry the load.[6]
  - Division of inheritance. This includes the vertical division of the ancestral house, the event that creates new households. The wider

family continues to act as one ritually. This unit is sometimes referred to as a *kawaḥ*. Occasionally one or two sons will claim their share of the inheritance and set up house on their own. In this case they are given their share in cash and land, sparing the physical division of the ancestral house.

- **Ritual division**
  Eventually, new households divide ritually, no longer observing festivals and life-cycle rituals together. Lineage Deity Worship continues to be performed, ideally, as a larger unit, not only with one's brothers but also with the wider lineage. Note that ritual unity may continue for a long time after economic division.

4.2. The traditional crafts of the Pengu Daḥ

The traditional crafts of the Pengu Daḥ are those that the Pengu Daḥ themselves perceive to be the crafts of their forefathers. It is not difficult to ascertain the details of these crafts as they are still, for the most part, practised by members of these lineages. Indeed, it is only a matter of a few decades since virtually every adult male of these *thar*s was engaged in them.

4.2.1. Hollow metal crafts

The type 'hollow metal crafts' distinguishes the work of the copper- and bronzesmith from that of the finer work of the gold- and silversmith. The working of gold and silver has traditionally been the province of the Vajrācāryas and Shākyas. The techniques have also extended to the finer working of brass. It is in the more mundane creation of vessels for everyday use that Tāmrakār Coppersmiths and Nyāchyā̃ Bronzesmiths made a niche for themselves.

a. History of hollow metal crafts

If the T'ang annals are reliable, the metalware industry of the Kathmandu Valley goes back at least to the fourth century BCE (R. Tamot 1995: 28). Kautilya, thought to have written his *Arthasasthra* at that time, described a number of metalware goods from Nepal. The Tishtung stone inscription, erected in 607 during the reign of Amsuvārman, mentions export of copper utensils (*tāmrabhānda*) (Vajracarya 1973: 309-311).

Metal statues of bronze and copper belonging to the sixth and seventh centuries have been found at Candesvari temple (Banepa) and at Sankhu. These are evidence that, during the Licchavi period, 'metallurgy and metal casting were in a high degree of excellence' (Gajurel and Vaidya 1984: 13). Chinese records of the same era also attest to this fact. It is a Newar custom for people to dedicate metal vessels to gods and goddesses especially on the death of a family member. Antique metal vessels are found nailed up at the top storey of temples and are probably 500 years old. Some of these brass and copper vessels may even be 1,000 years old (ibid.: 31).

Coppersmiths are divided over the origins of their craft. According to some, the technique of copper working and the shape of the vessels are different from those of Indian coppersmiths (such as those of Rajasthan). They deduce that their ancestors came from Tibet, which seems to be highly speculative to my mind. The likelihood is that the early coppersmiths, did in fact, migrate from India.

One Tāmrakār was of the opinion that the beating of brass began, in the Valley, only 300 years ago, though the lost wax technique of casting was known long before.[7]

b. Typology of metal workers

Raju Tamot (1995) constructs a typology of metal workers in Taksār (Bhojpur) according to their products (I reproduce his typology as it is given. Note that some of his italicized words are Nepali.):

- goods made of bronze by the cire perdue method: e.g., *kasaudi*, *kachaurā*, *ankhorā*, *karuwa*, *anti*, *sukundā*, *panas*, *nhyaka mu*, *sinha mu*, and *ghanta*;
- goods made of plain copper and brass sheets: e.g., *ghaḥ*;
- serving spoons: *dhāgaḥ* and *catā*; and
- bronze dinner plate: *chares thāl;* big serving bowl: *dabaka*; and cymbals: *jhyamta.*

Traditionally brasscasting (*dhalāy yāyegu*) has been the craft of the Shākyas, not of the Tamvaḥ or the Kasāḥ. It is the technique rather than the products, however, that distinguishes these various groups. The techniques employed in the making of brass vessels such as the drinking pot (*karuwa*) are those of casting and turning.[8] A more sophisticated typology of the working of copper and its alloys in Nepal takes account of these criteria (Figure 3).

The technique of repoussé, in which thin sheets of copper or brass are wrought into relief designs with light blows of a small hammer, is the traditional craft of the Shākyas and, as such, is not dealt with here. Furthermore, the other alloy of copper—bronze, an alloy with tin—is noted but not described in detail, as its working, in Lalitpur, was traditionally the province of the Kasāḥ (Mulmi/Nyāchyã Shresthas). Bronze plates are now finished by the Tamvaḥ (and their workers) with the first, and harder part of the process—that of beating the ingot into a two-dimensional disc—being completed in the factory. The description that follows is that of the working of pure copper and brass sheets in the formation of hollow vessels which is the traditional provenance of the Tāmrakār coppersmiths.

c. Raw materials

Copper (*sijaḥ*) mines are found throughout Nepal. Among these are a mine in the hills west of Kathmandu, three in the hills to the south of Lalitpur, one each in the Sun Kosi and Bhote Kosi valleys east of Panauti, one in the hills south-east of Panauti, and one in the Arun valley just to the south of Taksār (Bhojpur)

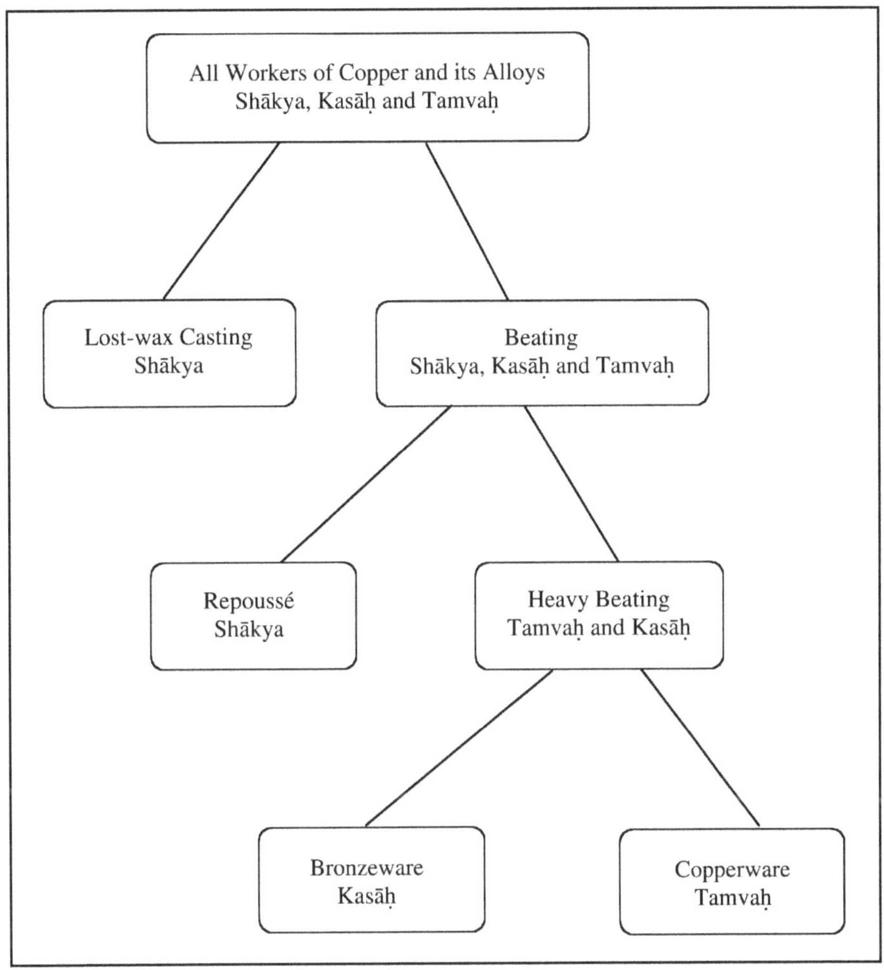

Figure 3. Typology of workers of copper and its alloys.

(OUP 1997: 9). Men of the Gurung, Magar, Gharti and Kāmi communities traditionally extracted and smelted copper ore (Gajurel and Vaidya 1984: 61f.). The resultant metal was then turned over to the government who sold the surplus. The complex process of extracting copper from its ore involves five different operations: concentration, roasting, smelting, bessemerization and purification (ibid.: 101). Zinc (*jastā*) is a cheaper commodity than copper. A few mines are found in western and central Nepal. Two are located in the Sun Kosi valley, east of Panauti (OUP 1997: 9). Tin (*kelã*) is a rarer commodity in Nepal with only one mine located in the far west. Resin (*thakura*) is obtained from chir pine (*salla*, N., *Pinus roxburghii*, L.; Appendix 4, p. 294), which, though much reduced still grows in the lower hills. Nowadays, apart from borax, which is found in India, most raw materials are imported from China and Singapore.

d. Alloys of copper

There are two distinct alloys of copper and zinc, both of which are called brass in English but that have different names in Newar. Malleable brass (*lī̃*), suitable for beating, has a low proportion of zinc (four parts copper are alloyed with one part zinc) compared with that used in the lost wax method (at least 36 per cent zinc). In the latter the higher plasticity of the alloy makes it ideal for creating cast brass (*dhalāy/dhalot*).

Bronze (*kā̃y*), a wrought alloy of copper and tin, was worked traditionally by the Mulmi/Nyāchyã Shresthas in Lalitpur and Kamsakārs in Kathmandu (both called Kasāḥ in colloquial Newar). Once it has been exposed to sunshine, bronze loses its malleability and shatters when dropped on a hard surface.

e. Properties of copper and its alloys

Copper and its alloys have a number of useful properties that have made it ideal for its use in the creating of hollow vessels (Alexander and Street 1951: 160). Pure copper, like several of its alloys (notably brass), is very ductile and malleable and can be pressed, forged or beaten into complicated shapes without cracking—very important in the construction of vessels for the holding of liquids. Copper has a high conductivity of heat per unit volume, higher, in fact, than for any other known substance except silver. Copper and most of its alloys can be joined with ease by such processes as soldering, brazing and welding and is resistant to many forms of corrosion. Finally, copper and its alloys possess an attractive appearance and colour ranging from red in the pure metal to chocolate, ochre, gold, yellow or white in its various alloys.

f. The coppersmith's workshop (*jyāsaḥ*)

The characteristic tool of the coppersmith is the 'soft hammer' (*nayu mugaḥ*). Hammers come in various weights according to the work to be performed: 1.5 *pau* (300g), 3 *pau* (600g) or 1 *darni* (2.2kg), the latter used primarily for beating out the water pot (*ghaḥ*). Other tools include the wooden mallet (*si mugaḥ*) for flattening out thin sheets of copper, steel and stone anvils of various different sizes and shapes, tongs, pliers, thick iron rods and crucibles.

The small furnace required for bringing the metal to high temperature is usually situated at the rear of the coppersmith's workshop. It is run on charcoal and, though in the past a hand bellows was used, today the coals are fanned by means of an electric blower.

g. Preparation of metal sheeting for hollow metal crafts

To get copper from the raw state into a state ready for working into a hollow vessel demands three basic steps, all of which these days are completed in preparation for selling to the local craftsmen:

> **Smelting**. Raw copper ore first needs to be smelted. Nowadays, pre-smelted copper is imported from Singapore or Malaysia. Scrap copper

is not as pure as 'Bright Berry' copper and, as such, is not subject to so high an import duty. There is no need to smelt imported scrap copper, as it is pure enough for pot making. Scrap brass that is brought from the locality, however, is not pure enough and needs smelting before it is usable. To smelt, the scrap is melted down with the flux. The dross is skimmed and the remaining liquid tested by removing a small crucible-full, letting it solidify and then working it with a hammer. The dross (*sijaḥ khi*) is not discarded but is mixed with black gram by the Kulu drum-makers for making the black circular resonating layer on the skin of the drum.

Casting. The casting of copper is not a straightforward process. If there is abundant ambient oxygen the copper oxidizes producing a brittle article. In the absence of oxygen, on the other hand, hydrogen is absorbed from the fuel gases or from moisture which, when the metal cools bubbles out of solution causing the copper to have a porous structure. The task of the refiner is to strike a happy medium with oxygen kept between 0.025 and 0.1 per cent (Alexander and Street 1951: 162). In the initial casting of brass for the production of hollow vessels, the proportion of zinc is crucial. With less than 36 per cent zinc, a single alpha solid solution is created making for a malleable alloy. If the proportion of zinc is greater than 36 per cent another, beta, solid solution would also be present. This results in a different kind of alloy that is difficult to work by beating but has a higher plasticity and therefore can be cast (ibid.: 165).

Rolling and Cutting. Gajurel and Vaidya describe the process of making bronze dinner plates (*kā̃y, kans,* Np.) (1984: 48-54). It would take four men—one to turn the plate and three to beat it (*kwai dayegu*). The same process was employed in the production of copper and brass vessels. A large pot would require three *darni* of copper, a smaller one two. Rolling mills have removed the hardest part of hammering the alloy into the required thickness leaving the artisan the job of hammering it into its third dimension. These plates are indispensable at the wedding ceremony.

h. The water pot—the characteristic product of the coppersmith

The Tāmrakār and Mulmi/Nyāchyā Shrestha have crafted a number of utensils in their workshops. (Full lists are given in Appendix 3, p. 293.) The characteristic product of the coppersmith—the water pot (*ghaḥ, gāgri,* Np.; *gāgra,* Skt.)—deserves closer attention. There are two forms of water pot crafted by the Newar coppersmith:

Newaḥ ghaḥ. Newar form with flat bottom, suitable for carrying on the hip, as is the normal practice in the Valley.

Magaḥ ghaḥ. Parbatiyā form with round bottom suitable for carrying in a basket (*doko,* Np.) with head-strap (*namlo,* Np.) as is common in the

> hills. Tāmrakār shopkeepers also jokingly call this attractively decorated pot the 'toorist ghaḥ' as visitors often buy it as a souvenir.[9]

Both water pots have a different shape to those found in India reflecting the different methods of carrying. This clearly illustrates the influence of ecology on the culture of both the Newars and the Hill Nepalese. This is how Gajurel and Vaidya put it:

> The typical water pot (*gāgri*) belongs to the historic past—not only for the peoples of Nepal, but for all peoples of the world. But as the centuries rolled on and technology grew up, people evolved out the forms and sizes of water pots best suited to their own social and domestic needs and environments. (1984: 37)

Either of the two water pots built by the Newar coppersmith may be constructed of either of two materials: copper or brass. The copper pot (*sijaḥ ghaḥ*) is considered good for health and is used for special purposes including that of *pujā*. The brass pot (*lĩ ghaḥ*), on the other hand, is kept more for ordinary use and, being an alloy, is tougher (*chā*) than the pure copper pot. The traditional water pot is still considered an essential part of Newar dowries, and with the increasingly unreliable water supply in the Kathmandu Valley over the past decade, the use of the *ghaḥ* for collecting water has had a new lease of life.

i. Construction of the water-pot

In the past the copper, or copper/zinc mixture, was melted and then poured into circular moulds after which it was beaten by hand into the required thickness. Now copper and brass discs are bought from local factories saving the most difficult and tiresome part of the labour.[10] Modern changes to the technique are very few, as machines, in general, cannot produce the pot in the way it is wanted. Some, however, are starting to use bottom and middle parts that are already pressed by a machine. This technique has disadvantages that make it undesirable to some coppersmiths. Among these are the wastage of metal as the machine-pressed part uses a larger initial disc, and the fact that the machine-pressed part is not the correct shape having vertical walls instead of walls that taper inwards towards the centre.

Starting with sheet metal, the construction of the *Magaḥ ghaḥ* is a seven-step process (R. Tamot 1995: 97-100).[11] The pot is made of five parts: crown, neck, shoulder, belly and base. The *Newaḥ ghaḥ,* in contrast, though constructed traditionally of three components (head, shoulder and base) is now built of four (crown, neck, shoulder and base).

> **Cutting**. The sheets are cut into the required shape.
>
> **Annealing**. The copper sheet is heated to a dull red with a gentle fire and then quenched to make it soft and malleable.
>
> **Beating**. The sheet is now beaten into shape by a range of hammers, including the round-headed wooden mallet, over variously shaped anvils, stakes or a hollow wooden block.

Joining. A small charcoal furnace is kept in the corner of the workshop. A mixture of borax and water is applied to the parts to be joined. This prevents oxidation and acts as a flux. When this is dry, a mixture of borax and powdered solder (75 per cent brass/25 per cent zinc) in equivalent proportions is applied as a paste along the edge-to-edge butt joint. It is then heated to a bright red with a gentle fire and, once joined, allowed to cool.

Cleansing. The pot is then dipped into a dilute (10 per cent) solution of sulphuric acid to remove surface oxides.

Planishing. The procedure that makes the distinctive sound of the coppersmith at work involves a process of work hardening the metal by means of fairly light, even, hammer blows (from a convex-faced hammer) over a convex stake anvil from a few inches height (Plates 2 and 3).

Finishing. Scrubbing with a mixture of ash, sand and lemon juice finishes the pot.

Certain coppersmiths gained a reputation for particularly fine work. Ganesh Lal Tamrakar of Cāka Bahi used to make such good and characteristic water pots that they were in high demand and referred to as 'Ganesh ghaḥ'. It is said that people could always tell a 'Ganesh ghaḥ' though they would not have recognized its creator on the street.

Plate 2. Narendra Tāmrakār planishing a Newar water pot (Newaḥ ghaḥ).

Plate 3. Bal Gopal Tāmrakār planishing a 'Magar' water pot (Magaḥ ghaḥ).

4.2.2. Woodwork

a. History

The origin of Nepalese woodcarving is unknown though the Chinese traveller, Wang Hsüan-t'sê, who visited the Valley in 673 CE did describe sculpted and painted wooden houses (Slusser 1998: I, 39). Woodcarving reached its zenith in Malla times, during the seventeenth century, when there was much patronage from the kings and their courtiers.

b. Timber

Most of the wood used in the Kathmandu Valley has traditionally been harvested from in and around the Valley itself and seasoned in wood-fired furnaces. In the past there was little problem with deforestation in Nepal, as harvesting of timber did not exceed natural growth. But since the advent of electrical machinery and exports of timber to India in the latter half of the twentieth century the reserves of quality hardwoods needed for woodcarving have been severely depleted. Wood prices have consequently risen sharply threatening the woodcarver's way of life. (Appendix 4, p. 294, lists each type of timber in use today.)

c. Woodworking tools

Newar carpenters use a variety of hand tools as well as, today, a few electric tools.[12] The hammer and adze are locally made (Plate 4). The blade of the hand saw is about thirty centimetres long and the teeth are inclined so as to cut by pulling. This variety of saw is peculiar to Asia. The Japanese have

Plate 4. Phul Babu Barahi cutting a spoke for the chariot wheel with his adze.

thought up several varieties of blades and teething suited to different kinds of work but the Newars have only two forms. The stock implements like the plane and rabbet plane were introduced from India around the 1930s. The chisel, heading chisel and gouge are locally made and resemble those used in Europe. The sculptors (various shapes of chisel) are smaller, made locally and do not have wooden handles.

The tools used by Bārāhi for building chariots are remarkable in their simplicity (Plate 5). Two saws—the hand saw (*koti*) and the band saw (*arawāl koti*)—are used to cut the timber into pieces. The rest of the work of shaping and cutting mortises is accomplished by use of the adze (*baḥcila*) and chisel (*hāḥ*). Wooden mallets (*simugaḥ*) of various sizes from the usual one-handed mallet to the massive two-handed twenty-kilogram maul are used with the chisels and for knocking sections together. The use of modern tools in the building of the chariots is strictly prohibited with the one concession being to an electric auger that is employed to bore through the middle of a new wheel hub. It is said that this concession was made because 'otherwise it would take a week'. The exception proves the rule, however: innovations have not been allowed in the building of the chariots. It is fairly safe to assume, then, that the above tools used on the chariot are the very same tools that were employed from the beginning of the Būgadyaḥ Jātrā in the seventh century CE.

Plate 5. Tools used by the Bārāhi on the chariots.

d. Woodworking techniques

Woodworking in the Valley has had to develop in the absence of a high degree of metallurgical development. Sitting on a mat or low stool and holding the wood with the toes is a practice that, though alien to Europe, is common to 'practically the whole of Asia, Japan and Korea' (Slusser 1998: I, 110). The Asian saw, with back-facing teeth, is particularly suited, ergonomically, to work on the floor. It is the sitting posture that forces the stronger stroke of the saw to be that of the draw, rather than the push as it is when standing.

Traditionally the Newar house is constructed of brick and wood, generally along the elongated rectangular plan. The house is separated from the road by a continuous raised threshold protecting the inside of the house from sudden localized floods during the monsoon. Walls are fabricated of brick and floors, roof frame, windows and doors are all constructed of wood.

The Newar window is a beauty to behold (Plates 6,7). According to Bernier, Newar windows display 'the fullest and most elaborate development of wood carving in Asia' (1975: 251, in Shepard 1985: 245, Bernier 1977). Different types of window are constructed for different floors (Appendix 5, p. 296). Windows are often decorated with religious motifs such as that of the Buddhist Trimurti: Buddha, Dharma and Samgha. Lattice windows (*tiki jhyāḥ*) bring out the residential and private character of the second floor. The strength of the window is in its complexity and many-piecedness because the climate produces frequent variations in weather. It is also easier to carve a

Plate 6. The five-fold Newar window (*nyāpā jhyāḥ*).

Plate 7. Kabindra Tāmrakār carving a piece for a small replica Newar window.

small piece. This is especially so when several carvers are working together in a cramped workshop, as is often the case.

Newar doors are no less resplendent. Shepard reports that, 'The large wooden doors might contain three hundred separately carved pieces' (Shepard 1985: 168). The posts and lintels as well as the doors themselves are often very finely and intricately carved.

Le Port points out that two joint forms in the construction of the peristyle angle of monument roofs are also used in France in similar cases to carry out very meticulous works (1991: 90). 'It may be noted,' he says, 'that despite the thousands of kilometres which separate them, men confronted with similar problems and materials have adopted the same aesthetic and technical solutions in order to solve problems.'

The isolation of the Rana times put technological innovation on hold and led to a decline in external woodwork (ibid.: 110). With the restoration of monuments in recent years, however, there has been resurgence in this skill.

4.2.3. Lapidary crafts

Stone carving in the Kathmandu Valley was well developed by the Licchavi era. The oldest datable artefact of the Valley is that of a life-size Kushan-period sculpture of King Jaya Varma dating from 184/185 CE (Tamot and Alsop 1996). The craft of stone carving developed through the centuries so that according to Slusser, 'There was a prolific output of Tantric stone images during the Malla Period' (1998: I, 75). The Krishna temple of Mangaḥ is an exquisite monument to the Malla era stone carver. Not only is the temple constructed largely without the aid of metal or wood, a finely detailed frieze depicting scenes from Krishna's life adorns the entire circumference of the temple immediately above the lintel. To build this temple it was necessary for King Siddhi Narasimha Malla to remove a lineage of stonemasons from Bhaktapur to Lalitpur. Whether this was in place of the local stonemasons or in addition to them is not clear although the entire group of seven Lwahãkaḥmi lineages claims to have been involved.

As the last stone carver in Jom Bāhāḥ died without heirs in 1980 (Shepard 1985: 216), stone carving does not figure in this study. In Lalitpur today stonework is carried out primarily by the Vajrācāryas and Shākyas of Binchẽ Bāhāḥ who, it is said, learned their trade from the Lwahãkaḥmi of Jom Bāhāḥ. Some Maharjans are also employed in this craft.

Ivory carving first appears in the Valley in the late Malla era. Today one household of Lwahãkaḥmi and one of Vishvakarma Sikaḥmi work ivory and semi-precious stone such as turquoise. The work is very intricate and demands very small chisels, bright light and fine motor skills. A finished piece can fetch a high price—a turquoise Buddha measuring ten centimetres in height was sold for Rs. 80,000 (US$1,300) in the late 1990s.

4.2.4. Sweetmaking

The Rājkarnikārs recognize that their sweets have a common origin to Indian varieties but nevertheless see Nepalese sweets as distinct. Bengali sweets, they will point out, are prepared with more milk. Certain sweets, such as the *ras bari* were introduced to Nepal only a few years ago. Others, such as the *panjābi* are clearly of Indian origin but were introduced before the living memory of the present sweetmakers. Anyone wanting to start a sweetmaking business does not require a large capital outlay as tools and ingredients are not expensive. Labour, however, is intensive, leading many sweetmakers today to hire workers for their shops.

The principal ingredients of Nepalese sweets are these: wheat flour (*chucũ*), rice flour (*pwacũ*), sugar (*cini*)—formerly molasses (*sākha*), and condensed milk (*khuwa*). Most sweets are deep fried in clarified butter (*ghyaḥ*), but vegetable oil (*cikã*) is an acceptable alternative. Other ingredients include spices and colours.

There are several different kinds of traditional Newar sweet. (A complete inventory is given in Appendix 6, p. 297.) It is important here to point out that confectionery is not valued merely as a foodstuff. Some sweets also have significant symbolic value in Newar culture. Sweets are very often offered as part of the *pujā* ceremony. They are always given as part of the presentation from wife-givers to wife-takers and vice versa as part of the formalities that seal the marriage contract and the *samdhi* relationship between in-laws. In this respect two particular sweets deserve special mention—*aĩta* and *lākha mari*. At the 'Giving the Areca Nut' (*gway biyegu*) ceremony, which seals the wedding plan, *aĩta* is presented by wife-givers to wife-takers. In a reciprocal gesture, on the arrival of the wedding procession at the bride's house *aĩta* is offered by wife-takers to wife-givers.

Sets of *lākha mari* are given by wife-takers to the bride's household at the time of settling the marriage contract. Whole *lākha* mari, or parts thereof, are then passed on to relatives as the invitation to the wedding. The amount given depends on the proximity of the relationship. If only a small piece is sent the invitation is intended for the recipient only, such as would be the case between friends. If a quarter is given the invitation is for the recipient and his or her spouse. Half a *lākha mari* is an invitation to a married couple and their children (*nimhatipu, macāchi*), and an entire sweet is for the whole household including servants (*culhai*). *Lākha mari* is also given by wife-givers to wife-takers at the ceremony of Samdhi Swayegu ('the making of/ fixing of in-laws').

4.3. The Pengu Daḥ in the modern economy

The focus of this study is a social and religious one. At this point, however, it is helpful to establish the material and economic context in which the Pengu Daḥ live and have developed over the centuries. Each of the groups that go to make up the Pengu Daḥ has traditionally been employed in one or another craft. In the modern socio-political context, however, handwork of any kind carries with it a certain stigma (Bista 1991: 130). Although seemingly not paralyzed by this, the young men of the Pengu Daḥ do seem to have taken on some ambivalence to their traditional trades. Older men affirm the value of work with the hands even though they may have laid aside their tools in favour of running a shop.

4.3.1. Modern Tamvaḥ economy

Almost all of the Tāmrakārs of Lalitpur have a family coppersmith business. Many continue to work copper by hand but even during the span of the research period this was markedly on the decline. The residences of the Tamvaḥ are clustered around a few courtyards that are off the main north-south trade route through Lalitpur. These courtyards are grouped into three adjacent localities—Cāka Bahi, Haugaḥ and Ikhā. It is often easy to tell that one has passed into a Tāmrakār locality. The multiplicity of copperware shops and the distinctive sound of the beating of copper are clear indicators. If one walks along the road from Uku Bāhāḥ in eastern Lalitpur towards Cāka Bahi there is a clear change of timbre in the sound of hammer against metal. Many of the Shākyas of Uku Bāhāḥ are employed in the crafting of 'curios'—the making of (in their case) images of the Buddha and Buddhist deities for the tourist trade. The hammer is small and the work is fine. The Tāmrakārs, however, in their production of larger, household vessels have to beat the copper much more vigorously with a heavier hammer. The change from the quick succession of light, high-pitched taps on the brass of the Shākyas to the more deliberate and heavy blows of the Tāmrakārs is quite remarkable.

Many, especially those with a house on the main road or on a lane in the

Plate 8. Antique pots for sale at a Tāmrakār's shop.

centre of town have a copperware shop. They themselves may or may not make the crafts but order them or buy them from their neighbours. Some of these shop owners have brass and copperware for hire for weddings and other such functions, which are displayed during the wedding season. Many sell antique copperware as well as modern (Plate 8).

Sambhu Raj Tamrakar said that when he was a lad, Tichu Galli would be 'full of the sound of hammering' and remarked that it could hardly be heard today. Thirty years ago very few Tāmrakārs had their own shop. There were a few copperware shops in Haugaḥ, mostly owned by Nyāchyā̃ Shresthas. But during the past ten years especially many Tamvaḥ have opened a shop. The advantage they have is that they own their own house on a main road. One

Tāmrakār who set up shop in 1993 took loans totalling Rs. 550,000 and was able to pay these off within a few years. Businessmen believe that the ease of travel on roads from the hills has caused the copperware business to flourish. The Nyāchyā̃, however, who have seen their market share drastically reduced in recent years, say that the Tamvaḥ took up selling their own products as a means to higher status.

Some Tamvaḥ have a workshop at their house or courtyard and employ four or five (or up to a dozen) Kāmi workers (Parbatiya Blacksmiths).[13] Today there are several dozen Kāmis working in copperware production in Lalitpur.[14] Only one Kāmi has started his own business, having migrated to Lalitpur from his village three years ago. He employs half a dozen other Kāmis and makes to order for the shops. Lack of capital has so far prevented any of these Kāmis from setting up their own shop. It would seem only a matter of time, however, before some of them do.

The more educated Tāmrakārs have office jobs or other businesses alongside the family business. Very few have abandoned coppersmithery altogether. Some Tamvaḥ businessmen are sceptical of the future of the copperware business and are seeking other avenues for their children to pursue. As Dil Mohan told me, 'People are no longer using copperware. They give it at weddings but just keep it. If they need a big pot for a feast they can hire it.' Several Tāmrakārs, then, have branched out into other sectors of business including the selling of general kitchenware, wooden toys and sweets (Appendix 7, p. 299).[15]

The White Everest Vyapar Company imports scrap copper from Singapore and Malaysia whenever there is sufficient demand. This public limited company is dominated by Tāmrakārs but shareholders also include Rājkarnikārs, Shresthas and Maharjans. Two rolling mills, owned by private limited companies, are situated at Patan Industrial Estate and a third at Bālāju. Here the imported copper and brass ingots are rolled into thick sheets and then stamped out into discs for sale to local businesses thus skipping the physically very demanding initial pounding process. Nyaro Mill has fifty shareholders and Sun Kosi Rolling Mill twenty-eight, every one a Tāmrakār. At the Sun Kosi Rolling Mill three Tāmrakār men manage a work force of thirty-five, including a large group of skilled Bihari (north Indian) machinists.

Retail trade of copperware is somewhat regulated in Lalitpur by the *Tama Pittal Vyavasayi Samgh Tadārtha Samiti* (Copper/Brass Tradesmen's Association Trade Committee). A printed list is put up in shops showing the regular price of copper and brass goods per kilogram. This is quoted as the starting price. For example, in 2002, a water pot sold at Rs. 260 per kilogram.[16] Bargaining can take half an hour or more for one item with the customer finally settling for a small fraction off the original asking price. The Association has fifty-five members—one from each copperware shop in Lalitpur. Copperware is sold all through the year but there is a great increase in sales during the wedding season—Mārga, Māgh, Phāgun, Vaishākh, and Jyesth—as much copperware is bought as a wedding present (*kwasaḥ*). People of all communities come to the shops in Lalitpur from the city and the surrounding hinterland, including the encircling hills.

It would seem that the present polity has brought a larger market to the copperware shops. Upwardly mobile people want to show off their consumption of copperware at the marriage of a relative. This seems to have led to an inflation of expectations on the part of those who get married and those who come to 'See the Face' of the bride. Relatives want to display the costliness of their gifts, and copperware is a prime choice.

4.3.2. Modern Marikaḥmi economy

Most Rājkarnikārs have a family sweetmaking business, according to their traditional occupation. It is for this reason that the Rājkarnikārs are so spread out over the city. People are happy to travel from all over the city to buy a copper water pot for their daughter's dowry but no one wants to go far to get perishables like sweets. Consequently the demand for sweets has led to the supply being scattered all over the city.

Many Rājkarnikārs are well educated and perhaps have diversified more than their fellow caste sub-groups. Many own a cold store, others are running large businesses (usually associated with food production; e.g., sliced bread),[17] and a few are in government service (Appendix 7, p. 299). Some have a catering business alongside their sweetshop. Competition for a share of the sweet market has also increased in recent years. Maharjans, Ranjitkārs, Tāmrakārs, Parbatiyā Brahmans and the recently arrived Marwaris from India all vie for the sweet tooth of the city's burgeoning population.

There is a perception among members of the Pengu Daḥ that the Rājkarnikārs are 'higher' than the other *thar*s both in wealth ('*arthik kshetra*') and education ('*baudhik kshetra*'). They do seem to have many more that are doctors, engineers, and other professionals. One older Tāmrakār man explained their success as the result of their having a tradition of working in shops where they met people, made connections and grew wise. The Tamvaḥ, by contrast, only started opening their shops during the 1980s.

4.3.3. Modern Lwahākaḥmi economy

Only two households of the Lwahākaḥmi use the honorific name 'Shilākār' (stonemason). In the past the entire *thar* were stonemasons (*lwahãkaḥmi*). As we have seen (§4.2.3), the Khwapa lineage was brought from Bhaktapur to help build the Krishna temple in Mangaḥ in 1637 during the reign of Siddhi Narasimha Malla (1619-1660 CE) in Lalitpur's 'Golden Age'. They are nearly all now working in the carving of wood. This switch to woodcarving seems to have begun around three generations ago. The Lwahākaḥmi themselves see this as a result of the Shah dynasty's lack of patronage in the building of temples. One family practises ivory carving and semi-precious stone carving.

The Lwahãkaḥmi assert that they first taught the Vajrācāryas of Binchẽ Bāhāḥ the craft of stone carving. Since then Binchẽ Bāhāḥ has gained a worldwide reputation for its craft.

The Lwahãkaḥmi carve a number of different items either on order from a buyer or to sell from the shop. These include carved building parts such as windows, doors and temple roof struts. Others carve tables and cabinets that are then sold in the shop, often as wedding presents. Others make replacement parts for renovating temples and other old buildings or for export to Europe or Japan for the building of a Newar-style temple or house. Such replicas of carved windows are also attractive to tourists who browse the shops in the season. Finally, a large number of Lwahãkaḥmi turn wood on the lathe to make components for chairs and tables (Appendix 7, p. 299).

4.3.4. Modern Sikaḥmi economy

Sikaḥmi men today are nearly all carpenters, mostly making furniture, picture frames and woodcarvings. The influx of many Madhesi carpenters from the Tarai has created an arena of high competition among woodworkers in the city. House carpentry is carried out largely by these migrants. Woodcarving, however, is the specialty of the Shilpakārs, both Vishvakarma Sikaḥmi and Lwahãkaḥmi. The Paḥmā Sikaḥmi make furniture but do not practise carving. Some Shilpakārs and Sthāpits turn table legs on lathes (*kunkegu jyā*) on a contract basis for furniture makers (Appendix 7). These apart, one Shilpakār Sikaḥmi household carves ivory for which it has received awards.

The Bārāhi continue to make the chariot of Bũgadyaḥ (Karunāmaya/ Matsyendranāth) each spring for which they are paid Rs. 265 per person per day by the government Guthi Corporation (1999). The rest of the year they are busy with various other woodcrafts such as the production of picture frames, and moulds for the brick industry. One Bārāhi household has become quite wealthy running a timber yard (Appendix 7).

4.4. Conceptualizing the relation between occupation and caste

Advocates of the occupational theory of caste, a variant of the materialist position, argue that caste is based simply on the occupations of the various groups that go to make up the society. Berreman (1960, 1971, 1972) takes such a position. According to him ritual status is a direct product of a person's economic status, which leads to a caste rank that is closely tied to occupation. 'It soon became evident,' he writes, 'that "secular status" is significant to caste ranking primarily as it is reflected in "ritual status", but not in and of itself' (1972: 210). Moreover, Berreman asserts that one can change one's ritual status merely by taking up a different occupation. The Bajgi Tailor-Drummers, for example, were forced to take up the occupation of the skinning and disposing of dead animals and thereby became untouchable to their fellow Bajgis. But this is one way only. Surely it is much more difficult for a group to climb together and be recognized simply on the basis of their change in occupation. So ritual status does have a separate meaning that is not completely explained by occupation. It is clear that some relationship exists between caste and occupation. A formal correspondence between the two, however, cannot be maintained in the face of the ethnographic data.

Rosser (1966) is another for whom, quite simply, differing status positions are derived from the distribution of political and economic power.

> For my own part, I take 'caste' simply to be a form of social stratification in which the necessary statements and judgements about relative status are couched predominantly in a traditional ritual language. In a particular caste system the differing status positions of the component groups are in my view derived ultimately and basically, as in all systems of hierarchical stratification, from the distribution of political and economic power within that system. The language of ritual behaviour is used conventionally to express and validate status achieved through and based upon the operation of political and economic factors. (Ibid.: 69)

Rosser opposes the commonly held emic view that ritual behaviour is the determinant of one's status. 'The superior position of the Brahman, depending mainly on the power and patronage of the ruler where it has not depended directly on his own political and economic power, has been made secure to the extent to which he has been able to disseminate these mystical theories' (ibid.). Rosser echoes Ibbetson who asserts that 'social standing, which is all that caste means, depends very largely on political importance...' (Ibbetson 1881: 174, quoted by Rosser 1966). Berreman, Rosser and others, then, characterize caste as simply a variety of 'social stratification' also found in other societies.

According to this theory then, one would expect to find a rigid connection between occupation and caste in Newar society. Those working copper, for instance, would all be accorded an equal status. The foregoing ethnographic data, however, militate against this theory. Today there are basically two completely separate castes creating hollow copper vessels—Tāmrakārs (the traditional workers) and Kāmi (Parbatiyā Blacksmiths) who have filled the gap left by the movement of Tāmrakār men into business and other professions. These two castes have strictly no ritual relations. They may not intermarry and have no commensal relations. One might contend that this is a relatively recent phenomenon and I would agree. It is also clear, however, that, at least throughout the Malla era men from certain other castes only could achieve acceptance into the Coppersmith circle. Not anyone could take up the trade. Monks from the monasteries could. Such households had no debilitating history such as, say, a Khadgi would have had. So existing Coppersmiths had no trouble absorbing them into their marriage circle.

Furthermore, the working of wood does not, and it is clear, also did not (in Malla times at least), make anyone a Sikaḥmi. Clearly there were carpenters in Lalitpur in the seventeenth century—somebody had to be building the houses. But for the building of a temple, such as the Taleju temple in the palace compound, the carpenter had to have the necessary ritual status as well as physical skill. The hiring of just any carpenter, then, was unthinkable. And since there were no Carpenters with the necessary ritual qualifications in Lalitpur they had to be brought from Kathmandu. Participation in a festival, such as that of the Bārāhi in the Jātrā, is not contingent on them being carpenters so much on their being Carpenters. It is true that they do actually have to be skilled at woodwork. But the point is that if they were not they would not cease to be Bārāhi. Not all Bārāhi work on the chariot. Some have other jobs that prevent them from doing so, including, for most of the time, the present supervisor (Nāyaḥ). Each one, though, is proud of his identity as a Bārāhi. The individual does not acquire status from his personal participation but from the participation of some from his lineage. Moreover, some carpenters are hired by the Guthi Corporation to augment the Bārāhi contingent. They may be Farmers—their work on the chariot does not make them Bārāhi. Two Tamang men hired by the Nāyaḥ to wield the twenty-kilogram maul for knocking the wheel parts together (a job that no Bārāhi seems to be strong enough for) claim no elevation in status. It is a case, then, not of status by participation but of status by *association*, and that association is one of *kinship*.

The occupational theory of caste also fails to offer an explanation for the regular occurrence of a multiplicity of occupational groups forming one marriage circle. As Fürer-Haimendorf (1957: 245) noted, 'many so-called [Newar] "castes" are nothing but occupational and non-endogamous segments of larger caste-groups' as we have seen in the case of the Pengu Daḥ.

Dumont is foremost among those who oppose the materialist theory of caste. Dumont (1972: 62-63) criticizes Weber (1958), for instance, on the grounds that the materialist view is ethnocentric and makes the religious aspect of caste secondary (Gellner 1982: 535). Quigley also takes the materialists to task: 'The reason for a caste's high or low ritual status cannot simply be a question of its economic position. If it were, then caste status and economic strength would always coincide and quite clearly they do not' (1993: 159). But Quigley cannot endorse Dumont's absolute disjunction between status and power. 'Dumont's mistake', writes Quigley, 'is to believe that because there is no automatic connection between ritual status and economic and political strength, there is no connection at all' (ibid.: 160).

What, then, is the relation between occupation and caste? Clearly there is some relation or a particular *thar* would not go by an occupational appellation. Occupation, then, must have had at one time a more significant defining role for a person's identity. It was occupation, for the householder and thence by extension to the entire household, that determined marriage relations. By virtue of the expansion in significance of the bond of kinship, however, occupation came to take a less significant role in the determination of ritual status. The current fluidity in attitude towards occupation (not total—you won't find a Tāmrakār cleaning public toilets) is not just a modern phenomenon, but one that is as old as the caste system itself.

Gellner (1995: 213-4) mentions an observation made by two writers on the Newars (Shepard 1985: 59; Lienhard 1989: 594) and two further writers on India (Ketkar 1909: 20; Pocock 1962: 85) that a hierarchy of artisans reflects the metals they work in. 'Such a homology gives the following, certainly very striking, correspondences: Vajrācārya/gold, Shākya/silver, Tāmrakār/copper and Kamsakār/bronze, Shilpakār/wood, Lohākār/iron' (Gellner 1995: 213). Gellner himself, however, observes that such correspondences are only approximate. Furthermore, this does not appear to be an emic construct at all. Pocock's own suggestion that the internal hierarchy of artisans may reflect the degree to which they are embedded in the *jajmāni* system seems to this writer to be most helpful (1962: 86-87). Those considered lower in the hierarchy, then, are the artisans that are less able to sell their products on the open market.

Quigley explains why we cannot equate caste and class:

> The essential difference between caste and class is not that the latter is a system of social stratification and the former is not. Both systems are manifestly hierarchical. The difference lies in the extension of kinship ties into the political arena. Caste works through the idiom of kinship because this is the only means of providing order in an otherwise unstable political climate. (1993.: 162)

The relation of occupation to caste now becomes clear: 'The clue to caste organization does not lie in the hereditary transfer of occupations, as is often supposed, but in the hereditary transfer of ritual functions which connect different groups to the palace or dominant caste' (ibid.: 164).

5. Ordered Space

> ...both in Hinduism and in Buddhism, space, as Oldenberg remarked, and in this case he meant 'ordered' as opposed to 'free' space, was conceived of as 'a lotus flower the petals of which are the cardinal points and at the four intermediary points.' To place a god or gods in this pattern was to order space; it was also to take the town which they protected out of the context of disordered space which surrounded it.
>
> Vergati (1995: 146) quoting Oldenberg (1919: 38)

> In its traditional form the Newar city is a royal site, consecrated by a king on an ancient commercial site.
>
> Toffin (1991: 75)

5.1. Introduction

On entering one of the old cities of the Kathmandu Valley the outsider is immediately struck by the sheer density of its population.[1] The compact construction of housing has reduced the entrance to many a courtyard to a tunnel through what would be the ground floor of one of the houses. I estimate that in places such as Jom Bāhāḥ up to 70 per cent of the land is occupied by buildings. It has not always been so dense, however. Even twenty years ago there were many more gardens within the city.[2] Nevertheless, we are confronted here with a particular approach to settlement. The issue at stake here, as we shall see as the chapter unfolds, is one of a sharp differentiation between the inside and outside of the settlement. As the city of Lalitpur developed the outer limits of the settlement were spread ever wider. This was always completed with careful planning. The medieval Malla city, at which we will look in more detail, was ringed by a wall that put a strict limit on urban sprawl. Nevertheless, King Siddhi Narasimha Malla managed to extend the city westward to include the new locality of Na *twaḥ.* The intention of his son, Sri Nivas Malla, to extend the boundary of the city further westwards and take in the outlying village of Puco, however, was left unfulfilled. Such expansions were not to be rushed into, which is perhaps why this particular one never materialized. In general, therefore, new building took place within and conspicuously not without, the confines of the city boundary. With such pressure on land the solution was to build ever upwards—a strategy that continues to the present day.

If, as it is said, limitation is the beginning of form, then what were the limiting factors that led the designers of Lalitpur, if one can call them that, to demonstrate such an approach to the use of space? I shall focus on three: the need to keep as much land as possible for farming, the need for security against the ravages of invading marauders, and the development of an epidemiology that imbued in the Newars a dread of the wild and disordered outside. The lack of irrigation of the dry tableland (*tar*) itself put a limit on the usefulness of much of the land for agriculture, so it is clear that this factor alone is not sufficiently explanatory. The incursions of the armies of Doya and Khasa, however, and the short-lived but earth-scorching raid by the iconoclastic hordes of Samas Ud-din in the early fourteenth century, faithfully recorded by the writer of the *Gopālarāja Vamshāvali*, must have left an indelible imprint on the collective consciousness of the Valley's population (Vajracarya Malla 1985: 143-55). I shall examine the Newar approach to disease in a later chapter (§7.25).

Space, as Levy points out, is one way of representing a community. I have looked already at the organization of space in the house (§1.8) and shall defer a discussion of the organization of space in the locality to the next chapter (§6.1). In this chapter I intend to explore the ways that the symbolic organization of space has been used to represent the community of Lalitpur as a whole.[3]

5.2. The historical development of Lalitpur

5.2.1. A settlement by a river

Hindu cities, as many cities around the globe, are often located next to, or nearby, a river. From the river comes the water necessary for agriculture and the watering of flocks, for washing and cleaning. Presumably in the early days of settlement, before the construction of aqueducts, the river provided water for drinking and cooking as well. Lalitpur is no exception. The Bāgmati River, which from its source high on the Shivapuri ridge at the Valley's northern rim wends its way across the valley floor between the old cities of Lalitpur and Kathmandu, forms the principal river of the Kathmandu Valley. Its tributary, the Vishnumati River, is the significant river for Kathmandu. An analysis of Lalitpur's location and economic and ritual life, however, demonstrates that the Bāgmati itself was crucial in the origin and development of the city.[4]

The early evolution of the settlement that was to become Lalitpur was based on wet rice agriculture, which evidently developed in the low-lying land of the Bāgmati River flood plain. On the Valley floor, the best land for the cultivation of rice is invariably found at the bottoms (*dol*) where the soil is clayey and keeps wet. Poorer land is found on the higher ground (*tar*), effectively the very top of the ancient lake deposit, which is sandy and dries out quickly (Webster 1983). With the best land in use for agriculture, the early settlements, that later coalesced to form Lalitpur, were situated on the river bluffs immediately above. From this position also, any attack on the settlement would have been significantly easier to repel. These ancient settlements are represented now by the localities of Konti, Cyāsaḥ, Nyautā, Cāpatā, Guita and Tyāgaḥ (Map 9).

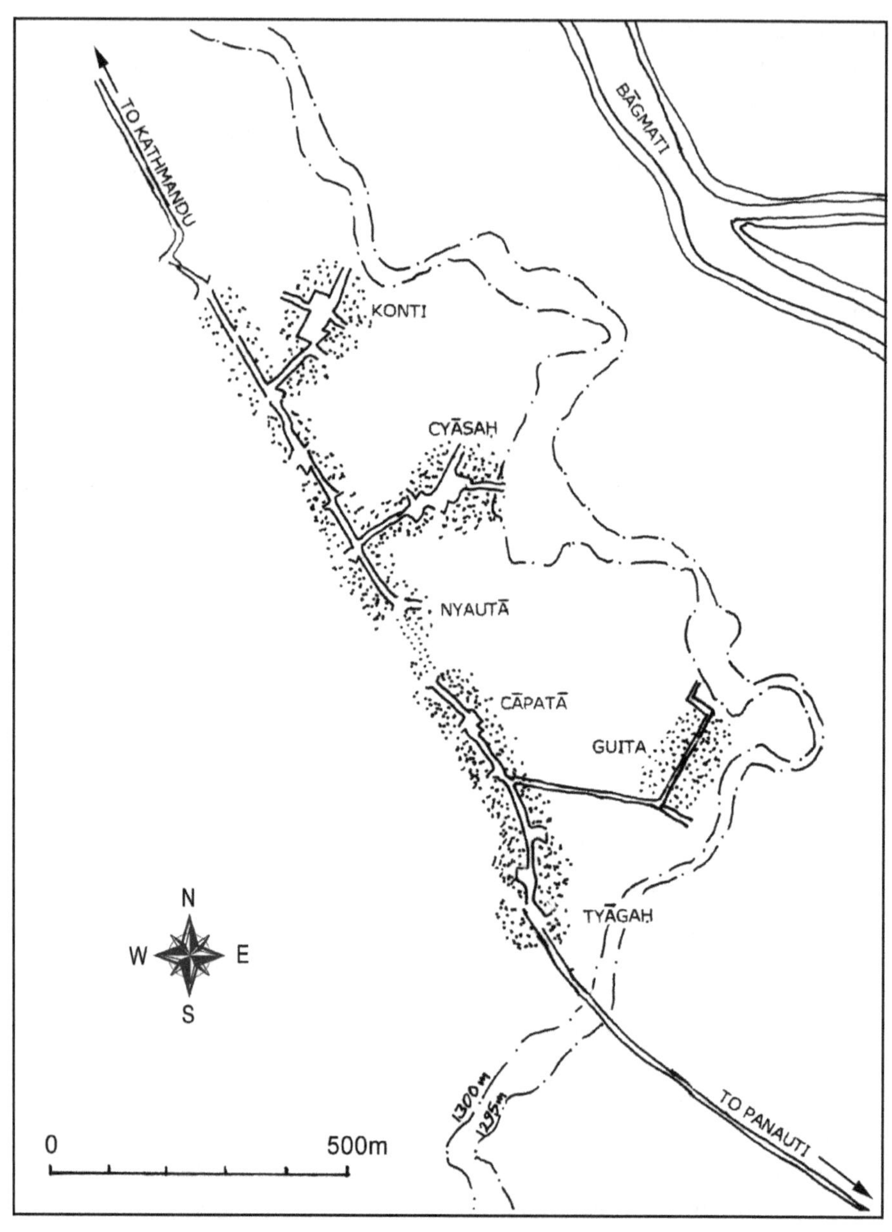

Map 9. Early settlement of Lalitpur (after Gutschow 1982: 157).

Today the waters of the Bāgmati River are considered sacred, as they are in rivers throughout the subcontinent, and popularly referred to as the Ganges (Ganga)—the archetype of sacred waters. Though everyone knows the Bāgmati is not *the* Ganges, it is known to be connected to it downstream and so is seen to be organically, or at least spiritually, one with it. The same is true of its tributaries.

It is worthwhile at this point to explore the meaning of the Bāgmati as a sacred river. As a tributary of the Ganges, the Bāgmati shares in its religious significance. Water is seen everywhere as a purifying substance or cleansing agent. This is not a question of their bacteriological purity but of their ritual and symbolic purity. As Diana Eck has pointed out, 'ritual purification by water is one of the great themes running through the history of Indian religious life...' (1993: 217). For Hindus the quality that gives river water its special significance is its flow. Throughout South Asia running water alone is used for cleansing.

The Englishman's pleasure at soaking in a hot tub (effectively in his own dirt!) is totally alien to the vast majority of South Asia's populace. It is the flow of the water that can both absorb impurities and carry them away. Bathing in the river, therefore, is thought to be efficacious not only for physical cleansing but also for one's spiritual life.

Furthermore, anything taken from the river is considered pure. Traditionally, the sand, which is required for the seedbed on the first day of Mohani, Nala Swanegu, is excavated from the Bāgmati River at the Shankamul *ghāt*s (§8.8.1). The marked increase in the physical pollution of the river has led many, in recent years, to travel all the way to Gujeshwari for their sand. Most of those who do so, however, would not venture to explain the precise relationship between physical and ritual pollution.

It is significant that the major Valley rivers are all located *outside* the boundaries of her cities. Purification, then, involves the material removal of dirt, and with it the ritual removal of spiritual impurity, by means of the physical transference of the impure from city space. It is this physical movement from sacred space to an apparently disordered, natural space, that seems to bear significance for Newar society. As Levy puts it for Bhaktapur's Hanumānte, the river forms a locus for dying, cremation and purification:

> [It] is outside the traditional boundaries of the city and takes much of its meaning (which it shares with the ideal symbolic Indian river, the Ganges) from its transitional position at a boundary to another world and its flow toward still another whose orders are other than that of the city. (Levy 1990: 153)

Each of the three main cremation grounds (*mashān*) of Lalitpur—Shankamul, Yappa and Bāl Kumāri are situated on a bank of the Bāgmati River or near one of its tributaries. Furthermore, items that have been used in Ancestor Worship (*shrāddha*), notably the *pinda*s are thrown into the river after the ceremony. Until he has deposited these items the one who has performed the *shrāddha* is considered highly impure. On his way to the river he is preceded by a friend who ensures that he is not touched until he has completed the ritual and bathed. Likewise, at the close of certain festivals, notably on the final days of Holi and Mohani, and at Swanti on the day following Kijā Pujā, the items used during the *pujā* are removed from the city to be thrown in the river.[5]

Generally, in South Asia, the true right bank of the river is considered to be the most auspicious for building a city or temple. Bhaktapur, in keeping with this ideal, is situated on the true right bank of the Hanumānte (Levy 1990: 153; Dutt 1977: 24). Interestingly, however, neither Kathmandu nor Lalitpur are on the true right bank of their rivers. Another notable exception to the ideal is that most holy of Hindu cities, Banāras (Varanāsi, Kāshi), which is on the true left bank of the Ganges. We may note simply that the founding of settlements such as these clearly must have preceded any attempt to formalize their ritual significance.

5.2.2. A commercial centre

Gutschow (1982) and Toffin (1991b: 76) have demonstrated the importance of trade links in the development of Newar cities. The Licchavi City of Lalitpur (or Yupagrāmadranga as it was then known) clearly developed around the intersection of two trade routes. One running roughly north-south would have linked Lalitpur with India via Wāy (Chapagaon), Lele and Makwanpur, and with Tibet via Sankhu. The other, running east-west linked the city with Kirtipur and Panauti. Trade was vitally important in the economy of the growing city (Map 10, p. 98). Once the wetlands had been opened up for rice cultivation by the invention of the short-handled hoe (*ku*) a surplus of grain led to this new dynamic in the city's development (Webster 1981).

5.3. Sets of deities

Space is also defined by reference to several sets of deities that are positioned at significant locations in and around the city. Gutschow (1982: 165, Map 182) shows a set of four Bhimsen shrines and four Nārāyana shrines which are all located within the city. Both sets of four shrines encircle the central palace area. Gutschow (ibid.: Map 183) also shows the locations of eight Ganesh shrines that are divided into two sets of four. One of these groups describes a polygon that, like those of the shrines of Bhimsen and Nārāyana encircles the palace area.

It is not clear what significance, if any, that these particular sets of deities have for the life of the city. They do not give rise to any specific festival nor are they visited, as far as I am aware, in any consecutive manner. Other sets of deities have very clear meaning, however, and it is to these that I shall now turn. But first, more on the boundaries which give the city much of its character.

5.4. City boundaries

As Slusser points out (1998: I,92-93 and II,plates 95,96) the old Malla cities were walled settlements punctuated at many points by gates. This is attested by contemporary and later accounts such as those of Kunu Sharma (1961) and Oldfield (1981: 1,95-96,102-103,111).[6] It is possible, as Slusser did herself,

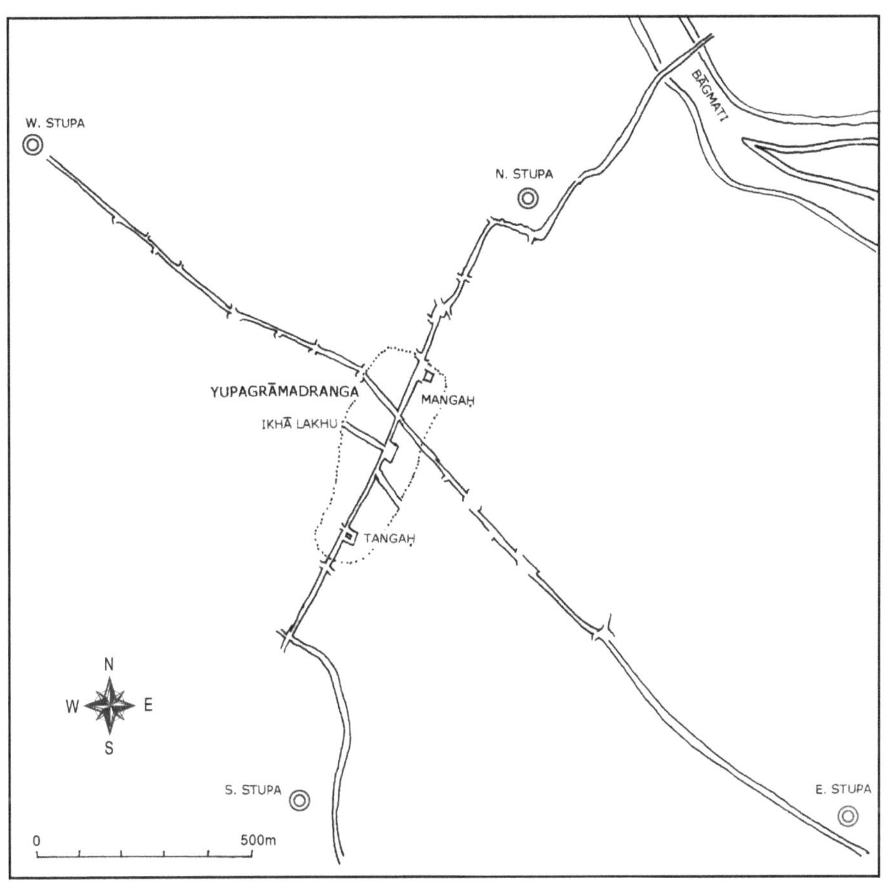

Map 10. The intersection of trade routes.

to trace the precise location of the old wall even though there is no extant substantial evidence. Local residents know the exact point at which they are within (*dune*) or outside (*pine*) the old walls. Place names such as Kwalkhu (Kwālakhu) and Ikhā Lakhu tell of former gates and boundaries going back, in the latter case, to pre-Malla times.

Local residents tell of twelve or more gates that used to perforate the walls of Malla era Lalitpur. When asked where exactly the gates were, however, they are often at a loss to give the precise locations of more than two or three of them. One map that was sketched for me, oriented with west at the top, had the names of only two gates: *taḥ dhvākā* on the west and *jhval dhvākā* on the east.

The easiest way to tell where several of the gates were placed, however, is by an analysis of the locations of some of the low castes. Although most residents of Lalitpur were not intentionally situated at any particular distance from the city centre, two low caste groups were clearly located on, or relocated to the boundaries of the city at some time in the distant past. The

Dyaḥlā Untouchables were placed immediately outside the old Malla city gates, whereas the (unclean but touchable) Khadgi Butchers were, for the most part, placed immediately inside.[7] Since these castes still live largely in their traditional localities the simple matter of distinguishing one caste from the other can lead to, at particular locations, precise mapping of old city boundaries (Map 11). The Dyaḥlā were to be located not simply outside the city wall but more particularly, outside the gates. In this way their polluted presence would protect the city from marauders or evil spirits (*bhut/pret*), which, like the city's inhabitants, would also find them repulsive.

Further evidence for this emphasis on the importance of the division between the inside and outside of the city is provided by an analysis of Lineage Deity

Map 11. Centre and periphery in city space.[8]

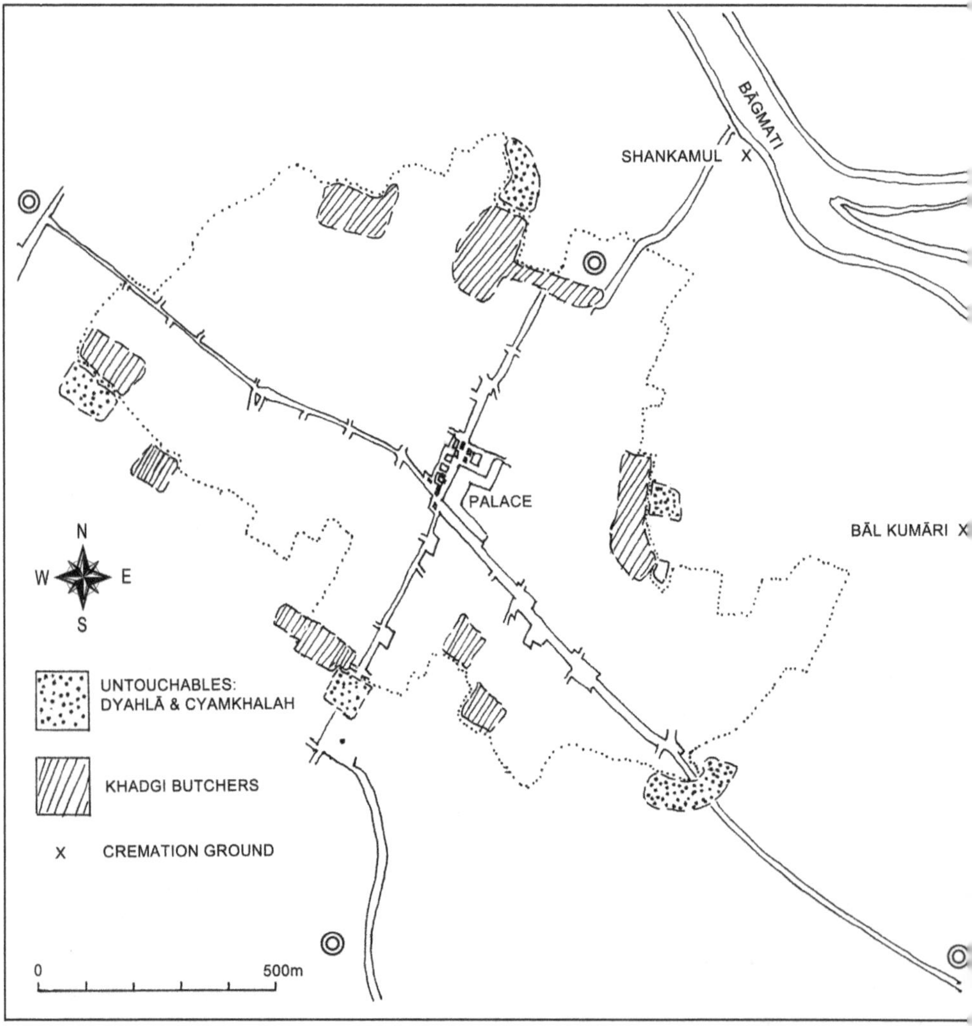

sites. Lineage Deities were always sited *outside* the settlement. The reason for this is not clear, although their resemblance as natural stones (*prākrit*), to the aniconic *pitha*s may have something to do with it. Perhaps also the relation of the cult of the Lineage Deity with the worship of dead ancestors (*pitri*) led to such an association. Many lineages retain an oral history of the establishment or relocation of their Lineage Deity (Plate 9, p.100). It is possible, then, by comparing these oral historical accounts with the actual cult and location of these shrines, to make some tentative deductions about the time in which a certain lineage migrated, or how the lineage in question was established in the first place (Locke 1985: 517; Gellner 1992: 239-40).

Why this preoccupation with boundaries? The Hindu town as an organized community had to be set apart from the unorganized outside. The nineteenth century Sanskritist Max Müller drew attention to the fact that (as quoted in Gutschow and Kölver 1975: 20):

> Hindu towns seem to bear out [the] notion [that] a town is a region that is, as it were, walled off from the surrounding country. Such land as was inhabited by an organized community had to be set off from the country, which was unstructured, uncultured, not 'urbanized'.

Hence the Sanskrit *pur* means both 'wall' and 'town' (as in Lalit*pur*). The wall therefore acted as a boundary between the structured, urbanized inside and the unstructured, wild outside.

Such a concern with boundaries goes back at least to Vedic times. Michael Witzel explains that the Vedas made a distinction between *grāma*, 'settlement',

Plate 9. Marikaḥmi Lineage Deity at Iti.

and *aranya*, 'wilderness' (1997: 519). The *aranya* was dangerous and full of threats. It was where the barbaric and uncivilized aborigines and dreaded demons lived. By demarcating the boundaries, therefore, the Aryan settlement became a sacred space resembling the Vedic offering ground. In this it seems the ancient Aryans were not alone. Jameson points out that the Newar city's concern with boundaries, particularly those between order and chaos, offers striking analogies with those of that other ancient Indo-European civilization, Greece (1997: 487).

5.4.1. Ashoka mounds

Gutschow and Kölver suggest that Lalitpur was subject to planning from a very early stage and that this became necessary in order to delimitate the new foundation on the fusion of the earlier separate settlements (1975: 20). The four mounds (*stupa*s or *thur*s) that ring the city seem to have been set up to give on the one hand an expression of unity to the space contained within, and on the other some sort of orientation to that space. Their location, though notionally at the cardinal points of the compass are up to twenty-four degrees off the true geographic axes. In this the mounds correspond to the major trade routes described above (Map 11; cf. Gutschow 1982: 154). Most of the streets of Lalitpur are laid out in a grid pattern roughly parallel to these trade routes. It would seem that the city grew up self-consciously oriented by the four mounds which themselves were built to sanctify the space within and lend some legitimacy, if it was needed, to the development of the city through its trade. Could it also be significant that, located as they are at the four entry points of what was, after all, a crossroads, the *stupa*s were intended to counteract the inauspiciousness of this node?[9]

5.4.2. Power-Places

In and around the city of Lalitpur there are thousands of Power-Places (*pitha* or *pigandyaḥ*) each consisting of a simple unhewn stone. These stones are often a metre or so below ground level with steps leading down for the convenience of the worshipper. Rarely are these 'hyperethral shrines', as Slusser calls them, covered, although, like the Bhavani Power-Place in the courtyard of 'House' of Mangaḥ, they may be surmounted by brass *nāga* serpents and related paraphernalia and surrounded by a stone border. Many, perhaps all, of these shrines have a Sanskrit name but it is clear that most, if not all, represent local cults that were later Sanskritized. Locals usually interpret these shrines as sites where pieces of Pārvati's decomposing body fell to earth when, according to the myth, the grieving and distraught Shiva carried her corpse on his shoulder.

Many residents make a distinction between 'true' Power-Places and those that are, as it were, interlopers. The number of True Power-Places, they say, is twelve, but a heated argument will often ensue when trying to define which of the plethora of possibilities are rightly included in the group. Although many

Power-Places are located within the old city boundaries, all twelve of the True Power-Places are located outside the city (Map 12, p. 103). The Twelve consist of the Eight Mother Goddesses (Ashtamātrika) with the addition of a shrine each belonging to Bhairava, Kumar, Ganesh and Siddhilakshmi (Table 5).

Power-Place Worship (*pitha pujā*) is an essential part of the autumnal festivals of Yẽnyaḥ and Mohani, and the equivalent vernal Mohani festival of Pāhā̃ Cahre. At Mohani, procession to the Power-Places begins on Kayashtami (Bhādra-*shukla*/Yãlāthwa 8) and goes on for a full lunar month (§8.4). Most Newars, including members of the Pengu Daḥ, visit the Power-Places in the mornings playing as they go the *dāmaru* (*dabu dabu*, small, one-handed double-headed drum) (cf. Gutschow 1982: 173, Fig.194). Maharjans, on the other hand, visit the Power-Places in the evening playing the *dhimay* (large, double headed drum) and *bhusyāḥ* (accompanying large cymbals).

The Eight Mother Goddesses (Ashtamātrika) are worshipped everywhere around the Kathmandu Valley as manifestations of Devi, the Goddess. The city of Bhaktapur can be neatly divided into nine sectors corresponding to the Eight Mother Goddesses plus a ninth, central goddess, that are situated at Power-Places around its perimeter (cf. Gutschow's map in Levy 1990: 155). In spite of Toffin's claim to the contrary (1984: 484) it is not at all easy to trace an eight-fold division in Lalitpur corresponding to the Eight Mother Goddesses. Rather, as Barré *et al.* (1981) have pointed out for Panauti (in Gellner 1984: 117), there seems to be only two, or perhaps three, of the Mother Goddesses that have a significant cult—Mahālakshmi, Bāl Kumāri and Vishnu Devi. If there is, in fact, an eight-fold division it is not at all as well developed as it is in Bhaktapur. Furthermore, there are no 'god houses' (*dyaḥ chẽ*) within the city that correspond to the Power-Places outside as there are in Bhaktapur (Levy 1990: 231; Vergati 1995: 39).

Table 5. The twelve 'true' Power-Places of Lalitpur.[10]

Batuk Bhairava, Lagankhel
Mahālakshmi*, Tasi (S)
Kumār Rājā, Kusunti
Vishnu Devi (Vaishnavi)*, Yappa (SW)
Brahmayani*, Neku
Maheshvari (Rudrayani)*, Palinka
Indrayāni*, Lwahãgalaḥ (NW)
Ganesh, Hasapataḥ
Dhum Vārāhi*, Dhantila (NW)
Cāmundā (Sikali)*, Sikabahi, Shankamul (N)
Bāl Kumāri*, Kwachẽ (E)
Siddhilakshmi (Siddhi Caran), Bangi

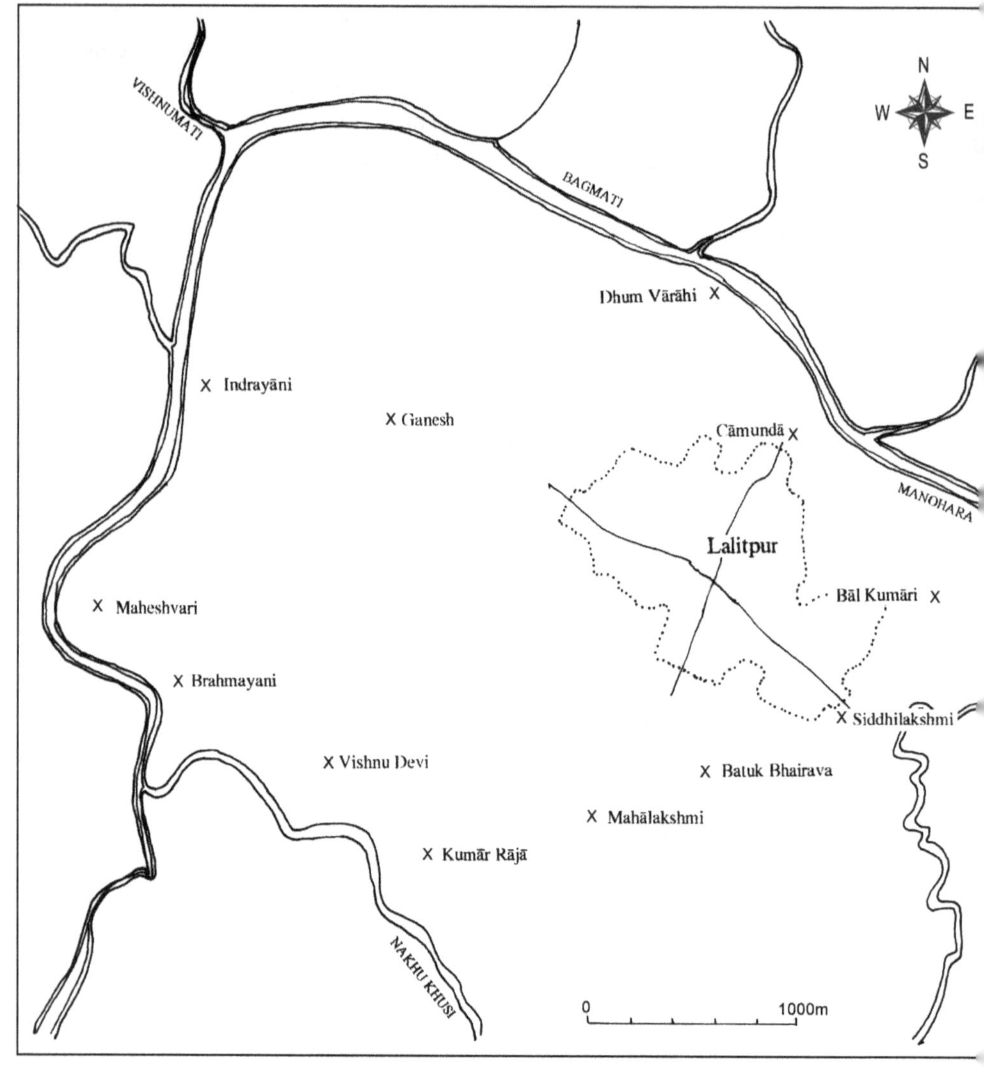

Map 12. The twelve 'true' Power-Places of Lalitpur.

Key: * denotes Mother Goddess, *mātrikā.*[11] (S), (SW), (E), (N) and (NW) indicate relative location.

Apart from the significance of the Eight Mother Goddesses for the festivals outlined above, Lalitpurians also do Power-Place Worship during the course of various life-cycle rituals. It is instructive to map the Power-Place Worship of various lineages. Among the Pengu Daḥ who still live within the confines of the old city, for instance, all Bārāhi, all Marikaḥmi, all Paḥmā Sikaḥmi and the following lineages of Tamvaḥ—Bhya, Haugaḥ (except Dhasi Hãe), Itāchẽ (except Bāgaḥ), Kothujhvaḥchẽ, Lachica—worship the Power-Place at Bāl Kumāri. All Lwahākaḥmi, all Vishvakarma Sikaḥmi and the following lineages of Tamvaḥ—Dhasi Hãe, Bāgaḥ, Jyoti, Kũḥchẽ, Kwaḥ, Naḥ Bāhāḥ, Nāyaḥ—all worship the Power-Place at Mahālakshmi. One lineage of Marikaḥmi that resides at Jawalakhel, however, does *pitha pujā* at Vishnu Devi. This data demonstrates that the attachment to a particular Power-Place is determined by two factors: descent and location.

Ultimately location wins over descent as, when a group moves on a permanent basis, they take up the worship of the Power-Place that is related to that locality. Their traditional Power-Place cult is not necessarily abandoned, however, and at important life-cycle events a *pujā* will be offered to both. Examples of this include the Bāgaḥ and Dhasi Hãe branches of the Tamvaḥ Itāchẽ lineage, and the Jawalakhel lineage of Marikaḥmi. Those who have migrated to other cities also adopt the Power-Place of the locality in which they settle as, for instance, the Panauti lineage has done.

The question arises as to the purpose of these Mother Goddess shrines. It would seem that we are dealing here with the systematizing of a number of existing deities into a set in order to give some form to them and raise their significance for the city as a whole. Gutschow and Kölver suggest that the system of the Eight Mother Goddesses 'was probably meant to *raise the status* of what had become a royal settlement' (1975: 21). It seems to me, however, that the system does more than this. Each of the Mother Goddesses is situated outside the city, in the wild, disordered land where the demons lurk and bandits may attack. In the same way as the Untouchable Dyaḥlā were positioned outside the gates of the city, presumably during Malla times, the Eight Mother Goddesses were neatly situated to ward off the danger of that other world. This is a connection that is not lost on locals. The reason that fierce gods and goddesses are better than benign deities as policemen of boundaries is because people are afraid of them (Gellner 1997c: 552). By making them into a set and giving them Sanskrit names, medieval Lalitpur was formalizing their protective role. A set of eight also speaks about unity in diversity. The medieval city was a disparate one with lineages and castes all pulling away from increasing central control. By making the eight into a set, the city was saying something about the unity of the city itself; a unity against outsiders that revolved around the royal centre from which processions to the outside would begin and to which they would return.

There is a further group of goddesses that we must examine here. These are the Ten Great Knowledges (Dashmahāvidya). Again, the exact complement of the Dashmahāvidya is contested (Table 6). Not all of the Ten Great Knowledges are of equal importance. The cult of Bāgalamukhi is important for all the city's inhabitants. Her propitiation is seen as important for the prevention of cholera (Slusser 1998: 322). As with the twelve 'true' Power-Places, the cult of the Dashmahāvidya is especially important on Kayashtami (Bhādra-*shukla*/Yālāthwa 8) when a Dashmahāvidya Pujā is held around all ten shrines (§8.4). The significant difference between the Dashmahāvidya and the Ashtamātrika is not so much in their number as in their location. With the exception of Vajrāyogini (Tārā) of Puco, each of the Great Knowledges, accompanied, in its vicinity, by an image of Bhairava, is located *within* the confines of the city (Map 13).[12] They are not, however, evenly distributed throughout as one might expect; none are located further east than Tripurasundāri in Cāka Bahi. Dil Mohan Tamrakar is of the opinion that the Dashmahāvidya represent an older group of protective deities that were once situated outside the boundaries of the settlement. Indeed, he reported a tradition that the image of Bāl Kumāri at Kwāchẽ is a copy of the one at Cāka Bahi, which is located adjacent to that of Tripurasundāri.[13]

Map 13. The Ten Great Knowledges (*dashmahāvidya*) of Lalitpur.

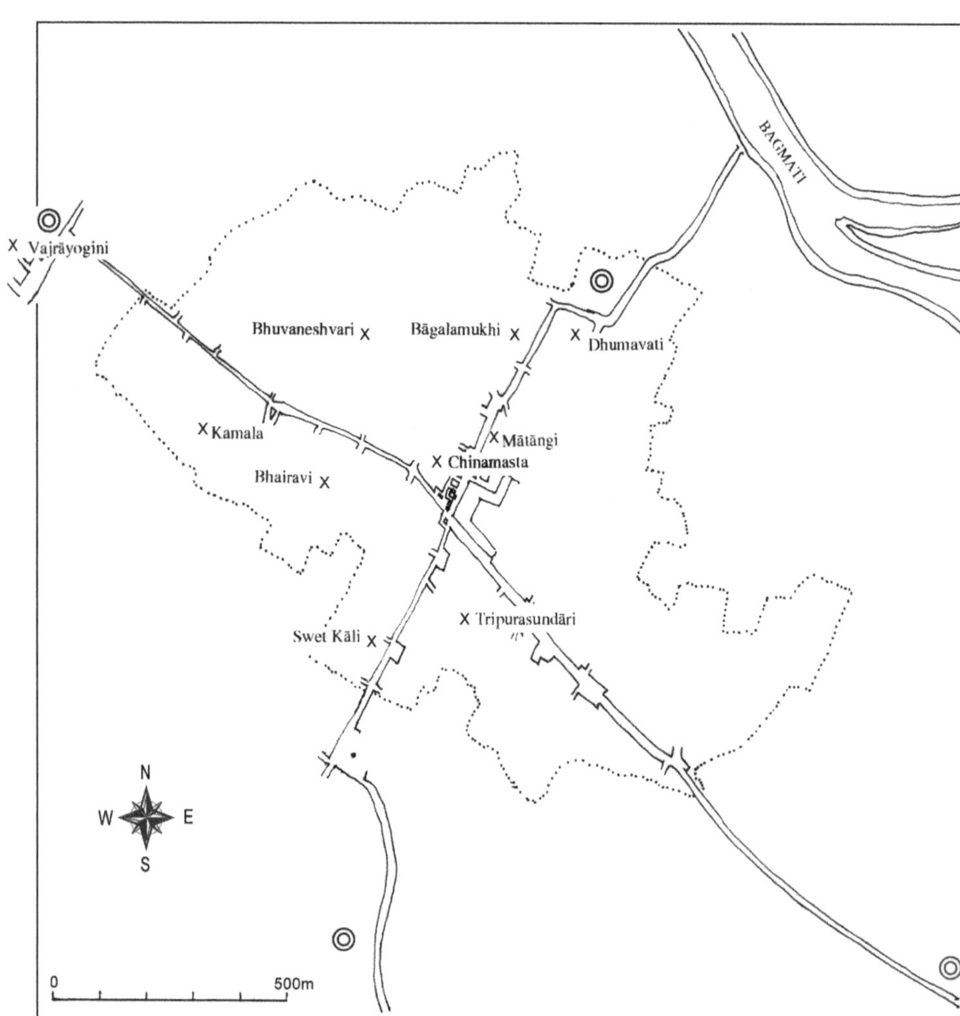

It seems highly probable, then, that the Dashmahāvidya were the protective deities, analogous to the twelve True Power-Places, of the Licchavi City of Yupagrāmadranga (§5.2.2).[14]

Table 6. The Ten Great Knowledges (*dashmahāvidya*) of Lalitpur[15]

Tripurasundāri, Bāl Kumāri, Cāka Bahi
Swet Kāli, Ta Bāhāḥ
Bhairavi, Bahālukhā
Kamala, Purnacandi
Vajrāyogini (Tārā), Puco
Bhuvaneshvari, Nakaḥ Bahi
Bāgalamukhi, Kumbheshvāra
Dhumavati, Dhum Bāhāḥ
Mātāngi, Swatha
Chinamasta, Mamadu Galli

5.4.3. Cremation sites

Related to the locations of the Eight Mother Goddesses are the cremation sites (*mashān*) of the city. Three of the cremation grounds—Shankamul *mashān*, Manohara Manimati *mashān* and Yappa *mashān*—are located adjacent to Mother Goddess shrines—those of Cāmundā, Bāl Kumāri and Vishnu Devi respectively.[16] The majority of Lalitpurians cremate their dead at Shankamul, which was refurbished in the nineteenth century under Rana patronage.[17]

Each of these three cremation grounds is located near a river. The Yappa *mashān*, however, located at the Vaishnavi shrine at Nakhu, is surprisingly at some distance from the river itself. Could this be because the river has meandered to a different course since the cremation ground was established? The Shankamul cremation ground is at the riverside itself and consists of a number of bathing and cremation *ghāt*s. It is similar in appearance though not in size to those at Banāras and Pashupati. It is also at some distance from its accompanying Power-Place, that of Cāmundā. One could surmise that the river had meandered away from the shrines since they were established. In the case of Shankamul the importance of the cremation ground enforced its relocation with the retreat of the riverbank.

Lalitpurians, in fact, make a distinction between the *mashān* at the riverside and the actual cremation platform (*depaḥ* or *dip*) which is usually up on the bank and, as we have seen, sometimes at some distance from the river itself. At Vishnu Devi there are three cremation platforms—one for Vajrācāryas and Shākyas, another, nearest the shrine, belonging to Maharjans and other high and middle castes, and a third at some distance from the other two for the Khadgi.

The cremation ground at Shankamul has four cremation platforms each with its own shelter (*phālca*). High castes and Maharjans may use the largest. Tandukārs, Khadgis and Vyanjankārs have one each. The 'Untouchable' Dyaḥlā do not have a cremation platform at all but burn their dead separately down by the river (Gellner and Pradhan 1995: 167). All castes throw the ashes of the dead in the river upon completion of the cremation.

We have already noted the significance of the river for cleansing. We have here only to add how the waters of the river not only cleanse the city from that most inauspicious and impure substance, the corpse, but also provide a means, as it were, to travel to the next life.

5.5. The central hub: The palace square

At the centre of the city of Lalitpur lies the palace area (*lāyaku*) referred to by locals as Mangaḥ and marked on maps as 'Darbār Square'. The present palace buildings were constructed, for the most part, in the seventeenth and early eighteenth centuries in place of previous palace buildings (Plate 10). The site now occupied by the palace seems to have been the seat of the monarchy from Licchavi times. The adjacent water fountain, the Mangaḥhiti, was built around 400 AD and is the oldest known structure in the locality. Local tradition relates that the palace was moved to its present site from a mound at Patuko, one block north and west of Mangaḥ, during Licchavi times. According to this tradition, the Patuko mound was built by the Kirāti kings (Shrestha and Malla 1971: 36; Gellner 1996: 129; Landon 1976: 209). The myths of origin of the nearby Kwā Bāhāḥ refer to oppression by the Kirātis who were forced

Plate 10. Mangaḥ (Lalitpur Durbar Square) from the south.

from their palace by hundreds of bees and chased to the locality of Cyāsaḥ to the north-east where 800 (*cyā saḥ*) of them died. Lalitpurians regard the Vyanjankār caste, which inhabits Cyāsaḥ, as the descendants of those who survived.

The relocation of the palace to its present site, precisely at the intersection of the two major trade routes seems to have been an attempt to express spatially what was already a reality politically—that the king was the centre of the life of the city. We will look at this more later on when we consider the movement of gods around city space.

The legitimation of the central role of kingship in Lalitpur was accomplished first and foremost by the construction of various temples within and in front of the new palace. The present-day arrangement of monuments in Lalitpur's palace square demonstrates a very carefully thought out strategy to sanctify the central, royal space by the establishing of a number of seats of the gods. The intended effect of this sanctification was no doubt to lend legitimacy to the king's reign. The amazing density of concentration of major temples of brick and stone in such a small area bears testimony to careful design. Although the buildings are of very divergent designs and built with various materials the overall visual effect is not crowded. Nineteenth and early twentieth century foreign observers marvelled at the beauty of the square as does many a tourist today. Since its designation as a UNESCO World Heritage Site in 1979 many of the monuments have undergone extensive restoration. The architect Sekler describes the design of the space thus:

> By having related heights, horizontal lines were carried from one building to the next and all this helped to unify the overall impression. Were it not for the unification through these means and through the underlying ordering principles of number and measure, the total impact might have been too restless, even disturbing, owing to the strong contrasts of shapes, textures and colors. As it is, unity and diversity balance each other in a most successful manner. (Sekler 1987: 66-67)

Why was it so important to design the square with such an approach? The architects were without a doubt expressing certain values by doing so.

> The strong visual order imposed on the buildings of the Darbar Square in all likelihood was based on an equally powerful and complex belief-system. This order, together with the outstanding artistic craftsmanship of the masters of the past and with the originally impeccable—now, alas, broken—hierarchy of scale, made Patan Darbar Square one of the great historic urban spaces of the world. (Ibid.: 67)

So the overall effect of the location and design of the Palace Square is to demonstrate the unity of the city around and under the rulership of her king. This centrality of kingship, though, since the conquest of Lalitpur by Prithvi Narayan Shah in 1768 greatly weakened politically, is still strongly expressed *ritually.* We will see how this works below.

5.6. Ritual movement through space

There are several procession routes (*pradakshinapātha*, Skt.) in the city of Lalitpur. Processions following these routes vary greatly in significance for the city. The great festival of Matayā, for instance, attracts many thousands of devotees, whereas the Narasimha Jātrā, which follows a different route, is essentially the province of only one caste.

It is helpful at this point to tease out a typology of the procession routes for the city and to try to discern the significance of each one within the overall context of the annual march of the calendar.

One could take as the most basic division between the processions, those that have the worship of a deity as their main *raison d'être* and those that do not. The only one that falls in the latter category, however, is the funeral procession, or 'Way of the dead'. Another basic division, at least for the vast majority of those processions that are for the purpose of worship, is between those in which the devotees visit fixed images of the deities, and those in which movable images are transported through city space.

Niels Gutschow has differentiated four types of procession route: centrifugal, linear, centripetal, and convoluted (1982: 190-193). The last two are, it seems to this writer, variations of the same category. Moreover, Gutschow counts Pitha Pujā as a centrifugal procession. Although it does include an excursion from the city I include it as a separate type of centripetal procession because it is, nevertheless, focused on the centre, as I will demonstrate. I have, therefore, constructed a new typology that attempts to take these factors into consideration (Table 7, p.110).

5.6.1. Centrifugal processions

Certain processions are centrifugal, that is, they start at the centre, or at least on the inside, of the city and work their way outside (Gutschow 1982: 193, Fig.233). The classic festival in which centrifugal procession plays a significant part is that of Gathā̃ Mugaḥ which takes place, as we shall see (§7.10), in the middle of the monsoon. Effigies of the demon Gathā̃ Mugaḥ are constructed by children during the day and in the evening carried out of the city on a clearly defined route to a place where it is burned.

The other procession to take a centrifugal character is that of the funeral (Map 14, p. 111).[18] On the death of a resident, pallbearers and other members of the death *guthi*, family members, and friends gather at the house of the dead. In a short time, the corpse is brought out, a procession forms and then moves at, what seems to a European, a hurried pace through the streets of the dead person's locality (*twaḥ*) and on through the city to the cremation ground outside. The route, the 'Way of the dead' (*silāpu*), is always the same. Everyone knows the route that he will take on his last journey from his home, should he have the fortune of taking his last breath there. The route followed by each locality is, in most cases, an apparently rational one to the outsider, though not always. In some places a diversion seems to be made so that the

Table 7. A typology of processions.

Centrifugal		Ways of the dead (*silāpu*) Gathā̃ Mugaḥ
Linear		Mahālakshmi Jātrā Bāl Kumāri Jātrā Vishnu Devi Jātrā Bū̃gadyaḥ Jātrā Kwenādyaḥ Jātrā
Centripetal	Royal	Sā Paru Nyaku Jātrā Matayā Ganesh Pujā Narasimha Jātrā Krishna Jātrā Bhimsen Jātrā
	Convoluted	Bāhāḥ Pujā Matayā Krishna Pujā Bhimsen Pujā Dashmahāvidya Pujā Vasundharā Pujā
	Excursive	Pitha Pujā

route is not the most direct. The most glaring detour is that followed by the residents of the localities south of the royal palace.

A funeral procession from Haugaḥ or Tangaḥ, for instance, makes its way down the main road towards the palace at Mangaḥ but then, instead of going straight down the road in front of the palace and the great temples of the palace square, turns one block west to Mahāpā. Only then does it resume its northward journey before heading east again at Konti to exit the city and finally arrive at Shankamul.

Two phenomena are noteworthy here. Firstly, the funeral procession does not exit the city at the nearest gate but heads, instead, across the city. Secondly, the procession makes an inefficient detour around the centre instead of going straight through it. These two phenomena lead me to conclude that the normal and ideal centrifugal pattern is modified by the importance of the site of cremation. This importance is almost certainly a measure of its antiquity. In the context of Bhaktapur, Gutschow and Kölver suggest that the Ways of the dead 'doubtless belong to the oldest materials that can be found' (1975: 27). If this is so, as one would expect, then the later superimposition of the palace on this pattern led to the need to modify the pattern in order to avoid that place of supreme purity. When I asked why the procession must avoid the palace area, informants told me that the king loved his subjects so much that he mourned whenever he saw a funeral procession. This was how Dipak Lal Tamrakar expressed it:

> The reason why the way of the dead is around Mangaḥ is so that the king would not see the procession from out of his window. If he did then he would grieve for the dead as for one of his family. Why give him grief and make him eat only one meal that day?

Map 14. Ways of the dead (*silãpu*).

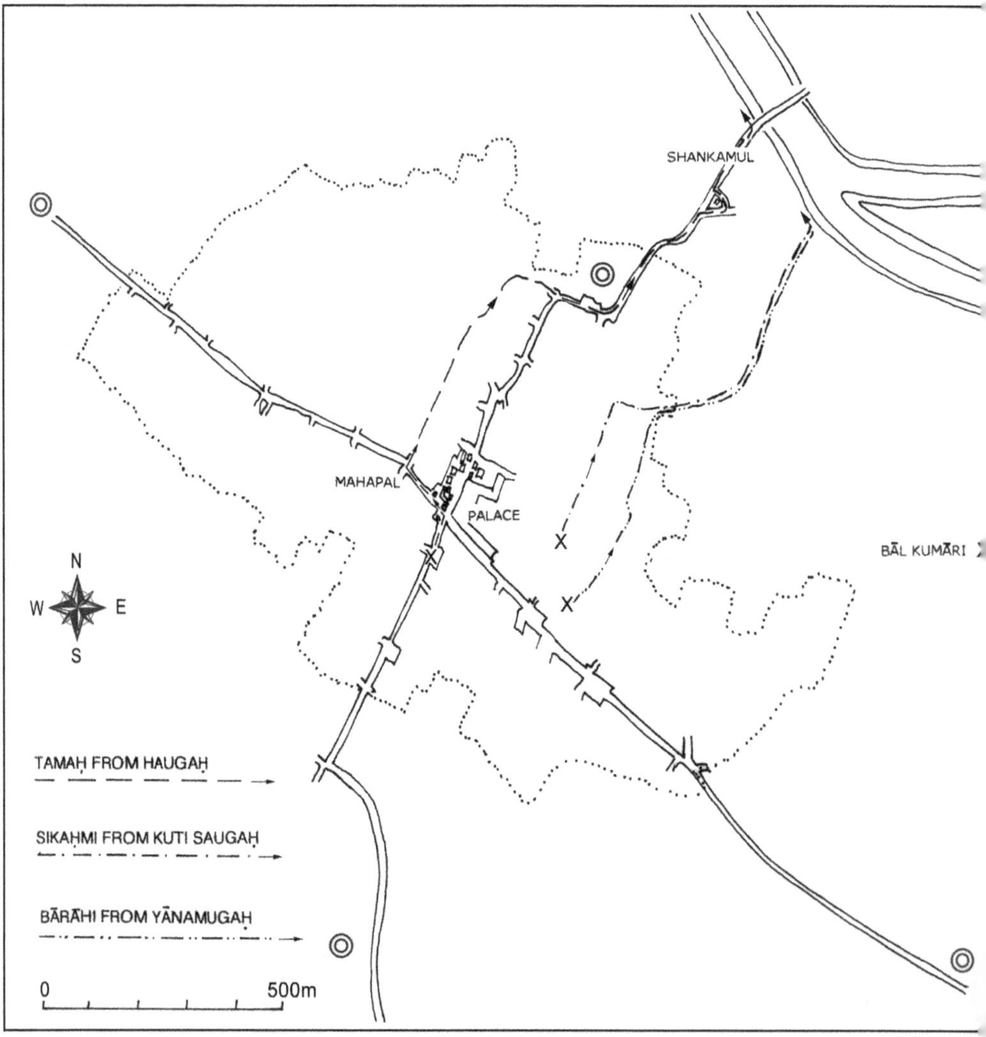

From the popular perspective, therefore, the processions took a detour to avoid giving the king unnecessary suffering. Such a story fits in with the devotion with which Nepalese, in general, honour their monarch.[19]

The main significance we must understand about centrifugal processions, however, is this need to remove impurity and vileness from the city. Both corpses and effigies of demons, representing the demons themselves must be taken out of the city. The city must be kept pure in order to function as a sacred space. All impurity must be removed. It can be said that the mundane daily task of the city's sweepers, a group still consisting largely of the 'Untouchable' Dyaḥlā, is also centrifugal entering the city as they do only to work back out with the debris of urban life. In Malla times, in fact, they were only allowed into the city at daybreak and had to be out again before it got dark. Even today, one can enter one of the localities of the Dyaḥlā and be hit by the overpowering stench of the putrefying carcasses of dead dogs, that have been removed from the confines of the old city and simply left in front of the dwellings of the Sweepers, who seem to be oblivious to the fetid atmosphere.

5.6.2. Linear processions

The movement of deities through city space is affected, first of all, by whether those deities normally dwell within or without that space. Linear processions are those that, again along prescribed routes, enter from the outside, continue through city space and exit again to return to the deity's home (Gutschow 1982). Several deities are carried through the city in this way. All are resident outside the city. Of these, three are of the Mother Goddesses, Mahālakshmi, Bāl Kumāri, and Vishnu Devi (ibid.: 173, Fig.195).[20] Another is of the powerful Tantric image of Ganesh, called Jala Vinayaka or Kwenādyaḥ (§8.14). Though Kwenādyaḥ has its own major temple at Co Bāhāḥ, south of the city, where the Bāgmati River flows through a gorge on its way out of the Valley, the large brass mask-like processional image is kept for most of the year at another temple at Puco. It is this heavy image that is mounted on a palanquin and carried through the south-western sector of the city on its annual *jātrā.* The great annual chariot festival of Bũgadyaḥ also describes a linear route, as one would expect of a visiting deity. More will be said about that later (§10.5, Map 16).

5.6.3. Centripetal processions

Centripetal processions are those that emphasize the integration of city space. By processing around city space—clockwise keeping the centre on ones respectful right—the festival integrates the diverse communities that make up the localities of the city. There are three types of centripetal procession: royal, convoluted, and excursive.

a. Royal centripetal processions

The majority of processions of Lalitpur follow a centripetal or integrative pattern. That is, by circumambulating the centre of the city they effect the unification of city space (Map 15).[21]

The main procession route of the city, this integrative *pradakshinapātha*, follows a route that wends its way around the centre of city space taking in as it does ten localities (*twaḥ*). Such centripetal processions are those that take place in the festivals of Sā Pāru, Nyaku Jātrā, Matayā Ganesh Pujā, Narasimha Jātrā, Krishna Jātrā, and Bhimsen Jātrā.

All centripetal processions follow a clockwise route—that is the centre of the city is always kept on the right of the processing devotees. There is an important exception here, however. At the point immediately to the north of the royal palace, the procession does not circumambulate the city centre and the palace by progressing to the east and through the localities of Valakhu and Nyautā. Instead, the procession route takes a direct line to the centre taking

Map 15. The royal centripetal procession route.

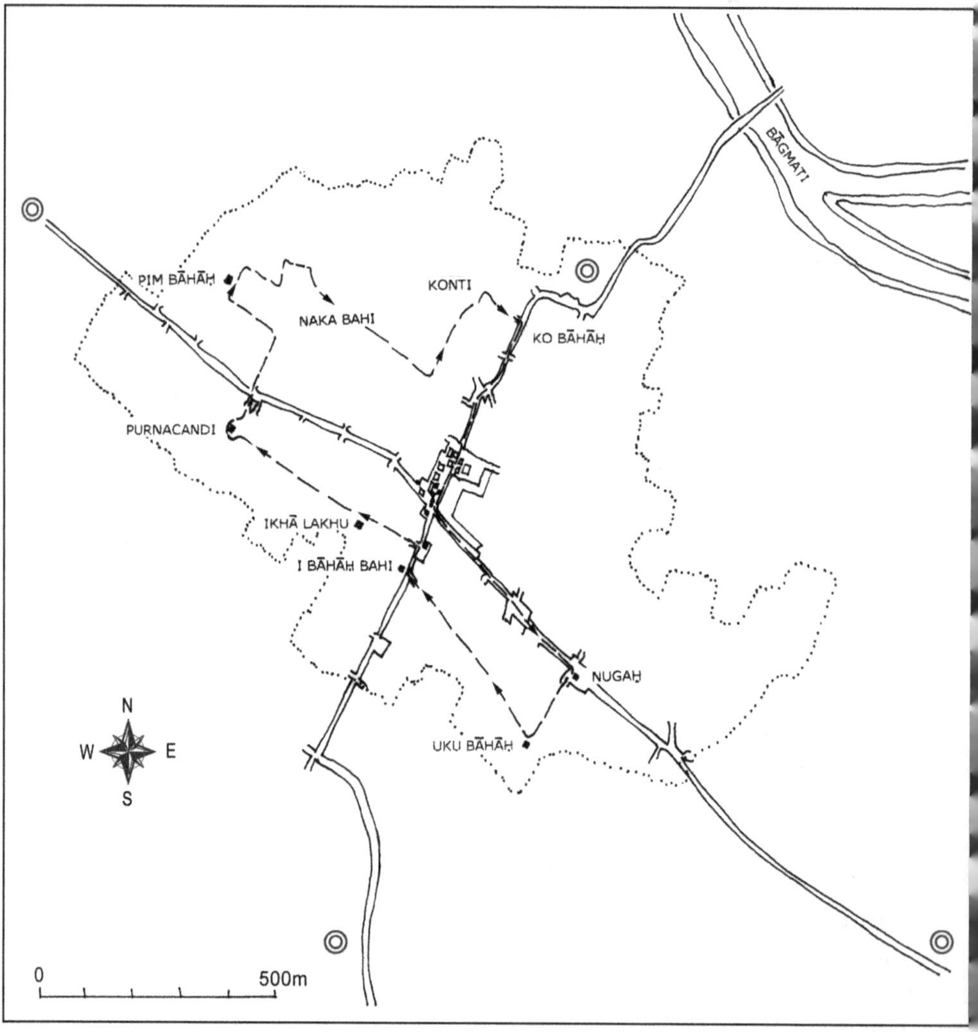

the devotees immediately in front of the palace and thence east to Saugaḥ and Nugaḥ.

This integrative or centripetal *pradakshinapātha* has been designed so that it winds directly in front of the palace. Why is this? One thing we can be sure of is that this *pradakshinapātha* does not describe an older city boundary as Barré *et al.* suggested for Panauti (1981: 41) and Gutschow himself suggested for Bhaktapur in an earlier paper (Gutschow and Kölver 1975: 21; cf. Toffin 1991b). The route does not follow any known boundary that has been discovered by historians. Furthermore, there is no concept of inside and outside as there would be if the route were considered a boundary such as a wall. Rather, such a *pradakshinapātha* binds the city together as Gutschow later realized (1982: 190). But furthermore, and this is what makes this procession route different from the other kind of centripetal route (the convoluted one to which I will turn shortly), this route is a royal route. The event consciously includes the king in a way that convoluted processions do not; hence, I call this the royal centripetal *pradakshinapātha.*[22] Interestingly, in addition to using the designation *thya* for those who are invited to a feast or similar event, Lalitpurians also use it to refer to those who are allowed to take part in the Matayā Nyaku Jātrā, in a sense similar to that reported by Ishii for Satungal (1978).[23] Certain localities (the ten through which the *pradakshinapātha* traverses) are *thya*–in, and certain are *ma thya*–out. The boundaries are very clearly and precisely understood. Haugaḥ, Cāka Bahi, Saugaḥ and Ikhā Lakhu are *thya*, but Yānamugaḥ, Kuti Saugaḥ, Cyāsaḥ and Tangaḥ are *ma thya.* It is those *twaḥ*, which are considered *thya*, that today still have the rotating responsibility for Nyaku Jātrā. Some residents are of the opinion that Tangaḥ, Kuti Saugaḥ, Yānamugaḥ and other such localities were not part of the city when the festival was inaugurated.

All the festivals that make use of the royal centripetal *pradakshinapātha* take place during the dark half of the month of Gũlā.[24] What is the significance of this? Tradition has it that Buddha himself chose this month for his worship because no other gods would. There is more to it, though, as most of the *jātrā*s that take place at this time, have nothing to do with Buddha at all. Sā Pāru, Narasimha Jātrā, Krishna Jātrā, and Bhimsen Jātrā in fact are unashamedly non-Buddhist. The explanation must be sought not in ideology but in structure. As I shall explain later (§7.10), this lunar fortnight follows hard on the heels of the *first* lunar festival of the year—Gathā̃ Mugaḥ Cahre. In that festival we see a symbolic enactment of the removal of all that is base and evil from the city. As such it is a negative festival. It is there to undo the worst effects of that period of chaos, which resulted in the collapse of the urban order during the first and heaviest half of the monsoon. With the festivals of Gũlāgā (Bhādra-*krishna paksha*) we have the beginning of the positive reconstruction of that order. It is as if the people are saying that urban unity is of utmost importance.

This writer suspects that the royal centripetal *jātrā*s of Gũlāgā (Bhādra-*krishna paksha*) are no older than the beginning of the Malla period, unless older *jātrā*s changed their route to conform. It seems highly likely to me that King Siddhi Narasimha Malla established the royal centripetal *pradakshinapātha* in the seventeenth century.

Large urban festivals both express and create cohesion in the city. As Clifford Geertz remarks: 'Culture patterns have an intrinsic double aspect: they give meaning, that is, objective conceptual form, to social and psychological reality both by shaping themselves to it and by shaping it to themselves'. (Geertz 1973: 93)

Or, as Levy puts it for Bhaktapur, the town's 'spatial divisions both give meaning to and take meaning from their special divinities, symbolic enactments and their associated legends and myths' (1990: 199).

b. Convoluted centripetal processions

Gutschow's fourth type of procession is, for want of a better term, a 'convoluted' one but one that is nevertheless centripetal. This kind of procession is exemplified by Lalitpur's Matayā festival (Gutschow 1982: 190, Fig.226). Such a procession is integrative in that it circumambulates city space but not royal in the sense that Sā Paru is, as it pays no attention to the central space itself. Matayā is, in fact, the archetype of such processions as its modern analogues to other deities demonstrate. The purpose of such festivals, which include the older Bāhāḥ Pujā as well as the modern Krishna Pujā and Bhimsen Pujā, is for each of the participants to visit each and every shrine of a particular deity within city space. In the case of Matayā this involves thousands of devotees walking, often barefooted, around the city on an extremely convoluted, but for all that ordered, route to each of the Buddhist votive shrines. These shrines are called *caitya*s (or, in more colloquial Newar, *cibhāḥ*s) (cf. Gutschow 1982: 170, Fig.190). During the course of the procession the devotees also circumambulate the four mounds (*thur* or *stupa*) that are positioned at the four cardinal directions around the city. To reach three of these mounds it is necessary to make a detour, as it were, outside the old city boundaries as they were never encompassed by the old city's urban encroachment.

The procession of Bāhāḥ Pujā, that takes place the day before Matayā, visits each of the dozens of Buddhist monasteries around the town. In doing so, the line of devotees is forced to cross the centripetal *pradakshinapātha* at Keshav Nārāyana Cok, the northernmost courtyard of the royal palace. This is a most interesting and telling phenomenon as, at precisely the same time, the self-consciously *shivamārgi* procession of Sā Pāru is making its way around the city on the centripetal *pradakshinapātha.*

The line of Buddhist devotees then has to cross the procession of Sā Pāru. The reason for this is historical. In order to allow for the northward extension of the palace compound (with the building of Keshav Nārāyana

Cok) the Malla kings of the early seventeenth century were compelled to uproot the monastery of Haḥ Bāhāḥ from its ancient site in Mangaḥ. It was then transplanted 400m westward at its present site in Ga Bāhāḥ. Not to be intimidated by such an act of royal aggression, the devotees at Bāhāḥ Pujā continue to offer *pujā* to Haḥ Bāhāḥ at its older site by placing fruit and other offerings on the step of the courtyard's golden door (Plate 11). It is this continued act of defiance that leads to the two processions to continue to cross each other's path. What was truly amazing to this writer was to observe the two processions going on in this way, without the slightest interest in, or even, acknowledgement of, the other's existence!

Matayā, though not following the route of the royal centripetal *pradakshinapātha*, nevertheless is related to it in three ways: firstly, the procession is organized by a committee, on a rotational basis, from one of the ten localities (*twaḥ*) on that route; secondly, the Nyaku Jātrā—the procession of musicians that plays on the same day as Matayā—does circumambulate the city on the centripetal route; and thirdly, it is also a clockwise integration of city space. What then is the relationship between the two routes? It is apparent that the royal centripetal *pradakshinapātha* is an invention of the Malla kings, and that Matayā was too well established, and too closely followed to allow the kings to change it. They did, however, bring it under some sort of central control by delegating the responsibility for its organization to the ten localities along the integrative route and ordering the Nyaku Jātrā to play along that route simultaneously.

Plate 11. Façade of Keshav Nārāyana Cok and the Golden Window.

c. Excursive centripetal processions

Power-Place Worship, which involves procession to each of the Twelve True Power-Places in turn, is also a kind of centripetal procession (§8.4).[25] The difference with this procession, however, is in the fact that this procession takes place, for the most part, outside the city. Each day a procession forms at the city centre, Mangaḥ and makes an excursion out of the city to the particular shrine of the day.

Having done the *pujā*, the procession retraces its steps to the palace (cf. Gutschow 1982: 173, Fig.194). The integrative character of the procession is in the set as a whole. This is reemphasized on the ninth day of Mohani (*syāko tyāko*; §8.8.4) when all twelve Power-Places are visited at one go.

5.7. Sanctifying city space

The location of deities in and around the city, and the movement of deities or, alternatively, the movement of their devotees through city space all have a symbolic significance. In relation to the Navadurga of Bhaktapur, Gutschow and Basukala suggest that the gods enact an 'elaborate set of processions which aim, in the broadest sense, at ritual taking possession of space, of a realm sacred to and sanctified by these gods' (1987: 147).

> The appearance of the Navadurga in the streets and lanes not only serves to substantiate the actual presence of the gods in town. It is in fact much more: the gods come to each and every quarter as if to prove that they form the component parts of the whole, the town of Bhaktapur with its heterogeneous spatial and social structure. Thus the appearance of the gods confirms and reaffirms the special quality of an urban as opposed to the rural environment. The gods represent the essence of the urban environment... (Ibid.: 155)

5.8. Mental maps

Mental maps are conscious and sub-conscious ways of perceiving space. Residents in any one locality may give any number of variations of what they see as significant space. There are often common themes, however, demonstrating a shared perception. In this section I want to examine two of these mental maps: the mandala and the moiety.

5.8.1. The city as a mandala

A number of observers have noted the significance of the concentric arrangement of Newar cities (Kölver 1976; Gutschow 1982; Slusser 1998; Shepard 1985; Zanen 1986; Pradhan 1986 and Levy 1990). This concentric arrangement is clearly modelled on the form of the mandala.

> A mandala is an arrangement of deities conceived of in sets (of four, eight, sixty-four or more) laid out along the axes of the cardinal points around a centre. (Gellner 1992: 190)

The cities, however, are not simply *like* mandalas; in the consciousness of the citizens who pursue their lives in them they *are* mandalas. The form of the mandala, therefore, was a statement of the city's central significance and its link to a cosmic order (Shepard 1985: 67ff.).

Two features of the mandala make it especially suitable as the template of the Newar city: its centre and its axes. The stronger of the two would seem to be that of the centre. In the visualization of the mandala, the devotee moves ever towards the centre in his quest for the divine. The centre is the goal, the point around which all else revolves. There is a clear hierarchy, then, from periphery to centre. The axes, however, have a different function in that they provide to the inhabitants of the city an orientation to the world outside. The mandala, then, must be entered in order to be of any significance to the devotee. That entry can only be gained through designated points: gates to the divine. Without gates the city has no connection with the outside world. Gates are essential for trade without which the city would collapse. Any person who wants to orientate himself within the city could take their bearings from the hilltops that ring the Valley (though this is less easy since modernity has led to the raising of ever-higher buildings). It is no accident then, that the summits of Jāmācwa (Nagarjun), Dhinco (Champadevi), Sipuco (Shivapuri) and Puco (Phulcoki) took on a cosmic significance as the cardinal points in the mandala that was the Nepal Valley (K.P. Malla 1996). Furthermore, there was the ever present, but for half the year invisible, chain of the Himalaya running across the northern horizon.

In one settlement, at least, a further dimension is added to that of centre-periphery—that of height. Levy notes that Bhaktapur, like very many cities, makes use of a hill—on which it is built— (as well as its bordering river) to add height to the more significant orientation of central-peripheral (1990: 153). Higher-status temples, palaces and residential areas are located on the crest of the hill. Lalitpur, however, is not so oriented. The city is located on a low plateau sloping upwards from the originally settled river bluffs southward to somewhat higher ground. Upper status space, then, in Lalitpur, is not higher than that of lower status actors. In fact a community of 'Untouchables', the Dyaḥlā is situated at one of the highest point of the city. Nevertheless, height is made use of even in Lalitpur. In Malla times there were strict limits to the upward extension of residential construction. In so doing the planners of the cities made a point of the value of height in its manifestation of divinity. In the popular mind of the Lalitpurian this was expressed as a rule that no building was to be higher than the chariot of Bũgadyaḥ. The Degutale temple within the palace grounds (26.5m high; Sekler 1987: 61,64) *is* higher than the chariot, however. It would seem, therefore, that the builder, under the patronage of Sri Nivas Malla, was making a point—if not that Taleju is of greater significance than Karunāmaya, that Karunāmaya and Taleju are intimately related. Moreover, as Slusser has demonstrated, the Newar-style temple is a three-dimensional mandala (1998: 145).

The importance of the centre in the life of the Newar extends beyond the spatial arrangement of the city's deities to other aspects of his life. As Lewis states, there are 'structural homologies between the pattern of organized shrines, religious art, the household center, and finally to the human body through the physiology of *kundalini* meditation' (1984: 133). The arrangement of deities around the city, therefore, is not the only way that space is ordered. Gutschow and Kölver note that the *sashtras* (*Shilpashastra* texts and many chapters in the *Purānas*) 'provided instruction on how the diverse members of the social body ought to be distributed within the city' (1975: 35). There appears, therefore, an ideal form of caste distribution that consists of concentric rings of ever-increasing status from outside in. On the ground, however, this is hardly discernible except at the very centre and periphery.[26]

When did this idea, of the *mandala* as an archetype for town planning, become significant? Vergati is of the opinion that this religious structuring of urban space belongs to the inspiration of the Mallas of the seventeenth century (1995: 144). This seems highly likely. As Gutschow and Bajracarya write,

> This process entailed a fundamental re-structuring of sacred space: shrines which had been founded immemorial times ago as the seats of pre-Hindu, and probably pre-Buddhist, deities were filled with a new content, were given new interpretations, and thus were absorbed into new spiritual patterns. (Gutschow and Bajracarya 1977: 2)

They also write that,

> The ideal symmetrical pattern (which we find expressed in a *mandala*) is of course in reality modified by the two factors of topography and history: that is, by the structure of the terrain, and by a tendency to use shrines of older gods and goddesses, which were reinterpreted and newly consecrated, to fit into the new system. (Ibid.: 4)

5.8.2. The city as a moiety

A number of scholars have remarked on the division of Newar settlements into two halves, commonly viewed as 'upper' (*thaḥne* or *cway*) and 'lower' (*kway*). The villages of Theco and Pyangaon where Toffin worked are two such settlements (1996a: 67). Various locals explain these halves in different ways but the consistent explanation is that it relates to the flow of the nearby river—upstream being the upper half and downstream being the lower (Levy 1990: 153,168; Vergati 1995: 179). Toffin makes much of this 'moiety system'. It is, he says, 'a sociological divide, an essential part of the fabric of Newar society' (1996a: 81). If this is true, then the 'moiety system' demands a careful examination.

The city of Kathmandu is one settlement that demonstrates a binary division. This division is acted out in conflict during the festival of Sithi Nakhaḥ in which youths from the upper and lower halves of the city clash on the dry bed of the Vishnumati River. Furthermore, each of the upper and lower sides of the city of Kathmandu has been associated until now with a particular lineage of Thakujuju (Malla), descendants of the former twelve Vaishya Thakuri Rāja who ruled the capital until Ratna Malla (fourteenth century) (ibid.). Bert van den Hoek has shown how they still play an important and central role as patrons of sacrifice in some festivals of the locality such as that of Indrayāni in the upper part of the city (1993: 360-361).

Toffin asserts that 'The moeity system manifests itself with special strength during the royal rituals performed within or around the ancient Malla palaces' and that this is especially the case in Kathmandu (Toffin 1996a: 69). Van den Hoek and Shrestha (1992) have described the dance drama that is enacted each Mohani at Hanumān Dhokā. The dance occurs when the four processional images of Taleju are brought down to the Mohani room and when they are carried back again. It is said that Daitya and Kumar, the two gods that are impersonated in the dance, protect Taleju Bhavani, the central *shakti* of the realm, from dangers that might be threatening her. Van den Hoek and Shrestha explain the opposition between Daitya and Kumar as a persistence of the old Vedic idea of a 'sacrifice of war', following J.C. Heesterman. Toffin finds it simpler and more accurate to interpret it in terms of the centrality of the king and his personal goddess Taleju in the city. 'What is stressed here is the king as the sustainer of the realm, the power that upholds the universe, the key figure transcending all oppositions around him' (ibid.: 70).

Kathmandu is not the only Newar settlement to experience fighting between the two halves. The Biskaḥ festival of Bhaktapur is another case in point. Newar fights, Toffin observes, occur at some critical moments of transition of the year (1996a: 73). Biskaḥ is roughly at the spring equinox. Sithi Nakhaḥ inaugurates the period of rice cultivation. Newar peasants name it: 'the festival of the married daughters, *mhyāy macā*', because Sithi Nakhaḥ ushers in a season where the house will be empty of all its members, busy in the fields, as it is when daughters leave their paternal house at the time of marriage' (ibid.).

Toffin goes on:

> These battles are conspicuous for their attempt to restore a primordial chaos, the confusion of origins, followed by a recreation and a return to a reanimated cosmic order flooding across structural boundaries. Every opposition is then overcome or transcended in a recovered unity. Such periodic oscillation between chaos and order, death and life is a salient feature of the Newar cycle of festivals. (Ibid.)

What can we learn from this apparent moiety system of the Newars? Toffin's thesis is that the binary division 'is of crucial importance for the understanding of the old civilization of the Kathmandu Valley' (1996a: 67).[27] The moieties could be compared to those hill populations of Nepal that speak Tibeto-Burman languages such as the Tamang and Gurung. All this is to restate Toffin's earlier argument that the Newars are originally a tribal people and that the present Hindu hierarchical social system is a layer over the previous structure. Toffin also observes that modern party political divisions seem to fall along the old binary lines which, if true, demonstrates the resistance of this structure to change. In relation to spatial design, therefore, two models stand out in marked contrast: the concentric model is a Hindu one and emphasizes hierarchy but the diametrical model suggests an egalitarian society based on reciprocity. Parish, however, who is at pains to emphasize the resentment and disaffection that caste generates among the 'subalterns', feels that the division of Newar communities into two antagonistic halves is 'dynamically generated by the Newar social system' (1997a: 155). So for Parish the moiety is a product of Hinduism.

Is the 'moiety system' Hindu or tribal? How can we evaluate this conflict? It is my opinion that we cannot call the concept of moiety within Newar communities a system at all. It is true that binary division is one way that many Newar communities express themselves. But to call it a 'system' one must surely demonstrate that such a concept is pervasive and dominant. These it is not. On the one hand, cities such as Kathmandu, one of Toffin's prime examples, have a middle division—*dathu*—that has not been taken into account. On the other hand, some Newar communities have no such binary division at all. Such is the city of Lalitpur. Lalitpur's discourse encompasses terms of 'high' and 'low' but these are never used in any absolute sense. One part of the city is higher than another, which is higher than yet another, and so on. Talk of two halves, then, is absent. Furthermore, Lalitpur has no festival such as Kathmandu's Sithi Nakhaḥ or Bhaktapur's Biskaḥ to sort out any kind of boiling binary antagonism. On the contrary, the city seems to be more properly divided into three according to participation in the Jātrā (§10.7), or four according to the rotation of Yẽnyaḥ festivities (§8.5). Is there any binary division at all in Lalitpur? There does seem to be something of an opposition in the design of the palace square between the gods of the palace (blood-drinking) and those in front of it (mostly vegetarian).[28] But there is no such division in the city as a whole. Is the case of Lalitpur, then, simply an exception that proves the rule? Or does it, in fact, have some other explanation? The answer, it seems to me, must come from an historical examination of the development of these settlements.

It is impossible to trace with any accuracy the development of the Newar cities. Niels Gutschow and his associates have done the most extensive work on the development of Bhaktapur and have concluded that the founding of the city involved the unification of a number of small villages that had developed in the area from about the third century (Levy 1990: 40). Gutschow and Kölver, however, also explain that the royal centre of the city shifted, in the fifteenth century, from Tacapāl, a point that is now well in the eastern half of the city to Lasku Dhokā (1975: 16-19). This was to become, with planned expansion, the western and 'lower' half of the city.

Very little can be learned from the past of one of Toffin's examples of a moiety, the village of Theco, but Toffin himself describes the development of the city of Kathmandu from the fusion of two separate settlements (ibid.: 81-82; cf. D. Vajracarya 1987: 360). The history of Lalitpur, however, reveals no such fusion. For sure, as in the case of Bhaktapur (and presumably each half of what became Kathmandu), the city was founded by the fusion of a number of villages. But at no point in the history of Lalitpur do we find anything approaching a binary division. By the end of the Licchavi period the dominant settlement was that of the village of Yupa which, by expansion and royal charter became the city of Yupagrāmadranga (ibid.: 361; cf. Vajracarya and Shrestha 2036 vs: 64-67). The historical evolution of Lalitpur, therefore, precluded the development of a moiety.

5.9. Conclusion: The centrality of kingship in ordered space

Although the bounded nature of settlements seems to have been thoroughly established in ancient times this does not seem to be true of their centredness to any great extent. The Malla kings, as masterful politicians, however, took full advantage of the sacred texts that sanctified the city as a mandala. Although the centrality of the palace was already an accepted notion they took it to a new plane. The value of centredness became equivalent to that of kingship. All roads in ancient Europe may have led to Rome, but in medieval Lalitpur they led, ideally at least, to the palace. We will look at the significance of this further in later chapters.

6. Territorial Organizations

> Conformity to a small number of institutions is perhaps the single most stressed value in Newar society and underpins the cohesion of local, caste-based groups….
>
> Declan Quigley (1986: 83)

6.1. The locality (*twaḥ*)

Much of the daily and seasonal life of the Lalitpurian, as of the inhabitants of the other major Newar settlements, is lived within his locality. Each locality (*twaḥ*) within the city to some extent constitutes, in microcosm, what the city is on a grander scale. As I noted in the introductory chapter, Levy calls the *twaḥ* the 'village in the city' (1990: 182): '*Twaḥ*s, or their major segments, are the face-to-face communities beyond the extended family where people know each other personally and where mutual observation and gossip are important sanctions' (Ibid.: 185).

The locality, almost invariably, is characterized by a central square that is clearly analogous to that of the city as a whole. The square, or in many cases the monastery (*bāhāḥ, bahi*), has its temples and its blend of religious and secular uses. Farmers spread out their unhusked rice to dry, women wash the family clothes at the well, vegetable-sellers display their produce, men sit and talk politics, a post-partum mother gets an oil massage, children climb on the temple guardians and play hide-and-seek. Furthermore, it is the site of many a feast. There is always a shrine to Ganesh somewhere in the locality. Such a shrine, in fact, often constitutes the central locus of the locality. Often there is a dance platform (*dabu*) which, when not being used for dance-dramas, may be used by moneychangers bringing religious legitimacy to vibrant commerce (Lewis 1995: 42). Everyone in the locality knows which is 'his' Ganesh shrine. A visit to the shrine is often the first act of the larger drama of a household ritual.

In many cases the precise boundaries of the locality are common knowledge. The boundary between Haugaḥ and Tangaḥ localities, for example, is exactly in the middle of the doorway of the monastery I Bāhāḥ Bahi. The precise enumeration of the localities of Lalitpur, however, defies the modern surveyor. It is sure that the new political 'wards' constitute a precise set, but these are seldom significant in day-to-day life. It is the traditional locality that forms the inhabitant's neighbourhood, the immediate, public sphere of daily life. But the limits of the *twaḥ* are set at different points depending on the context in which it is to be defined. The Shilpakārs of Ikhā, for instance, belong to Jom Bāhāḥ or Tichu Galli depending on whether they live inside the monastery courtyards or outside in the lane. Moreover, they may belong to Haugaḥ or Ikhā Lakhu when it comes to participation in Nyaku Jātrā. All the time, however, they will visit the Ganesh shrine whose shrew (*tichu*) guardians give the lane its name and in so doing regard themselves as residents of Ikhā *twaḥ*.[1]

It is important for us to note here that territory transcends Newar lineage or caste ties. This is highly significant. We have already noted the strength of the lineage and the caste and cannot but recognize how debilitating such strong ties could be to the genesis and maintenance of city unity. The locality, however, can often cut right across the boundaries of these groups. It is my contention that, though they did not design such a situation, the Malla kings nevertheless took advantage of it. The effect of this was to weaken the bonds of lineage and caste. Festivals such as Matayā, with their lack of centrifugal emphasis (§7.18.2), could be centralized to a degree that previously they had resisted, by organizing them on the basis of territory.

We have already noted the analogous nature of the *twaḥ* to the city as a whole. This goes further than a simple central square. Each locality has its boundary to the outside world as well. Faced with the problem that the border of the locality also happens in most cases to be the border of another locality, and therefore could not be used for the removal of impurity, Newars of the *twaḥ* went down. That is, impurity was to be removed by means of certain gateways underfoot—interfaces to another, equally impure and dreaded world. Every household knows where to deposit impure substances such as an umbilical cord, soiled menstrual cloth or clothes in which a person has died. The spot, the Remains Deity or *chwāsā*, marked by an aniconic stone embedded in the ground, can be found in all localities. Often they are multiple. The *chwāsā* can be understood as a sort of sinkhole of impurity within the city. The city must be kept pure. Macrocosmically, pollution such as that embodied in a corpse is removed from the city by transferring it physically beyond the city's boundaries. Microcosmically, however, it is sufficient for unclean substances to be left at the *chwāsā* from where their impurity will be absorbed.

The *chwāsā* are often located at a crossroads, which as I have already mentioned, is considered to be the haunt of evil spirits such as the reverse-footed female demon, the *kicikini*. After the eating of the ceremonial dish (*thāy bhu*), as at a Marriage or Mock Marriage celebration, a lighted wick is placed in a leaf plate containing the left-over food and placed at the *chwāsā* to ward off such evil (Nepali 1965: 226). The *chwāsā* is also understood to represent the local goddess of smallpox, Ajimā or Hāriti, whose principal image is enshrined at Svayambhu. This is the same deity worshipped by the Aji at the ritual of Birth Purification. Ajimā is considered a dangerous deity with whom it is not wise to meddle. *Pujā* to Ajimā, therefore, is propitiatory with grave consequences for those who neglect it. 'If we don't do *pujā* to Ajimā she will get us by the throat'. On one occasion, early on in my research, I was talking to a Tāmrakār man in Tichu Galli when my interlocutor urged me, with some anxiety and embarrassment, to move to the other side of the lane as I was unknowingly standing on the local *chwāsā.* In keeping with the myth of the ogress Hāriti, children's illnesses are particularly attributed to the *chwāsā* Ajimā (Nepali 1965: 335).

This chapter explores the life of the locality from the perspective of its institutions. Certain, very important, organizations exist within the locality which regulate much of the social and ritual interaction of its inhabitants. Foremost of these are the *guthi*s and to these I will now turn.

6.2. *Guthis*

All Newars have traditionally attached great importance to the socio-religious association called *guthi* or *gu.* Among the Parbatiyā *guthi* means land-tenure (M.C. Regmi 1976), whereas in the Newar community its most basic and fundamental denotation is as a type of association. Land has probably been more important in the past among Newars also but a combination of confiscation of lands after 1768/69 and land reform in the 1960s have weakened that significance (Quigley 1985b: 7). Locke describes *guthi*s as endowed 'trusts set up for the maintenance of foundations or the continued performance of religious or civil works' (1997: 10). *Guthi*s have a long tradition and are known to have existed in Licchavi times. The earliest *guthi* described in Nepal is a 'lamp *guthi*' (*pradipagosthi*, Skt.) mentioned in a seventh century inscription in Lele (D. Vajracarya 1973: 282-3). It is clear that the Newars have had a great many *guthi*s in the past and that, though somewhat reduced, the *guthi* continues to play an important part in their life. This is clearly seen among the Pengu Daḥ for whom *guthi* membership, oftentimes multiple, is a significant part of daily life.

Membership in the *guthi* is formal and limited. That is, *guthi*s are to a greater or lesser extent exclusive. If one qualifies for membership of a particular *guthi* there are two possible ways to gain access. If one is the eldest son of a *guthiyār* then he automatically has a right to a place in the *guthi* on the death of his father. All he has to do is to turn up at the next gathering. On the other hand, membership of some *guthi*s can be acquired on request and the payment of a registration fee. In 1998, the fee for joining the Tamvaḥ Cidhã Guthi was Rs. 1,500. An eligible Marikaḥmi man may join the death *guthi* of that *thar* simply by feeding all the other members good luck food (*sagã*).

Often, membership of a *guthi* is denoted as an ideal number. The Bārāhi Daḥ Guthi, for example, consists ideally of twenty-four members (*caubis jawān*), one of which is Bũgadyaḥ himself. The actual number of *guthiyār*s in membership at any one time, however, may be quite different. When I told Surya Lal Barahi, the then *thākāli*, that, in fact, there are only nineteen members in his *guthi* he insisted vehemently that I was wrong: 'No, don't write 19, write 24', he said. Upon completion of the assembling of the Bũgadyaḥ chariot each spring, the Bārāhi *thākāli* invites eligible men to become *guthiyār*s. Any such individual simply rises to his feet, bows to the deity and to each of *guthiyār*s older than he and takes his place according to his seniority.

Membership of a *guthi* is normally barred against the children of men who have married outside the limits of the prescribed marriage circle. One man bearing the patronymic Bārāhi is barred from membership of the Bārāhi Daḥ Guthi because his mother is a Chetri. He is also barred from working on the chariot and so is denied the status of his lineage.

Fighting between *guthiyār*s is almost proverbial in Newar society; very often such a fight results in the break-up of the *guthi*. In the past it is clear that such a break-up would have invariably resulted in the creation of another *guthi* as we can see has happened to the death *guthi*s of the Tāmrakārs and Shilpakārs (§6.2.4). Both Fürer-Haimendorf (1956: 36) and Toffin (1977: 44) make the assertion that periodic fission is natural and inevitable, and has happened in each generation; but as Quigley points out *guthi*s ideally, like households, never split (1985b: 48). Such a process is a concession to the inability of the *guthiyār*s to get along.

Now I will turn to the three basic principles of *guthi* organization.

6.2.1. Basic principles of the *guthi*

Gellner (1992: 248) agrees with Fürer-Haimendorf (1956: 36) that the three basic principles that underlie the organization of the *guthi* are seniority, rotation and territory. He then reduces the first two to the principle of equality. In the discussions below I will argue that the principle of territory is fundamental and will ground my argument primarily on data collected from the plethora of *guthi*s belonging to the Pengu Daḥ.

a. Seniority

Seniority in the *guthi* is expressed in a number of ways. Juniors (*kwakāli*) bow to their seniors (*thākāli*) on ritual occasions.[2] At a feast, *guthiyār*s sit on straw mats in order of age always with the elder member on the right hand of the junior. All *guthi*s with a membership larger than eight express the seniority of the eight elders (collectively termed *thākāli*) in the ritual division of the head of the sacrificial animal in the feast (*sikāḥ bhu*). In the Bārāhi Daḥ Guthi, furthermore, ideally a second group of eight *guthiyār*s joins the elder eight to form a wider body of *thākāli*s. If a space among the elders comes available on a death then the qualified *guthiyār* may be inducted into the group. This induction is called '*nāyaḥ luyegu*'.[3] Seniority makes no difference to the obligation that a *guthiyār* is expected to fulfil in the event of a death all are obliged to attend regardless of position.

b. Rotation

The second organizing principle is that of the rotation of responsibilities. *Guthi*s have a very clear order of membership, which gives rise to the passing on of responsibilities from one member to another. 'Pāḥ kāyegu' (to take a turn), 'pāḥ phayegu' (to promise, to undertake one's turn), 'tā [or tācā] kāyegu' (to take the key) are all expressions used to take one's turn (Gellner 1992: 233). Ordinarily this means that the responsibility of organizing the usually annual *pujā* and feast falls on the shoulders of each *guthiyār* in turn. For those of the Tamvaḥ Tadhã Guthi this is an onerous responsibility as the membership totals sixty-five. The other side of the coin, however, is that in such a large *guthi* one would normally be expected to fulfil one's obligation only once in a lifetime.

The combining of members into groups often modifies such a system of rotation. In this way ones turn comes more often but the cost is shared among the group, thus is not so burdensome. Among the Pengu Daḥ these *guthi* sub-divisions are called *wala pala* or *wala pā.*[4] Such divisions operate differently in different *guthi*s. The Tamvaḥ Cidhã Guthi, for instance, has three *wala pā* each supervised by a *nāyaḥ* selected from among the members.

The three *nāyaḥ*s function together as a committee to oversee the operation of the *guthi*, its finances, etc. The *wala pā* have no function during the annual feast that takes place during the cold season (*cikulā*). At this time, the turn-holder sponsors the *pujā* and feast. The summer (*barkhā*) meeting, however, is run by the *wala pā* in its turn. This would seem to indicate precedence for the winter event.[5] The Tamvaḥ Tadhã Guthi, however, organizes its five *wala pā* by a different system. After a member of the first *wala pā* has his turn it is passed to the next member of the second *wala pā*, etc. Furthermore, winter and summer feasts are counted separately so that the turn-holder does not have to pay for both in the same year. The *wala pā* system also modifies the addition of new members, who are added to each *wala pā* in strict rotation, notwithstanding the loss of a member.

The Rājkarnikār death *guthi*, which has sixty-four members, is divided into four groups, each of sixteen members. Rotation of *guthi* duties is according to group so that each has its turn every four years. The group leader (*nāyaḥ*) is a hereditary position, a situation that is opposed by younger, more democratically inclined *guthiyār*s who would prefer a direct election.[6] Furthermore, the *guthi thākāli* is called the *pancanāyaḥ* and is the eldest of the *guthiyār*s after the four *nāyaḥ*s. At feasts the four *nāyaḥ*s are given precedence over all others. One wonders whether such a situation reflects the original (four?) lineages of Marikaḥmi descended from the brothers that, according to oral historical accounts, migrated to Nepal (§2.6.2).[7] The Shilpakār Tadhã Guthi also has hereditary *wala pala nāyaḥ*s. This seems to reflect the eight lineages (seven Lwahãkaḥmi and one Sikaḥmi) that go to make up the *thar.*[8]

In the Bārāhi Daḥ Guthi four *guthiyār*s are appointed in strict rotation of age for each year. The groups they constitute are temporary, as the total number of *guthiyār*s is usually not a multiple of four.

c. Territory

Although, as Gellner reports (1992: 232), the role territory plays in the organization of *guthi* life varies, it is my contention that territory plays a most basic role in determining the organization of a *guthi.* Quigley, studying the Shresthas of Dhulikhel, found that locality is fundamental. *Guthi* membership, he asserts, is 'constrained by residence' (Quigley 1985b: 11). The *guthi* is essentially a territorial social group. This territoriality is modified by factors of lineage and caste but nevertheless demonstrates an important value.

> It is these associations which pre-eminently provide the residential element of Newar social organization and which ensure that identity is not simply a matter of affiliation to lineage and caste. Lineage and caste are themselves defined in terms of a ritual attachment to a locality. (Ibid.)

It is normal, therefore, for a family to transfer membership to a different death *guthi* on moving to a different location (Toffin 1995b: 251). This would not normally be considered necessary today unless the family moved completely out of the Kathmandu Valley. The death *guthi* of the Rājkarnikārs exists till today as one organization despite the fact that members are to be found scattered across the wider metropolitan area. Such a *guthi*, however, has instituted changes in order for it to function practically as two units whilst maintaining its ritual integrity. Such a change involves the mutual understanding that only those *guthiyār*s that reside on the same side of the Bāgmati River as the deceased member are obliged to be present at the funeral. I will look again at this adaptation to modernity below. Suffice it to state at this point that it would seem to be one expression of a change in value and emphasis in Newar culture as a whole.

6.2.2. Types of *guthi*

Various authors have attempted to come up with helpful typologies of *guthi*s. Nepali lists a number of '*guthi*s' that are in reality festivals at which the *guthi* in question gathers for a feast (1965: 193). The Tamvaḥ Cabāchẽ lineage Rām Navami Guthi, for instance, has the same membership as the Cabāchẽ lineage Sixteen [Day] Ancestor Worship (*sohra shrāddha*) *guthi.* In any particular year one *guthiyār* will be the turn-holder for both *guthi*s and in talking of the group in a general way it may be considered one *guthi.* When the events are discussed, however, they are referred to as different *guthi*s since they meet at different times for different purposes. Another example is that of the Pwāḥsyāḥ lineage of Tamvaḥ, which has, as they would put it, a Lineage Deity *guthi* and a Sixteen [Day] Ancestor Worship *guthi.* In this way also the Vishvakarma lineage is another that has, as they say, 'three *guthi*s'—a Yẽnyaḥ *guthi*, a Sixteen [Day] Ancestor Worship *guthi* and a Tantric Worship (*desi pujā*) *guthi.* The fullest example of this tendency among the Pengu Daḥ is that of the Bārāhi Daḥ Guthi. This particular *guthi* (in the sense of group) meets for ritual and feasting purposes a total of ten times each year, by far the most ritually active *guthi* of all that belong to the Pengu Daḥ. Each event has a different name and is considered a different '*guthi*' even though the same turn-holders are responsible for each event throughout the year. Although one wishes to acknowledge such semantic breadth, for analytical purposes it is best if a distinction is made between the group and the event. I will use the term *guthi* only in reference to the group unless otherwise indicated.

From the point of view of land tenure there are three types of *guthi*: private *guthi*s that are self-regulating, private *guthi*s that are registered with the Guthi Corporation (*Guthi Samsthān*), and *rāj guthi*s that are administered by the Guthi Corporation (Gellner 1992: 235). This is not such a helpful typology from a sociological perspective, however. Vergati's (1995: 98) tripartite typology of *guthi*s linked to lineage, caste or territory is surely too confusing to be helpful, as death *guthi*s, for instance, are based on caste *and* territory and neither death *guthi*s nor Lineage Deity *guthi*s are ever multicaste. Quigley's (1987b: 11) tripartite typology of Lineage Deity *guthi*, death *guthi* and temple or festival *guthi* is better but still includes many overlaps. Furthermore, Quigley's typology was based on the marginal Valley town of Dhulikhel which, though thoroughly Newar, does not have the range of caste and complexity of one of the Valley's cities.[9]

Gérard Toffin distinguishes six principal types of *guthi*: death *guthi*, worship association, Lineage Deity (*digu dyaḥ*) *guthi*, caste council, economic *guthi* and youth club (1984: 178f.). This is more comprehensive and yet still not representative of the major Newar settlements. Youth clubs, for example, exist in Lalitpur but are not organized as *guthi*s (a matter to which I will return later, §6.4.1). For this reason Gellner adapts Toffin's typology by dropping the one which functions as a youth club noting that it seems to be a peculiarity of Pyangaon (1992: 236-7). To the remaining five, however, he adds the 'public utility' *guthi*, which he explains were founded for the upkeep of such public amenities as the shelter (*phalcā*) and water fountain (*hiti*). The nearest to such a *guthi* I have come across in my fieldwork among the Pengu Daḥ is that of the Tamvaḥ Mahālakshmi Guthi and do not give it a separate category.

One of Toffin's categories, the caste council *guthi* deserves a brief treatment at this point. Toffin reports the existence of a *deshla* (or *deshanaḥ*) *guthi* belonging to the Citrakār of Bhaktapur (1984: 213-5; 1995b). Such a *guthi* serves to regulate the activities of the caste including economic competition between its members. Toffin reports, furthermore, that such *guthi*s in Kathmandu and Lalitpur have almost disappeared (ibid.: 253ff.). Among the Pengu Daḥ one *guthi* stands out as having such a function. The Bārāhi Daḥ Guthi operates, on one level, like the *deshla guthi*s of the Brahmans and Citrakārs, as a sort of board of reference for the supervisor (*nāyaḥ*) and his brother (*bhai nāyaḥ*) covering the apportioning of work each year on the Bũgadyaḥ and Cākwāḥdyaḥ chariots. The Bārāhi, it will be noted, share a brace of characteristics with the Brahmans and Citrakārs apart from this. Like these other castes, the Bārāhi are few in numbers and find their identity in the significant ritual role they play in the religious life of the city.

It seems to me that the best way to categorize *guthi*s is under three principal types according to their degree of social closure: agnatic *guthi*s, *thar guthi*s and multicaste *guthi*s. A virtually complete catalogue of Pengu Daḥ *guthi*s is summarized in Table 8 (p. 130) (there are bound to be some Sixteen [Day] Ancestor Worship *guthi*s and optional lineage *guthi*s that I have not discovered).

6.2.3. Agnatic *guthis*

I have coined the label 'agnatic *guthi*s' to refer to a large group of *guthi*s that fundamentally limits membership to various nested categories of agnatic (patrilineal) relatives. These include, from the narrower to the wider: Sixteen [Day] Ancestor Worship (*sohra shrāddha*) *guthi*s, Tantric Worship (*desi pujā*) *guthi*s, and Lineage Deity (*digu dyaḥ*) and Mohani *guthi*s.[10]

a. Sixteen [Day] Ancestor Worship (*sohra shrāddha*) *guthis*

The agnatic *guthi* with the narrowest membership is the Sixteen [Day] Ancestor Worship (*sohra shrāddha*) *guthi*. Small groups of agnates congregate at the house of the *thākāli* on a specific day during the lunar fortnight of Yālāgā (Ashvin-*krishna*, September) (§8.6). The day is always the same for each *guthi* and, according to some, is fixed to the day of the fortnight (*pratipada*, *dvitiya*, etc.) on which their common ancestor died. The domestic priest performs a special Ancestor Worship (*shrāddha*). Such a ceremony is repeated across the Kathmandu Valley during this time. Most such groups performing the rite are not organized as a *guthi*. Those that are, however, eat the formal feast together and take turns, as in all *guthi*s, to sponsor the *pujā* and prepare the feast. Among the Pengu Daḥ those who continue to observe Sixteen [Day] Ancestor Worship as a *guthi* are the Tamvaḥ Jyoti and Nāyaḥ lineages. The Tamvaḥ Cabāchẽ lineage also meets as a Sixteen [Day] Ancestor Worship *guthi* and includes a *pujā* to the Tantric Deity at Naḥ Bāhāḥ on this day. Some Sixteen [Day] Ancestor Worship *guthi*s meet at other times during the year. That of the Tamvaḥ Nāyaḥ lineage is such a *guthi*: when the Bũgadyaḥ chariot is at Lagankhel the *guthiyār*s visit the shrine of Bũgadyaḥ's mother, the Mā̃ju Simā, to sacrifice a duck.

Sixteen [Day] Ancestor Worship *guthi*s frequently split into smaller units and never seem to attain the breadth of participation that other *guthi*s do. It seems that continued participation in this *guthi* is, in many cases, the defining factor in the determination of one's ritual proximity to an agnate, expressed in the degree of mourning one observes.

b. Tantric Worship (*desi pujā*) *guthis*

Tantric Worship (*desi pujā*) *guthi*s are also agnatic organizations in that their membership is strictly limited to men who are (really or imagined to be) patrilineally related. Tantric Worship *guthi*s tend to have a wider membership than those that are for Sixteen [Day] Ancestor Worship. This does not

Table 8. *Guthis* of the Pengu Daḥ.

	Sixteen [Day] Ancestor Worship	Tamvaḥ		Nāyaḥ *khalaḥ* Cabāchẽ *khalaḥ* Sukuḥ *khalaḥ* Talachẽ *khalaḥ* Jyoti *khalaḥ* Itāchẽ Phalcachẽ *kawaḥ*	
		Sikaḥmi		Vishvakarma *khalaḥ* Paḥmā *khalaḥ*	
agnatic	Tantric Worship	Tamvaḥ		Nāyaḥ *khalaḥ* Cahre Guthi	
		Shilpakār	Lwahãkaḥmi	Combined Yāka, Hukā Bāgaḥ, Khica and Katilāḥ *khalaḥ*s *desi pujā guthi*	Combined Shilpakār *thar desi pujā guthi*
			Sikaḥmi	Vishvakarma *khalaḥ*	
	Lineage Deity Worship and Mohani	Tamvaḥ		Greater Jhvaḥchẽ *et al.' khalaḥ* Pwāḥsyāḥ *khalaḥ* Kwaḥ *khalaḥ*	
		Marikaḥmi	(unnamed lineage)	*bhujyaḥ guthi*	
		Sikaḥmi	Bārāhi	Daḥ Guthi	
	optional lineage	Tamvaḥ	Haugaḥ	Akshaya Tritiya Guthi	
			Naḥ Bāhāḥ	Gũlā Paru Guthi	
			'Greater Jhvaḥchẽ *et al.*'	*pāthyāye guthi*	
			Cabāchẽ	Mahālakshmi Guthi Rām Navami Guthi	
			Kũḥchẽ	Krishna Guthi	
			Pwāḥsyāḥ	Garsa Guthi	
		Marikaḥmi	Palmā	Pancadān *guthi*	
			(unnamed lineage)	*bhujyaḥ guthi*	
		Sikaḥmi	Vishvakarma	Yẽnyaḥ *guthi* Cibhāḥ *guthi*	
			Paḥmā	*sãnhu guthi* Yẽnyaḥ *guthi* *pāthyāye guthi*	
			Bārāhi	Cathaḥ Guthi	
thar	death	Tamvaḥ		Tadhã Guthi Cidhã Guthi Daru Guthi Rām Navami Guthi (larger) Rām Navami Guthi (smaller) (Pauca Guthi)	
		Marikaḥmi		*sanā guthi*	
		Shilpakār (Lwahãkaḥmi & Vishvakarma Sikaḥmi)		Tadhã Guthi Cidhã Guthi	
		Sikaḥmi	Paḥmā	Sila Caḥre Guthi	
			Bārāhi	Daḥ Guthi	
	optional *thar*	Tamvaḥ		Bāl Kumāri *bājã guthi* Bhimsen Guthi Mahālakshmi Guthi	
		Marikaḥmi		Yẽnyaḥ (Bhairava Khwāḥpāḥ) Guthi	
		Lwahālaḥmi		Basuwa Siwa Guthi	
multicaste		Harkhãdyaḥ Guthi (Tāmrakār, Kayastha, Shākya) Bhairavanāth Guthi (Tāmrakārs, Shilpakārs, Citrakārs, Ranjitkārs) Nasantya Dāphā Guthi (Shilpakār, Tāmrakār, Rājkarnikār, Maharjan)			

necessarily mean that their membership is more numerous but, rather, that it may include persons whose personal knowledge of agnatic relations with the others is derived solely from their mutual membership in the *guthi*. The Lwahãkaḥmi Tantric Worship *guthi* consists of four *guthiyār*s—one from each of Yāka, Hukā Bāgaḥ, Khica and Katilāḥ lineages. All *guthiyār*s are required to have taken Tantric Initiation (*dekhā*) from a Vajrācārya priest.[11] The *thākāli* of each of these four lineages takes a month-long turn to do daily worship (*nitya pujā*) at the temple of the Tantric Deity which is situated in an upstairs room of an old house behind Cibhāḥ Nani, Jom Bāhāḥ. Membership is limited to these four lineages alone and demonstrates an older grouping of Lwahãkaḥmi that existed before the Khwapa, Gãyrāsimga, and Kāji lineages supplemented the four original lineages. On the winter solstice (reckoned as Paush-*krishna*/Thilāgā *dasami*; §9.4) a special, three-day *pujā* to the Tantric Deity commences. Two Vajrācārya priests join the four *guthiyār*s and two married women from the turn-holder's household. Each day's *pujā* is followed by the eating of the ritual meal (*samay baji*) and feast (*bhway*).

Tantric Worship *guthi*s are not restricted to *buddhamārgi*s (i.e., those who employ the services of a Vajrācārya domestic priest) although some of my Pengu Daḥ informants are under that impression. Lineages of *shivamārgi* Tamvaḥ, such as the Nāyaḥ *khalaḥ*, also have such *guthi*s. As with the Lwahãkaḥmi Tantric Worship *guthi*, the Nāyaḥ lineage Cahre Guthi regulates the worship of the Tantric Deity, in this case above the temple to Vishvakarma in Tichu Galli. *Guthiyār*s take turns for a month at a time to offer the daily worship and keep the temple clean and tidy. The name of this *guthi* is derived from the annual feast that is held on Gathã Mugaḥ Cahre (§7.10). The phenomenon of Tantric Worship *guthi*s among the *shivamārgi* Tamvaḥ, where the god worshipped is Buddhist and the priests involved are Vajrācārya, led Mahila Shilpakar of the Vishvakarma Sikaḥmi lineage to insist that this proved that the Tamvaḥ 'used to be *buddhamārgi*'. This is, as we have already seen, an assertion that the Tamvaḥ themselves usually deny.[12]

The Vishvakarma lineage of Sikaḥmi also has a Tantric Worship *guthi* that operates to worship the lineage Tantric Deity situated behind one of the houses of Bega Nani, Jom Bāhāḥ. Membership of this *guthi*, like that of the Lwahãkaḥmi, is strictly limited to agnates. The Shilpakār Tantric Worship *guthi*, however, breaks this strict rule of agnatic membership. Membership of this *guthi*, includes persons of not only all the seven lineages of Lwahãkaḥmi but also of the Vishvakarma Sikaḥmi. Thus, it defines that group of lineages that, though known to have no agnatic relationship, constitute the Shilpakār *thar*. No one claims in this case that a shared *guthi* for Tantric Worship proves that all the participants are agnatically related, however distantly.

c. Lineage Deity (*digu dyaḥ*) and Mohani *guthis*

The third type of agnatic *guthi* that I examine here is constituted of the Lineage Deity (*digu dyaḥ*) and Mohani *guthi*s. Lineages that have an ongoing strong solidarity observe the two major festivals of Dewāli and Mohani together. These are commonly referred to as two *guthi*s but, as I have already stated, for the purpose of analysis I shall treat them as one since they have a coextensive membership. Among the Pengu Daḥ, two lineages that observe both festivals together as a lineage *guthi* are Kwaḥ and Pwāḥsyāḥ *khalaḥ*s.

The Lineage Deity *guthi* is similar to the Tantric Worship *guthi* in that its explicit purpose is the worship of a (real or imagined) lineage-specific deity.[13] Lineage Deity *guthi*s, though apparently very important to the Pengu Daḥ in the past, are much fewer than they were even two decades previously—a trend that seems to be repeated throughout Newar society. Of the almost forty lineages of the Pengu Daḥ only a few now have any active Lineage Deity *guthi*. One lineage of Marikaḥmi does Lineage Deity Worship vicariously through the current turn-holder. In this case the *pujā* is performed immediately after the offering of *bhujyaḥ* to Bũgadyaḥ at Lagankhel giving the organization its name of *bhujyāḥ guthi*.[14]

Although Lineage Deity Worship remains important to nearly all Newars, the institution of the *guthi* as the appropriate instrument to mediate that no longer has the following it once seems to have had. Moreover, many of those smaller units (sub-lineages or simply households in many cases) that do Lineage Deity Worship together these days content themselves with a much-attenuated version of the full ritual. Among the Pengu Daḥ only two lineages continue to perform the full Lineage Deity Worship—the Bārāhi and the wider Jhvaḥchẽ lineage of Tamvaḥ, the former taking four days and the latter (performed by the *thākāli* and thence called *thākāli pujā*) lasting an arduous six.[15]

d. Optional agnatic *guthis*

There are a number of *guthi*s that are restricted to the lineage and yet are different from the *guthi*s that we have examined so far. Although all *guthi*s involve the worship of a deity, the emphasis of the foregoing types of *guthi* is social rather than religious. There are agnatic *guthi*s, however, that, though they do have a strong social aspect, do not fundamentally express the solidarity of the lineage. These *guthi*s usually have been set up by an ancestor of the lineage and have the worship of a particular deity as their focus. Although I characterize them as 'optional' they are not optional for members. The initial founding of the *guthi* was optional—the founding *guthiyār*s made a supererogatory gift in the initial establishment of the *guthi*.

Among the Pengu Daḥ in Lalitpur there have been four common types of optional agnatic *guthi*: the *sãnhu* (or *sãlhu*) *guthi*, the *pāthyāye guthi*, the Yẽnyaḥ *guthi* and the Pancadān *guthi* (cf. Gellner 1992: 243, 1995b: 231). Among the Pengu Daḥ there are two Yẽnyaḥ *guthi*s belonging to the Vishvakarma and Paḥmā Sikaḥmi lineages.

*Sãnhu guthi*s are common throughout Lalitpur. On the first day of each solar month hundreds of worshippers throng the sites of Būgadyaḥ and Cākwāḥdyaḥ to worship Karunāmaya-Matsyendranāth. Commonly, having done *pujā*, the *sãnhu guthi*, which usually consists of between six and fifteen members, eats *samay baji* together. In some cases the turn-holder alone visits the shrine of Būgadyaḥ where the image is kept (at the village of Būga, at Ta Bāhāḥ, Lalitpur, or on the chariot during the festival). After worshipping the image, he brings back *prasād* for the other members who then eat a feast together (Gellner and Pradhan 1995: 178). *Sãnhu guthi*s used to be more common than they are today. The only *sãnhu guthi* of the Pengu Daḥ that I was able to record, that of the Paḥmā Sikaḥmi, is now defunct.

Several Pengu Daḥ lineages have a *pāthyāye guthi*, which while having the same object of worship as the *sãnhu guthi*, differs from it in its mode of operation. Until recently, the *pāthyāye guthi* of the Sikaḥmi Paḥmā lineage used to light 108 lamps to Būgadyaḥ on the chariot's arrival at Lūhiti, Nugaḥ. The Tamvaḥ Jhvaḥchẽ lineage *pāthyāye guthi* continues to pay a local Vajrācārya priest to do a daily *pujā* to Būgadyaḥ from the day the image is placed on the chariot to the day before it leaves Thati for Jawalakhel. The *guthi* has two feasts each year—one on the day the deity is brought from Būga and the other on the day it is taken back.

The now defunct Pancadān *guthi* of the Palmā Sikaḥmi lineage would, until recently, feed the Vajrācāryas and Shākyas of the 'Fifteen *bāhāḥ*s' who would come to Kuti Saugaḥ on Yālā Pancadān (§7.13). The Tamvaḥ Garsa Guthi, on the other hand, continues to give one *pāthi* each of several grains as an offering (*dān*) to Shākyas and Vajrācāryas on this day.

There are a number of other *guthi*s belonging to this subcategory. The Tamvaḥ Kūḥchẽ lineage Krishna Guthi is one that organizes the annual *jātrā* of the Krishna image of Kūḥchẽ on Krishnashtami (Bhādra-*krishna*/Gūlāgā 8, §7.20.2). The Vishvakarma Sikaḥmi lineage operates a Cibhāḥ Guthi in which they visit the *cibhāḥ* in the nearby Cibhāḥ Nani to offer *pujā* on a designated day each year. The Tamvaḥ Cabāchẽ lineage Rām Navami Guthi does *pujā* to Mahālakshmi on Rām Navami (§9.16.2).

Corporate worship often involves the singing of traditional hymns. The music played in this connection falls into one of three different types: *dāphā*, *bājā* and *bhajan*.[16] Not all groups that sing hymns are *guthi*, and *bhajan* music groups are never so constituted. Here I will examine one *guthi* representative of the *bājā* tradition. Later (§6.2.5) I will look at the *dāphā* tradition and then (§6.3) at *ad hoc* musical ensembles, which play music from either the *bājā* or *bhajan* traditions.

There are several *bājā* musical associations that involve the Pengu Daḥ. Some are constituted as *guthi*s, while others are not. The Naḥ Bāhāḥ Gūlā Pāru *guthi* is made up of an ideal number of twenty-two *guthiyār*s all belonging to the Tamvaḥ lineage of that name. This *guthi* sings *bājā* hymns at Naḥ Bāhāḥ (Cakravarti Mahāvihāra) in the locality of Cāka Bahi each day of the

Buddhist holy month of Gũlā (§7.11), and each *sãnhu*, *shukla-ashtami* and Wednesday evening throughout the year. The *guthi* celebrates just one feast on completion of Gũlā (Gũlā Pāru, §7.24) from which it takes its name.

Instruments played in the *bājā* tradition include *harmin*, *jhyāli*, *kartal* (two-piece one-handed percussion instrument), *magaḥ khĩ* (*mādal*, Np., a small two-headed drum), *cinta jhyāli* (a pair of cymbal tongs), *tainai* (a triangle) and *tamal bām* (*tabala*, Np., a pair of drums).

6.2.4. *Thar guthis*

Among the Pengu Daḥ some *guthi*s have a membership wider than that of the lineage but fundamentally restricted to the *thar.* Among these are the death *guthi*s and a number that, like the optional agnatic *guthi*s, are explicitly for the worship of a particular deity.

a. Death *guthis*

For many Newars, the death (*sanā*) *guthi* is the most important kind of *guthi.* A Newar who belongs to no other kind of *guthi* will nevertheless usually belong to a death *guthi.* Some observers have stressed the role of the death *guthi* so much that one might conclude that the lack of such membership is most debilitating. Quigley reports that in the early 1980s, for Dhulikhel Shresthas at least, the threat of expulsion from the death *guthi* was a very powerful form of social control (1995a). The situation of Dhulikhel Shresthas, however, like all Shresthas to some extent as Quigley points out, imposes an abnormal weight of importance to the *guthi* institution, as it is membership of the *guthi* that is the prime determinant of one's marriageable status. Data on the Pengu Daḥ, on the other hand, show that the death *guthi* does not have the same significance for all Newars. For the Pengu Daḥ it is not necessary to belong to a death *guthi* to prove one's credentials. Everyone in the locality can vouch for one's caste *bona fides*.

If not so universally important for marriage, the death *guthi* has, nevertheless, till very recently been of great importance for death. Newars are obsessed by death, and they are obsessed by the dramatic consequences that can arise if the funeral rites are not carried out according to tradition. All Newars that I have met, whether they are peasants, merchants, priests or painters, display the same mixture of incomprehension and fear with respect to those people who live on the edge of society: ascetics, for example. How, if they are deprived of their caste and of all family support, can these people be cremated or buried when they die? Who will take care of the funeral rites? For the Newars this is a singularly important question. Death *guthi*s are a collective way of responding to it (Toffin 1995b: 259).

It is also clear, however, that for funeral services alone the death *guthi* no longer has the monopoly it used to enjoy. The Marwari funeral service, for example, is available to anyone who wants to use it. Some Newars, including members of the Pengu Daḥ, therefore, have left their death *guthi* and now arrange funeral services themselves. This casting off of traditional institutions demonstrates again the significant impact of modernity on Newar culture. As one middle-aged Shrestha man told me, 'These days everything is possible... if you have money'.

The death *guthi* is not, however, simply a funeral co-operative. It is a religious association. Nowhere is this seen more clearly than in the annual *pujā* and feast. The worship of the tutelary deity (each Thursday by the turn-holder) and the act of feasting in the company of the deity give the death *guthi* a distinctly religious character.[17] The *guthi*'s tutelary deity can be any god that the *guthi* may have chosen. The Tamvaḥ death *guthi*s, for instance, worship one of two local deities outside the city. One is the Lineage Deity of the *thar*, Tamkadyaḥ (Ugracandimai), to the west and the other is Mahālakshmi to the south.[18]

Another '*guthi*' is mentioned in the literature in connection with the death *guthi* that is, the '*bicā guthi*' (cf. Locke 1980: 174; Gellner 1992: 246). Among the Pengu Daḥ, the *bicā guthi* operates as simply one function of the death *guthi*—the main feast of the year of the Shilpakār Tadhã Guthi, for instance, is called *bicā guthi.* At this event the welfare of the families of the *guthiyār*s is discussed.

The question arises as to the basic organizing principle of the death *guthi*, whether it is based on agnatic relationship or territory. As can be seen below, certain death *guthi*s of the Pengu Daḥ, the two Tamvaḥ Rām Navami Guthis and the Paḥmā Sila Caḥre Guthi for instance, are comprised solely of agnatic relations. As Toffin reports (1995b: 261, n.20), the death *guthi*s of Lalitpur's Citrakārs, likewise, are lineage-specific, as are some Maharjan death *guthi*s (Gellner and Pradhan 1995: 178).

As tempting as it would be to deduce from these data that the death *guthi* is based on the principle of agnatic relationship, this would be premature. All the above examples are of small lineages, the members of which, if no longer in practice at least in theory, live in close proximity to one another. An analysis of the larger Pengu Daḥ death *guthi*s, however, demonstrates that the principle of agnatic relation is secondary, and often overridden by the principle of locality. It is not possible by looking at the organization and membership of the Lalitpur Tamvaḥ death *guthi*s, however, to come to any final conclusion about organizing principle since (until very recently) all the Tamvaḥ have lived in close proximity to one another. It is nevertheless clear that agnatic relationship is not the principal factor as all three of the larger Tamvaḥ death *guthi*s and both Shilpakār death *guthi*s cut right across lineage boundaries with apparent abandon.[19]

There seems to be an ideal, at least among the Pengu Daḥ, that each *thar* should constitute a single death *guthi.* In reality, however, splits have led to division of most of the erstwhile *thar*-wide institutions. Members of the Tamvaḥ Daru Guthi assert that theirs is the original Tamvaḥ *guthi* and that it was established when the Lineage Deity was brought to Jawalakhel around the seventeenth century. Furthermore, the Tamvaḥ Cidhã Guthi claims precedence over the Tadhã Guthi, which broke away from the former some time in the distant past—a relationship that is expressed today by the precedence of the Cidhã Guthi in the *pujā*. The Tamvaḥ Rām Navami Guthi (also called Ikhã Guthi by outsiders) split into two about 1900 CE. No connection between the Rām Navami Guthis that have Mahālakshmi as their tutelary deity, and the other Tamvaḥ death *guthi*s that have Tamkadyaḥ as theirs, is remembered.[20]

Death *guthi*s have feasts at least annually and very often two or three times a year. At these gatherings a major *pujā* is offered to the tutelary deity. This can go on for up to five days as in the winter feast of the Tamvaḥ Tadhã Guthi. This *guthi* meets as *wala pā* on the first and fifth days with the *guthiyār* and with one other from his family attending. On the intervening days the entire *guthi* gathers together. At each of these *pujās* a goat is sacrificed to the tutelary deity. In contrast to the *pujā* done at Lineage Deity Worship (to the same deity in this case) the goat does not have to be pure black. As at Lineage Deity Worship, the head is divided among the eight elders of the *guthi* (*sikāḥ bhu*). In all the Pengu Daḥ *guthi*s, the winter feast is the most important of all with the handing over of accounts, keys, etc., to the next turn-holder at the close.

There is a popular perception among Pengu Daḥ *guthiyār*s that if one were to leave his *sanā guthi* and try to join another he would be rejected. One Shilpakār, however, did just that a few years ago, leaving the Tadhã Guthi that had been racked by intra*guthi* conflict and joining the Cidhã Guthi.

b. Optional *thar guthis*

As with the optional agnatic *guthi*s (§6.2.3), those that I categorize as optional *thar guthi*s have been set up at some time for the explicit purpose of worship of a particular deity. Among these is the Tamvaḥ Bhimsen Guthi, which does a procession to all Bhimsen shrines in Lalitpur on the ninth day of the waning fortnight of Bhādra (Bhādra-*krishna*/Gũlāgā 9). Another is the Bāl Kumāri *bājā guthi*, which is made up of eleven Tāmrakārs from the locality of Cāka Bahi adjacent to the shrine of the Mahāvidya that gives the *guthi* its name.

*Guthiyār*s are very clear that participation in this *guthi* is open to all Tamvaḥ of the locality (*twaḥ*). The social focus of this *guthi* then is not the lineage but the locality. On Jugaḥ Cahre (§7.22) another similar Tamvaḥ *guthi*, the Mahālakshmi Guthi, visits Mahālakshmisthān, a two kilometres or so to the south of the old city, to clean two brass flags that were placed at the temple by the ancestor of one of the *guthiyār*s. There is no worship on this day but they eat a feast straight after their work is done and return a few days later (on Bhādra-*shukla*/Yãlāthwa *pancami*) to do a *pujā* and eat another feast.

Another variation on this theme is the Basuwa Siwa Guthi (lit., 'Thursday Service Guthi') of the Lwahãkaḥmi, which has as its tutelary deity the

Lwahãkaḥmi Lineage Deity at Mani Dwã. During the year the turn-holder does *pujā* to the deity each Thursday as the turn-holder of the *sanā guthi* does. *Guthiyār*s do not need to have taken Tantric Initiation but only those who have so taken can worship. On Sithi Nakhaḥ the *guthiyār*s visit the Lwahãkaḥmi Lineage Deity at Mani Dwã in order to bring a movable image of the deity back on a palanquin to the turn-holder's house for the special *pujā* for which two Vajrācārya priests are needed. *Guthiyār*s say that the *pujā* is very complicated and expensive, as a lot of paraphernalia is required. Before the *pujā*, in a reversal of the usual procedure, *guthiyār*s eat *pãcāku* (five pieces of *chwaylā* and three *sali* of *aylaḥ*).[21] After the *pujā* the image is returned to Mani Dwã.

6.2.5. Multicaste *guthis*

It is an interesting fact that no *guthi* exclusively represents the Pengu Daḥ as a whole. All one finds when one casts the net wider are multicaste *guthi*s. There is no *guthi* that is open to a plurality of Pengu Daḥ *thar*s that is not also open to other castes from outside the group. Having said that, multicaste *guthi*s that include members of the Pengu Daḥ are not common. In the course of my research I was able only to find three: Harkhā̃dyaḥ Guthi, Bhairavanāth Guthi and Nasantya Dāphā Guthi.[22]

The Harkhā̃dyaḥ Guthi meets on Yẽnyaḥ Punhi. This small multicaste *guthi* was founded two generations ago by three friends, a Tāmrakār, a Kayastha and a Shākya, who established an image of Harkhā̃dyaḥ[23] in a nook near the Krishna temple in Mangaḥ and donated land and paraphernalia for its upkeep and worship. On Yẽnyaḥ Punhi the *guthiyār*s visit the *murti* and feed people homebrewed beer (*thon*) through a pipe in the image.

Two multicaste musical *guthi*s include members of the Pengu Daḥ. The Bhairavanāth Guthi is a *bājā guthi* whose twelve members include Tāmrakārs, Shilpakārs, Citrakārs and Ranjitkārs. The Nasantya Dāphā Guthi, on the other hand, is an ensemble for the worship of Bũgadyaḥ through the musical idiom of *dāphā*. This *guthi* has a complex tradition that is worthwhile examining in detail. The Nasantya Dāphā Guthi meets for worship at dawn (*nasantya* means 'dawn') during the Jātrā wherever the image of Bũgadyaḥ happens to be stationed.[24] The tutelary deity of the group is the Nāsadyaḥ of Nāsa Nani, Haugaḥ. *Dāphā* ensembles, as Grandin (1989: 77) points out, are usually comprised of Maharjans though Vajrācāryas and Shākyas also participate.[25] The membership of the Nasantya Dāphā Guthi, however, is mostly drawn from the Tāmrakār *thar.* A few Rājkarnikārs are also members, as were Shilpakārs in the past. The lead instrument is the *khĩ* drum, other instruments being *jhyāli* (small cymbals), *tāḥ* (bells) and *harmin* (harmonium).[26] The group also includes two Maharjans who play the *pwanga* horn. As with other *dāphā* groups all songs are prescribed and are sung in Newar and Sanskrit. There is no room for choice (*pharmās*) of repertoire as there is for other types of corporate worship. This group is unique among all the music groups of Lalitpur as, when all other instruments are not to be played between Sithi Nakhaḥ and Gathā̃ Mugaḥ, this group is expected to continue to do so (§7.10). The antiquity of this guthi seems beyond doubt: manuscripts of *dāphā* hymns are found from the time of Siddhi Narasimha Malla.[27]

The Nasantya Dāphā Guthi has a complex organization. Apart from the annual rotation of *guthiyār*s as turn-holders, the *guthi* is also divided into three *wala pā.* The *guthi* celebrates a total of seven feasts throughout the year (§8.7). The three *wala pā* are each responsible for one of the following feasts: *dyaḥ laswa pujā*, *kiki swā̃* and Bicā Pujā. Today, with the smaller membership of the *guthi*, the first and third groups have been combined. The second group, for its part, has taken on the responsibility for the feast at Sasu Pujā. The other feasts are all the responsibility of the current turn-holder.

6.2.6. *Guthi* as social identifier

The importance of the *guthi* as an instrument of social control has been a moot point in the literature. Things have clearly changed in the decades since Nepali and Quigley did their fieldwork. Nepali makes much of the *guthi* as a system of cohesion and social control (1965: 420). Writing of Dhulikhel in the early 1980s Quigley asserts that, 'Without membership of the *guthi*s, one has no lineage and therefore no caste status. In Newar terms this amounts to losing any meaningful identity' (1985b: 59). By contrast, however, when one looks at the ease with which the cities' inhabitants will leave this institution at the turn of the twenty-first century it is clear that the *guthi* has lost much of its importance in Newar society.

The *guthi* system is clearly collapsing for reasons that seem to be mostly economic: population pressure on the land, land reform and corruption by tenants and trustees registering land in their own names (Locke 1997). It is clear that the Land Reform Act of 1964 dealt a deathblow to many *guthi*s (Malla 1997). The embezzlement of *guthi* land by the tenants is a recurring theme in the *guthi* discourse of the Pengu Daḥ. As the Bārāhi *thākāli* Surya Lal put it: 'The *mhāy* [Jyāpu and Parbatiyā tenant farmers] are not bringing the grain from the [*guthi*] land that they are supposed to. It is a big problem. They tell us to prove it is our land but there are no papers.'

There is another reason for the decline in the fortunes of the *guthi* system. Modern, liberal democratic values are often seen to be in antipathy to the organizational principles of the *guthi.* The *guthi* is an institution that values maleness, age and local tradition—each of which has been under attack by modernity through the channels of rationalistic education, the electronic media and the globalized economy. The defiant comment of one young Shilpakār man whose family had just left the death *guthi* expresses a now common sentiment: 'If a member of our family dies we will work it out. *Guthi*s are just organizations and organizations don't have to be like that.'

6.3. *Ad hoc* musical ensembles

Ad hoc musical ensembles (*khalaḥ*) are found all over the city and play music from either the *bājã* or *bhajan* traditions. There is clearly a significant difference between an ensemble that is a *guthi* and one that is not. Membership of the *ad hoc* ensemble is somewhat fluid and, though caste and territory are significant principles in their organization, there is little loss in expulsion and therefore little social control can be exerted. The *guthi*, on the other hand, has a formal membership, a basic principle of equality between the members and, ideally, an endowment.

Localities (*twaḥ*) have their own *bājã* ensembles that play at auspicious life-cycle rituals such as Old-Age Initiation and certain annual festivals. Such *ad hoc* ensembles are not constituted as *guthi*s but, nevertheless, do have certain formal characteristics. *Bājã* ensembles of the locality are made up of members of each of the castes of that community. Others, no less territorial, comprise members of one particular caste. One such is the Tamvaḥ *dhāḥ bājã khalaḥ* of Cāka Bahi. Local Tāmrakār men, supplemented by other Tāmrakārs from nearby localities, sing Newar hymns and play the *dhāḥ* (double-headed drum) with accompanying ensemble. They are divided into two groups with four *dhāḥ* and two pairs of *bhusyāḥ* (accompanying large cymbals) in one group, one *naykhĩ* (smaller double-headed drum) and one pair of *cusyāḥ* (accompanying small cymbals) in the other. Though they play together in some of the music the two groups have a different repertoire, the music often alternating from one group to the other. Traditionally the *dhāḥ bājã khalaḥ* included two Kāpāli *muhāli* (shawm) players. These days, due to the availability of better-paid work and the degrading association of shawm playing, the Kāpāli do not play for this ensemble (§3.4.3). In their stead a group of three Damai are paid to play one Western oboe and two trumpets. The instruments of the ensemble, all portable, enable the group to play through the streets at the front of the Old-Age Initiation procession. Though the ensemble is constituted solely of Tāmrakārs, territoriality seems if not to take precedence over caste, to be equally important.[28]

Multicaste *dhāḥ bājã* ensembles play at an important annual city-wide festival, that of Nyaku Jātrā/Matayā. Each of the ten localities through which the royal centripetal procession route passes has its own *dhāḥ bājã* ensemble. Each locality, in rotation, is given the honour of leading the Nyaku Jātrā procession and in preparation for this the *dhāḥ bājã* ensemble must learn and practice several dozen hymns over the period of several months preceding its turn. The music *guru*s and those who hold the positions of *dhāḥ nāyaḥ* and *bhusyāḥ nāyaḥ* are accorded great honour in the community with each of these men being dressed in white turbans (*betali*) during the festival. Play always begins with the worship of the musicians' tutelary deity, Nāsadyaḥ. The procession of Nyaku Jātrā includes stops to sing hymns at thirty shrines around the centripetal *pradakshinapātha.* Each deity has a particular hymn with a particular combination of tune (*rāga*) and rhythm (*tāla*). G.R. Shakya (1995) reports a decline in the importance of the *dhāḥ bājā̃*; the long period of training required to learn the repertoire of the *dhāḥ* puts off some young men from getting involved.

The other type of *ad hoc* musical ensemble found in Lalitpur is the *bhajan khalaḥ*. Whereas some *bājā̃* ensembles are constituted as *guthi*s, *bhajan* groups are never so formally organized. Each *bhajan* ensemble is for the worship of a particular deity. One such is the Krishna Mandir Bhajan Khalaḥ, which meets to sing hymns to the deity at his important temple at Mangaḥ, playing the *harmin*, *tabala*, etc. All members of the ensemble are *shivamārgi*.[29] Another *bhajan* group is the Mahālakshmi *nagara bhajan khalaḥ*, which gathers at the Nhutunthi Cuka Mahālakshmisthān in Ikhā each evening during the lunar month of Yãlā. This ensemble consists of a dozen Tāmrakār men and plays the *nagara*, *tāḥ*, *jhyāli*, *bhusyāḥ*, *kartal* and *samkha* (conch) instruments.

The Tāmrakār Mridanga Bhajan Khalaḥ, drawn exclusively from the Tamvaḥ Kũḥchẽ lineage, is for the worship of Bũgadyaḥ. Participation is voluntary and it is not established as a *guthi*. In contrast to the *dāphā guthi*'s repertoire the songs are not set but are considered optional (*pharmās*). The Mridanga Bhajan Khalaḥ presents its musical offering to Bũgadyaḥ on Sundays, Thursdays, full moon days and Eighth (*ashtami*) days while the deity is at Ta Bāhāḥ. They then sing each evening at the site of the deity from the day of the bathing ceremony up to and including the last day of the Jātrā when the *bhoto* is shown.

A multicaste *khī̃ bhajan khalaḥ* has a central role to play in two city festivals. On Jyesth Punhi (§9.26) the group gathers on the dance platform (*dabu*) at Mangaḥ and performs all thirty-two hymns ascribed to King Siddhi Narasimha Malla while the throne of his son Sri Nivas is displayed on the plinth of the adjacent Krishna temple. The ensemble includes Tāmrakārs, Maharjans and Shresthas playing two *khī̃*, the harmonium, and bells (*tāḥ*). The other occasion on which the *khī̃ bhajan khalaḥ* performs is as accompaniment to the autumn dance-dramas called Kati Pyākhã, also held at the dance platform at Mangaḥ. Similarly the Mridanga Phagun Bhajan Khalaḥ sings hymns to Krishna before his temple in Mangaḥ each evening of Holi (§9.12). The members of this ensemble are drawn from Tāmrakār, Shrestha, Citrakārs and Maharjan castes.

There are differences between the three forms of music traditionally played by Newar ensembles. Whereas the instruments of the *dāphā* and *bājā̃* ensembles, such as the *dhimay*, *dhāḥ* and *kvacakhī̃* are seemingly indigenous, the instruments of the *bhajan* ensemble are shared by non-Newars (Grandin 1989: 66). The *magaḥ khī̃* and *nagara* for instance are shared with the Parbatiyā of the hills and seem to point to a sharing of culture that was not present when *dāphā* was developed. There is, furthermore, a difference between the *bhajan* ensemble that plays at the Krishna temple and the others that are described above. The Krishna temple ensemble with its playing of the harmonium and *tabala* has a clear and unambiguously Indian character whereas the others, though not as indigenous as the *dāphā* and *bājā* ensembles, do nevertheless have more of a Nepalese feel.

As Grandin explains, Nepal was reconnected to the circuit of Hindustani *sashtriyā sangit* (classical, scriptural songs) in the late nineteenth century as the Ranas introduced them at court (ibid.: 92). As the *bhajan* groups have grown in popularity the *bhakti* dimension of Newar religious life has been emphasized (Lewis 1984: 187).[30] In contrast, the music of *dāphā* appears as 'a closed, compartmentalized subtradition that merely reproduces itself' while the *bhajan* is 'open, inclusive, assimilative, and innovative' (Grandin 1989: 179). It seems likely that *dāphā* groups will continue to decline even as *bhajan* groups gain new members. But is this, as Grandin implies, a result of repertoire? Surely it has as much to do with the difference of social structure between the two groups. *Dāphā*'s decline is linked to the decline in the fortunes of the *guthi*.

6.4. Modern organizations

6.4.1. Modern territorial organizations

Modern territorial organizations include locality improvement committees, youth clubs and prestige organizations.

In recent years many neighbourhoods have organized a Locality Improvement Committee (*tol sudhār samiti*, Np.). One such is Ikhā Tol Sudhār Samiti, formed in the late 1980s. The purpose of such organizations is to ensure a corporate approach to the care of public property in the locality. In a place like Ikhā this largely means maintaining the Tichu Galli road and sewer system beneath it. Other cleaning committees will organize the cleaning of wells and ponds on Sithi Nakhaḥ. Webster (1987) has described a system of work groups that is similar to these locality committees. These work groups, called *bolajyā* are a formal organization for mutual work on fields among Maharjan farmers. According to Webster, *bolajyā* is:

> A system of mutual help, not based upon hierarchy, but rather upon the idea of working as equals, not just within a caste, but irrespective of caste. The determining concept in this system is that of fraternity, of brotherhood and sisterhood, rather than caste differentials and duties. (Ibid.: 297)[31]

Locality Improvement Committees are *not* called *bolajyā* groups they include neither *pujā* nor feasting. They are, nevertheless, like *bolajyā* groups in that they are territorial and emphasize mutual co-operation rather than hierarchical interdependence.

Many localities today also have a youth club named, significantly, in a mixture of Nepali and English: '*yuva club*'. Such organizations, often based at a local, public shelter (*phālca*) are the means to purchase and look after games equipment. There is often a small library. Such groups are often given the responsibility for marshalling the crowds in such processions as Matayā.

A number of international prestige associations such as the Jaycees and the Rotary Club have branches in the Kathmandu Valley. I include these as modern territorial organizations because, though they are branches of a wider group, they invariably meet on a territorial basis; e.g., the Rotary Club of Kathmandu Mid-town. Attachment to a locality is, however, pragmatic rather than principled; branches are expected to divide whenever they grow beyond a dozen members or so. Typically these organizations attract wealthy businessmen and women irrespective of ethnicity, though many Newars are involved. English is the medium of communication within many of these groups. Their explicit purpose is usually framed in terms of public works such as the support of education projects. It is clear, however, that such associations benefit the members themselves as well with opportunities to form business ties as well as social interaction with others of similar socio-economic standing.

Other modern voluntary organizations exist to further the aspirations of the Newar language movement. Such a group is the *pāsāpuco*, for the educating of the children of the members and the encouragement of the use of Nepāl Bhāsha. Newar is self-consciously the medium of communication within the group, which theoretically includes Newars from all castes.

Jhigu Samāj (Our Society) of Dharān is a group, like the *pāsāpuco*, that is self-consciously Newar. Jhigu Samāj is actually the result of the transformation of a former death *guthi*, which had been established two generations ago. The modern organization explicitly admits members from all clean castes and runs on the principles of other modern organizations with a committee and voting.

6.4.2. Modern caste-based organizations

There is a clear distinction between modern, territorial organizations and caste-based organizations. Caste-based organizations pay scant notice to issues of territoriality but rather emphasize the solidarity of the caste in a manner that transcends territorial boundaries. Gellner comments on the rise of such 'caste-based' organizations: among the Newars, there are so far, organized bodies representing the Brahmans, Vajrācāryas, Kamsakārs, Maharjans, Nakarmis, Mānandhars, Citrakārs, Tandukārs, Khadgis and Kāpālis (1999: 16).[32] There is also an *ad hoc* committee to represent the wider Urāy community though no rules or aims of the committee have yet been published. No such group has been created among the Pengu Daḥ although during the course of my research the Tāmrakārs, Rājkarnikārs and Lwahākaḥmi have formed their own societies.[33] As we have seen (§3.4.2), Gellner describes what he calls an 'ingenious solution' that the Urāy have come up with to deal with the vexed question of whether the Rājkarnikārs are part of the Urāy or not. The Urāy organization is open for the time being to those Urāy of Kathmandu thus excluding the Rājkarnikārs until a national body is set up (ibid.: 17). This is, in fact, a traditional solution since the castes themselves were largely only ever really substantive as city-bound units. It is, though, as Gellner remarks, a modern conundrum. In the not-too-distant past there would have been no great felt need to define such neatly bounded units. Here I will describe two such caste-based organizations that represent different groups of the Pengu Daḥ: the Ugracandimai Service Committee and the Rājkarnikār Society.

The Ugracandimai Service Committee (Ugracandimai Sewā Samiti, Np.) has been constituted to bring together all *bona fide* Lalitpur Tāmrakārs in one organization. At the time of writing there are around 300 members including many who live in the hill bazaars but whose ancestral home is Lalitpur. Applications for membership have to be proposed by a member of the committee and can only be approved after the applicant's lineage has been adequately demonstrated. Panauti and Bhaktapur Tamvaḥ are barred from membership as are those who are descended from Tamvaḥ that had married Jyāpunis or Mānandhars. The senior male (*thākāli*) from each household is counted as a member with all others in the household having a sort of associate membership as in a *guthi*. The executive committee has eleven members and is run on lines of a modern committee discarding rules of seniority. Voting for committee members is carried out every two years. Although there is a provision in the constitution for voting on other issues, all other decisions, in a situation that will be readily recognized by observers of decision making across Asia, are arrived at by consensus. The committee has a regular income from the rent of four shops that have been built on the side of the road on the land belonging to the Ugracandimai temple. There is a certain endowment, which is invested in a bank, but until now it has never been used. A nominal subscription of Rs. 5 is collected from each member. If there is any major need, such as when the temple had to be rebuilt in 1982, then a voluntary offering is taken.

As a virtually *thar*-wide organization the committee seeks to establish solidarity between its members. Furthermore, it has sought to use its power to legislate on social problems encountered by its members. In 2002 a booklet of rules was published by the committee legislating how much expenditure was acceptable at weddings, etc. This includes an agreement not to hold public Taking the Areca Nut (*gway kayegu*) and Going to See the Face (*khwā swā wanegu*) celebrations, which have become an opportunity for great demonstrations of wealth over the last twenty or thirty years. Concretely one may not present more than five trays of gifts at such an event. The agreement is both to protect the prestige of those who are less well off as well as to cut unnecessary expenditure.

The purpose of the Rājkarnikār Society (Samāj) is, I was informed, threefold: to raise the Rājkarnikārs up (socio-economically), to reduce the effects of inflationary competition among its members in social events, and to help other castes. The Society runs programmes not traditionally handled by the caste *guthi.* These programmes include a prize giving for the children of members who pass the School Leaving Certificate. Like the Tāmrakār committee, membership of the committee of the Rājkarnikār Society is not determined by seniority but by ballot. The committee has recently, like its Tāmrakār counterpart, drafted a set of 'rules of behaviour' to be followed by all Marikaḥmi at the celebration of a life-cycle ritual. As with the Tāmrakār society the number of trays one may present at the Taking the Areca Nut and Going to See the Face (*khwā swā wanegu*) rituals is strictly limited. But the limit is more 'liberal' than that of the Tāmrakārs one may give up to twenty trays.[34] Hem Lal Tamrakar suggested to me that this was because the Rājkarnikārs are 'higher' than the Tāmrakārs both in wealth (*'arthik kshetra'*) and education (*'baudhik kshetra'*). This was, however, an opinion with which Ram Govinda Rajkarnikar could not agree.

6.5. From territory to caste—The transformation of Newar identity

The old *guthi* system was based on *locality.* Membership in those territorial organizations was essential to Newar identity and life. Attachment to locality provided a countervailing force to the other defining institution of caste. By cutting across caste boundaries and bringing together members of different castes (within limits) within its institutions, the locality reduced the power of caste to define loyalties and in so doing gave the royal centre the instrument to increase its control over the city as a whole. It is clear, however, that modern Newar society is going through a transformation. The reasons for this are threefold: the demise of the city as the capital of an independent political unit; the migration of the city's inhabitants from the localities to outlying 'suburbs' and further afield; and the developing sense of Newar identity as an ethnicity with the subsequent growth of solidarity of caste-based organizations as subsets of that ethnicity. Territory as an organizing principle, therefore, no longer has the power it once had. Caste also, in the traditional sense as an integrated system, is also in decline with the growing strength of the nation state and the impact of modernity. Individual castes, however, have responded to this milieu by organizing themselves into what amounts to quasi-ethnic groups. In the case of the Newars this has led to the development of a stronger pan-Newar ethnic identity.

7. The Renewal of Order I: Restoring Civic Space

> When Matayā began there was just one couple playing their horns. The man got lost so his wife searched for him, playing her horn, which sounded like she was calling, 'Where are you?' He would reply on his horn, which sounded like, 'I am here!' At this time there is so much rain there is the liability of flooding. No one must sleep during this night otherwise the world will turn over. So the *nava bājā̃* go around keeping people awake.
>
> Buddhi Raj Tamrakar

7.1. Introduction

So far in this study I have described Newar society in terms of its structures of kinship and caste. I have, furthermore, analyzed the way the city of Lalitpur is structured spatially and the relation of territorial organizations to the other social structures. This is all static. Newar culture, however, like all living cultures, is far from static. It is dynamic, ever-moving and changing. That dynamism is nowhere better seen than in the festivals.[1]

In this survey of Lalitpur's festivals I will attempt to dig up the structures that define the order with a view to teasing out the major influences in the development of the city's calendar. In keeping with the overall focus of this study, I will also examine each festival to discover the roles of kinship and kingship to see if they can help us to make any sense out of the caste system. Not all festivals are equally significant. Some, in fact, are trivial from the perspective of the city as a whole. Those that are of greater importance to the city are given more attention. Those that are minor are given a short summary. Many of the minor festivals do not seem to fit any discernible pattern. Perhaps it is this feature alone that has resulted in their lack of importance.

In a study of Nepal's festivals it is important to note that many are distinctly local. Very few of Nepal's festivals, in fact, are observed nation-wide. The city of Lalitpur, as with any locality, has developed its annual scheme of festivals by selecting (as it were) from a vast menu of South Asian options. Some festivals, such as Gatilā, Mukhaḥ Ashtami, Swā̃yā Punhi and Disi Pujā, are celebrated almost exclusively by those who are self-consciously Buddhist. Other festivals, such as Sā Pāru and the Narasimha Jātrā, are celebrated exclusively by those who would identify themselves as *shivamārgi*s.[2] The vast majority, however, are not restricted to those of any particular religious path.

Two calendars are in use for determining the precise timing of the annual festivals solar and lunar. To adjust the discrepancies between solar and lunar months it is necessary to add six lunar months in every cycle of nineteen solar years (or roughly one month in every three years, Slusser 1998: I, 381). The intercalery period is called *malamāsa*, meaning 'filth (or faeces) month' (often corrupted to *manamāsa*), or more euphemistically as Purushottam.[3] It is considered inauspicious and inappropriate for any life-cycle rituals (*samskāra*) or festivals; no major auspicious event can be accomplished during this time. Bũgadyaḥ's chariot, for instance, cannot be moved from Lagankhel to Jawalakhel during this time as this movement is determined by reference to the heavenly bodies (§10.7.6). The Jawala Jātrā, however, is not affected, nor is the return of Bũgadyaḥ to Bũga (Bũgamati). Furthermore, though *pujā* can still be offered, no animal may be sacrificed. If one is born during this month it is considered a bad thing and his birthday is ascribed to the same date on the following lunar month.

Relatively few festivals are observed according to the solar calendar. Rather than examining them separately I shall do so as they crop up during the course of the lunar calendar.[4]

7.2. Note on non-annual festivals

Before I begin my survey of annual events, and for the sake of completeness, I include here a short note on the few non-annual festivals. The Samyak festival is held every five years on Phāgun-*shukla tritiya* (Cillāthwa 3) (Gellner 1992: 181). All the images of Dipankara Buddha from around Lalitpur are brought to the courtyard of Nāg Bāhāḥ and placed in a line. Then, from very early in the morning, thousands of local people come to stand in line and do *pujā* to each image. Among the worshippers are the members of the Nasantya Dāphā Guthi, who visit to sing hymns to Bũgadyaḥ, which is also brought on a palanquin to the festival (§6.2.5, and Chapter 10).

Another non-annual festival is the twelve-yearly arrival of the god dance troupe, the *dyaḥ pyākhã*, of Khokana that performs dance-dramas at a number of platforms in Lalitpur. Furthermore, the major festival of the city—the Jātrā—is enacted in a grand way every twelve years with the pulling of the chariot all the way to Lalitpur from the village of Bũga and back again.

7.3. The lunar calendar

Several observers have commented on the lunar calendar and its use in Newar societies (Gellner 1992: 215-7; Levy 1990: 643-57; Lewis 1984: 343; Slusser 1998: I, Appendix 1; Tuladhar 1996: 455-62). Newar use of the lunar calendar is inflected by each Newar settlement (and those of Hindus broadly) in a unique way lending each a distinct character. Broadly though, many of the festivals of each of the Newar cities are celebrated in parallel with each other and, in some cases, notably Mohani and Lakshmi Pujā, with communities across India.

Each lunar month is divided into two halves—a waxing or bright half (*shukla pakshā*) and a waning or dark half (*krishna pakshā*). The eleventh day of each fortnight (*ekadasi*) is sacred to Vaishnavites who do an Observance (*vrata*) to Nārāyana on this day. In the same way, the eighth day (*ashtami*) is sacred to Buddhists as the day to do an Observance to Amoghapāsha Lokeshvara. Certain taboos are observed on significant days of the lunar month. No animals, for example, are to be slaughtered on either of the *ekadasi*s or on the new moon. The former is clearly of Vaishnava influence (Klostermaier 1990: 172; Eck 1993: 256).

As with other Hindu cities, such as Banāras (Eck 1993: 257), each deity has its special months. Bhimsen, for example, is worshipped especially during the month of Dillā (July) and the Devi during Yālā (September).

The chariot festival of Bũgadyaḥ—'The Jātrā' as it is called locally—is another festival whose beginning, at least, is determined by the lunar calendar. The Jātrā is the most important local festival for the people of Lalitpur. In its breadth of involvement and emotional appeal it is very closely analogous to the Biskaḥ festival of Bhaktapur (Levy 1990) and the Indra Jātrā of Kathmandu (Toffin 1992). The other great local festival of Lalitpur, the monsoon Buddhist festival of Matayā, matches the Jātrā in attracting large numbers of participants and great enthusiasm (Gellner 1992: 88). Of the two, however, the Jātrā is clearly the more significant as it involves the entire community and lasts much longer. At the Jātrā, if at no other festival, the citizens of Lalitpur must invite their married-out women and their families (*samji khalaḥ mhyay macā*) for a feast. The celebration of Mohani (Dashaĩ, Np.) is on a level with the Jātrā in the importance given to invitations and feasting and the breadth of participation with the lineage group (*phuki khalaḥ*). Nevertheless, as it takes place largely in the confines of the home it does not have the same public feel as the Jātrā. Furthermore, it is at the Jātrā that the Jyāpu Farmers of Lalitpur (Maharjans and Dãgols) traditionally invite their new sons-in-law to stay at their home for four days (Gellner 1991: 119). Because I consider the Jātrā to be worthy of special examination, I devote the entire Chapter 10 to it.

At what point does one jump on the roundabout of Lalitpur's annual cycle of festivals? In a sense this can be quite an arbitrary decision. Levy (1990: Ch. 13) has chosen to enter it at the point of the New Year of the Nepāl Samvat calendar. It is true that the start of the formal calendar year does carry with it a real sense of a new beginning. Gellner, on the other hand chooses to begin his survey in the spring with the bathing of Karunāmaya on Caulāgā 1 (Vaishākh-*krishna pratipada*) (1992: 215). I believe, however, that entering the lunar year at the beginning of the inauspicious period of Caturmāsa has certain advantages. The first advantage is that this is the way locals approach the calendar: the first major festival one arrives at in this way is Gathā̃ Mugaḥ, which locals, in fact, designate the first festival of the year. The second is that, at this time, in a way more concrete and raw than at the formal New Year, there is a deep sense of the redawning of life after a period of much uncertainty and anxiety, as Marc Gaborieau (1982) has demonstrated in the Parbatiyā ('Indo-Nepalese') context. The period from Sithi Nakhaḥ to Gathā̃ Mugaḥ is, as I will demonstrate, one of deep disorder. The festivals that follow it have one grand purpose: to restore order to the city. Although there is overlap it may help to conceive this period of renewal in two parts: first the restoration of city space and second the restoration of the society that inhabits that space. I will come to the second part in the next chapter. Here I will describe the festivals of the first part. The beginning of Caturmāsa falls within the lunar month of Dillā. But before I jump on the roundabout and examine its parts, I must step back and view the whole at one glance. How does one view the whole? What questions must one ask in order to approach a general understanding?

7.4. Approaching the festivals

Why do Newars, or anyone for that matter, celebrate festivals? Most Newars would answer by saying that it is what they have always done. Rarely does one ask why, or for what purpose, the festival was instituted or developed. But I will attempt to address this question repeatedly as we advance through the festive year.

Gérard Toffin has emphasized that communal festivals are of particular relevance to Newar society, for 'they often correspond to a critical moment in the annual calendar...' (1987: 225):

> The festive ritual's first aim is to dramatize this critical moment and to repair the cosmic order. In other cases, communal festivals can be understood as a return to the primeval mythical time of the origins. They reenact the crucial transition between the chaotic condition of nature and the ordered state of culture. These ritual reenactments of the act of creation and foundation of settlements thus emphasize the cosmogonic renewal of the locality and of society. They entail a rejuvenation of the socio-cosmical order, a moment in danger. (Ibid.)

As I hope to show in the ongoing description and analysis, Toffin's comment hits the nail on the head. The festivals involve an interaction between the world of mortals, the social order, and the realm of deities, the cosmic order. In so doing a certain kind of order is established that, though it is annually corrupted, is reconstructed and displayed for all to see and take note. There is, then, an annual cycle to the festival routine, a cycle that is intimately related to the seasons.

It is very difficult to come up with a watertight typology of festivals as each household seems to throw up another variation on the theme and neighbours argue with each other over what the categories are anyway. Newars use the rather loose term *nakhaḥ* to label important festivals. The festivals in general are usually referred to as *nakhaḥ-cakhaḥ*. Sometimes people feel a need to try to distinguish between *nakhaḥ*s and *cakhaḥ*s but this is futile, as there is no such category as *cakhaḥ*. It is only used in the compound form with *nakhaḥ* as a sort of umbrella term for all such annual events. Each important annual event in which a *pujā* is offered is considered a *nakhaḥ*. In nearly all such events a feast (*nakhaḥtyā*) is eaten, to which one's married-out daughters and their children (*mhyay macā*) are invited. Often one's sisters' children and *their* children (*bhincā macā*) are also invited if the occasion is considered of sufficient importance. In Lalitpur, on two occasions (at least among the Pengu Daḥ), the husbands of one's daughters and sisters are also invited—Mohani and the Jātrā.

Events that are not considered *nakhaḥ* are often occasions for a procession (*jātrā*) or are simply not important to the individual. Such an occasion might be considered optional (*pharmās*). Others, such as Nāg Pancami and Sri Pancami, are not optional but are, nevertheless, not important enough to invite one's *mhyay macā*.[5]

7.5. The annual cycle of seasons

There are various ways of viewing the seasons as they occur in South Asia. The Western scientific perspective recognizes three: a cold, dry season lasting from around October to February, followed by a hot, dry season from around March to early June, followed by a hot, wet season (the 'monsoon') from late June to September. According to the ancient Hindu calendar, however, there are no less than six annual seasons.[6] These are based on lunar reckoning as follows:[7]

Vasanta:	from Māgh-*shukla*/Sillāthwa 5 (Sri Pancami)
Grishma:	from Caitra-*shukla*/Caulāthwa 5
Varsha:	from Jyesth-*shukla*/Tachalāthwa 5
Sharad:	from Shrāvan-*shukla*/Gũlāthwa 5 (Nāg Pancami)
Hemanta:	from Ashvin-*shukla*/Kaulāthwa 5
Shishir:	from Mārga-*shukla*/Thilāthwa 5

These six seasons have very little meaning for most Newars. Very few would even recognize them. It would seem that Newars generally distinguish only two seasons: the cold season (*cikulā*) that begins on Nag Pancami and the hot season (*barkhā*) that starts on Sri Pancami. The interesting thing about the way the seasons are marked is that to the visitor the season seems still to be in full swing just when the Newars observe a change to another. This seems to demonstrate a certain way of experiencing the climate. It is the *change* of the seasons (*mausum hilegu* or even sometimes *yuga hilegu*)[8] that is significant to the Newar. It may be still hot but there is a slight nip in the air so the cold season is beginning and should be marked in a public way by a festival and in a private way by the consumption of a certain special foodstuffs in the home. The coldest part of the year is still at its most intense but the air has a feeling of change so a new season is beginning. There may be snow on the surrounding hills in mid-February (as there was unusually in 1989) but it is considered the hot season nevertheless.[9] The great festivals, then, like their Vedic precursors, are tied to liminal points in the transition from one season to another and one year to another. 'They function,' Witzel puts it, '... as rites of passage of the year' (1997: 518). Now I come to the festivals themselves.

7.6. Dillā Pujā

The month of Dillā is Bhimsen's month. Every household will do a special *pujā* to Bhimsen (Bhindyaḥ) at his temple in Mangaḥ at least once during this month, with some visiting the temple every day. As Bhimsen is the husband of Draupadi, Krishna's younger sister, this is also a special month for the worship of Krishna.

7.7. Caturmāsya Vratarambhaḥ (Ashādh-*shukla*/Dillāthwa 11)

This July day, though not an important day as the festivals of Lalitpur go, is nevertheless the first day of the four-month period of Caturmāsa, the very important period of the year, in Vaishnavite reckoning, in which Vishnu is said to be sleeping. From this day onward the life of *shivamārgi* Newars is characterized by heightened devotion. Devotees take weekly trips to their favourite temples. Brahmans read the *Rāmayana* and *Mahābhārata* (especially *Bhagavad Gita*) texts. During this time also, Maharjans and others make regular visits to the image of Ganesh at Kwenā (Kwenādyaḥ or Jala Vinayaka) every Tuesday (Gellner 1992: 79).

Gellner reports that Caturmāsa corresponds to the ancient Indian rainy season (1992: 354, n.9). Diana Eck calls Caturmāsa the 'rainy season retreat' as, at this time, many *sannyasin*s settle down, rather than wander (1993: 261). The monsoon, she says, is known for its 'good sleeping weather' (ibid.). The whole of Caturmāsa is understood to be a period of disorder when demons are particularly threatening (Gellner 1992: 214-8). Caturmāsa, then, is not the season for auspicious life-cycle rites such as Marriage. In Lalitpur no weddings, or any other moveable life-cycle ritual, such as Loincloth Worship, will be performed (except perhaps on Kārttik-*shukla*/ Kachalāthwa 5 and 10).

In approaching this period, we will go first to look at an event that takes place, not at the beginning but right at the end—the Kati Pyākhã dance-dramas. The Kati Pyākhã, named after the month Kārttik during which they take place, constitutes a series of dances and dramas, performed on the platform (*dabu*) in front of the old palace in Mangaḥ that extend through the last week or so of the lunar month. Having been instituted by King Siddhi Narasimha Malla in the seventeenth century, the repertoire of this dance-drama was boosted by his son and grandson until it extended the full length of the month from Kati Punhi to Sakimilā Punhi (Wright 1993: 245). The dance-dramas fall into two categories: comic repertoire by the Bāthaḥ, the three jesters or clever fellows; and the dramatic god dances (*dyaḥ pyākhã*), in which deities wrestle with the forces of evil. Half a century ago the dance-drama fell on hard times and for a while was discontinued altogether. In recent years, however, the series has been revived and attracts great crowds of onlookers

The programme of the dance-drama is structured around this pivotal moment. Before the auspicious night, the Bāthaḥ act out their folk stories with slapstick tomfoolery.[10] They are followed by two *dyaḥ pyākhã:* The Art of War (Yuddha Kala) and the Goddess Dance (Devi Pyākhã). In the dance of the pivotal day itself (Kārttik-*shukla*/Kachalāthwa 11), Vishnu awakes and slays the demons Madhu/Kaitan freeing the world of their terror. The two final days are similar in that the central figure in each is an *avatār* of Vishnu—Vārāha, then Narasimha. In each, demons strut about the stage until the *avatār* makes his dramatic appearance and rids the earth of the evil being.

Levy asserts that, for Bhaktapur at least, Vishnu's sleep is not salient (1990: 438). Other major deities in the Hindu tradition also leave the world to sleep at various times and typically for four months. In Lalitpur, however, as I hope to show, Vishnu's sleep is a key concept in unlocking the festivals of the following months. I will come back to the Kati Pyākhã repeatedly as I explore the significance of Caturmāsa.

7.8. Tulasi Piye (Ashādh-*shukla*/Dillāthwa 12)

The day after the beginning of Caturmāsa *shivamārgi* Newars plant the herb basil (*tulasi*) in pots at their homes. This plant will then be worshipped as Vishnu each day throughout the four months until the thirteenth day of the lunar fortnight that ends the period (Kārttik-*shukla*/Kachalāthwa 13).[11]

7.9. Dillā Punhi/Guru Punhi (Ashādh-*shukla*/Dillāthwa 15)

This day, falling on the full moon of the month of Dillā, is a special day for the worship of, and the giving of gifts to, one's guru (Guru Pujā). Functions are held at schools. Within the memory of my informants this has never been an important event.

7.10. Dillā Cahre/Gathā̃ Mugaḥ (Shrāvan-*krishna*/Dillāgā 14)

We now arrive at the first major festival (*nakhaḥ*) of the year Dillā, or Gathā̃ Mugaḥ Cahre. The day begins with a special *pujā* to household deities that are normally worshipped in a more perfunctory manner on other days. The ritual food, *samay*, is offered to the deities.[12]

Each household would traditionally tie a bunch of straw, corn stalks, stinging nettles and some other creepers in a bundle. After *pujā* is offered to the 'head' of the effigy, it is lit and carried to each room where the smoke is understood to expel evil spirits (*bhut*/*pret*).[13] The bundle is then thrown at the Remains Deity (*chwāsā*, §6.1). On this day many households drive iron nails into the lintel of the main doorway to their house. Levy reports that some wear iron rings for days afterwards (Levy 1990: 519).

Traditionally the young men and children of the locality would gather at the *chwāsā* to bundle straw together to make an effigy of the demon Gathā̃ Mugaḥ (Ghantakarna, Skt. and Np., 'Bell Ears'; cf. Levy 1990: 518, Fig. 28).[14] The children would hold a string across the road and extort money from the drivers and cyclists who were unfortunate enough to pass that way. In the evening the children would then paint their faces and beg from door to door with a phallic representation of Gathā̃ Mugaḥ on a winnowing tray (*hāsā*; cf. ibid.: 522, Fig. 29). The day finishes with the removal from the city of the effigy of Gathā̃ Mugaḥ along a prescribed, centrifugal route (§5.6.1). Young people from Cāka Bahi would set fire to the head of the effigy and carry it southwards out of the city to the Priya Pukhu (Priya Pokhari) pond where it would be thrown.[15] On return, revellers would have to wash the face and bathe before entering the house, otherwise it was believed that demons would enter with them.

On this day also the Nasantya Dāphā Guthi does a special concluding *pujā* to Nāsadyaḥ. The significant fact here is that the *guthi* may have been playing all through the period from Sithi Nakhaḥ to today. This period of around seven weeks is a most significant period of the year. It is the busiest period of the season for the farmers who are heavily engaged in rice transplantation. It is also considered an inauspicious time. The heavy rains will normally have come and gastrointestinal diseases will be rife. As such, it is the one period of the year that all music groups are forbidden to play (Michaels 1987: 191) except, that is, for the Nasantya Dāphā Guthi. By contrast this group *must* play during this time. The worship of Karunāmaya is essential to ensure an abundant rice harvest. Now their duty is done and they can put away their instruments until the next cycle begins some months later.[16]

The festival of Gathā̃ Mugaḥ is the first major unit in a whole series of purification rituals that are done at this time as the heaviest period of rains gives way to the lighter and drawn out latter monsoon. Newars have a very clear concept of the trouble that is brought upon the city during the season of rice transplanting that finishes on this day.[17] The farmers have been hard at work in the fields. Inevitably they have brought dust and dirt into the house and into sacred urban space. With that dirt evil, in the form of malevolent spirits, has been brought into the city and into the house. As Gutschow and Basukala put it, 'During the period of growth and fertility, the town is stripped of the protection of the gods and, in a sense, is left exposed to evil spirits' (1987: 164).

The festival of Gathā̃ Mugaḥ, therefore, is the first ritual of expulsion. The evil spirits that are thought to be in the house need to be expelled by means of invoking them into the straw bundles. They are then burned at the *chwāsā* or destroyed and dragged out of the city to a more powerful ritual dumping ground outside the walls. The period of disorder can only be brought to an end if the evil spirits that have entered the city, and more significantly in this case, the house, are expelled or exorcized. This can be done by means of rituals that physically embody the spirits. It is only after this that they can be taken out of physical space. The festival of Gathā̃ Mugaḥ then, brings a partial restoration of the civic order (cf. Levy 1990: 521).

7.11. Gũlā Dharma (Shrāvan-*shukla*/Gũlāthwa 1–Bhādra-*krishna*/ Gũlāgā 15)

The month of Gũlā, falling roughly in August, is the most important month in the Newar Buddhist calendar.[18] Legend has it that the Buddha chose this month, known to be inauspicious with its high incidence of illness and suffering, because no other god would take it. The first day of this month, Gũlāthwa *pratipada* marks the beginning of the intensive daily worship of Buddha. Buddhists fast and read sacred texts. The festival is centred on the sacred Buddhist hilltop mound of Svayambhu to the west of Kathmandu, where many devotees go each morning of the month for worship. *Bhajan* groups such as the Gũlā Pāru Guthi (§6.2.3) meet at each monastery early in the morning and each evening to sing hymns of worship. Moreover, the month of Gũlā is a favourite one for women to do an Observance (*vrata*). During the month animal sacrifice is forbidden to all except those who butcher for a living.

The beginning of Gũlā also marks the start of the nightly processions (*bagi wanegu*) of *bājā̃ khalaḥ* associated with Nyaku Jātrā/Matayā (§7.18.1).

7.12. Nāg Pancami (Shrāvan-*shukla*/Gũlāthwa 5)

The second major event during Caturmāsa, Nāg Pancami, takes place just a few days after Gathā̃ Mugaḥ on the fifth day of the waxing lunar fortnight of the month of Gũlā. On this day the *nāga*s, serpent deities that are thought to inhabit the ground and especially wells, ponds and lakes, are worshipped. A newly hand-painted picture of the *nāga*s is pasted over the door of the main entrance to the house and *pujā* is offered. *Nāga* serpent deities are seen as having a protecting role for the house. They are propitiated at the digging of the foundations of a new house and are considered to have a malevolent streak if offended. Anderson retells a story of the killing of three baby *nāga*s in the field by a farmer (1988: 91-92). This led to the revenge of the mother *nāga* on the farmer and his family. The carnage was only halted as the last daughter of the family pacified her by offering milk. The cult of serpent worship is not limited to Nepal. Klostermaier (1990: 311) reports that Nāg Pancami is still quite popular in India, especially in the South, where many people regularly feed the cobras in the house with milk worshipping them as guardians. Eck reports that, in Banāras, Nāg Pancami is the most important festival of the ancient serpent deities (1993: 264). She writes that the monsoon has always been an important time to worship the snakes, as the water will often push them up into houses and courtyards. According to the *Garuda Purāna*, the worship of *nāga*s on Nāg Pancami brings peace and prosperity. The *Narad Purāna* says that if one offers cow's milk to the *nāga*s on this day he will be safe from snakebite the whole year (Deep 1999: 54).

Newars see this day as the beginning of the cold season in much the same way as they see Sri Pancami as the beginning of the hot season (§9.9). Although there is no special feast on this day, cows' milk must be drunk in order to protect from the rigours of the coming cold weather. To the visitor from cooler climes it strikes one as odd that this should be considered the beginning of the cold season. Temperatures still regularly reach 30°C (86°F) during the day and fall only slightly during the night. Newars, however, will don a light cardigan or switch to thickly woven clothing on this day. Formally, Nāg Pancami also heralds the beginning of the season of *sharad*, which, like all the official, textual seasons will last two months.

This festival constitutes a part of the overall process of reestablishing order out of the chaos, cosmic and physical, of the past two months. In this case the order that needs to be reestablished is literally foundational. The *nāga*s reside in the fields that have been worked over during the rice-planting season and it may be that some *nāga*s have been killed or otherwise offended. So they need to be placated in order that their malignant aspect should be repressed. Also they are in the water through which gastrointestinal diseases are spread. The disorder brought about by the rains and the necessary disturbance to the realm of the *nāga*s needs to be overcome. This is accomplished through *pujā*.

7.13. Yala Pancadān (Shrāvan-*shukla*/Gũlāthwa 8)

On this, the auspicious Eighth day (*ashtami*) of the lunar fortnight, Buddhists give alms to the monastic community (Samgha) of Shākyas and Vajrācāryas.[19] Traditionally, members of the Samgha visit public shelters in the localities where local people offer them unhusked rice, husked rice, lentil seeds, wheat and salt.[20] Locke reports that these gifts are given in honour of a visit of Dipankara Buddha which, according to tradition took place on this day (1980: 234).[21] On this day, as has already been observed, the Tamvaḥ Kwaḥ lineage visits its own Tantric shrine at Kwā Bāhāḥ to do *pujā* (§2.6.1).

7.14. Bahidyaḥ Bwayegu (Shrāvan-*shukla*/Gũlāthwa 12—Bhādra-*krishna*/Gũlāgā 5)

During this roughly eight-day period Buddhists visit monasteries to view images of Buddha. Locke reports that it used to be the custom to display deities in monasteries throughout the month of Gũlā but that now it has been reduced to four days, or even one day, because of the theft of images (1980: 235).

7.15. Gũ Punhi (Shrāvan-*shukla*/Gũlāthwa 15)

The festival of the full moon of Gũlā, Gũ Punhi (Janai Purnimā or Rakshā Bandhān, Np.), important to *shivamārgi*s across South Asia actually begins the day before the full moon day (Gũlāthwa 14).[22] On this day of preparation,

Levy reports, Newar Brahmans, in parallel with Brahmans throughout South Asia eat only once, bathe and, traditionally, have their head shaved (1990: 441; cf. Klostermaier 1990: 309).[23] This annual purification ritual is in anticipation of the festival of the following day and those that follow in quick succession thereafter. That evening also, at Konti the Nava Bājā ensemble performs the first in a series of four concerts in the precincts of the Kumbheshvara temple.

In the morning, the Rājopādhyāya Brahmans bathe in the river and change their sacred thread in a ceremony that reestablishes their sacred authority (Levy 1990: 441). Those who act as domestic priests then visit their patrons' houses and, muttering mantras, tie thread (*gũha puca*) on their patrons' wrist. Various items are wrapped in a small piece of red and gold cloth (*asan*) and tied to the wrist by means of the thread.[24] This is widely understood to bring security to the wearer. One Brahman informant explained the need for security in ecological terms the early monsoon with its combination of heat alternating with rain being a prime cause of illness. Normally the thread is only removed at Lakshmi Pujā, some two or three months later, when it is tied to the tail of a cow, but some are not bothered if it comes off before.[25] High caste *shivamārgis* (Parbatiyā Brahmans and Chetris, and Newar Brahmans, and some Shresthas) also change their sacred thread (*jonā*) on this day.

In Lalitpur, the focus of the festival is the temple to Shiva at Kumbheshvāra. In a grand *melā* thousands of devotees throng the precincts of this important temple from early in the morning. Dozens of Parbatiyā Brahman priests line the precincts ready to tie the thread on the wrist of the devotees, many of which have travelled from outside the city for the festival. Further afield, crowds flock to the important valley Buddhist religious centre of Svayambhu.[26] At Kumbheshvara, worshippers offer *pujā* to the Shiva *linga* in the main temple and receive *prasād* from the priests in form of vermilion (*sinha*) and a sprinkling of water. Then, on the northern side of the precincts, devotees line up to do *pujā* to a special gilt sheath (*kosa*, *kavaca*) of spiralled serpents (*nāgas*) crowned with a *purna kalasha.* This sheath has been mounted on the main Shiva *linga* throughout the previous month. At midnight it is removed and mounted on a platform in the middle of a pond or tank where it remains for twenty-four hours. The tank, it is said is fed by the waters of the Goshaĩkunda lakes way to the north in the Jugal Himāl. Men and boys plunge into the waters from the *ghāts* and surrounding walls and enjoy what is clearly a lot more than a token ritual bathing.[27]

Back in their homes, local Newars prepare leaves with a mixture of various foodstuffs for the ritual of Feeding the Frogs (*byăca bwa*). Pieces of sweets, beans, radish, flower petals, and small rice cakes (*gwajā*) are placed on the leaf and mounted at a point on the outside of the house to feed the frogs. Anderson says that this is observed mostly by farming communities (1988: 98), but in fact conservative Newars of many castes participate. Frogs are considered auspicious creatures as it is said that they invite the monsoon rains with their croaking. The Feeding of the Frogs is in acknowledgement of the part they have played in bringing a hitherto successful monsoon season and a supplication that their work would not cease too soon. Furthermore, Levy reports that farmers regard frogs as having a protective influence from malevolent spirits on their fields (1990: 441).

Today and on the days immediately following, a special soupy dish (*kwāti*) is eaten.[28] Newars attest to the health-giving properties of this nine-bean dish especially regarding it as efficacious against intestinal diseases. 'This is scientifically proven to be profitable to one's health', a Tāmrakār man asserted. 'It breaks the mosquito's leg,' said another. Some people add *lalica* to the soup. This grass-type plant is found in the 'jungle' and they say that if you eat it, it causes *baula*, a sort of temporary madness which is manifested in the funny costumed groups that process as part of Sā Pāru and Matayā on the days immediately following. Perhaps it is this madness that lends a sort of legitimacy to those who criticize the authorities as, on this day and the days immediately following, satirical newspapers are produced and sold in the streets.[29]

How do we approach an understanding of this important event? Dil Mohan Tamrakar recounted to me the following myth:

> Once there was a king called Balidev who was powerful in *dharma.* At that time the kingdom was rich. By his *dharma* the acts of the earthly king shook the throne of the heavenly king, Indra. Indra sent his servant (Narad) to earth to discover why this was happening. He discovered that it was Balidev's *dharma shakti* that was causing it and returned to Indra to report this. Indra went to visit Nārāyana in *vaikuntha* to ask for his rescue. Nārāyana told him that he would save him from this calamity and Indra returned home. So Nārāyana took on the form of a Brahman and came to earth. He wandered about begging for alms. He came to Balidev and begged him for alms. Balidev, being a rich king, replied, 'Ask whatever you want and it will be given you'. Nārāyana then asked him to allow him to take three steps. Balidev, still not aware of his real identity, granted him this request, thinking that he could not get far with only three steps. But Nārāyana reverted to his real form. He then went back to heaven with one step and with his second step covered the earth. Then he asked Balidev, 'Where should I put my third step?' Balidev then told Nārāyana to step on his head, which he did. Balidev went down. But he asked Nārāyana if he might visit *vaikuntha* each year. This he does on Gũ Punhi wearing his gold bracelets. So that is why we wear a yellow thread bracelet on this day because it represents gold.

There are three main characters in this story—Balidev, the human king; Indra, the god of rain and king of the gods; and Vishnu/Nārāyana who takes the form of a Brahman in order to deceive Balidev. Balidev is growing more and more powerful by his *dharma.* This was such that the proper relationship between men and gods was in danger of being inverted. The king of men was threatening the king of the gods. Indra is powerless to remedy the situation and so has to appeal for help to a greater god, Nārāyana. Nārāyana takes on the form of a Brahman, who I have noted, would have just gone through a purification ritual. He comes to Balidev and deceives him into granting him three wishes. Nārāyana takes advantage of this and puts Balidev in his place. The kingdom of the gods is secure for another year. The connection of man to heaven, however, is not completely severed. He may have access to Nārāyana in his realm once a year, by the leave of the great god himself.

To come back to the festival, this event is clearly a ritual of protection. A Brahman must tie on the thread because Nārāyana himself appeared as a Brahman. He alone can give protection from the malevolent forces that are so threatening at this time of year. The thread may be removed at Yẽnyaḥ after order has been partially reestablished with the restoration of the king's authority (§8.5), or on Lakshmi Pujā when order has been completely renewed (§8.10.3).

7.16. Sā Pāru (Bhādra-*krishna*/Gũlāgā 1)

The following day, Sā Pāru (Gai Jātrā, Np.) is another major event in the annual cycle of Newar festivals and is an occasion of Valley-wide importance. In a shadow of the grand carnival of Bhaktapur, however, only a minority of Lalitpur's inhabitants participates in her procession. As in that most Hindu of the Newar cities, only *shivamārgi*s participate.[30] As most Lalitpurians are *buddhamārgi*, however, the Sā Pāru jātrā is a much more low key event.

The occasion begins, like many Newar festivals, with a special *pujā* in the homes. Today as on the previous day, the special bean soup, *kwāti*, is eaten as part of the meal. For many Lalitpurians, including *shivamārgi*s, this is the extent of their participation in any given year. For those who have lost a relative since the last Sā Pāru, however, the festival takes on great importance. The morning will be spent in preparation for the procession later in the day. The Citrakār may visit to paint cow masks for those who will be performing the bovine impersonation (Toffin 1995b: 241).

The festival as a city event begins with a special *pujā* to Krishna conducted by Rājopādhyāya Brahmans at his temple in Mangaḥ.[31] A *pujā* is then offered to the Krishna *bandhu*. Children dressed in brightly coloured ceremonial outfits play this group of deities, Krishna, Rukhmani, Satyabhama and Balabhadra, and their attendants.[32] After the initiatory *pujā*, the Krishna *bandhu* slowly moves out and on to the main road in front of the temple. A long white cotton sheet is unrolled onto the road along which the group will process. At this point devotees who have lost a family member during the past year may present an optional offering of sweets, fruit and flowers to the Krishna *bandhu* group with the help of their domestic priest. The families of the boys and girls who comprise the group keep these offerings.

Around noon the participants form a procession and begin to move out along the centripetal *pradakshinapātha*. A column of brightly dressed and heavily made-up young Brahman girls follows two hired men carrying tall, decorated cloth-covered poles.[33] After this follow small groups of devotees who have lost a family member in the preceding year. Unlike the hundreds of groups that process through the streets of Bhaktapur on this day, the Sā Pāru procession of Lalitpur is joined by a fraction of that number. Some groups process with a live cow. Others have a picture attached to a child's head or chest. A large ceremonial umbrella covers each group. Some groups push a decorated trolley with Hindustani instruments—*tabala* and harmonium. Others play flute or violin. Men walk with the trolley singing Newar *bhajan*s translated from the Rāmayana. As they proceed these groups also give out Sā Pāru *dān*—little packets of cucumber, *pāsi* (Nepalese pear), sweets (*mari*), and pomegranate (*bãsi*). Each participating family joins the procession at the nearest point to their homes. Finally, after all the participating groups the Krishna *bandhu* takes up the rear.[34]

In Sā Pāru devotees get an opportunity to accrue merit for the deceased. Participants are keen to explain that those who have died go straight to heaven (*svarga*) through the merit of their involvement. The giving of *dān* is not so unambiguous. Givers and takers alike do not usually like to admit that there is any problem with the gift. In the north Indian context, however, gift giving is clearly seen as problematic (Parry 1986; Raheja 1988a). Those that receive *dān* are helping to remove the pollution caused by the death in the family. Gellner discusses the relevance of the 'Parry-Raheja model' for the Newar context (1992: 119-24). He admits that sometimes *dān* may be understood to carry sin (*pāp*) or inauspiciousness (*ashubh*, *ashānti*, *mabhĩgu*) but that such is not the only opinion. Furthermore, there are methods of preventing any unwanted transfer such as the reciting of an appropriate verse. He concludes that the differences with north India may be due in part because of the presence of Buddhism. In the context of Sā Paru, however, with its clear association with death the gift must surely be inauspicious. This is often not understood by the receivers who appear to accept the *dān* with few qualms. The givers of the *dān*, however, acknowledge that it carries an inauspicious connotation and would not accept it themselves. In 2001 Dil Mohan Tamrakar attempted to give *dān* to the Brahman *pujāri*s who conducted the four-hour long *pujā* at his expense. They refused to accept the gift, however. The foodstuff was divided up. Some was used in a *pujā* to Bāl Kumāri at Cāka Bahi and distributed as *prasād* to the worshippers (the local *bājā khalaḥ*)—the new status being deemed harmless. The Mhāy Nāyaḥ took the rest to Pashupatināth where it was distributed to *sannyasin*s and others who were glad of the good food.

This festival would seem to be one that was instituted, as a copy of the great festival of Bhaktapur, during the seventeenth century. The evidence for this conclusion comes first and foremost in the route taken by the procession. The centripetal *pradakshinapātha*, as we have seen (§5.6.3) seems to have been established by the great Malla Kings Siddhi Narasimha Malla and his son Sri Nivas once they had begun their ambitious program of palace and temple building in the central locality of Mangaḥ. The association of the festival with the great central Krishna temple (built in 1637 CE) bolsters this argument.[35] In the days following Sā Pāru a number of other processions follow this same route.

7.17. Bāhāḥ Pujā (Bhādra-*krishna*/Gũlāgā 1)

On the same day that the *shivamārgi*s are celebrating Sā Pāru, the *buddhamārgi*s of the city celebrate the festival of the monasteries, Bāhāḥ Pujā. Each monastery has its own festivities in connection with the worship of the various images of that institution and the reading of sacred texts such as the Perfection of Wisdom (Prajñā Pāramitā) (Gellner 2001: Ch.7). The significance of this festival to the city as a whole, however, is that a procession forms to visit each of the eighteen main monasteries and four *stupa*s.[36] A *dhāḥ bājā* ensemble, accompanied by a handful of Damai musicians, heads the procession (§6.2.6). After the ensemble, priests lead the devotees in their worship. Hundreds of women, mostly from the *Bāhāḥ*s themselves, often in groups with matching traditional dress, process with trays and baskets of *pujā* materials to offer at each shrine on the route. The entire *pujā* takes about six or seven hours to complete. During the procession the devotees have to cross the line of the Sā Pāru procession at Keshav Nārāyana Cok to offer *pujā* at the former site of Haḥ Bāhāḥ (§5.6.3).

7.18. Nyaku Jātrā/Matayā (Bhādra-*krishna*/Gũlāgā 2)

The high point of this greatest of all Buddhist months is the festival of Matayā, which follows the day after Bājāḥ Pujā. The festival attracts more involvement than any other in Lalitpur except perhaps for the Jātrā which, while perhaps not involving so many people together in one event, includes *shivamārgi*s as well as *buddhamārgi*s and extends over a much longer period. Nyaku Jātrā/Matayā comprises a set of events that culminate in the great procession of this second day of the waning lunar fortnight (Gũlāgā 2).

7.18.1. Preparatory rituals—Bagi Wanegu

Preparation for Matayā begins on the first day of the month (Shrāvan-*shukla*/ Gũlāthwa 1) on which, just after midnight, a procession forms in the locality that is in charge of the festival for that year.[37] Instruments are played and a crowd of hundreds of folk from the immediate locality and beyond gathers together to join the procession. This procession, Bagi Wanegu ('to go on *bagi*'), is the first of a series of occasions in which the men of the organizing locality display the repertoire of the *dhāḥ bājā* and associated instruments of the Nava Bājā, which they have been learning for some months. On this and the following few nights the Nava Bājā ensembles process through the streets and lanes of Lalitpur following closely the path of the officiating Vajrācārya priest to each and every public or private Buddhist shrine of the city (Plate 12).[38] The most significant feature of this procession is the blowing of the buffalo horns (*nyaku*) in each lane and at every corner and temple. Men and women walk in between these groups and do *pujā* to the votive shrines (*cibhāḥ*) and other deities that lie along the path by casting husked rice, vermilion and coins as they pass. In doing so they prepare the path for the later, much grander, procession of thousands of devotees to take place a fortnight later on the actual day of Matayā. As one informant put it: 'They have to go out at night at this time to prepare the path for Matayā. There are many lanes and people will get lost if we do not do this. There is a lot of disturbance. This ritual makes it better.'

7.18.2. Matayā

The high point of the festival is the actual procession of Matayā, which takes place on the second day of the dark half of Gũlā. Many thousands of devotees (perhaps ten times the number that participated in Sā Pāru the day before) gather at dawn at the same starting place that the Bagi Wanegu procession began. Today they must walk often bare-footed and fasting, in procession around all four Ashoka *stupa*s and past each of the 1,400 votive shrines of Lalitpur. The procession takes all day with the devotees following the precisely described route as already prepared, so to speak, by the *nyaku* horns and their accompanists, two weeks beforehand (Gutschow 1982: 170, Map 190).

Plate 12. Haugaḥ *dhāḥ bājā khalaḥ* on Bagi Wanegu with two *muhāli* players.

Inhabitants of Lalitpur are obliged to participate if they have lost a relative during the past year. Some *shivamārgis*, such as the Tāmrakārs, participate in Matayā even though they have already done their part in Sā Pāru the previous day.[39] Those who are particularly going through austerities for the merit of their deceased loved ones wear sacking over their near-naked bodies to protect them as the prostrate themselves before each shrine that they visit. The offering of lamps to Buddha is to signify his enlightenment. According to legend, while Shākyamuni Buddha was in deep penance to attain Nirvana the Māras disguised themselves as demons and damsels in order to corrupt him. He overcame the temptation and as a result became Buddha. Then the Māras came to confess their sins to Buddha and worshipped him (Deep 1995).

In spite of the seriousness of the occasion, being as it is associated with death and merit making, the event has a strongly festive, even carnival atmosphere in common with the celebration of Sā Pāru in Bhaktapur the previous day (cf. Levy 1990: 594ff.). Groups of friends participate in a common uniform Maharjan women in traditional *hāku pātāsi* dress; men in traditional *daura suruwāl* and *dhākā*-weave cap (*tapli*; *topi*, Np.); girls wear matching dresses. Some groups of men dress up as demons or ghosts (*lakhe*) or wild animals such as monkeys and lions.

7.18.3. Nyaku Jātrā

The other major event of the day is the procession of Nyaku Jātrā. In a manner almost independent of the great procession going on around all the Buddhist shrines, the Nava Bājã ensemble processes along the centripetal *pradakshinapātha* stopping at each of the temples en route. The participants of Nyaku Jātrā, identical to those who walked the Matayā route in the preparatory procession of Bagi Wanegu a fortnight before are drawn from the inhabitants of the locality that is hosting the festival for that year. Led by the *dhāḥ bājã* ensemble, as before, the procession moves off, in a relaxed manner, in the late morning after doing *pujā* to Nāsadyaḥ, the patron deity of musicians.[40] As with the Bagi Wanegu procession the most important instrument in Nyaku Jātrā is the *nyaku* buffalo horn. It is believed that when the *nyaku* horn is sounded the spirits of the dead gain merit and peace for their next life.

The highlight of the Nyaku Jātrā is the performance of the Nine Instruments (Nava Bājã). No matter from where the procession begins, the Nava Bājã always perform in front of the Keshav Nārāyana Cok of the old Malla palace below the Golden Window (*lũjhyāḥ*). The ensemble arranges itself in front of the Golden Window with the gurus sitting in front directing the proceedings. A crowd gathers and the three-hour programme begins. The performance of the Nine Instruments (today there are usually over sixteen or so) involves a succession of solo and duo performances interspersed by the playing of the *dhāḥ bājã* which joins in with each as a sort of chorus (Plate 13). Each performance ends with the playing of the *nyaku* horns.[41] After the performance, the procession moves on and finally completes the circuit late in the evening.[42]

7.18.4. Concluding rituals—Matayā Ganesh Pujā and Buddhabārdyaḥ Wanegu

The final events in the Nyaku Jātrā/Matayā series are the Matayā Ganesh Pujā and Buddhabārdyaḥ Wanegu.[43] The date for these varies as they are always held on the first Tuesday and Wednesday after Matayā.

The Matayā Ganesh Pujā involves a procession of devotees drawn mostly from the locality that has sponsored Matayā that year. Gathering together in their *twaḥ* in the afternoon, groups of local women, dressed as for Matayā in matching saris or *hāku patāsi*, line up with baskets of *pujā* materials to offer to all the shrines of Ganesh along the centripetal procession route. Each image of Ganesh is presented with a huge leaf plate, which is then piled high, with the various components that go to make up the ritual meal, *samay baji.* Leading the procession is the *dhāḥ bājā* with the Kāpāli playing the *muhāli* and the Damai playing their western wind instruments.[44] After the completion of the *pujā*, the procession hands over the responsibility for sponsoring the festival to the inhabitants of the next locality.

The next day all the participants of Matayā go on pilgrimage to Baregaon south of Lalitpur on the way to Godavari where they do *pujā* to Buddhabārdyaḥ ('Wednesday god'). The Matayā participants will have one more outing before they are done, on Yẽ Pancadān (Bhādra-*krishna*/Gũlāgā 13) when they

Plate 13. Haugaḥ *dhāḥ bājā khalaḥ* with Krishna Kapali on *muhāli* at I Bāhāḥ Bahi.

will make a pilgrimage to Svayambhunāth to offer alms to the Shākyas and Vajrācāryas of Kathmandu.[45]

7.18.5. Understanding Nyaku Jātrā/Matayā

Although, on the surface, Matayā and the twin procession of Nyaku Jātrā are about accruing merit for the deceased, these rituals would further seem to be meant to have a purifying effect on city space. The Matayā procession and that of Bagi Wanegu that precedes it are intended to reestablish the spatial order. The monsoon is still lashing the streets and houses. There is still the potential for disaster as the comment by Buddhi Raj Tamrakar in the epigraph makes clear.

In Nyaku Jātrā/Matayā the integrity of city space is reestablished through the procession of participants through the intricate maze of courtyards to visit each and every votive *cibhāḥ* and *stupa* in and around the city. The boundaries are secured again by the physical visiting of the four principal *stupa*s during the course of the procession. The centrality of the king in this festival is expressed in a number of ways. Like all the centripetal processions, that of Nyaku Jātrā passes right in front of the palace. Furthermore, the highlight of the procession is the performance of the Nava Bājā in front of the Golden Window. This window is without equal among all the resplendent windows of the palace. Its exquisitely carved gilt surround is pregnant with powerful symbols. Dating from Sri Nivas's reign (1660–1684), the Buddhist *bodhisattva*, Sristikārtri-lokeshvara ('Lokeshvara emitting all the gods'), a form of Karunāmaya, is depicted emitting all the gods. Forms of Vishnu above and his mount Garuda below frame the whole icon. When the king appeared at the window he would be framed as Vishnu also thus identifying the king and the god.

The integrity of the city is also demonstrated by the rotation of the responsibility for organizing the festival among the ten central localities. All the castes that constitute a *twaḥ* work together to make this event work. As I have already pointed out (§6.1) the integrity of the *twaḥ* acts as a break to the power of the caste. One may marry across localities within one's caste but alliances are prevented from becoming too powerful by the need to work with other castes in one's locality.

7.19. Narasimha Jātrā (Bhādra-*krishna*/Gũlāgā 5)

The next festival of this, the densest fortnight of festivals in the annual calendar, is the Narasimha Jātrā. The Narasimha Jātrā is run, and only participated in, by Lalitpur's Rājopādhyāya Brahmans.[46] As with Nyaku Jātrā/Matayā, the procession starts and ends at the point on the centripetal procession route belonging to the organizing lineage.

The festival begins with a *pujā* to Narasimha, the man/lion *avatar* of Vishnu. The lineage *thākāli* offers *pujā* to Narasimha played by a boy who takes the part for the day's festivities. Dressed in red and gold and wearing a mask, Narasimha is flanked by boys playing the goddesses Sarasvati and

Lakshmi. In addition *pujā* is offered to Prahlāda—the honoured devotee of Narasimha.[47]

When the *pujā* is complete the procession begins. At the front two Brahman men push a decorated trolley on which is mounted an amplified harmonium, *tabala* and microphone. Every few dozen yards they stop the trolley and sing Newar *bhajans*. Six pairs of girls follow in exactly the same manner as they do in Sā Pāru. The focus of the procession is the cast of deities played by the boys. Prahlāda comes first walking backwards, hands clasped in obeisance, followed by Narasimha, Sarasvati, and Lakshmi.[48] The Narasimha Jātrā, like those of Nyaku Jātrā and Sā Pāru, takes place around the centripetal procession route. As with the performance of the Nava Bājā a few days before, the Narasimha Jātrā stops for a while in front of the golden window of the palace before moving on and completing its circumambulation of the town centre.

7.20. Krishna Janmashtami (Bhādra-*krishna*/Gũlāgā 8)

This focal Krishna-cult event of the year takes place on the day that has traditionally been observed as Krishna's birthday. Worship of Krishna takes place with much enthusiasm at all Krishna temples and shrines throughout the Valley, as it does across South Asia (Eck 1993: 266).[49] In Lalitpur this is especially focused on the great Krishna temple in Mangaḥ, which has not just local but national significance. In fact, local people are often cool to the event viewing it as belonging much more to the Parbatiyā than to their own community. Krishna devotees from miles around throng the temple from the evening before to do *pujā.* The auspicious focal event is at midnight precisely, as this is the time Krishna was born in the *bandha griha* (the prison house) at Mathurā (Klostermaier 1990: 309). Worship continues all night and throughout much of the following day. In deference to Vaishnavite sensitivities, no animals are to be slaughtered on this day.

In Lalitpur, *pujā* also goes on at the Krishna temples in the locality of Nugaḥ and at the Kũḥchẽ *phālca* at Tangaḥ which later become the starting points for the Krishna Jātrā. Apart from worship taking place at these various shrines two citywide events deserve our attention—Krishna Pujā and Krishna Jātrā.

7.20.1. Krishna Pujā

Krishna Pujā, initiated only in the 1930s, involves the worship of all of the roughly 300 public Krishna images in Lalitpur.[50] The Krishna Pujā has a number of characteristics that are reminiscent of such gatherings in north India, the heartland of Krishna-*bhakti*. Large orange triangular flags with the Sanskrit symbol 'OM' and other *sloka*s bedeck the temples, some devotees attend in saffron, and Hindi devotional music is played over loud speakers. The attraction of large numbers of non-Newars, moreover, gives this event a very different feel to some of the other festivals that have been going on during the previous week.[51]

The procession begins about eight o'clock in the morning with *pujā* to local deities. An all-Kāpāli, Western-style *ben bājā̃* takes the lead, followed by Brahman priests and devotees. As at other such processions groups of women and children in matching dress, along with a few men, line up to give various offerings to the succession of Krishna images as they proceed (Plate 14). The total number of participants in the late 1990s was around 700–800. As ever a *dhimay bājā̃* group takes up the rear.

7.20.2. Krishna Jātrā

In the evening the second focal citywide event of the day takes place, Krishna Jātrā. Two images, one from Kũḥchẽ *phalcā* in Tangaḥ and the other from the Krishna *phalcā* in Nugaḥ, are carried in procession around the centripetal *pradakshinapātha*. Each of the processions is entirely independent.[52] At dusk the procession begins with the singing of hymns to Krishna in Newar by the local men accompanied by the *dhāḥ bājā̃*. Each image carried on a palanquin by the young men of the locality is preceded by the *dhāḥ bājā̃* ensemble of that place. They accompany the music of the Damai group (in past days these would have been Kāpāli *muhāli* players). Two Maharjans constituting the *dhimay bājā̃* take up the rear. The procession moves rapidly along the *pradakshinapātha* stopping to sing *bhajan*s every now and then and taking two hours to complete the course.

7.21. Bhimsen (Bhindyaḥ) Pujā and Jātrā (Bhādra-*krishna*/Gũlāgā 9)

Although Bhimsen (Bhindyaḥ) theoretically has the previous month of Dillā as his own, the city's major festival to this deity falls here in Gũlā.[53] In the morning thousands of devotees visit the various Bhimsen shrines to offer

Plate 14. Children dressed up for Krishna Pujā.

pujā. The focus for this worship is the temple in Mangaḥ where hundreds of devotees wait in line for their turn to offer not only vegetarian offerings but also chickens and chicken eggs as Bhimsen is one of the deities who receives offerings of blood. Hundreds of buffaloes, chickens and ducks are sacrificed here throughout the day. On this day, as on the previous day, two different processions take place: Bhimsen Pujā and Bhimsen Jātrā.

7.21.1. Bhimsen Pujā

In the morning hundreds of people flock to the starting point of the Bhimsen Pujā procession, which, like the processions it is modelled on, Krishna Pujā and, more fundamentally, Matayā, begins and ends at the locality whose turn it is to organize it. The procession is not very old at all, having been instituted by the residents of Haugaḥ in 1979. Unlike Matayā, no attempt is made to visit any of the private images of Bhimsen, as they are so ubiquitous it would be practically impossible, every business having a small shelf for *pujā* to this deity.

As in other such processions the women and girls of the turn-holding locality turn out in festive groups with matching traditional clothing. At the front of the procession walks the local *dhāḥ bājā* ensemble with Damai group. Following them, the men and women of the locality bring offerings to place before each shrine including foodstuffs to offer *samay baji.* Among the worshippers the *nagara bājā* ensemble walks and sings *bhajan*s to Bhimsen and Shiva among others. As usual, the *dhimay bājā* takes up the rear. The entire procession, circumambulating the city centre via the centripetal *pradakshinapātha*, takes three or four hours.[54]

7.21.2. Bhimsen Jātrā

In the evening the important Bhimsen Jātrā takes place.[55] Thousands of devotees throng the Palace Square and visit the shrine of Bhimsen upstairs in his temple at Mangaḥ. Inside the temple the air is stifling hot and thick with the sweet smoke of incense. Bells are rung and devotees take *prasād* from the temple god guardian (*dyaḥ pālā*). Outside also, as the evening progresses, hundreds of thousands of incense sticks are held aloft, creating a most intense aromatic atmosphere. Devotees exit the temple and visit the large brass portable image of Bhimsen, which is already mounted on his palanquin ready for the procession. A number of musical ensembles play and sing *bhajan*s around the square.[56] This festival belongs overwhelmingly to young men who, with great shouts from the crowd, eventually bend their inebriated shoulders to the carrying poles of the palanquin, and convey the heavy brass image around the city's centripetal *pradakshinapātha.*

7.22 Jugaḥ Cahre (Bhādra-*krishna*/Gũlāgā 14)

This minor pre-New Moon festival is marked again by the drinking of *kwāti* soup. It is said that this final imbibing now puts right any diseases that were not cured by the drinking of *kwāti* on Gũ Punhi.[57]

7.23. Bāya Khwā Swayegu (Bhādra-*krishna*/Gũlāgā 15)

The new moon day that completes this festival-packed month is the day for 'Seeing the Face' of one's father. On this *nakhaḥ* children across the country give gifts to their father. A special meal is eaten and the father gives them his blessing. Those who have recently lost their father must make a pilgrimage to the important Shiva temple at Gokarna on the north side of the Valley to do Ancestor Worship (*shrāddha*).[58] Thereafter, on successive father's days the bereaved son must give *dān* to his domestic priest.[59]

For the particular family, the day ceases to be a *nakhaḥ* on the death of the father. Married-out daughters will no longer visit their natal home on this day.

During the night Kāpāli men will tour the lanes playing the conch shell and making a racket in order to drive away evil spirits from the localities. In the morning they return to collect *dakshina.*

7.24. Gũlā Pāru (Bhādra-*shukla*/Yãlāthwa 1)

The celebrations of the month of Gũlā are finally brought to an end on the day after the new moon, Gũlā Pāru. Those who have been doing special worship of Buddha during the month eat a feast and celebrate the ending of the festival of Gũlā Dharma, in much the same way that Muslims celebrate the ending of the month of Ramadan.

7.25. Ritual and physical purification

We have seen that the period immediately following that of rice transplantation is chock full of festivals, most of which have a connection with purification. While purification is viewed largely in ritual terms, however, pollution is not

Plate 15. Many festivals provide happy entertainment for hard-working women.

merely ritual. There is a strong material view of dirt associated with rice planting. This perspective finds expression in the exegesis of illness and other kinds of misfortune. Traditionally, Newars have viewed illness to be caused by either or both of two groups of phenomena: the actions of malevolent beings (dangerous deities, ghosts or witches) and environmental conditions.

As we have already seen, a whole class of deity is considered dangerous. If they are offended they may retaliate. They must, therefore, be propitiated. As Slusser points out, it is the female deities that are responsible for such diseases as cholera, malaria and meningitis (1998: I, 328). Children's illnesses are particularly attributed to the *chwāsā Ajimā*—the Remains Deity (Nepali 1965: 335).

Up until a few decades ago the Valley was particularly susceptible to devastating outbreaks of smallpox (*taḥkai*). The disastrous epidemic at the end of the eighteenth century is particularly embedded in the collective consciousness of the people. It was in this epidemic that King Rana Bahadur Shah's favourite queen died and, in a desperate attempt to keep his son from catching the disease, the king tried to expel all the children from the Valley (Slusser 1998: I, 329). The ravages of the last epidemic of 1963–64 can still be seen, etched into the faces of its victims. Again, Ajimā was usually suspected to be the cause of these outbreaks. Later, when vaccination became readily available, as a child was inoculated, family members would take offerings to Ajimā or, in Lalitpur, to Sitalamai at Konti.

The chronicles and diaries of visitors to the Valley are replete with evidence of major epidemics. The traveller Si-tu Panchen (1700–1774 CE) describes such an epidemic, which was raging in the summertime (though not in the winter) of 1723 when he was visiting. Once stricken by the disease most people died within thirty hours. The king reported that on a single night during the rainy season over one hundred dead bodies had to be removed from the town (Lewis and Jamspal 1988: 199). The king also told his guest that this had gone on for three years and that two-thirds of the population had perished.

Cure for such illness is effected by the worship of the goddess who is considered to have brought the misfortune. Often Newars will also resort at such times to a traditional doctor (*vaidya*), a medium (*dyaḥ waimha*), or other practitioner (Gellner and Shrestha 1993; Gellner 1994). Sometimes a Citrakār is called for healing purposes. He will paint powerful symbols, such as lions, on a patient with a skin problem, for example (Toffin 1995b: 243).

It is clear that the monsoon with the period immediately preceding it, has always been the period with the highest incidence of illness. This is as true today as it has been in the past, although the spread of such epidemics and their impact has been much reduced with the advent of biomedicine. Nevertheless, strongly held beliefs about the causes and cure of illness continue. Only a generation ago many children were still dying in the Valley from diarrhoea because the traditional cure was to restrict fluids, which caused serious dehydration and death. This is still a problem today, especially in more remote parts of Nepal. Water, then, has been seen traditionally as a mixed blessing. Without it no one can live, no crops will grow and famine will follow. But with it comes disease. It is no wonder that the intake of water was considered bad for the child suffering from diarrhoea. Furthermore, there is a common conception that one will most likely become ill from getting wet. One Brahman informant told me stomach upsets are also attributed to the constant changing from wet to hot during the monsoon.

Water is not the only problem, however. Nepali reports that red clay is not supposed to be brought into the house during the whole month of Shrāvan (1965: 75). There is a conception, then, that the soil itself might cause disease during this time. Such are the environmental causes that are linked to the occurrence of disease.

The district hospital of Lalitpur, Patan Hospital, is located just a couple of hundred metres south of the old city walls in Lagankhel. Staffed by local and expatriate medical workers, the hospital functions not only to treat those who are referred by local doctors but also as a grand mall of outpatient clinics. With very low costs, the clinics serve especially the poorer sections of Lalitpur district's population, with over a thousand patients being seen on any given day. Raw numbers of outpatients are kept for each clinic.

It is possible from these statistics to plot a graph of epidemiology (the occurrence of illness) against time.[60] To do this, I selected six from the eighteen separate clinics for statistical analysis over the three successive years 2056–2059 VS (1999–2002 CE). The clinics that were left out were judged to be less likely to reveal any difference through the year, such as the Surgical Referral (SRC), and Antenatal (ANC) Clinics. The six clinics selected were the Female (FC), Male (MC), Medical Referral (MRC), Paediatric Referral (PRC), Dermatological (SKIN) and Children's (UFC) clinics. The results are set out in Figure 4.[61]

It is immediately apparent from the graph that illness does indeed follow a seasonal pattern. There is a steep climb in the graph as the hot season gets hotter and the peak is reached in the early monsoon month of Ashādh, falling off only gradually as the monsoon wears on.[62] The smaller peak at Mārga is readily explained as an anomaly due to the fall in numbers in the previous month with the hospital being closed for several days during both Mohani and Swanti, and many farmers being busily engaged in their fields at rice harvest.[63] It is not clear at this point why there should be a dip at Vaishākh. Indeed, the year 2056–57 VS recorded no such dip.[64]

If water is so strongly linked to the spread of disease why does the graph show an inexorable climb through the hot, dry season from Phāgun to Jyesth? Part of the answer to this is that water-borne diseases, multiplying in the hot weather, are spread largely through cross-contamination of the domestic

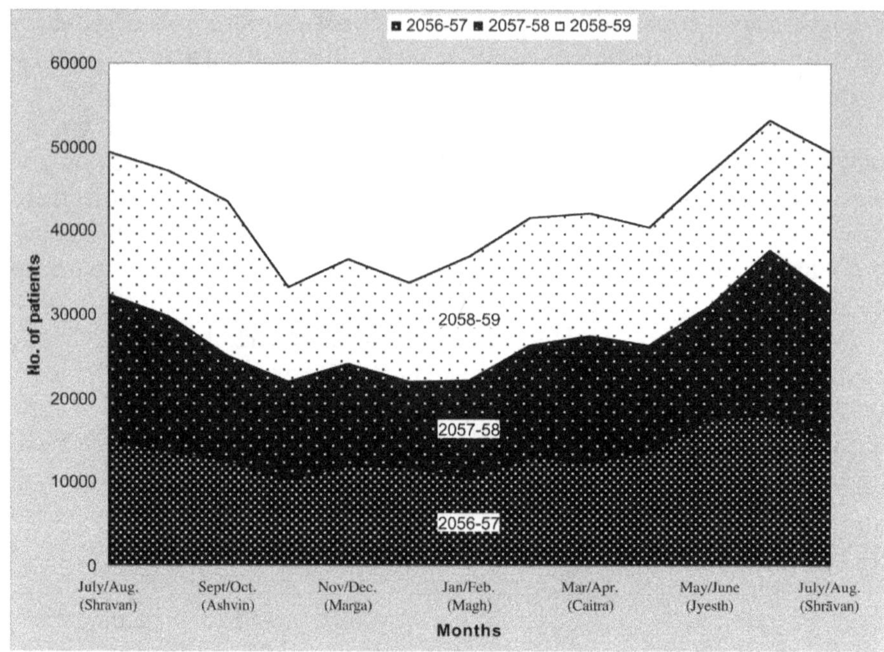

Figure 4. Selected outpatients at Patan Hospital.

water supply from the sewers. Prevention of cross-contamination is achieved in other countries by pumping the domestic supply at high pressure. In the Valley, however, as the pressure drops with the decline of water availability through the hot, dry season so cross-contamination increases.[65]

7.26. The story so far

We have come to a junction in our survey of the annual festivals of Lalitpur. The emphasis of the festivals so far has been on renewing city space. This spatial renewal has been effected largely by the ritual expulsion of the decay and corruption that had entered the city during the season of rice transplantation. That was a period during which the important distinction between the city and its environment, ordered space and unordered space, form and unfettered freedom had collapsed. By moving around city space deliberately and systematically in the various processions that followed the spatial order was once again reestablished. The city as the abode of men and gods has now been recovered. But that renewal is not yet complete. I will attempt to demonstrate how it is completed in the next chapter.

8. The Renewal of Order II: Restoring Civic Society

> Oh Lord: may there be mercy for us at the request of the speaker.
> Arise and make your appearance, O Nārāyanaju.
> Make it possible, O Nārāyanaju, for shri-Jaya Bhaskara Malla to obtain universal kingship.
>
> Song to Nārāyana composed by King Jaya Bhaskara Malla of Kathmandu (1700–1714), in Lienhard (1992 [1974]: 29)

8.1. Introduction

The month of Gũlā is now finished. The great centripetal processions that mark that month are complete. City space is, to a large extent, restored. The society that inhabits that space, however, has not yet been restored in quite the same measure. It has not yet regained its pre-monsoon order. Three great festivals, Yẽnyaḥ, Mohani and Swanti, complete the process that has already begun. All are situated, with a few minor ones filling the spaces, in the three months that follow.

8.2. Cathaḥ (Bhādra-*shukla*/Yãlāthwa 4)

The fourth day of the waxing lunar fortnight of Yãlā is Ganesh's birthday and the main day of the year for his worship (Klostermaier 1990: 309). Lalitpurians as others around South Asia visit their local Ganesh shrine to offer a special *pujā*, which must include the sweet *laddu* that Ganesh particularly enjoys.[1] People worship Ganesh on this day to ensure that no charge of thievery will come against them. Deep recounts the myth behind this festival (1999: 89).

It was a full moon day and Lord Ganesh was riding on his mount to a council of the gods. When the moon laughed at him and teased him for riding such a small animal Ganesh cursed the moon saying, 'From now on you will have no more light on my birthday and those who look at your face on this day are sure to turn out to be thieves'. The moon went to Lord Shiva and asked for his grace to overcome this curse. Shiva made an arrangement with his son, Ganesh, according to which the moon was to have his full light back once a month. The second part of the curse, however, was never rescinded.

In the evening then, soon after sunset, without looking at the moon, Newars offer a special *pujā* to it as Chataḥdyaḥ, the thief god. They then hide themselves indoors until they hear a dog cry. The moon, it is thought, has taken the dog and now it is safe to come out. Deep (ibid.: 87) reports that the gods are also suspect of thievery on this day and for this reason the windows of the Bhimsen temple at Mangaḥ are closed.

8.3. Kwakha Jā Biye (Bhādra-*shukla*/Yãlāthwa 5)

On this minor festival, women do a special *saptarshi*[2] *pujā* followed by a special offering of boiled rice to the crows.[3]

8.4. Kāyāshtami (Bhādra-*shukla*/Yãlāthwa 8)

This day marks the beginning of observances for the great autumnal festival of Mohani. Today Dashmahāvidya Pujā is performed in which a few hundred pilgrims process around the city to the Ten Great Knowledges (§5.4.2).[4]

Pilgrimage to the '12 *pitha*s' of the city, *yalasiba*, begins today and continues throughout the following lunar month (§5.4.2). This marks the beginning of activities associated with Yãlā Pujā, this month being especially important for the worship of the Goddess (Devi). For many residents this day has no significance and passes unnoticed.

Most Newars, including those of the Pengu Daḥ, visit the Power-Place in the morning, walking in a group playing the *damaru*. Each morning the group starts from the palace at Mangaḥ and returns after the *pujā*. Maharjans, on the other hand, visit in the evenings playing the *dhimay bājā*.[5] Each Power-Place is worshipped in strict order, the most important Power-Place for any given household coming last.

8.5. Yẽnyaḥ (Bhādra-*shukla*/Yãlāthwa 1 1—Ashvin-*krishna*/Yãlāgā 3)

The eight days surrounding the full moon of Yãlā constitute a set centred on the worship of Indra. Although an important festival in Lalitpur, Yẽnyaḥ (Indra Jātrā) has not attained the huge significance that it has in Kathmandu. Indra Jātrā in Kathmandu is the greatest of all that city's local festivals. Though it does not rival the duration of the chariot festival of Bũgadyaḥ in Lalitpur, the breadth of participation and the intensity with which it is celebrated is just as great.

8.5.1. Yẽnyaḥ Pujā

As in Kathmandu (Toffin 1992a: 73) and Bhaktapur (Levy 1990: 458), apart from some preparatory rituals, Lalitpur's festivities begin on the fourth day before full moon (Yãlāthwa 12) with the raising, in several localities around the city, of ceremonial poles called Yẽnyaḥdyaḥ.[6] One such is the Yẽnyaḥdyaḥ of Cāka Bahi, which is raised by the Maharjan Tangaḥ Mahālakshmi Guthi. The Yẽnyaḥdyaḥ is a two-metre high wooden pole with a bunch of leaves tied to it and a wooden mask of Indra attached to the top. The *guthi* does *pujā* to the mask and to the stakes that support the post on the day it is raised and on the full moon day, Yẽnyaḥ Punhi. The *thākāli* does the *pujā*. *Samay baji* is eaten and then offered to passers-by.

The important days of the festival are the central four: Yãlāthwa 13—Yãlāga 1. On these days the focus of the festival shifts around the city, clockwise from quarter to quarter, in the following sequence: Kwalkhu—Cyāsaḥ (Yãlāthwa 13), Tangaḥ—Guita (Yãlāthwa 14), Haugaḥ—Mangaḥ,

Bhimsensthān (Yãlāthwa 15), Ikhā—Patan Dhokā (Yãlāga 1). On the day of one's turn special *pujā* is offered to the gods of the locality. One of the most elaborate of these local celebrations takes place at Purnacandi, where twelve plates, each with a mountain of boiled rice (*bhujyāḥ*) and various other foodstuffs including the sweetbread *lākha mari*, are presented to the deity.

The day of one's turn, boiled rice is eaten as usual in the morning. In the evening, however, *samay baji* is eaten, the essential component of which is the lentil cake *waḥ*. Some inhabitants then hand out small leaf dishes of the *samay baji* to passers-by out in the street.

Dangerous gods, such as Bhairava and the various forms of the Goddess, the Eight Mother Goddesses (Ashtamātrika) and Ten Great Knowledges (Dashmahāvidya) are especially worshipped during this festival. Power-Places are worshipped locally. At Cāka Bahi a special *pujā* is done to Tripurasundāri (one of the Dashmahāvidya). In it a buffalo is sacrificed slowly to the deity with the animal's entrails being pulled out from its neck before it is dead. In the evening a brass crown is brought down from the monastery across the road by local Maharjans who place it on the stone and offer it *pujā*. Hymns are sung and a feast is eaten (Plate 16). Just down the road at Haugaḥ Bāhāḥ, in a ritual apparently unique in Lalitpur but common in Kathmandu, the Rājkarnikārs exhibit and worship a mask of Bhairava. A plate of *samay baji* is set before the mask for passers-by to partake of.

Yẽnyaḥ is a particularly important festival for artisans. On the day of their turn these craftsmen, such as the Pwāḥsyāḥ lineage of Tamvaḥ display their

Plate 16. Tāmrakār men of Cāka Bahi singing *bhajans*.

handicrafts in public courtyards. On the last day of the festival, Yãlāgā 3 (Ashvin-*krishna tritiya*), the images of Yẽnyaḥdyaḥ are taken down. This is also the day for the observance of Gatilā which I will describe shortly.

As an important *nakhaḥ*, Yẽnyaḥ is brought to completion with the calling of one's married-out daughters and their families for a feast (*nakhaḥtyā*), usually a few days after the festival itself. In Lalitpur Yẽnyaḥ is a unique festival in that it is the only one that may be legitimately observed with feasting during the year after there has been a death in the family and hence it is called locally the Death Festival (*si nakhaḥ*). The connection with death is even stronger in Kathmandu, where an important event during Yẽnyaḥ is the procession for the dead made by recently bereaved Buddhist Newar families on the fourth day (Toffin 1992a: 85).

8.5.2. Yẽnyaḥ as a royal festival

Bajracharya (1959) and Toffin (1992a) have both written on the celebration of Yẽnyaḥ in Kathmandu where, of all the Valley communities, it is celebrated with the most panache.[7] The central focal event of the festival is the raising and lowering of the huge *yaḥsī* pole in front of the old palace at Hanumān Dhokā, in a ritual analogous to that performed in Bhaktapur at Biskaḥ. A golden elephant, the mount of Indra, is placed at the foot of the *yaḥsī* symbolic of strength and kingship. To understand the *yaḥsī* and its link with kingship we have to look to Hindu tradition. Indra is the king of the gods and the 'prototype of sovereignty' (Toffin ibid.: 78). His strength is said to be prodigious. A similar royal ritual was performed in ancient India. In classical India the Indra festival was closely associated with theatrical performances in which the king appeared on stage. The *yaḥsī* spatially reinforces the central location of the palace in the city emphasizing the centrality of the king.[8]

According to local tradition the origins of the Indra Jātrā in Kathmandu go back to the creation of the city. Toffin demonstrates how central the place of the king is in this festival. This festival, therefore, enhances the existing Nepalese monarchy and also keeps alive the 'glorious past' of the Newars. Moreover, the festival is preceded by the demon dance (Lakhe Pyākhã) expressing the disorder that threatens the universe. The raising of the pole, then, may express the strength and authority of the king over disrupting forces. '… Indra Jātrā can be seen as a ritual of renewal of royal power, putting an end—at least temporarily—to anarchic elements and restoring the king's order' (ibid.: 82).

Why is Yẽnyaḥ in Lalitpur and Bhaktapur celebrated with less complexity than it is in Kathmandu? Levy suggests that some of the analogous events in Bhaktapur are transformed in meaning because they are not put in the context of a major integrative festival. 'Indra Jātrā in Kathmandu is the period in which the living goddess, Kumāri, makes her main public appearance, and establishes her relationship to the Gorkha king' (1990: 457). In Bhaktapur this happens during Mohani. In Lalitpur, likewise, Yẽnyaḥ does not have to fulfil the same set of requirements as it does in Kathmandu. One of the events that give Kathmandu's Indra Jātrā its complexity is the component of procession for the dead. Its equivalent in Lalitpur, as I have described (§7.18.1), has already taken place in the previous month so that element would be redundant in this festival. The participation of the Kumāri is also not necessary at this point in Lalitpur, as she has a series of outings during the Bũgadyaḥ Jātrā (§10.7.4).

Yẽnyaḥ, in Lalitpur, is more like an original Indra festival without the accretions that make it so important to Kathmandu. To understand it, then, I must repeat the salient features. The festival is nominally a *pujā* to Indra, the old Vedic king of the gods. It is apparent, however, that Indra does not take centre stage in this festival. He is there, in the form of the mask on the Yẽnyaḥdyaḥ pole, and receives worship each day of the celebration. But it is the two sets of dangerous deities, the Eight Mother Goddesses (Ashtamātrika) and the Ten Great Knowledges (Dashmahāvidya), with their consort Bhairava, who receive the greater attention. The relationship between Indra and the goddesses can be likened to that of the old, feeble king and his young swashbuckling musketeers. Indra, as I have already demonstrated (§7.15), is viewed as a weak, ineffective ruler. He is still sovereign. It is he who grants the rain to water the rice, which by now is reaching maturity. But there are evil forces at work, over which Indra is powerless. Nārāyana is still asleep. The goddess, Devi, alone is powerful enough to counter that evil. The cult of the goddess and her many manifestations, springs from this logic.

As I have already noted (§7.8), the second of the two god dances (*dyaḥ pyākhā̃*) of the great dance-drama sequence that plays during Kārttik (Kati Pyākhã) is the 'Goddess Dance' ('Devi Pyākhã'). This is always performed on the evening immediately preceding Haribodhini Ekadasi (Kachalāthwa 11), the day that Vishnu awakens from his four-month slumber. The Goddess Dance, a very entertaining drama involving both human and divine characters, begins with a slapstick comedy by vulgar Untouchable Fishermen (Dyaḥlā, played by Maharjans). The two men, ridiculously dressed in cloth hats and clothes with fish and frog motifs, swagger around the stage drunk, flinging fishing nets out to catch cloth fish that are teasingly cast towards them by the audience. They make lewd gestures and shout vulgarities at each other in a manner that would normally be considered offensive.

The Dyaḥlā dance is followed by that of the Kãwã, the skeletal demon who strikes fear into the heart of stouthearted men. He rushes about the stage, making ribald gestures and shouting obscenities at the audience who find it all very comic. After the Kãwã comes the Khya, the goblin with the lolling red tongue. He dances by standing on his head. The message is clear: things are awry, the world is in chaos. Untouchables, those ever-present reminders of another, unwelcome order, are unbridled, unrestrained in their behaviour. Demons wreak havoc in the city. Then the Devi dance begins. Bhairava,

Kumāri and Mahālakshmi enter the stage and, after a few movements sit to receive *pujā* from the hands of a Brahman priest. Thus worshipped, the three powerful deities, with energetic rushes and dynamic twirls, perform their show of strength. With lunging jabs and trenchant swipes of the sword they rid the earth of evil and restore the world to its proper order. The Devi Pyākhã of Lalitpur is equivalent to the more complex dance-drama of Bhaktapur, the Nine Durgas. As Levy reports, they function in exactly the same way: '...the Nine Durgas' *pyākhã* can be interpreted as being about the struggle between disorder and order, about what happens to individuals who violate order, and finally, about what has to be done to restore that order' (1990: 573).

Thus, the festival of Yẽnyaḥ is one more step on the road towards the renewal of the urban order. The handing out of leaf plates of *samay baji* to passers-by is another opportunity to pass off the accretions of evil that have plagued the household since the monsoon began with the giving of the inauspicious prestation (*dān*; §7.16).

In Lalitpur, just as it is in Kathmandu, the royal centre is also emphasized, though to a lesser extent. Two distinct phenomena bear this out. I have described how the *pujā* is performed in four parts of the city on different days. All four parts are not, however, sectors of the city. Three are. The third, on the full moon day itself is not. Though the main day for *pujā* revolves around the city in the customary clockwise direction, the centre of the city, which of course includes the palace, is separated out for the full moon day itself. This event, then, reestablishes the royal seat of power after the disintegration of the early monsoon.

The second phenomenon that emphasizes the royal nature of this festival is the fact that households in mourning are also expected to participate. There is a notion, seldom expressed, that the king must not be burdened by the sorrows of his subjects (§5.6.1). In this quintessential royal event, therefore everyone must participate and not dull the king's own festive pleasure.

8.6. Sixteen [Day] Ancestor Worship (*sohra shrāddha*, Ashvin-*krishna*/ Yãlāgā 1-15–*pitri pakshā*)

The waning lunar fortnight of Yãlā is the occasion for a special Ancestor Worship (*shrāddha*). It is believed that during this fortnight ancestors return to the houses of their descendants seeking worship and homage (Anderson 1977: 139). Each day hundreds of worshippers go to the temples, holy places, and sacred rivers and, in the Valley at least, especially to Pashupatināth to perform Ancestor Worship (*shrāddha*) to their departed ancestors, an event also observed in India (Eck 1993: 267).

During this period a male ancestor must be worshipped each day but the *shrāddha* is performed on the particular day (*tithi*) of the nearest common ancestor's death. The focal point of the *pujā*, as with other *shrāddha*s, is the formation and worship by the senior male of the household (*thākāli*) of rice balls (*pinda*s). On this occasion, however, a total of sixteen balls are worshipped in contrast to the normal three. During the ritual all ancestors, all other deceased relatives and those of the domestic priest, king and tenant farmer are remembered by name. On the ninth day (Mātri Navami) special ceremonies are enacted for the worship of female ancestors, especially deceased mothers. According to Anderson many men refrain from shaving and cutting of nails throughout the fortnight although it is only forbidden on the actual day (1988: 140). Others have their head shaved especially in preparation for the event.

Ideally this event is an occasion for the entire patrilineal clan, as well as the married-out daughters and their families, to come together. Many of these units still operate as a *guthi* (§6.2.3). As with other *shrāddha*s, the domestic priest is called to officiate. For those lineages that constitute a *guthi*, the *pujā* is followed by the eating of the ritual meal (*samay baji*) and later, the feast (*bhway*).

Sixteen [Day] Ancestor Worship is a preparatory ritual for the focal autumnal celebration of Mohani, which I shall look at shortly. The solidarity of the agnatic lineage is renewed by the corporate observation of this ritual. At least some Vajrācāryas and Shākyas did at one time celebrate this festival. Such self-consciously Buddhist *thar*s have since ceased to participate in line with the wider gradual 'de-Hinduizing' of their religion.

8.7. Gatilā (Ashvin-*krishna*/Yālāgā 3)

This day is special for the Observance (*vrata*) of the Buddhist deity, Vasundharā. A *pujā* is performed in each locality to Vasundharā, Kumāri, and Mahālakshmi in order to ensure a good harvest. As part of the ritual of this day, the Lalitpur Kumāri is worshipped at the Tantric shrine of her official residence by the elders of her monastery, Haḥ Bāhāḥ, flanked by paintings of Vasundharā and Mahālakshmi. In recent years a Vasundharā Pujā procession modelled after Matayā has been instituted.

8.8. Mohani (Ashvin-*shukla*/Kaulāthwa 1-15)

The waxing lunar fortnight of September/October is the occasion for the celebration of the most important festival of the autumn season and, in Lalitpur at least, of the waning half of the year.

Preparation for this festival has already taken place in the preceding fortnight with the worship of ancestors (§8.6). Furthermore, pilgrimage to the important set of twelve Power-Places has been going on since Kāyāshtami, three weeks previous. The festival of Mohani (Dashaĩ, Np.; Dashara, H.) is essentially focused around the patrilineal clan. Close patrilineal relatives (*syāḥ phuki*) are defined partially by their solidarity in the celebration of this event. Unlike the festival of Yẽnyaḥ, households in mourning do not participate. Their participation is effected vicariously, however, by the celebration of the ritual on their behalf by other caste-mates of a different, unpolluted lineage.

Local people believe that the autumnal Mohani was instituted as an alternative to its celebration in the spring. The vestige of that older, original Mohani is still observed but in a much attenuated form as I will describe in due course (§9.16). It is not clear why the festival was shifted to the autumn although Newars have some thoughts on this. One opinion is that it was moved from the spring because it is hot then and people do not much feel like eating a feast.

In parallel with other lineages of the city, the erstwhile royal lineage also celebrates Mohani. Today this is accomplished under the patronage of the Guthi Corporation. I will look at both how ordinary citizens celebrate the festival and how the rituals are performed in the old palace to get a feel for how the Malla kings used to follow it. As I hope to demonstrate, ordinary citizens do largely the same rituals as the king, though, as one would expect, with less grandeur. With this in mind, then, I shall take each day in turn and describe the activity around the palace's Mul Cok in Mangaḥ and the parallel activities in the homes of ordinary people.

8.8.1. Naḥlā Swãne (Ghatasthāpanā, Np.) (Ashvin-*shukla*/Kaulāthwa 1)

On this first morning of Mohani, the house is cleansed with the normal mixture of red clay and cow dung. Later, a mixture of barley (*taḥcwa*, Nw.) and corn (*kaḥni*, Nw.) seeds are sown by the *thākāli* in the Tantric god house or other special room set aside for this purpose. For the seedbed, sand is brought from the sacred Bāgmati River. In the past this was always collected at Shankamul but in recent years many go to Gujeshwari, up river from Pashupatināth where it is considered less polluted. A sacred flask (*kalasha* or *ghata*) is then consecrated, and having planted the seeds, the *thākāli* then does *pujā* to both *ghata* and seeds and takes *prasād* for him and all the other members of the lineage. The seedbed, resting in a clay pot or wooden box, is then covered, causing the barley shoots to grow up pale. The box or pot will not be opened until the tenth day.

Over at Mangaḥ the same mixture of seeds is sown in the Mohani temple of Taleju on the south side of the Mul Cok of the old palace by Rājopādhyāya priests, the chief of whom is the descendant of Siddhi Narasimha Malla's own domestic priest (*purohit*). As in the homes of ordinary residents, a sacred flask (*ghata*) is also established as Taleju in this room. This small temple will be the focus of worship throughout the festival.

Today also the special daily worship (*nitya pujā*) to blood-accepting deities begins. Apart from the Mother Goddesses, Bhimsen, Ganesh, and Bhairava are also offered special *pujā*, which, along with the normal daily worship articles, consist *samay baji* with the customary meat and alcohol. From today till the full moon, two weeks later, only pure foods will be eaten, chicken, tomato, onion, and garlic being among the foods avoided.

In the evening the first of a series of dance-dramas by the Gan Pyākhã dance troupe is performed. King Sri Nivas Malla established these dance-dramas in the seventeenth century.[9] Like the Nine Durgas dance troupe of Bhaktapur that figure prominently in Levy's *Mesocosm* (1990, Ch. 15), the Gan Pyākhã troupe comprises a group of dangerous deities,[10] played by young men in elaborate costumes and brightly painted masks.[11] The dancers of the Gan Pyākhã are all either Shākya or Vajrācārya.[12] Each has to remain in a state of purity throughout the period of the performances.[13]

The performance kicks off on the first evening with a simple *pujā* to the masks. The young men then don the masks for the first time and immediately the sound of aṇkle bells is heard as the dancers begin to shake under the influence of the deity. After a dance at the Nakaḥ Bahi platform in front of the monastery the troupe then moves slowly out and along the lane to Mangaḥ. During the dances the Panca Tāla Bājã accompanies the troupe.[14] On arrival at Mul Cok, to the tolling of the great Taleju bell, the troupe is given a ritual welcome by the chief Brahman *purohit*, following which they enter the courtyard and take their seats in a circle before the watching crowd.[15]

After a short *pujā* to the patron deity of music and dance, Nāsadyaḥ, the singing of *bhajan*s begins. Then four actors, playing the part of men,[16] enter, do a simple dance, and invite the deities to stand and receive *pujā* from their hands. The four human characters then dance in front of Bhairava. One of them takes out a scroll (the *hukum patra* of the king) and reads it aloud, giving notice to all that the king has done the *pujā.* After this the deities each dance in turn.[17] Upon returning to Nakaḥ Bahi late in the evening the musicians perform a short *pujā* to Nāsadyaḥ.

The following five days (Kaulāthwa 2-6) are the slow days of the festival.[18] The *ghata* and the growing shoots of barley and corn (*naḥlā*) are worshipped each day in homes across the city by the senior house female (*thākāli nakĩ*) or other woman. In the worship, instead of the normal offering of sound on a bell, the small twin-headed drum, the *damaru* is played.

Over at the Mohani room at Mul Cok, the chief Brahman *purohit* and his assistants carry out the same rituals that are performed in the homes. Furthermore, on each of these evenings the Gan Pyākhã troupe repeats the performance of the first day.

8.8.2. Swã Swãne (Ashvin-*shukla*/Kaulāthwa 7)

This is the first of the high days of the festival. In the local houses, once the normal daily Mohani *pujā* has been completed, the morning meal of boiled rice is eaten as usual. After this, the members of the household perform a ritual purification. All uneaten boiled rice is removed from the house, and the floors of the house are smeared with the usual mixture of red clay and cow dung. From this time on till the tenth day boiled rice will not be consumed except after redeeming it by adding sugar, milk or clarified butter (*ghyaḥ*).

At Mul Cok an important ritual is performed whereby, at the auspicious moment, the images of Taleju, that are normally ensconced in the Degutale and Bhavani temples, are worshipped and then carried down by the chief priest and his assistants and placed in a small room in the Mohani temple.[19] Along with the images of Taleju, the king's sword and shield are also carried to the Mohani temple and placed with the deities (Plate 17). Here they stay for the remainder of the festival. Once the images are established a sacrifice is offered to Taleju in the courtyard.[20]

That afternoon the Gan Pyākhã troupe arrives at Mul Cok. Today the dancers sit in a circle in the south-east corner of the courtyard, marking a transition from their performances inside the palace to those outside on the platform in front of the Cār Nārāyana temple opposite. After the usual simple programme that has been conducted over the past week the troupe performs seven more complex dances. At the close of this programme the troupe returns to Nakaḥ Bahi.

In the evening, in an almost completely unconnected ritual, the *swã swãne* (*phulpāti*, Np.) belonging to the present Shah dynasty arrives from Nuwakot in a 'recapitulation of the conquest of the Valley' (Gellner 2001: 76). This procession carries a ceremonial flask (*ghata*) and a palanquin (*dholi*, Np.) filled with flowers to each of the palaces of the former Mallas. The arrival of the procession to Kathmandu at Hanumān Dhokā is celebrated

Plate 17. A priest carries the image of Taleju Bhavani and the sword of Sri Nivas.

elaborately with military bands and a gun salute in the presence of the king and government ministers. The event in Lalitpur, not being the present capital city, is much simpler. Once at Puco, just outside the old city, the procession to Lalitpur is met by a group of men under the employ of the Guthi Corporation who escort the procession straight to Mul Cok.[21] On arrival at the Mul Cok the *ghata* and *dholi* are placed on a specially prepared area of the courtyard in front of the entrance to the 'Chetri Dashaĩ' room which is next door to the Mohani temple.[22]

Later that evening, the Gan Pyākhā troupe returns to Mangaḥ as before but on this occasion they perform on the platform opposite the palace. The reason for this change, as is readily explained by locals, is that 'Some days are for the king and others are for the people'. Later that night, at Mul Cok, the Butchers of Cyāsaḥ sacrifice a buffalo and three goats.[23]

8.8.3. Tāpā (Mahā Ashtami, Ashvin-*shukla*/Kaulāthwa 8)

On this day, the daily Mohani *pujā* is supplemented with a special *pujā* (*tāpā*) to a sorority of five deities in the form of five pots: Indrayāni, Brahmayani, Cāmundā, Rudrayani, and Vishnu Devi. Each pot contains one of the following liquids: water, powerful spirits (*aylaḥ*), homebrew beer (*thon*), red beer (*hyāū thon*), and *khay* (yoghurt mixed with oil and salt).[24] Later, many of Lalitpur's households will make a visit to the Kumāri temple at Ta Bāhāḥ to do a special Kumāri *pujā*. The sharing of the ritual meal (*samay baji*) follows this.[25] An important part of the celebration of Mohani, among Parbatiyā and Newar alike, is the slaughter of animals, particularly goats and ducks. Though many Newars and Parbatiyā sacrifice their animals on this day, most wait till the following day.

The focus for the city as a whole is again the Mul Cok in Mangaḥ. Here the Butchers from Cyāsaḥ sacrifice five buffaloes and five goats and, that evening, the Gan Pyākhā perform their programme of dance-drama on the platform as they did the day before.

In the evening the first of three feasts is consumed.[26] This feast is called the *kuchẽ bhway*, from *kul chẽ* (whole family) which shows that the meal is meant to be eaten in one's ancestral home. In this feast the *thākāli* is given a large quantity (two *mana*s)[27] of beaten rice on a banana leaf. Others are given a nominal measure of two *mana*s by stuffing paper into the measuring pot before charging it with beaten rice. During the feast, those who have made an animal sacrifice share the animal's head between the lineage elders (*sikāḥ bhu*) (Nepali 1965: 409).

Orthodox Hindus, Anderson tells us (1988: 148), fast all day in preparation for the Kālarātri (Black Night) in which hundreds of buffaloes, goats, sheep, and ducks are sacrificed at Mother Goddess temples around the Valley. Dozens of buffaloes and goats are slaughtered on this night in the Mul Cok.

8.8.4 Syāko Tyāko (Mahā Navami, Ashvin-*shukla*/Kaulāthwa 9)

For the Newars, at least, this is the main day for sacrificing to Durga and the Mother Goddesses. With the exception of Vajrācāryas, Shākyas, and others who are influenced by the doctrine of non-violence (*ahimsā*) so important to both Buddhists and Vaishnavites, most Newar homes offer sacrifices of goat and duck to Durga. This is accomplished by slitting the throat to allow blood to flow on to the image. Others simply lop off the head off the animal with a quick downward chop of the curved Nepalese knife (*khukuri*).

Sacrifice is also made to Durga to request her protection on motorbikes and cars for the coming year. Blood is directed onto the wheels and bumpers of the vehicles along with intoxicating spirits, flowers, rice, and vermilion. Those who want to participate but do not want to take life offer as alternatives duck or chicken eggs. Furthermore, *pujā* is offered by the house *thākāli* to Vishvakarma in the form of the household tools (*jāwāḥ*) which, in the case of Tāmrakārs, for instance, is in form of hammer, scales and weights.

On this day Power-Place Worship, which has been going on for some days now, takes on a different form: pilgrims go on procession around all twelve of Lalitpur's *pitha*s. On arrival back at home they share *samay baji.* In the evening, they eat a feast including, again for those who have sacrificed an animal, the sharing of the sacrificed head (*sikāḥ bhu*) by the lineage elders.

Over in Mul Cok, the Cyāsaḥ Butchers have returned to slaughter dozens of buffaloes, goats, ducks, and chickens as sacrifices to Taleju. The sacrifice is slow and made so that entrails are pulled out and blood is spurting out before the animal has died, as at Yẽnyaḥ (§8.5.1). Sugarcane and ginger are also offered. Here, in the evening, several different rituals are performed. The sacrifices to Taleju continue with the slaughter of five buffaloes and nine goats. The Gan Pyākhã troupe performs their programme of dance-drama on the platform in Mangaḥ as they did the day before. Later, a Vajrācārya priest from Du Bāhāḥ enters the courtyard and does a *pujā* to Taleju in preparation for the arrival of a group of small girls dressed as Kumāri.

Five men from the Guthi Corporation[28] walk along the road to Haḥ Bāhāḥ where the Lalitpur Kumāri is waiting, sitting in her shelter at the entrance to the monastery.[29] The chief Rājopādhyāya priest of Taleju is here, also dressed in a red shirt and white *doti.* A number of small girls are carried in by a relative and set down in a row on the side of the courtyard.[30] Each is dressed up like the Kumāri herself in red clothes and brass crown. These girls are potential Kumāris. When the incumbent Kumāris menstruates or has some other defect the next is chosen from among this group. This is done every year so that there is always a girl ready to take her place.

With the chief priest in the lead, the girls are taken into a secret room upstairs at the back of the monastery. Here they are shown the heads of the buffaloes that were killed that afternoon in Mul Cok. The girls are watched as to their reaction; those that cry or are otherwise distressed are deemed unworthy candidates. From Haḥ Bāhāḥ they are taken in procession to Mul Cok preceded by two Kāpālis playing the *muhāli.* On arrival they are given a ritual welcome and led into the courtyard by the Bāya and past the bodies of several decapitated buffaloes that had been sacrificed that afternoon. Here they stand in a copper bowl and have their feet washed by the Bāya. The ceremony is completed now as the priests carry the girls upstairs into a room where they are worshipped and feasted and then returned to Haḥ Bāhāḥ. Later, at the auspicious time (*sāit*), the incumbent Kumāri herself is taken in one of her few official outings, in similar procession to Mul Cok where she too is feasted.

8.8.5. Cālā (Vijāya Dashami, Ashvin-*shukla*/Kaulāthwa 10)

On this, the greatest day of the feast, the waiting period is completed. The barley and corn shoots (*naḥlā*) are brought out from the *pujā* room where they have been worshipped each morning for ten days. Everyone is in festive spirits. This is the final day that the lineage will gather but before they do so the heads of each family finish *pujā* in their homes. The lineage then gathers at the house of the *thākāli* to participate in the main ceremony—the ritual of the cutting of the pumpkin (*phāsi palyu*). In preparation for this a Citrakār comes to the house and paints the face of the demon Mahishasura on a large, unripe pumpkin. Then, when all are gathered, and everyone has had a chance to do *pujā* to the pumpkin, it is 'sacrificed' by a male member of the lineage by striking it with a sword (*khwã*).[31]

The *thākāli* takes the offered flowers and presents some to each member in order of seniority, along with vermilion, fruit, *naḥlā* seedlings, representing Durga's sword, a taste of each of the *tāpã*, and red and white strips of cloth, as *prasād.* Each member then receives vermilion from each other member senior to himself and, in turn, gives it to each of his juniors. Each, as they receive, bows down to his elder. This *prasād* is exclusively for the lineage. Married-out daughters and their families are not allowed to partake, as they do not belong. The lineage then sits down to eat *samay baji* together.

In Mul Cok the chief Brahman *purohit* and his assistants do a special *pujā* to Taleju from early morning. Later in the morning there are further sacrifices of goats, sheep, and buffaloes to Taleju. Early in the afternoon the Cyāsaḥ Butchers arrive to take their portion of the buffaloes that had been sacrificed on the eighth day. The now putrid flesh of two buffalo heads is cut up there in the courtyard and then removed for the Butchers to eat as *sikāḥ bhu* that evening.

The priests offer a final *pujā* to Taleju and then, in a ceremony like that of the seventh day, the images of Taleju are brought out and carried in procession back to their usual temples on the north side of the courtyard. One of the assistant priests carries the Malla king's sword and shield. Another goat is sacrificed and the main ritual of Mohani is completed. At this time the Gan

Pyākhã arrive at Mul Cok to perform exactly the same programme as they did on Day 7. During the dance the chief Brahman *purohit*, having completed the ritual of replacing the Taleju images in their usual temples, wanders into the circle and hands out *prasād* from Taleju to all the musicians and dancers. With this the performances of the Gan Pyākhã for the city are complete.[32]

In the past it would now be the turn of the Gathu Pyākhã troupe who would arrive at this time, just as the Gan Pyākhã troupe is leaving. Having received a ritual welcome from the chief Brahman *purohit* they would perform the first of their dances. This now seems to have been discontinued. The Gathu who constitute this troupe are a caste of Gardeners from the village of Theco a few miles south of Lalitpur (Toffin 1996a: 79).[33] The deities that make up the Gathu Pyākhã troupe are identical to those of the Gan Pyākhã but unlike the latter they accept *panca bali*: the blood sacrifice of buffaloes, goats, sheep, fish, and duck. Furthermore, the dances of the Gathu Pyākhã are entirely unlike those of the Gan Pyākhã. During their repertoire a buffalo is sacrificed by a *guthiyār* from the village. The character of Bhairava further sacrifices a goat and gives blood to each of the Mother Goddesses to drink. That night the deities would sleep at Mul Cok. In the evening, in the various localities around the city, lineages enjoy their third and final feast of the event.

The next morning the Gathu Pyākhã troupe traditionally performs its dance routine, again with further sacrifices, before returning to Theco. The dancers would repeat their performances on each successive day until the full moon.

The remaining days of the fortnight (Kaulāthwa 11–15) are relaxed and pleasant days for visiting and feasting at the homes of relatives. Married-out daughters and their families (including their husbands) visit their natal homes; and all visit the home of their mother's brother, to receive *prasād* in the form of vermilion, fruit, and seedlings and to enjoy a feast (*nakhaḥtyā*) together. This demonstrates an importance unparalleled in Lalitpur by any festival except that of the Jātrā. In the evening of the thirteenth day, the Kumāri is brought in procession from Haḥ Bāhāḥ to Mul Cok where she too is fed a *nakhaḥtyā*, just as if she were a married-out daughter or sister of the Malla king.

8.8.6. Kati Punhi (Np. Kojāgrat Purnimā, Ashvin-*shukla*/Kaulāthwa 15)

The full moon day is the last day of Mohani on which relatives may visit each other's homes, be fed, and receive *prasād.* On this day, the *pujā* items are removed from the house and either thrown in the river or, alternatively, deposited at the *pikhā lakhu.* This is the final day of the Gathu Pyākhã. On this day also Buddhist votive *caitya*s are reconsecrated (Plate 18; cf. Gellner 1992: 216).

8.8.7. Understanding Mohani

Gellner (1997c: 555) tabulates the contrasts between Levy's accounts of Biskaḥ and Mohani, which form the basis for the construction of Bhaktapur's

Plate 18. A Buddhist *caitya* at I Bāhāḥ Bahi.

symbolic order. A similar contrast can be made for Lalitpur between Mohani and the Bũgadyaḥ chariot festival, the Jātrā.

The Mohani festival is clearly tied to the agricultural cycle with the symbolism of the barley and corn shoots. Indeed the festival 'heralds the beginning of harvest' (Gutschow and Basukala 1987: 141). As such, therefore, Mohani is the most important event of the autumn season. This has been the case since at least the seventeenth century, as the chronicles seem to indicate (Wright 1972: 238). The festival is essentially focussed on the lineage. This is expressed in a number of ways. Other relatives, such as one's married-out daughters may not see the *naḥlā.* They will visit only after the *pujā* is complete. The two great festivals of the lineage are Mohani and Dewāli—the season for Lineage Deity Worship (§9.23). It is important in these two great festivals for the entire lineage to come together to do *pujā.* Whereas Lineage Deity Worship occurs immediately before the onset of the monsoon, Mohani is celebrated at the time of the rice harvest when the monsoon comes to an end.

The focal deity of the ritual is the Goddess—Devi. It is she who receives the *pujā* in her various Tantric manifestations and in the form of Taleju at the palace. It is she also, in her manifestation as Durga, who defeated the demon Mahishasura. The Goddess, as I explained with regard to Yẽnyaḥ (§8.5.2), is the one who has put evil to flight in the months subsequent to the period of chaos and disorder during rice transplanting. Chaos has threatened the social order as well as the spatial order. It is this festival that restores the order within the lineage. Seniority is reestablished by the giving of vermilion (*sinha*) on the tenth day.

It is also reestablished in the traditional leaf-plate feast (*laptyā bhway*) which, in this festival as well as that of Lineage Deity Worship, is celebrated as a lineage. The traditional feast, especially when served to the *guthi*, has a number of significant features that both reflect and mould Newar notions of order. Participants in the feast sit on long straw mats and are served on large plates made out of large leaves sewn together with fine slivers of bamboo. It is important that all are served together.[34] No one sits down until invited to do so by the host. The plates are set before the participants are seated and various dishes are served in a careful mandalic spatial arrangement that mirrors on the plate the arrangement of the Mother Goddesses around the city and in a more profound way the very order of the universe itself. Senior participants are invited to sit in order of age, the juniors keeping seniors to their right.[35] When all are seated the staple beaten rice is dealt out, servers moving down the line from elders to juniors. The meal begins. A cursory *pujā* is offered to deceased ancestors by placing a few fingers-full of each of the starters on the floor next to the plate. The meal is eaten slowly, by pitching the food into the mouth with the fingers of the right hand. More dishes are served. Light banter pervades the atmosphere in stark contrast to the quiet serious manner in which the daily meal of boiled rice is eaten. The large variety of dishes is served in a strict order. The dishes vary in taste, colour and texture, the main requirement being that the overall effect should be balanced.

There are four courses in all. Each course is based on the consumption of beaten rice and attended by the recharging of the small clay dish (*sali*) with strong rice liquor poured out of a silver flask (*anti*) from a height of sometimes a few feet. These two ingredients give continuity to the feast, contrasting with the diversity of the various accompanying dishes.

Each course has its own essential accompaniments and others are added optionally. There is an almost seamless transition from one course to the next with all feasters moving at the same pace.

The sheer volume of food consumed at a feast is remarkable. It is important that everyone leaves the feast totally satisfied. Beaten rice has the effect of swelling in the stomach, which can leave the eater feeling full several hours afterwards. Newars make much of the healthful properties of the feast. Not just the dishes themselves but also the particular quantity and strict order in which they are served are thought to be very good for the body. This would not be so if the ingredients were consumed raw. The process of cooking transforms raw foodstuffs from a wild, uncivilized state into one that is 'domesticated' and fit for consumption (Witzel 1997: 511). The feast, therefore, serves to symbolize the lineage itself. There is a precise order to the lineage. If that order is observed then the lineage will prosper. If it is not the lineage may lose its integrity and breakdown completely.

Mohani is also very important for the city as a whole. Although on one level the events that take place at Mul Cok are the king's own lineage rituals, there is more to it. On another level the king's Mohani ritual is for the kingdom too. With the independence of the king, that of the kingdom is also expressed. In 1648 CE (768 NS), the *Buddhist Vamshāvali* reports, a queen of Pratap Malla of Kathmandu died (Wright 1993: 238). Siddhi Narasimha Malla of Lalitpur did not go into mourning though he was Pratap Malla's paternal uncle (and therefore of the same lineage). He celebrated Mohani as usual. Furthermore, though Mohani may not have been celebrated in the usual way after a death in the royal family itself, the rituals were considered indispensable. In the year that 'Sri Sri Jaya Sri Jyoti Narasimha' died (1652), though Mohani was not publicly celebrated, the king and priests still performed the ceremonies (ibid.: 240).[36]

The celebration of Mohani in Lalitpur and, more broadly, throughout the Kathmandu Valley has parallels throughout the Hindu world such as that of the Navarātri in Mewar, Rajasthan and Dashara in Mysore. The Navarātri is often described as *the* festival (*utsāva*) of kings and *kshatriya*s. Moreover, Navarātri is the most important ritual of kingship across India (Fuller 1992: 108). The demon Mahishasura represents the forces of ignorance and chaos. King Mahishasura's reign began when he overthrew the gods and forced them to live on the earth oppressed by the demons.

In other words, he turned the cosmic order upside down, specifically by usurping the throne of Indra. Durga's victory enables the gods to regain their kingdom and so to restore the universal *dharma* predicated on rule by a rightful king (ibid.: 109).[37]

Mohani, then, is a royal festival. The king's sword, the ultimate symbol of his sovereignty, is brought down and placed in divine custody, in the Goddess's Mohani room for the duration of the high point of the festival. The king needs the sword for battle and it will be relinquished to him for that purpose once the *pujā* is complete.[38] The king and the Goddess are 'allies wielding the same weapon in the same cosmic war' (ibid.: 119). The transfer of state sword at the close of the festival serves to demonstrate the delegation of power and authority from deity to king. So, as Fuller reports, 'a ritual of legitimation seems to have been an intrinsic part of Navarātri festivals' (ibid.: 120).

Furthermore, the worship of tools and vehicles on the ninth day harks back to another royal and *kshatriya* ritual. Worship of elephants and horses as well as weapons of war seems to have been a universal at royal Navarātris and it was generally held on the ninth day (ibid.). The weapons are imbued with divine power for the coming campaigning season.

Biardeau (1989: 309) demonstrates that it would be wrong to take the *Devi Mahātmya* or other texts as a kind of script for royal Navarātri celebrations (Fuller 1992: 117). Rather, a common core of symbolic themes is developed at both ritual and mythical levels. The king is the patron, *jajmān*, of the sacrifice.

'By the symbolic logic of sacrifice, the buffalo must be seen as a substitute for him (and his subjects)' (ibid.: 118). But as each buffalo sacrifice reenacts the slaying of the demon, the king is also identified with the victorious goddess.

8.9. Vishnu worship—Alāmātā Cyākyu ('To light the lamp') (Ashvin-*shukla*/Kaulāthwa 15—Kārttik-*shukla*/Kachalāthwa 15)

We are now drawing towards the end of the period of Caturmāsa. From Kati Punhi a month of special events focussing on the worship of Vishnu/Nārāyana takes place ending on the following full moon, Sakimilā Punhi.

This is also a special month for Buddhists as they make the daily pilgrimage to the important out of town Karunāmaya shrines at Bũga (Bungamati) and Co Bāhāḥ (Cobhār). Hundreds of devotees from Lalitpur as well as some from Kathmandu, Newars and Parbatiyā alike, walk or ride early in the morning to these two sacred spots to observe a fast. This pilgrimage is a favourite for young men especially, who keep each other company as they walk and make the journey one of pleasure rather than austerity. In town, however, at Kwā Bāhāḥ women undertake a month-long Observance (Kārttik *vrata*) in which they fast for all but a handful of water each day.

There is here a conflation of the identities of Nārāyana and Karunāmaya. Both deities are worshipped throughout this month and both are associated in some way with the notion of salvation. This association goes back at least as far back as the seventeenth century when King Siddhi Narasimha Malla gave it a great boost, and probably much further (Gellner 1996: 140). I will demonstrate the significance of this later when we look at Karunāmaya's great chariot festival, the Jātrā (§10.8.4).

During this period the people of Lalitpur, each evening in their localities, present offerings of light to Nārāyana.[39] Newars and non-Newars alike light lamps and place them on the roof terrace (*kaḥshi*), in an upper window, or on a tall pole (*yaḥsĩ*).[40] Along with these lamps, foodstuffs such as corn, soybean, lentil cakes (*waḥ*), chickpeas and peas are offered. Nārāyana, it is believed, is asleep in the Himalaya. It is time to wake him up.

We have already encountered the *yaḥsĩ* pole in our survey of the annual festivals (§8.5). We have seen that the word *yaḥsĩ* could be from the old Newar *yalasĩ*, which designates the sacrificial stake associated with important cosmological significance. It is likely that the colloquial name for Lalitpur, Yala, may also have the same etymology. The Sanskrit equivalent *yupa* may then be the origin for Lalitpur's honorific Licchavi name, Yupagrāma (Yupa village; Gellner 1996: 131). So the use of the pole in Lalitpur's rituals goes back at least to Licchavi times.[41]

8.10. Swanti (Kārttik-*krishna*/Kaulāgā 13—Kārttik-*shukla* Kachalāthwa 3)

With the arrival of Swanti (Tihār, Np.) we come to the conclusion of the long sequence of festivals that began four months previously at Dillā Cahre (Gathā̃

Mugaḥ; §7.10). The festival consists of five days of worship and feasting. Each day a different deity is worshipped. The festival has further significance as the Nepal Era New Year takes place during its course.

8.10.1. Kwaḥ Pujā (Kārttik-*krishna*/Kaulāgā 13)

The first day of the festival is set aside for the worship of the crow. Small leaf dishes are set out containing food, coins and burning incense. Crows are ubiquitous and usually feed on carrion such as the rats that are trapped and thrown out onto the lane each morning. They are feared as bad omens—woe betide the person on whose head a crow alights.[42] The crow is, in fact, worshipped as the messenger of Yamadyaḥ, the lord of the realm of the dead, also called Yamarāja.[43]

8.10.2. Khica Pujā (Kārttik-*krishna*/Kaulāgā 14)

The following day is the day for the worship of dogs. Dogs belonging to the household, as well as mangy street dogs, are fed and offered *pujā* in the form of vermilion on the head and garlands of marigolds. The dog also has a connection with death for he is the guardian deity at the gates of Yamadyaḥ's kingdom. Though on any other day a dog's existence is not the pleasant life of the doted pet, on this day, at least, it is treated most royally.

Like the previous day this one is a relaxed affair. Most people continue their daily work in the workshop or at the office. But an atmosphere of jollity pervades the streets. Unlike Mohani, when the slaughter of so many animals gives the festival a more serious feel, Swanti is a festival of light entertainment. Traditionally this is the only festival during which gambling was permitted, and that for five days only. Still today, everywhere there are knots of men, heads down throwing dice onto a cloth, or counting out coins as stakes for the cards.

8.10.3. Lakshmi Pujā (Kārttik-*krishna*/Kaulāgā 15)

This is the first of the three important days of the festival. Houses are swept clean and daubed with a fresh mixture of cow dung and red clay. The household must now prepare for the visit of Lakshmi, the goddess of wealth.

In the morning, before the worship of Lakshmi, the cow is worshipped. Cows are bathed, and vermilion and yellow colours are applied to the cows' head and horns. As with dogs the previous day, garlands of marigold are hung around the cow's neck. The sacred thread (*gũha puca*) that was tied onto the wrist of the devotee on Gũ Punhi, three months before is now removed and tied onto the tail of the cow. The cow (as I have already noted, §7.16), like the crow and the dog, has a strong connection with the god of the dead, Yamadyaḥ. It is the cow, it will be remembered, who will assist the worshipper to enter Yama's kingdom when he dies. Moreover, the cow is worshipped as the earthly form of Lakshmi who will be further worshipped in the evening.[44]

Early in the evening the house is decorated with flowers and tinsel. The *pikhā lakhu* boundary stone is cleansed with the usual mixture of cow dung and red clay. A path from the stone to the door of the house and on up to the treasure room (*dhukuti*) is prepared with the same mixture. On the prepared *pikhā lakhu* a sacred diagram (mandala) is drawn with powdered colours. A small clay saucer (*sali*) is charged with mustard oil, fitted with cotton wick, lit and placed on the mandala. Footprints of red ochre paint are printed on the path to the house and flickering oil lamps (*cāyu pala*) set at intervals to guide the way for the goddess. Clay oil lamps are placed around the house to attract Lakshmi and to make a pretty display. Nowadays houses are often festooned with elaborate displays of electric lights. This is the new moon day so there is no natural light to illuminate the path.

The senior male of the house then conducts a *pujā* to Lakshmi in the treasure room. Garlands are placed over her picture and vermilion added to her forehead. A new supply of money is placed in the treasure box with the petition that it be multiplied and a light is kept burning all night in the deity's honour.

Later, the household eats the first of a series of three feasts. On this night, groups of women and children go from door to door singing the traditional *bhaili ram* song and receiving small gifts from the household. The food that is offered to Lakshmi, however, is not supposed to be given to anyone from outside the house until the four following days are completed. Lakshmi Pujā will continue over the following days until Swanti finishes on the third day of the waxing fortnight.

8.10.4 Nhugu Dã (New Year) and Mha Pujā (Worship of One's Body or Self) (Kārttik-*shukla*/Kachalāthwa 1)[45]

The first day in the waxing lunar fortnight of Kārttik is a special occasion in Nepal only for the Newars. For Parbatiyā, hill tribes and Tarai dwellers alike this day holds no significance. Lakshmi Pujā continues this morning with the offering of a special plate (*thāy bhu*) of eighty-four dishes.

The importance of this day lies in the fact that, according to the Nepal Sambat (Nepal Era, the traditional calendar of the Kathmandu Valley) it is the first day of the New Year. This is an occasion that has taken on great political significance in recent years. Newar activists have championed the cause of their cultural and linguistic rights with this festival and the use of the Nepal Era. This is true especially in Lalitpur where the main thoroughfares are decorated with paper Buddhist flags and everyone goes about giving New Year greetings. In the evening young men ride around town in a motorbike cavalcade shouting '*bhintunā*'—'best wishes' (i.e., best wishes for the New Year).[46]

That evening the family gathers together for the ritual of Mha Pujā—Worship of the Self or Body. The senior house female (*thākāli nakī*) does *pujā* to household members. In this ceremony the mother pleads to the god Yamarāja to prolong the lives of her husband and children beyond their allotted time (R.P. Pradhan 1996: 188n.). The large open room of the house (*cwata*) is cleansed in the customary way and the family members are seated on straw mats around the sides of the room, in order of seniority.

The *thākāli nakī* then draws a mandala on the floor in front of each household member with vermilion, rice flour and *potay* (a yellow paste made with rice and oil). Eight mandalas are then drawn on the right of the *thākāli* representing the Ashtamātrika. After *pujā* to the household gods, the *thākāli nakī* does *pujā* to each of the family members in turn by offering them seasonal fruit, flowers, and walnuts. Traditional household implements such as the winnowing tray (*hāsā*) and broom (*tuphi*) are also worshipped.[47] Finally, the good luck food (*nyā sagā̃*) is given to each member of the household to protect them from evil spirits over the coming year.[48] The family feast follows the ritual.

At this point it is necessary to ask why the threshold of the Newar year should fall at this time. Padmagiri's Chronicle gives us an account of a popular myth explaining the beginning of Nepal Samvat (Hasrat 1970: 49-50; Anderson 1988: 171). There are two other possible reasons, however, for its situation at this point in the year. On the one hand, as Witzel points out, various New Year festivals of South Asia have shifted to various times in the year and seem to be related to different subsistence calendars (1997: 520).[49] On the other hand, however, it seems highly likely that the New Year celebration is connected with the ritual of Mha Pujā. Mha Pujā is a ritual of protection for the family. Kashinath Tamot believes that the festival was instituted after the fire at Mānesvara, which burned down so many homes and forced many people, including the ancestors of today's Tāmrakārs, to migrate to other settlements of the Valley (§2.6.1).[50] This epochal event, then, was the occasion for the beginning of the Nepal Era; the ritual of Mha Pujā, unique to the Newars, is a protective ceremony to ensure that such a disaster is not repeated.

8.10.5. Kijā Pujā (Kārttik-*shukla*/Kachalāthwa 2)

The last great day of Swanti is a time when every male in the Valley, in common with those of many communities across Nepal and India, must be worshipped by his sisters (Eck 1993: 271). All married daughters (with their children) visit their natal home for this important ritual.[51] The brothers sit on mats along the wall of the room and, in a ritual very similar to that of the previous day, the sisters draw mandalas and offer them flowers and fruits as well as the ubiquitous vermilion. One of the garlands is of the *gway* flower, a small purple flower that blooms at this time of year and which, when hung up to dry, lasts a long time. All understand the symbolism of longevity.[52] As with Mha Pujā, the ritual is an elaborate plea to the god Yamarāja to prolong the lives of their brothers.[53] After the *pujā*, vermilion is given to each person present by one of the women, and the whole family sits down for a feast.

8.10.6. Lakshmidyaḥ Bhu Kwakāyegu (Kārttik-*shukla*/Kachalāthwa 3)

This morning the final *pujā* of the season is offered to Lakshmi. This is followed by the distribution of *prasād* to all the family members and married-out daughters and sisters and their families (*mhyāy macā*/*bhincā macā*). This takes the form of vermilion and participation in the food from the *thāy bhu* that was offered to Lakshmi on Mha Pujā.[54] No one else may participate. After the meal, items used in the *pujā* are tossed into the river.[55] With this, the festivities of Swanti come to an end.

8.10.7. Understanding Swanti

The Newar festival of Swanti differs from its counterparts in neighbouring areas. Newars and Parbatiyā alike differ from their neighbours in the plains in that the latter observe only Lakshmi Pujā.[56] The Newars are further differentiated from the Parbatiyās in their additional observance of Mha Pujā. The festival, as both Parbatiyās and Newars observe it, has the additional elements of Kwaḥ Pujā, Khica Pujā and Kijā Pujā. Each of these elements has a symbolic association with death. The crow and the dog, as well as the cow (a symbol of Lakshmi) are all agents of Yama, the king of the dead. Each of these animals receives a *pujā* for the dead. Furthermore, Kijā Pujā and, for the Newars, Mha Pujā are both rituals to ensure the long life of members of the family. In the former, sisters visit their brothers to wish them long life. In the latter, the household senior woman pleads for the long life of the whole family.

This festival is overwhelmingly a family event every bit as much as Mohani is a lineage event. In the days that follow Kijā Pujā (usually on Lakshmidyaḥ Bhu Kwakāyegu) the family calls its married-out daughters and nieces and their children (*mhyay macā* and *bhincā macā*) to a feast (*nakhaḥtyā*).[57] Husbands of the women are not invited. This is for blood relations only. We are now drawing towards the end of Vishnu's four-month sleep, Caturmāsa. The festival of Swanti, therefore like that of Mohani and Yẽnyaḥ, contributes to the reestablishing of the social order after its collapse four months before. The family order too is now renewed.

8.11. Mukhaḥ Ashtami (Kārttik-*shukla*/Kachalāthwa 8)

The following Eighth Day Observance is considered the most important of these days of the year (Gellner 1992: 216). Buddhists fast on this day, as on all Eighth Day Observances. For the most part, only Vajrācāryas and Shākyas observe this day. This particular Eighth Day Observance has special significance at the temple of Pashupatināth where, in a unique ceremony, Buddha's crown is placed on the top of the *linga*.[58]

8.12. Kārttiksnāna Caturmāsya Vrata Samapti (Haribodhini Ekadasi, Kārttik-*shukla*/Kachalāthwa 11)

After a long four-month wait, Caturmāsa, the period of Nārāyana's sleep finally comes to an end. Kārttik, the month of special worship for Vishnu/Nārāyana comes to a climax as thousands of devotees gather at his temples around South Asia to offer their *pujā*. In Lalitpur, hundreds of red sari-clad women line up in front of the Cār Nārāyana temple in Mangaḥ to offer worship. Many who have undergone a partial fast for the last four months now observe a full fast in observance of the day. The following four days, until the full moon, Nārāyana temples around the Valley, such as the great temples of Buddhanilkantha and Cāngu Nārāyana are thronged with devotees.

On the thirteenth day of the fortnight the worship of the basil plant (*tulasi*) comes to an end with the offering of the rough lemon (*kāljami*; *Citrus jambhiri*, L.).

Pilgrimage to the Buddhist sites of Co Bāhāḥ and Būga continues until the full moon day, four days later. Women also join in at this point to take part in a short version of the Observance (*vrata*) in which they fast (*apasā cwane*) from all except a handful of water each day. The women stay at these shrines for the complete four days. Those at Kwā Bāhāḥ have now been fasting for a full month. It is critical that their husbands must come to bring them home on this day as not to do so signals the end of their marriage. In fact, some women will do the fast in order to bring a contentious marriage to a crisis and test their husband's faithfulness.

Back in Lalitpur, on this night the pivotal dance-drama 'Jalashāyan' (The Slaying of Madhu/Kaitan) is performed. Nārāyana sleeps on his bed at the back of the stage. Lakshmi sits submissively at his feet and Brahma sits on a lotus flower behind him. The demons Madhu and Kaitan enter and dance vigorously to the beating of the drums, slashing and lunging with their swords and imbuing the world with fear. They run back to Brahma's post and attack him by hacking at the stem of the lotus flower. Nārāyana slumbers on. Then Mother Earth (Māmāya or Prithvimātā) enters the stage, wearing a full bright red mask, red dress, and black hair and wielding her sword. Surely she will rid the earth of this terror? Mahāmāya and the demons clash. The music of the *dhāḥ bājā* speeds up and the dancing becomes more aggressive. But after all Mahāmāya is powerless to destroy the evil. She bows to the sleeping deity and exits. The dance is nearing its climax. Will Nārāyana finally awake? Will his *shakti* work where that of Mahāmāya didn't?

The instrumentalists lay down their *dhāḥ* drums and pick up the *khẽ*. The *pwanga* horns join in. At last Nārāyana awakes and rises from his bed. He engages the demons and they fight a bitter battle. It seems even he cannot defeat them. Again the instrumentalists pick up the *dhāḥ* and accelerate the tempo of their drumming. Nārāyana and the *daityas* dance, attacking one another vigorously with their weapons. Again the *khī̃ bājā* plays. Finally, Nārāyana stands opposite the demons and speaks: 'I'm impressed with you, ask a blessing of me.'

The demons reply, 'If you cannot defeat us how can you give us a blessing? You should ask a blessing of us.'

'You are right,' Nārāyana responds, 'please give me a blessing.'

Madhu and Kaitan walk across the stage to Nārāyana to give him a blessing but it is a trick and he swiftly slays them with a deft touch of his discus (*cakra*). Evil has been destroyed. The world is saved. At least for now, such salvation is not eternal. History is cyclic. The world is periodically swamped by evil. Nārāyana will need to come again to defeat evil. That he will do as one of his *avatar*s.

The next two nights are the final performances of the Kati Pyākhã. The story in each follows the now-familiar pattern. Demons control the earth. In the first Indra, typically, is powerless to do anything (§7.15). The masked Vārāha, the boar-*avatar* of Vishnu (played by a Shrestha) enters to great hoots from the audience. He is larger than life, dressed in a red and gold skirt, bedecked with a plethora of garlands, his blue/green face and great mop of grey hair surmounted by a headdress rich in flowers and tinsel. The *avatar* dances around the stage vigorously (all the more surprisingly that he is played by an elderly man) engaging the demon Hiranyaksha and his minions in serious battle. Neither prevails. Now, in a dramatic hiatus, Vārāha sits to receive *pujā* from the chief Brahman priest and descendant of the Malla kings' *purohit.* Thus empowered, the battle is rejoined and Vārāha easily defeats his enemies.

The last night is the climax of the Kati Pyākhã performance. Large crowds gather from early evening but the drama does not get going until quite late. The antagonist on this night is the demon-king Hiranyakashipu, played by a young Citrakār man. He and his minions dance aggressively. Enters Prahlāda, the demon-king's son who, much to Hiranyakashipu's disgust, is a devotee of another of Vishnu's *avatar*s, Narasimha.[59] The demons tie up Prahlāda to a post and threaten him severely.[60] Things look grim. The demons have the upper hand. The audience is thoroughly engaged. They are being carried along as the tempo of the drumming increases and the night wears on. The atmosphere is tense with anxiety.

Finally, just as all seems lost, the hero, Narasimha himself, bursts onto the stage through a paper screen. The crowd goes delirious. The masked Narasimha (played by a young Brahman man) cavorts around the stage energetically. He is dressed in orange, bedecked with a score of garlands, and wears a tremendous headdress surmounting his electric hairdo. The cosmic combat is intense but neither side gets the upper hand. The two sides retire. Each of the dancers receives a much-needed wipe of the brow from his attendant. It is way past midnight. Oil lamps cast shadows across the audience who have now been standing for several hours to watch this spectacle.

Now, as the day before, the chief Brahman *purohit* performs the empowering *pujā.* The music resumes, the climax of the drama approaches. The crowds surge and need to be held back. The demon-king looks increasingly anxious as Narasimha gets the upper hand. Hiranyakashipu is now near his end and he knows it. He is sweating profusely and knows that he cannot overcome this powerful deity. Attendants get ready to catch him. It is all over. Hiranyakashipu falls slain into the arms of the young dancer's father. The crowds go wild and invade the stage. A sheet is placed over the young man who has fallen unconscious and his headdress is removed. He is then carried hastily by his troubled family to a house in the lane behind the Car Nārāyana temple. 'Our son is dead, will he be revived again?'[61] The young man's 'corpse' is laid on a bed of straw. A Brahman priest of Taleju then plays his part as the healer (*vaidya*). He revives the young man by chanting mantras over a flask of water that is then poured into his mouth.[62] Back at the stage, the drama is resolved. Prahlāda is released and the deity receives *pujā* once again. The play has ended and with it, for another year, the world has been restored to its proper order. The audience can go home and rest. It has been an intense night.

Once again the role of the king in the period of Caturmāsa comes to the fore. The seventeenth century Malla kings consciously developed a clear identification with Vishnu/Nārāyana. This was manifested in a number of ways. The association of the palace with the great temples to Nārāyana and his *avatar*s (Krishna and Narasimha especially) in the Palace Square is an obvious one. Another is the design of the Keshav Nārāyana Cok with its Golden Window overlooking the Palace Square. As I have already indicated, the window is replete with iconography (§7.18.5). The way that Vishnu frames the whole sends a powerful message to observers: the principal Buddhist *bodhisattva* is, 'in fact', a form of Vishnu (Gellner 1992: 94-9). Not only so but the king, when watching the festivities below would be framed by the whole. There is, then, a further identification of the king himself with Vishnu that would be inescapable.

The Kati Pyākhã was another opportunity to express this powerful identification. It is not serendipitous that the actors playing the various gods and goddesses use various rooms of the palace to get dressed. On most days the actors don their make up and dress in one of the rooms of the Degutale temple. On the last two days, however, the protagonist in each of the dramas not only prepares for his part in the adjacent Keshav Nārāyana Cok but also receives a special *pujā* from the chief Brahman priest at that place. Furthermore, it is Narasimha, the lion-man *avatar* of Nārāyana who brings the play to its great climax. The king who instituted the dance-drama was, of course, King Siddhi Narasimha Malla himself. Could it be that he even played the part himself? Either way, the identification could hardly be more conspicuous.

8.13. Sakimilā Punhi (Kārttik-*shukla*/Kachalāthwa 15)

The last two events of this period are somewhat anticlimactic. The last day of the celebrations that mark the end of Caturmāsa is the full moon day, Sakimilā Punhi. On this day Newars offer a food item called '*halimali*'[63] to Nārāyana as they have done throughout Kārttik. *Halimali* is then taken home by the devotees to be eaten as *prasād* as part of a feast called '*halimali bhway*' or '*hi saki bhway*'.[64] Some people on this day also take part in a special pilgrimage to all four Valley-wide important Ganesh temples, the four Vināyaks.

8.14. Kwenā Jātrā (Kārttik-*shukla*/Kachalāthwa 14—Mārga-*krishna*/ Kachalāgā 1)

This minor festival of Kwenādyaḥ involves the procession of the image from Puco to its other temple in Co Bāhāḥ. Kwenādyaḥ is the colloquial name for Jala Vināyak, one of the four important Ganesh shrines of the Valley. The temple at Puco houses the movable image of Kwenā, while the original image is housed in its temple at the foot of the Co Bāhāḥ hill. This temple sits at the point at which the Bāgmati River gushes out of the cleft on its way out of the Valley, just a couple of miles southwest of Lalitpur.

On the first day of the *jātrā* (Kachalāthwa 14) the image of Kwenādyaḥ, a huge brass mask, is brought on a palanquin from its temple at Puco to Co Bāhāḥ, via the temple of Purnacandi at Ga Bāhāḥ. Two Khadgi Butchers, playing *naykhĩ* and *cusyāḥ* walk in front of the palanquin. The procession is led by a Tulādhar of Co Bāhāḥ, one of eight *thākālis* of the sponsoring *guthi*. On arrival at Co Bāhāḥ the *guthiyār*s eats a feast.

The following day, Sakimilā Punhi (Kachalāthwa 15), Kwenādya is offered a special *pujā*. The movable image is re-empowered by the sacrifice of a buffalo as it sits adjacent to the other, permanent image, in its home shrine. The movable image is then taken back on its palanquin to its usual home at Puco by a different route, via Cāka Bahi, Haḥkā Galli and Mangaḥ. Another feast is eaten. The festival concludes with a final feast the following day (Kachalāgā 1).

8.15. Order restored

It is fitting that the festivals that we have examined over the course of the last two chapters should come to completion at this point. Order has now been restored. City space is once again a sacred arena. The social order, likewise, has been renewed so that the actors can play their part, as they should. The final ritual act, as it is also performed upon completion of a Marriage or Lineage Deity Worship (§9.23) is a *pujā* to the powerful Kwenādyaḥ.

9. The Approach of Disorder I: The Season of Anxiety

It's the time of rice planting,
lightening has struck,
the showering of rain sang a song;
the clouds clapping [the rhythm]
the river jumped up—
made my heart dance.
The ornamentation of mud
imprinted on the blouse
is beautiful today;
today we laugh,
today we sing.
Tomorrow, oh my God! who weeps
because death has taken away!

'The Fifteenth of the Month of Ashādh' by Lakshmi Prasad Devkota,
translated by M.G. Treu (1993: 158f.)

9.1. Introduction

In our survey of Lalitpur's festivals we have now come to a critical juncture. The chaos that swept into the city, collapsing the moral and social order, has now been thoroughly sorted out. The rice harvest, the vital crop that inevitably brings its alter ego, chaos, with it, has been gathered in. Farmers, and all that depend on their produce, can sit back for a while and enjoy the sunny days and cool nights. Mats (*sukuḥ*) are woven in the courtyards. Jobs left undone throughout the busy rice season are finally addressed. It is a time for relaxing, for soaking in the sun and getting an oil massage. But as the days and months go past and the melody of life is played out another, darker, tone is detected. The heat is coming and is followed, as it must be, by the monsoon again. The darker tone of anxiety grows louder as the months wear on and as the dust picks up across the fields and in the alleys. Will the monsoon come, as it should? What will come with it? Will there be sickness, as always? The coming months, then, are a season of preparation. The right rituals and heartfelt supplication to the gods must once again ensure a bountiful harvest. Lineage solidarity must be expressed and reasserted in the teeth of the constant danger of dissolution. Lalitpur has once again, over the centuries, developed its own programme of events to express this. Chief among these is the chariot festival of Bũgadyaḥ, which will be examined, in the following chapter. The other festivals are less integrated but, nevertheless, form a movement of their own. These are described here. This chapter and the next are not in series as the two previous chapters, but in parallel, the two sets of events running concurrently.

9.2. Note on solar festivals

The first day of each solar month (*sãnhu* or *sãlhu*) is a special day for the worship of Karunāmaya. As we have seen (§6.2.3) hundreds of worshippers, many in *sãnhu guthi*s throng Ta Bāhāḥ and Tangaḥ Bāhāḥ on this day to worship Bũgadyaḥ and Cākwāḥdyaḥ.

Apart from these regular monthly observances, Lalitpur has only two festivals that are pinned to the solar calendar. Each is celebrated three weeks after the sun moves across one of its important boundary markers—Ghyaḥcāku Sãnhu is celebrated after the winter solstice and Biskaḥ after the vernal equinox. Equinoxes and solstices were regarded in ancient times as particularly threatening times of the year. It is as if one could never be sure whether the sun, in changing course from its southerly migration, would, in fact, head back north to bring the summer so essential for life. The two essentials for the growth of crops—sun and rain—are both dependent on the sun's presence in the Northern Hemisphere. A hot summer, though in many ways uncomfortable and attended by disease and death, is essential to ensure a plentiful monsoon. There is 'no wet without sweat, no rain without pain,' as English-speaking locals may tell the uncomfortable visitor. So the winter solstice is a time of anxious celebration. Lalitpur's festival of the vernal equinox, for its part, in contradistinction to that of Bhaktapur, is not attended by such grand festivities. The reason for this will be explored below.

It is clear that the winter solstice festival did in ancient times indeed fall on the solstice itself. Due to the method of calculating the Hindu calendar the festival has precessed to its present position (Gutschow and Basukala 1987: 148). This must also be true of Biskaḥ. Now we come to the festivals of this period.

9.3. Bālā Cahre (Mārga-*krishna*/Kachalāgā 14)

The fourteenth day of each waning fortnight is especially sacred to the worship of Shiva. On this particular *cahre* (a minor festival for Lalitpur) Newars, especially but not solely *shivamārgi*s, who have lost a family member during the past year go on pilgrimage out of the city to do *pujā* at the great Shiva shrine of Pashupatināth.

9.4. Thilā Punhi (Yaḥmari Punhi, Mārga-*shukla*/Thilāthwa 15)

This major festival is observed across much of South Asia, including the Kathmandu Valley, as the winter solstice festival (Klostermaier 1990: 311). This is at odds, then, with the clear textual evidence that Ghyaḥcāku Sãnhu once marked the solstice, as we have seen above.

On this day the special rice cake, *yaḥ mari*, is offered to gods everywhere.[1] The *yaḥ mari* is made of rice flour formed into the shape of a fig and filled with brown cane sugar and sesame seeds. After *pujā*, people eat the sweet as part of their feast.[2] Maharjans eat their feast after mixing *yaḥ mari* among piles of unhusked rice in the storeroom. This festival then marks the end of the rice harvest. By now all the rice should have been gathered in. It is said that by placing the *yaḥ mari* with the rice store a miracle may cause it to multiply.

Among the Shilpakārs of Ikhā an unusual custom has been observed for some generations. The Shilpakārs, it will be remembered, are made up of two craft groups: Sikaḥmi Carpenters and Lwahākaḥmi Stonemasons. The Sikaḥmi make and eat *yaḥ mari*, but the Lwahākaḥmi may only eat those made outside of their house. The reason for this is that, some time ago, after eating *yaḥ mari* a little Lwahākaḥmi girl died. This was thought to be because of eating the cake so the Lwahākaḥmi refused to cook it again. When octogenarian Mahila Shilpakar was a boy the Sikaḥmi used to cook *yaḥ mari* for the Lwahākaḥmi. This practice has since become defunct. Many *guthi*s join together for a feast on this day. Large companies of Maharjan men, for instance, can be seen feasting with their tutelary deity at Puco.

The night of Yaḥmari Punhi is observed as the longest of the year just as Jyesth Punhi is the shortest (§9.26). It is important that on this night no one should sleep the whole night through. To do so is to invite accusations of indolence: 'Is no night long enough for you?'

9.5. Sisā Pāru (Paush-*krishna*/Thilāgā 1)

The following day, the first in the waning fortnight, a special *pujā* is offered to the gods of the locality and to certain Mother Goddesses. Among the Pengu Daḥ the Tamvaḥ Pwāḥsyāḥ lineage does *pujā* to its mandalic deity Mahālakshmi at her shrine south of the city. It looks likely that the *pujā* to the mandalic deity of that locality is a protective rite at this anxious time of the sun's transit from its southward to its northward course.

This day is also an important day in the calendar of the Būgadyaḥ chariot festival. On this day the Bārāhi Carpenters visit the forest that is the source for the main beams of the chariot and select trees for the chariot's construction (§10.7.1).

9.6. Disi Pujā (Paush-*krishna*/Thilāgā 10)

On the tenth day of the waning fortnight another winter solstice festival is celebrated. On this day, those who have taken Tantric Initiation offer special *pujā* to the esoteric deity Cakrasamvara (Gellner 1992: 61).

9.7. The solar festival of Ghyaḥcāku Sānhu (Māgh 1)[3]

Early in the morning of the first day of Māgh, members of the Pengu Daḥ, like other Newars, visit their domestic priest (*purohit*) to give a special gift (*sira dān*). The gift consists of the following uncooked foods: one *mānā* of rice, lentils, turmeric, spinach, molasses, clarified butter (*ghyaḥ*), salt, ginger and, optionally, wood for cooking. They then walk to the temple at Agni Sāla for a special *pujā* considered compulsory by many Lalitpurians. The *thākāli* of the

Lalitpur Rājopādhyāya *guthi* attends the eternal flame that burns here.[4] *Pujā* (an oblation of sandalwood, common wood, *ghyaḥ* and cereals) is offered to the flame through the priestly intermediary to ensure the longevity of its devotees. A further *sira dān* is given to the Rājopādhyāya *thākāli.*[5]

On arriving back home on this important *nakhaḥ* the eldest married woman of the household (*thākāli nakī*) anoints all household members with oil. The anointing is followed by a ritual meal (*samay baji*). Married-out daughters then visit their natal homes (*thaḥ chẽ*) to receive anointing from their mothers and to eat a *nakhaḥtyā* (special family festival feast). Until she has given birth her husband is not invited. The feast includes a number of special foods: molasses (*cāku*), *ghyaḥ*, yam (*tarur*), a sweet ball of sesame (*hāmwa*) and molasses, and a special kind of spinach grown by the Vyanjankārs (Tepay *palaḥ*).[6]

The festival continues on through the month of Māgh. During this month Newars must at least once eat a dish called *may goja.* This dish, which is prepared by boiling rice and black lentils together in the same pot is seen as having healthful properties to ward off sickness in the middle of the winter. As such, it is the counterpart to the eating of the black lentil dish at Dasa Harā during the summer. As on that festival stinging nettles (*naykā̃*) are also added to the dish.

Newars do not see this festival as the winter solstice. Yaḥmari Punhi (§9.4) is seen as the winter solstice festival (though it is reckoned by the lunar calendar). Rather they see it as heralding the approach of the hot season. They say that the anointing with oil is to wish good health on the family. Locke suggests that the health-giving foods eaten on this day are to 'ward off diseases during the cold season,' and that 'the people should eat these foods from the beginning of this month until the warm weather' (1980: 222). In the common mind the festival is still considered to be a protection against the many diseases, such as cholera and smallpox, which plagued the people of the city in the hot weather until very recently (ibid.). In the Indian tradition, however, Māgh Samkrānti marks the beginning of the sun's path northward—the 'waxing' half of the year (Kane 1968-77: V, 211ff.; Eck 1993: 274).[7] This aspect of the festival is completely lost on the Newars.

It would seem, therefore, that Ghyaḥcāku Sãnhu is a later addition to the plethora of Newar festivals perhaps, one would surmise, introduced by migrants who settled in the Valley.

9.8. Milā Punhi (Paush-*shukla*/Pohelāthwa 15)

The full moon of January marks the beginning of the Observance (*vrata*) of Svasthāni. Each evening until the following full moon (Si Punhi) the Svasthāni *bākhā̃* (a series of stories about Shiva) is read aloud in the home. This celebration is also called Cyāla Punhi as on this day *cyāla* (a curry made from bamboo shoots, potatoes, peas and other vegetables) is prepared.[8]

9.9. Sri Pancami (Māgh-*shukla*/Sillāthwa 5)

During the month of the Svasthāni Observance a festival is held throughout South Asia in honour of the goddess of learning, Sarasvati (Eck 1993: 275). Today, a national holiday, is Sarasvati's birthday and schools put on special programmes. Some students fast throughout the day though this is not compulsory. At the great *stupa* of Svayambhu an important *melā* is held. Thousands of Buddhists flock there from around the Valley to offer special *pujā* to Manjushri, the Buddhist counterpart to Sarasvati. Sarasvati Pujā (Sasu Pujā, Nw.) is offered at any time between this day and Pāhā̃ Cahre, seven weeks later.

Sri Pancami, like Nāg Pancami, six months previous, marks the beginning of a major seasonal change. This is the beginning of the hot half of the year. From this day on water on the road will evaporate.[9] This day is very important for moveable life cycle rituals, especially weddings and the Mock Marriage. It is one of three or four days in the year that such rituals may be performed without the necessity of determining the appropriate auspicious time (*sāit*) as this is the day on which Shiva and Pārvati were married.

9.10. Si Punhi (Māgh-*shukla*/Sillāthwa 15)

This full moon day marks the end of the Svasthāni Observance (Svasthāni Vrata Samapti).

9.11. Sillā Cahre (Shivarātri, Phāgun-*krishna*/Sillāgā 14)

Shiva's Night is the major annual festival for the worship of Shiva. A great *melā* is held at Pashupatināth and crowds of devotees throng to the site to do *pujā* and enjoy the festive atmosphere, an event that is repeated throughout the Hindu world (Klostermaier 1990: 311; Eck 1993: 276). Children enjoy this day as one on which to extort coins from hapless drivers and cyclists as they do on Dillā Cahre. On this day also, a ritual takes place at the temple in Ta Bāhāḥ, in which a Tantric bone is placed on the head of the image of Bũgadyaḥ in a clear identification of Karunāmaya with Shiva (Locke 1980: 278f). As on Krishnashtami and Rām Navami, no animals are to be slaughtered on this day. My informants were divided as to whether this event is considered a *nakhaḥ*. Even for those who do so, however, it is not considered of sufficient importance to invite *mhyay macā* for a feast (*nakhaḥtyā*). The reason for this is not clear, though it appears to be linked to the other *nakhaḥ* of Pāhā̃ Cahre (§9.14). From this day to Sala Yaḥ guests are invited in and fed. In the evening, bonfires are lit in the streets of all the settlements of the Valley. People warm themselves in front of the fire, which is set up in front of a deity as it is thought that the latter will want to warm itself as well. Pious devotees stay up all night singing hymns of devotion to Mahādyaḥ, the Great God. Although three weeks after Sri Pancami, this day is considered the last day of the cold months (*cikulā*). From tomorrow the hot season will begin and fires will no longer be necessary. In fact the weather does warm up dramatically at this time of year.

9.12. Holi (Phāgun-*shukla*/Cillāthwa 4-15)

Although the festival of Holi is the focal spring festival throughout neighbouring north India, it does not have anything like the same importance in Nepal. In India it is a time of gaiety and colour, especially colour, as this is the event on which people daub each other with vermilion. Newars have an ambivalent attitude to the festival for reasons we will explore in due course. First, I will describe the festival as it is celebrated in Lalitpur. Here, of focal importance to the festival is the *cir* tree, which is set up in the palace square at Mangaḥ as a sign that the season of Holi is underway.

9.12.1. Sāit Swayegu (Phāgun-*shukla*/Cillāthwa 4)

The festival begins with the 'Seeing of the Auspicious Moment' (*sāit swayegu*). Officials under the Guthi Samsthān make a visit to a Joshi astrologer to determine the *sāit* at which time they should depart and in which direction they should go to find the tree.

9.12.2. Cir Swayegu (Cirotthanā Holikārambhaḥ, Phāgun-*shukla*/ Cillāthwa 8)

At the auspicious moment the procession of Guthi Corporation officials sets off in search of the *cir* tree with a Kāpāli preceding them playing the *muhāli.* Once the appropriate tree is found they do *pujā* to it. It is then cut down and brought to Mangaḥ where it is set up in front of the Krishna temple. The tree is trimmed and set up so that all the remaining branches point directly at the palace.

Devotees offer *pujā* to the tree in the form of vermilion, and tie pieces of red, blue, white and gold cloth to the branches. This is the sanction for the beginning of Holi. People come to bow to the tree and take a little vermilion to put on their foreheads as *prasād.* The *cir* is said to represent the tree on which Krishna hung the garments of the Gopis while they bathed in the Jamunā River unaware of his gaze (Anderson 1988: 250). From now until the full moon Holi 'play', the throwing of water and colour in courtyards and streets is sanctioned.[10] Each evening throughout the festival the Mridanga Phagun Bhajan Khalaḥ sing Nepali, Maithili, Bhojpuri and Newar *bhajan*s to Krishna in front of his temple at Mangaḥ accompanied by the *mridanga* (*pacimā*, Nw.). With the ensemble sits their sponsor, the turn-holder from the Cir Guthi—a *guthi* of fifty or sixty Shrestha men of Ikhā Lakhu.

9.12.3. Holi Punhi/Cir Wāchwaygu (Phāgun-*shukla*/Cillāthwa 15)

This is the high day of the festival. In the Valley, in contrast to the riotous behaviour of young men in north India, the throwing of red colour and water in streets has until now been restrained.[11] Today, however, a weak attempt is made to imitate that anarchy. Water and colour are thrown from roof-terrace to roof-terrace and onto passers-by as they run the gauntlet through the streets. Neighbours play in their courtyards throughout most of the morning and often well into the afternoon. Nowadays, police discourage play in streets but friendly courtyard battles often spill over into the by-ways.

In the evening the tree is brought down (*cir wã̆chwaygu*) and taken in procession to the Bāgmati where it is thrown in the river, signalling the end of Holi.[12]

9.12.4. Understanding Holi

There are at least two myths that are employed to explain Holi. Both Anderson (1988: 252) and Eck (1993: 277) relate the story of Holikā:

> Holikā was the wicked sister of the demon-king Hiranyakashipu [whom we met in the Kati Pyākhã, §8.12]. Being angered by her nephew Prahlāda's devotion to Vishnu and believing herself to be immune to death by fire she snatched Prahlāda and leaped into a burning furnace she had made for the purpose. In spite of her intentions, Prahlāda was saved by his great devotion to Vishnu and the fire consumed Holikā.

In another myth, Holikā terrorized the country so terribly that a child had to be offered to her daily (Klostermaier 1990: 311, Anderson 1988: 253). In order to deter Holikā eating the only child of a poor woman a good *sadhu* gathered all the local children together to heap abuse and throw filth on her leading her to die of shame.

The two myths contain three common elements in the following order: threat, disorder and resolution. In the first the threat is toward the *bhakta* of Vishnu. There is the liminal event while the demoness and Prahlāda are in the fire. Finally, there is a satisfactory resolution with the triumph of devotion over evil. The latter myth differs somewhat. There is no mention of devotion. The threat is there. The liminal event occurs when the normal order is overthrown and abuse and filth are employed to defeat the evil character. It is notable that it was a *sadhu*, a wandering ascetic standing outside the normal social order, who leads the children into their effective anti-social behaviour.

Holi has all the hallmarks of a New Year's celebration. The old year is dissolved with the order that gives shape to normal social life. There is the liminal period during which anti-social behaviour is deemed acceptable, within limits. Young men chant bawdy songs. Men and women play together touching and showering each other with vermilion. The normal social order is, as it were, turned on its head. Rules are discarded. It is, then, a time of social reversal and anarchy, albeit a carefully controlled anarchy that threatens to get out of hand but never really does so. The liminal period comes to an end with the lowering of the *cir* tree in an act that is remarkably similar to the New Year celebration in Bhaktapur—Biskaḥ.[13] Eck sees Holi as a 'New Year rite par excellence' (1993: 278). And indeed it is in all but name. Lalitpurians do not, in fact, recognize this festival as marking a New Year at all. This is clearly due to the fact that the year has other starting points that are more clearly marked by other festivals.

The association of Holi with Krishna gives some further indication of its meaning. The *cir* tree, as we have seen, is set up in front of the great Krishna temple in Mangaḥ. The play between men and women is seen as having its roots in the erotic play of Krishna with the Gopis. I suggest, therefore, that the festival also has roots in an ancient spring fertility rite that was later Sanskritized, an opinion also held by Lienhard (1995: 30).

Levy reckons that Holi's 'popularity in Kathmandu and Patan, along with other Krishna festivals, may attest to a relative breaking away from traditional priestly Hindu civic organization at the time of its introduction in contrast to the more conservative and traditional Bhaktapur' (1990: 430). That may be part of the story but there seems to be more to it. Bhaktapur, as Levy demonstrates, has a very important New Year festival of its own, Biskaḥ, that includes many of the elements that are part of Holi in Lalitpur and Kathmandu, which takes place just a few weeks earlier. Lalitpur's own Biskaḥ festival does not even approach the grandeur of Bhaktapur's (§9.17). Biskaḥ in Bhaktapur and Holi in Lalitpur function in analogous ways dissipating the threat of real anarchy by means of ritualized anarchy. The two festivals differ in their mythological content with Lalitpur's drawing heavily on that of Krishna, and Bhaktapur's Biskaḥ drawing on that of Bhairava and Bhadrakāli. Bhaktapur has a relatively undeveloped Krishna cult. Lalitpur's Krishna cult is more complex with the major Pujā and Jātrā revolving around his great temple in front of the palace during the monsoon (§7.20). Furthermore, the pulling of the chariots through urban space in Bhaktapur's Biskaḥ has parallels in Lalitpur's great spring festival, the Bũgadyaḥ Jātrā. Lalitpur's Holi, then, is overshadowed by the chariot festival, which begins just one month later.

I suggest that the development of Holi in Lalitpur was a conscious move of the great seventeenth century Malla kings who were so closely identified with Vishnu and his avatars. It was King Siddhi Narasimha Malla who built the Krishna temple, dedicating it in 1637 CE. And it is before that temple that the *cir* tree is set up, a tree that has been doctored so that its remaining arms reach toward the palace begging for the king's identification with the deity. The king, then, is at the centre of this event guiding the city through another great transition.

But it has to be asked why Lalitpurians (and Kathmanduites) are so ambivalent towards the festival. It is not considered a *nakhaḥ.* Most inhabitants do not even offer a *pujā.* No feast is eaten and relatives are not invited. It is clear, as I have said that Holi is a later Malla-era accretion to the festival calendar in keeping with the Vaishnavite leaning of the seventeenth century kings. That leaning was never fully absorbed by the local population, however. Vishnu-*Bhakti* remained largely a royal, and not surprisingly Brahman, emphasis. Furthermore, the uncertainty and reversal of the vernal equinox, expressed in Holi, is already expressed adequately in another pair of festivals that bracket this season—Sillā Cahre and Pāhã̄ Cahre. I have already described the former. The latter would come next were it not for another, minor, Krishna festival that intervenes.

9.13. Varsabandhana (Phāgun-*shukla*/Cillāthwa 10)

This minor festival celebrates the anniversary of the great Krishna temple (Lienhard 1995: 29). Celebrations are largely confined to those who are intimately connected to the temple, *shivamārgi* Shresthas and Rājopādhyāya Brahmans. For the bulk of the city's population it has no significance at all; most do not even know of its existence.

9.14. Pāhã̄ (Pāsā) Cahre (Caitra-*krishna*/Cillāgā 14)

This inauspicious day is when *pishāca* (demons) are thought to be particularly active. As on other *cahre*s (§9.3, §9.11) the focus of worship is Shiva. On this day, however, Shiva is worshipped in his form as the Luku ('hiding') Mahādyaḥ. Images of Luku Mahādyaḥ are often situated in a dark corner of a courtyard, covered with a stone, below ground level, where they are often besmirched with rubbish and dirt.[14] Anderson writes that Luku Mahādyaḥ is understood as being possessed by a *pishāca* on this day (1988: 264). By offering him *pujā* it is hoped that the evil spirit will be pacified.[15]

Although in Lalitpur this festival does not have the same importance as it has in Kathmandu, it is still considered a *nakhaḥ*. As on Sillā Cahre (§9.11), however, married-out daughters are not invited for a feast (*nakhaḥtyā*). Friends (*pāsā*), on the other hand, are invited into the home to be fed as guests (*pāhã̄*). In welcoming relatives and friends to one's house it is hoped that evil thoughts and harmful spirits will be dispelled (ibid.: 265). Why is it that *mhyay macā* are not invited to their natal home during the period from Sillā to Pāhã̄ Cahre, but friends are? I have demonstrated the clear association of Holi with the vernal equinox and the temporal collapse of the social order. That festival, not considered a *nakhaḥ* by Lalitpurians, does seem to be the product of a later influence from India. If this is so, then it may be that the period for inviting guests, which also falls over the equinox, may represent an older stratum of event that persists to the present, somewhat obscured by Holi. Like Holi, the inviting of guests rather than one's *mhyay macā* represents a reversal of the normal social order. That order is especially threatened, at this time, by malicious spirits (*pishāca*). Even Mahādyaḥ, the focal deity of every *cahre*, is possessed by the *pishāca*, so that he hides in the filthiest corner of the courtyard. Pāhã̄ Cahre, then, brings to an end this period of reversal. It is to be expected, then, that Lalitpur would place less emphasis on this event. In contrast to the festival in her sister city, the strong Krishna cult of Lalitpur around the central temple in Mangaḥ has stolen some of the significance from Pāhā̃ Cahre and placed it on Holi instead.

9.15. Sala Yaḥ (Sala Bwāki, Caitra-*krishna*/Cillāgā 15)

This new moon festival is far more important in Kathmandu than it is in Lalitpur. Since the return of Jung Bahadur Rana and his retinue from their European tour, a great *melā* (Ghodā Jātrā, Np.) has been held on the Tundikhel parade ground in what is now the centre of town. Horses are raced across the parched grass in front of crowds of onlookers including the king himself. Many Lalitpurians will visit this festival rather than participate in the local version. In Lalitpur, the festival takes place at the temple of Bāl Kumāri, Kwāchẽ, just outside the old north-east gate of the city. In a mockery of the serious racing in Kathmandu, a rider straddles a one-eyed, drunken horse backwards and the poor animal is made to gallop about for the sport of the onlookers. In the evening, the Bāl Kumāri Jātrā takes place. The movable image of Bāl Kumāri is mounted on a palanquin and paraded into the city around the north-east quadrant of the city (§5.6.2).

9.16. Caitra Dashaĩ—The Minor Festival of Rām (Caitra-*shukla*/ Caulāthwa 8-9)[16]

Caitra Dashaĩ (Mohani) is the equivalent spring festival of the great autumnal celebration that takes place six months earlier (§8.8). As we have seen, locals reckon that at one time the main Mohani celebration was, in fact, this one. The emphasis shifted over the centuries so that the autumnal festival has become much more important, so much so that many Newars view the spring festival, as its common name suggests, as belonging to the Parbatiyās rather than the Newars. I shall address the reasons for this in due course. Although the original festival was (and still is in north India—Levy 1990: 433, Eck 1993: 258), like its autumnal namesake, nine nights long, this is entirely lost today. Festivities begin on the eighth day of the fortnight and are completed the following day.

9.16.1. Pitha Pujā (Caitra-*shukla*/Caulāthwa 8)

On this day Newars make pilgrimage to the various Power-Places in and around Lalitpur for Pitha Pujā. In recent decades this has been formalized as a procession around a number of Power-Places following the format of Matayā and Bhimsen Pujā. Local men playing the *dhāḥ bājā* and *naykhĩ bājā*, accompanied by a group of four Damai playing the clarinet and trumpets, head the procession. The number of Power-Places visited is not fixed. Lalitpurians say that these days the procession visits fewer than it used to because, as I was informed now 'people are not religiously minded anymore'.[17]

9.16.2. Rām Navami (Caitra-*shukla*/Caulāthwa 9)

The following day is Rām's Ninth (Rām Navami). There is a remarkable absence of a cult of Rām in the Kathmandu Valley. There is no major temple to Rām in Lalitpur, although small shrines do exist in various homes and courtyards. On this day then, in stark contrast to the major celebrations going on in places like Ayodhyā in India, the worship of Rām is largely confined to the home, where a short *pujā* may be offered at the household shrine.

Pitha Pujā continues on this day from the day before. On this day several *guthi*s visit Mahālakshmisthān to do a *pujā* and eat a feast together.[18] All are from localities located within the area of the city over which Mahālakshmi is said to provide protection. The *pujā* includes the sacrifice of a goat as a blood offering to this Mother Goddess.[19]

Furthermore, on this day, until recently two Mahālakshmi processions used to be organized. The Lũchẽ Mahālakshmi Jātrā was run by a group of Maharjans of Lũchẽ, Cāka Bahi. This procession would run from Mahālakshmisthan and back via Mangaḥ, Nugaḥ, Uku Bāhāḥ and Cāka Bahi.[20] The Kewa Nani Mahālakshmi Jātrā was run by a Maharjan *guthi* of Kewa Nani, Mahāpā until the mid-1980s when the movable image of Mahālakshmi was stolen. The route of this *jātrā* was from Mahālakshmisthan to Kewa Nani via Kusunti, Iti and Ikhā.[21]

9.16.3. Understanding Caitra Dashaĩ

The 'small Dashaĩ' of Caitra seems to be connected to the vernal equinox (Witzel 1997: 526). Its relative unimportance in Nepal in contrast to the festival's celebration in other parts of South Asia would seem to reflect the contrasting importance of the autumnal Mohani. Furthermore, the almost complete lack of a Rām cult can be understood by reference to the *Rāmayana* (Levy 1990: 433). In that great epic, the hero Rām worships the Goddess in order to secure her help in his battle against Ravana. So on this day, in the Newar cities at least, this aspect of the epic is emphasized instead of devotion to Rām himself. Levy sees this emphasis in Bhaktapur as a product of that city's symbolic organization and thematic link to Mohani. The same is apparently true of Lalitpur.[22]

9.17. Solar New Year Festivities: Biskaḥ (Vaishākh 1)

On the last day of the solar year (Caitra last) a *yaḥsĩ* pole is raised in Lalitpur at Bāl Kumāri analogous to the major event in Bhaktapur (Levy 1990: 476). It is just five metres high, though it said that it was once as big as the one at Bhaktapur. This is then taken down the next morning signalling the beginning of the new solar year.[23] Pilgrimage to one of the mandalic peaks of the Valley is a subsidiary feature of this festival. Devotees from around the Valley climb Dhinco (Champadevi, Np.), Sipuco (Shivapuri, Np.), or Puco (Phulcoki, Np.) on the last evening of the year, returning home the next morning. Some light fires and stay up all night returning home in the morning. Those who have dug a well during the past year make an offering to the *nāga*s at Puco hill to the south of Lalitpur.

The following day, New Year's Day by solar reckoning is celebrated as Khai Sãlhu. On this day Lalitpurians drink a special kind of pea soup (*kwāti*). As the legumes are different this is a different kind of *kwāti* from the one that they will drink later on in the year, on Gũ Punhi and Sā Pāru. It is instructive at this point to compare Lalitpur's celebration of Biskaḥ with that of Bhaktapur. Parish sees the element of disorder in Bhaktapur's Biskaḥ festival as significant (1997a: 151).

Implicitly constructed as chaos, disruptive challenges to the festival's constructions of order and hierarchy are used to give felt value and reality to the formulations or order and hierarchy that are contested. This 'chaos' is contained by assertions of the power, legitimacy, naturalness and sacredness of the social order (Parish, ibid.)

This can hardly be said of Lalitpur's celebration of Biskaḥ, however. A relatively short pole is hardly threatening to anybody. In Lalitpur the message of the threat of chaos finds expression in two lunar festivals—that of Holi a little before the equinox (§9. 12), and that of the Jātrā immediately afterwards (§10).

9.18. Lhuti Punhi (Caitra-*shukla*/Caulāthwa 15)

As other full moon days, this is a special day for Buddhists. This particular *punhi* has special significance as, according to the *Svayambhu Purāna*, on this day the first Buddha sowed the sacred lotus seed into the primeval Valley lake causing the blooming of a lotus with 108,000 petals and giving rise to the sacred Svayambhu flame. Those who have lost a family member during the past year climb Jāmācwa peak (Nagarjun) on the north-west rim of the Valley where, it is said, in an echo of the Buddhas planting of the sacred lotus seed, they throw the skull bone of the deceased into the air. The following morning pilgrims from all over the Valley bathe in the waters of the Bālāju water garden at the foot of Jāmācwa.

9.19. Bũgadyaḥ Nhawã (Vaishākh-*krishna*/Caulāgā 1)

Today Bũgadyaḥ and Cākwāḥdyaḥ are given a ritual bath (*snāna*) marking the beginning of the festivities of the Jātrā (§10.7.1). From now on for the next few weeks many days are marked by events connected with the Jātrā which will be dealt with in its own chapter (§10; Appendix 8, p. 301, for comparison).

9.20. Maya Khwā Swayegu (Vaishākh-*krishna*/Caulāgā 15)

Today is the day for 'Seeing Mother's Face' in ritual parallel to that on the new moon in Gũlā, eight months before (§7.23). On this *nakhaḥ*, family members give gifts of food and cloth to their mother and receive *sagã̄* as a blessing in return. As on fathers' day it is vital that married-out daughters visit their natal home on this day for not to do so would cause great offence.[24]

They whose mother is no longer alive may go to the Mātā Tirthā ponds, six miles south-west of Kathmandu just off the Thānkot road. In the past some would walk for days to get there from outlying districts. They bathe in the larger pond and then climb stone steps to reach the smaller pond where they perform Ancestor Worship (*shrāddha*) and toss rice, sweets, fruit, coins, and vermilion into the pond and light oil lamps in devotion to their departed mother. At this time also some give prestations (*dān*) to their domestic priest. As on Bāya Khwā Swayegu (§7.23), for the particular family, the day ceases to be a *nakhaḥ* on the death of the mother. Married-out daughters will no longer visit their natal home on this day.

9.21. Akshaya Tritiya (Vaishākh-*shukla*/Bachalāthwa 3)

This day, the 'Eternal Third', marks the beginning of the season (Dewāli) for Lineage Deity Worship (*digu dyaḥ pujā*) for many Lalitpur *thar*s (Quigley 1985b: 15).[25]

9.22. Swãya Punhi (Buddha Jayanti, Vaishākh-*shukla*/Bachalāthwa 15)

This full moon observance marks the anniversary of Buddha's birth, enlightenment and death and, as a Theravādin festival, has only been observed in Nepal since that particular movement was brought to the Valley in 1926 (Gellner 1992: 215). Newars do *pujā* to local Buddhist shrines. Groups of men who identify with the modern Buddhist movement—Shākyas, Vajrācāryas, Maharjans, and others—make a procession around the centripetal procession route accompanied by the *dhimay bājā.* Though locally the focal point of celebration is Nāg Bāhāḥ many Lalitpurians make the journey to the centre of the festivities at Svayambhu.[26] In deference to Buddhist sensitivities, no animals are to be slaughtered on this day.

9.23. The Dewāli period—Lineage Deity Worship

The term Lineage Deity, *digu dyaḥ*, is a generic term, rendered *kuladevatā* in both Nepali and Sanskrit. These deities usually consist of a single aniconic stone flanked by several others, somewhat smaller, on either side, and situated in a field (*khyaḥ*) outside the confines of the old city wall as I have already mentioned (§5.4). The location of the stones, as Quigley rightly asserts, rather than the stones themselves seems to be of primary significance (1985b: 18; cf. Van Kooij 1978: 7).[27] Often the Lineage Deity of any particular clan may be one of several in close proximity. The stones are usually surrounded by a low wall and may have a small bell mounted to one side. Occasionally, the deity has a cult that is much more developed than usual. These are surmounted by a multi-roofed temple structure and adorned with all the paraphernalia of the *pujā* including banners, flags, lamp stands, and larger bells. Such are the Lineage Deities of the Bārāhi at Purnacandi and the Tamvaḥ at Jawalakhel.

Such deities have a well-known Sanskritic name, though this epithet must have been given some time after the god's establishment. In the case of Siddhilakshmi Purnacandi at Ga Bāhāḥ, the Lineage Deity is now well within the confines of the old city.

There has been much discussion over the identity, or otherwise, of the Lineage Deity (*digu dyaḥ*) with the Tantric Deity (*āgã dyaḥ*) (Quigley 1985b: 27-8). Vergati (1979: 122,124,127) believes the *digu dyaḥ* is precisely identified with the *āgã dyaḥ*. Toffin, however, disagrees (1984: 558). It is tempting to draw a parallel here between the relationship of the Tantric Deity to the Lineage Deity and that of the shrines of the Mother Goddesses and their Power-Places. Such a parallel holds in Bhaktapur where the cult of the Eight Mother Goddesses is particularly developed (Levy 1990: 228-34). The Mother Goddess shrines that ring the city of Lalitpur, however, unlike those of Bhaktapur, have no temple within the city. The identification of *āgã dyaḥ* with *digu dyaḥ*, therefore, seems to be entirely lost on most Lalitpurians. This is certainly true of the Pengu Daḥ.[28]

The great majority of Lalitpur's patrilineal groups, if not all, do Lineage Deity Worship at some point during the period of Dewāli.[29] For most Lalitpurians this period begins on Akshaya Tritiya. For all, it comes to an end on Sithi Nakhaḥ some four weeks later.

As an example of Lineage Deity Worship (*digu dyaḥ pujā*) I shall describe the *thākāli luyegu* as it is practiced by the 'Greater Jhvaḥchẽ *et al.*' lineage (Appendix 1, p. 288) of Tamvaḥ. This is by no means typical. In fact it is the fullest example I have come across in the course of my fieldwork, taking six days to complete.[30] Other Tāmrakārs acknowledge that their lineages also used to do the full complement of ritual but that now people 'have to go to the office', and don't have time for such lengthy commitments. The cost of the ritual for the *thākāli* and his family is also considerable and has led many to switch to following the shorter version, *lher pujā.*

The *thākāli luyegu* ritual practiced by the 'Greater Jhvaḥchẽ *et al.*' lineage is always the first by any Tamvaḥ during the Dewāli season. Other households of the lineage follow immediately after the *thākāli*'s. Then the other lineages are free to do theirs. Lineage Deity Worship always takes place either on a Thursday or a Saturday.[31] Certain days are busy at Tamkadyaḥ as several lineages do Lineage Deity Worship in succession. On such days priority is on a first come, first served basis.

9.23.1. Chwaylā Bhu (Day 1)

The first morning begins with the eating of a boiled-rice meal as on other days. Then the house is purified (*ni yayegu*). As on the seventh day of Mohani, the women of the house clean all the vessels, especially those that have had boiled rice in them so that there would be no boiled rice in the house. There will be no eating of boiled rice until the fourth day and no eating outside the house until the complete series of rituals is over with Kwenā Pujā on the sixth day. All household members bathe. Then the woman of the Barber (Nāpit) caste, the Nauni, arrives to 'touch the toes' (*lusi thiyegu*) of the family (§3.4.3). As on other visits, this may or may not involve the actual paring of the toenails. The household is now in a heightened state of purity.[32] From now on household members must abstain from garlic, chicken meat and eggs until they have completed the entire six-day ritual. The household has a lot of *pujā* materials to prepare for the following day. That evening, the *thākāli*'s family eats the preparatory feast of *chwaylā bhu.*

9.23.2. Digu Dyaḥ Pujā (Day 2)

The second day is the main day for Lineage Deity Worship proper. The household walks and drives to the Lineage Deity of Tamkadyaḥ (Ugracandimai) at Jawalakhel. Elaborate *pujā*s are offered, first to the aniconic stone image (*prākrit*) and then, after it is placed over the *prākrit*, to the brass image by the Brahman domestic priest, taking four or five hours to complete. Along with the worship of the Lineage Deity a special *pujā* is offered to the Nyākakhwāduma Mahādyaḥ (Five-Faced Shiva) whose shrine is opposite that of Tamkadyaḥ.[33] Then comes the sacrifice of a pure black goat (*nyākhuru dugu*).[34] In preparation for this, the domestic priest whispers mantras in the ear of the goat. The goat is sprinkled with water and everyone waits for it to give consent to its killing by shaking its body. The goat is killed by the household tenant farmer (Mhāy Nāyaḥ) by slicing through its jugular vein. The spurting blood is directed in an arc over the image. The *purohit* then does Lineage Deity Worship all over again. A male member of the lineage then climbs onto one of the roofs of the temple and unfurls streamers (*pātaḥ cayo*) so that they hang down from the top of the temple. The casting of *yaḥmari* sweets to the devotees below follows, in a ritual analogous to that which takes place at the 'Dropping the Coconut' during the Jātrā, and is clearly a form of *prasād.* An offering of 108 lamps of *ghyaḥ* is then lit in front of the deity. All the kinsmen with their priest then gather around the deity for the taking of *prasād* (*du samay kayegu*). If they cannot fit inside the temple then they hold up a sheet so that no one else can see them and eat *prasād* together by putting fingers to mouth thus eating polluted food (*cipaḥ ciyu*). Women then offer *pujā* to Lineage Deity and put vermilion as *sindhur* in their hair.[35] The morning's ritual is completed with the eating of *samay baji* and everyone returns to the house. From this time on for the next four days, the movable image is kept in *baigaḥ* not in its usual god room.

That evening, the family eats a feast together, which includes the sharing of the head of the sacrificial victim (*sikāḥ bhu*). In the past the Karmācārya Tantric priest would do a special ritual called the Gift of Life (*jiv dān*) in which the remains of the victim's head would be taken in a dish to the *chwāsā.* The Karmācārya would speak mantras over them in the belief that the life would return to the goat and it would wander off again.[36]

9.23.3. Kaulā (Day 3)

The third day begins with daily worship (*nitya pujā*) to the movable image of the Lineage Deity in the *baigaḥ*. The offerings, of *gulimali*, *aylaḥ*, and fruit, are the same as that given on Saturdays and Sundays to the movable image during the year. The normal *nitya pujā* through the year on Mondays to Fridays is simpler and does not include *aylaḥ*. *Samay baji*, including fried organs (*butan*) from the sacrificed goat, is eaten and, in the evening, this is followed by another feast.

9.23.4. Dyana bhu (Day 4)

The fourth day begins with *nitya pujā* as the day before. This is followed by the first meal of boiled rice (*dyana bhu*) since the first day. Boiled rice is also offered to the movable image and then deposited at the *chwāsā*. The day, as usual, finishes with a feast.

9.23.5. Caturdasi Pujā (Day 5)

The fifth day begins, as it has done now since the day before yesterday, with *nitya pujā* in the *baigaḥ*, after which the household again makes a visit to Tamkadyaḥ. This time, however, they do not take the image in the *pujā* basket but instead take a Flask (*kalasha*). After *pujā* to the Flask, *samay baji* is eaten. Once the evening feast is over the movable image is taken down from *baigaḥ* and replaced in its usual room on the *mātā̃*.

9.23.6. Kwenā Pujā (Day 6)

The final ritual of Lineage Deity Worship, as at various other ceremonies, involves the offering of a *pujā* to the Ganesh at Kwenā, Puco. Materials offered include a chicken egg, garlic (*lābā*), radish (*layẽ*, 'Ganesh's tusk'), and the deity's favourite sweet, *laddu.* As always the *pujā* is completed with the eating of *prasād* after which the household returns to the house. The ritual is now complete. From now on meals can again be taken outside the home, as there is no need to keep a special level of purity. *Samay baji* is followed, in the evening, by the last feast. For this married-out sisters and nephews and their families are invited.

9.23.7. Variations on a theme

The attenuated version of Lineage Deity Worship as the Tamvaḥ celebrate it, *lher pujā*, lasts three days rather than six. No domestic priest may be called and no Flask Worship is performed. Bārāhi Lineage Deity Worship lasts four days and is an integral part of the Jātrā, being celebrated after the chariot reaches Thati (§10.7.6). The four days are Chwaylā Bhu, Lineage Deity Worship (always on a Thursday), Lya Swayegu (The Checking of Accounts), and Cyā Bhu (Feast of the Eight Elders).

The performance of Lineage Deity Worship is a strong marker of one's caste credentials. Tāmrakārs, for instance, insist that if one of their number has married a Maharjan then they are excluded from the Lineage Deity cult.

The sharing of Lineage Deity Worship is the most important marker of one's fraternal proximity. When a larger lineage splits into two or more smaller units, as happens periodically, members of now separate groups no longer perform birth or death pollution for each other except in the perfunctory sense. Only those of the intimate group, who also share in the feast at Mohani (§8.8), are considered close patrilineal relatives (*syāḥ phuki*; §2.3).[37]

It is considered very important to do the Lineage Deity Worship correctly for failure to do so may incur the wrath of this dangerous god. After the break-up of the large Marikaḥmi lineage, the explosion of a coffee machine in one of their shops, which killed two staff, was attributed to the wrath of this deity. Animal sacrifice, under the influence of Theravāda Buddhism, has become increasingly unpopular among some sections of Newar society in recent years. Because of this some have considered discontinuing the practice altogether. Not to present an offering of meat and alcohol to a dangerous deity such as the Lineage Deity, however, seems to many to be inviting trouble. After considering this issue, the same Marikaḥmi lineage decided to refer the question back to the deity itself by putting two pieces of paper in front of it with the words 'yaḥ' ('like') and 'mayaḥ' ('dislike') written on them. A small child was told to draw the lot, which was negative, so they decided that the deity would not be happy if they discontinued. No such scruples seem to have prevented the Lwahãkaḥmi from dropping animal sacrifice altogether. When they do Lineage Deity Worship, today, a duck's egg is offered to the adjacent Ganesh but no meat is offered to the Lineage Deity itself. This seems to reflect a general ambivalence towards this festival among the members of this *thar.* Very few Lwahãkaḥmi do Lineage Deity Worship as a lineage anymore, most simply completing a perfunctory ritual on Sithi Nakhaḥ. The same is true of the Paḥmā lineage of Sikaḥmi.

9.23.8. Understanding Lineage Deity Worship

The significance of Lineage Deity Worship must be sought in its strong expression of clan solidarity. It is not, as I have demonstrated (§2.5), that the worship of the same Lineage Deity expresses such clan solidarity but rather the *corporate worship* of that deity. Many different lineages may worship the same deity during the Dewāli season. Each is expressing the integrity of the lineage. But there is no indication that the simple identification with a common Lineage Deity has any strong social significance.[38] Clan solidarity is not only expressed by corporate worship but also, and very strongly, in the corporate meal. After worship, *samay baji*, and later the evening feast, is eaten in the presence of the deity who also receives a plate. The meal is eaten as much as possible together, as a complete lineage. The preparation of the meal is also done together. There are no servants. Men and women work alongside each other. This is an affair for the lineage and no one else.

There are some significant similarities between the festivals of Mohani and

Lineage Deity Worship. Both involve the lineage in corporate worship. Both involve animal sacrifice. Although both last several days, the main period lasts for four during which the lineage must be in a heightened state of purity. In both, boiled rice is eaten on the morning of the first day and then any remaining is cleared out of the house. Boiled rice will not be eaten again until the fourth day. Each festival includes the eating of food in secret, away from the prying eyes of outsiders. Each, then, places a high premium on social exclusion.

Furthermore, the focus of worship on the Devi at Mohani has parallels in the cult of the Lineage Deity. Like the Power-Places of the Mother Goddesses, the Lineage Deity is always both outside the city boundaries and represented by an aniconic stone. Clearly the Lineage Deity, like the Devi, is regarded as a dangerous deity that requires propitiation with blood. This is borne out by some of the Sanskritic names that have been given the deity—Ugracandimai and Siddhilakshmi Purnacandi. The identity of the Lineage Deity is, therefore, conflated with that of the Devi. The two great festivals of the lineage, Lineage Deity Worship and Mohani frame that most dangerous period of the year—the monsoon. If, as I have tried to demonstrate, Mohani expresses the need to reestablish the social order after the monsoon, then Lineage Deity Worship can be understood as a preparatory ritual. The lineage is about to undergo a severe threat to its existence and solidarity. The worship of the Lineage Deity, then, is, at the very least, a rite of protection. Indeed, K.B. Bista, writing of the cult of his own Lineage Deity states that 'The principle aim of worshipping Kuldevatā is to avoid diseases and epidemics, acquire wealth and achieve success' (1972: 6, my translation).

9.24. Sithi Nakhaḥ (Jyesth-*shukla*/Tachalāthwa 6)

After eleven months we have now come to the final event in the lunar calendar, as it is conceived locally. It is a festival of completion in more ways than one. This is the final day for Lineage Deity Worship. All those who have not yet visited their external Lineage Deity during the Dewāli period will do so on this day. Furthermore, even those who have done Lineage Deity Worship as a lineage will now send a representative to the site for a final ritual. Essential to the ritual is the sharing of the beaten rice meal, which must include the lentil cake, *waḥ*—a protective food for the coming rainy season.

Early in the morning serious devotees rise and have a ritual bath in the river. The house is then purified with the normal mixture of cow dung and clay. This is also Kumār's birthday, so an important *pujā* is offered to this deity, Ganesh's brother, at his shrine in front of the house, the *pikhā lakhu*. Furthermore, a special *pujā* is offered to an unbaked brick as the Earth (Prithvi), a significant act to an agricultural society (cf. Levy 1990: 512). Being the end of the dry season, the water table is at its annual lowest. Rivers are virtually dry and ground water is harder to obtain. This day therefore is the day to clean wells and ponds. Such an intrusion into the realm of the *nāga*s would normally be considered a precarious enterprise but today the *nāga*s are also away doing their Lineage Deity Worship so it is ideal. In the evening, or on a following day, married-out daughters and their families are invited for a feast (*nakhaḥtyā*).

Some Lalitpurians call Gathā̃ Mugaḥ the festival of women (*mista nakhaḥ*). Today, in contrast, is the festival of men (*misa nakhaḥ*). These two festivals are the two major events that form the boundaries of a period that is, for the most part, devoid of festivities. Tomorrow is the beginning of the rice transplanting (*wā piyugu*) season. Work in the fields is heavy throughout this period. No instruments will be heard during this time; musical instruments are placed in the care of Nāsadyaḥ until the heavy work is done.[39] Only rice planting songs associated with rice transplantation (*sināјyā myẽ*) may be sung.

Levy notes that Sithi Nakhaḥ is a significant festival for it marks the change from old to new:

> Sithi Nakhaḥ is a threshold day, the ending of some of the year's activities and a preparation for something new. What is being prepared for with the anticipation of the seasonal rains is an encounter with nature vital to agriculturally based Bhaktapur, an encounter full of risks. This 'nature' is the environing and supporting realm of Bhaktapur's public moral, civic life. (Levy 1990: 512)

As if to emphasize the liminal character of this season, obscenity is 'extensively and publicly licensed' (ibid.: 516). Young men and old, and occasionally women too shout lewd cat calls to each other across the paddy fields. I was once the victim of some coarse joking on the part of a leathery old thrice-married Maharjan. I had explained that my wife was pregnant.

'Is it a boy or girl?'

'I don't know.'

'You should know. While you are making it you should think 'Boy... Boy... Boy!' and it will be.'

Lakshmi Prasad Devakota's poem 'The Fifteenth of the Month of Ashādh' describes a typical day in the rice-planting season with its festive joy and hard work. Near the end of the poem Devakota quotes a song which forms the epigraph for this chapter (Treu 1993: 158-159). It is worth quoting a few lines from this song here:

> It's the time of rice planting,
> (...)
> today we laugh,
> today we sing.
> Tomorrow, oh my God! who weeps
> because death has taken away!
> There is laughter, there is song. But, sobering thought, there will be sickness and death.

9.25. Dasa Harā (Jyesth-*shukla*/Tachalāthwa 10)

This calendrical event is a minor one for Lalitpur as it is for Bhaktapur though it is common throughout the Hindu world (Levy 1990: 437). Levy suggests that in its traditional Indian version it was a day for the removal of sins through bathing in the Ganges and other large rivers. In Bhaktapur, however, the emphasis is rather on protection from external misfortune (ibid.)

In Lalitpur, though some take the opportunity to bathe in the Bāgmati, this day is more important as the first day in the season for the eating of greens such as spinach, green onions, green garlic and the like. On this day as at Ghyaḥcāku Sãnhu (§9.7) a special lentil dish is prepared with black lentils, stinging nettles (*naykã*), and green chilies. In addition, the large leafy vegetable called *pākã* is either added to the lentil dish or fried separately. This food is regarded as a healthy food to eat at this time—the middle of the summer season—in the same way as *may goja* is consumed during the cold season in the month of Māgh.

9.26. Jyesth Punhi (Jyā Punhi, Jyesth-*shukla*/Tachalāthwa 15)

This full moon day is celebrated, by Newars, as the summer solstice festival (though, like the winter solstice festival of Yaḥmari Punhi it is determined by the movement of the moon). On this day traditionally one would shut up shop, or lay down tools a little early. Not to do so would demonstrate a continual lack of satisfaction with one's work.

Plate 19. Jyesth Punhi *bhajan khalaḥ*.

On this day Siddhi Narasimha's throne is displayed on the plinth of the Krishna temple, in front of the old palace. Locals view the throne as a symbol (*prākrit*) of the king himself, who would himself have sat outside in the evening to listen to the singing of the *bhajan*s by the ensemble (Jyesth Punhi *bhajan khalaḥ*; Plate 19).

The *bhajan* ensemble is made up largely of Tāmrakārs with a few Joshis and Shresthas, is organized under a committee, and is identical to the group that plays for the autumn dance-dramas, the Kati Pyākhã. They play two *khĩ* drums, a harmonium, and *taḥ* bells and sing thirty-two hymns attributed to Siddhi Narasimha Malla, which takes them through the afternoon and into the early evening.

It is said that during the singing of the *bhajan*s the monsoon must begin. As this festival happens usually in early June it is not unlikely that the monsoon will, in fact begin, at this precise time. The allusion here is to the king as rainmaker. The seat of royal authority, now vacant, is brought outside. The erstwhile king, as patron of the worship, sits on a throne that includes as its most significant element a nine-*nāga* gilt copper back. It is the *nāga*s that bring rain and it is by their blessing that the king reigns. By submission to the *nāga*s the king causes rain to fall on the land and the rice crops to grow.

10. The Approach of Disorder II: Sri Nivas has Come!

> Like a great ship staggering through a heavy sea—its curved prow terminating in a gilt figurehead of Bhairav, apparently forcing its way through the seething mass of humans who like billows surround it in one capacity and another—the great god Matsyendra in his car, with strain and cry makes his annual journey.
>
> Percy Brown (1997 [1912]: 108-9)

> The inhabitants... run about beating and playing upon every kind of instrument their country affords, which make an inconceivable noise.
>
> Father Giuseppe (1801: 310)

10.1. Introduction

In the study of the festivals of Nepal many scholars have noted the importance of the chariot festival of Karunāmaya (Matsyendranāth) that takes place in and around the old city of Lalitpur each summer. The most significant work to emerge on the chariot festival is Bruce Owens', *The Politics of Divinity in the Kathmandu Valley: The Festival of Bũgadya/Rāto Matsyendranāth* (1989). Owens describes almost the entire festival in great detail and is a mine of ethnographic data. John Locke's study, *Karunāmaya: The Cult of Avalokiteshvara-Matsyendranāth in the Valley of Nepal* (1980) recounts the history of the cult and takes us on a tour of the various cults of Karunāmaya in the Kathmandu Valley. Locke sets the chariot festival in the context of the worship of the various manifestations of Avalokiteshvara that are found in the Valley.

The principal deity of the Jātrā is Bũgadyaḥ (lit. 'god of Bũga'). Bũga (Bungamati, Np.) is a Newar village a few miles to the south of Lalitpur. Bũgadyaḥ is the main deity (*kwāḥpāḥdyaḥ*) of the monastery of Bũga–Bũga Bāhāḥ (Amaravatinama Vihārā). How it came to such prominence will be examined in due course.

I would not be the first to suggest that a Newar festival could be likened to a drama (cf. Levy 1990). As I hope I have demonstrated, all of Lalitpur's cyclic events entail an element of drama. At the risk of appearing unimaginative, however, I want to propose that, of all the festivals of Lalitpur, the Jātrā has tremendous appeal as an enacted play. This dramatic structure serves as a useful entry point in the exploration of the event's meaning.

If, as Shakespeare's Jaques declared, 'All the world's a stage,'[1] there are nevertheless moments, events in which the big themes of life seem to be enacted in a vivid and memorable way. Robert Levy remarks that part of the fascination of the Biskaḥ festival flows from 'watching the major figures in the hierarchical order symbolized by themselves,' carried swaying and lurching dangerously on the chariot of Bhairava (ibid.: 499). This is, I contend, equally true of Lalitpur's Jātrā. Levy continues: 'It is not enough for... [symbolic] forms to be meaningful, they must also be *engaging*' (ibid., original emphasis). People must be actively involved in the festival in order to fully appreciate and affirm the order that it is envisioning. I will come to the play itself in due time. First, it is necessary to introduce the play's principal actor by recounting some of his legends.

10.2. The legends of Karunāmaya/Matsyendranāth

There are several versions of the legend surrounding the origin of the Jātrā. Apart from being transmitted orally these legends also figure in the chronicle of Padmagiri and others (Hasrat 1970: 22). Khatry (1996: 93f.) and Locke (1973: 39-60, 1980: 285-8) recount various versions of the legend. In the following version I draw heavily on these as well as on oral accounts:

> One day Gorakhnāth was tricked by the *nāga*s into losing a bet. Gorakhnāth's response was to use his power (*siddhi*) to bind the *nāga*s at Mrigasthali near Pashupatināth causing no rain to fall for twelve years. After much investigation, King Narendra Deva's pandits discovered the cause of the drought, which had decimated the Valley. They advised him that the only way he would be able to get Gorakhnāth to rise and release the *nāga*s was if he can persuade his *guru*, Avalokiteshvara Karunāmaya, to come from Kamuni in Assam. Narendra Deva set out with his learned *ācārya*, Bandhudatta and a peasant named Rathãcakra in order to bring Karunāmaya to the Valley. Arriving at Kamuni they found Karunāmaya living as the youngest son of the king of that place. They managed to trick the king to let him go but his mother prevented him from leaving. Departing to the city of Kāmarup, Bandhudatta used his Tantric power to cast a spell on the boy who was able to sneak out of the palace over the sleeping form of his mother. The demons (*yaksha*s), which always seemed to be in alliance with the queen, snatched the boy away so that Bandhudatta had to call on the Four Bhairavas for help. Seeing the Four Bhairavas the boy was released and was carried on a palanquin by the Bhairavas to Nepal. As they neared their destination, however, the *yaksha*s again cast a spell causing the weight of four mountains to be brought down on the palanquin. The ever-resourceful Bandhudatta overcame this with his own spell, which turned Karunāmaya into a bumblebee. The bee flew into a flask (*kalasha*) which was then covered and brought safely to the outlying village of Bũga by the Bhairavas. On hearing of his *guru*'s arrival in the Valley Gorakhnāth rose from his seat releasing the *nāga*s and bringing rainfall once again to the parched fields.

Some versions then go on to explain other phenomena related to the cult of Karunāmaya such as how his mother came to stay at Lagankhel:

> Once the rain had started the party decided to continue to the city of Lalitpur. Approaching the city Bandhudatta ascertained that Karunāmaya's

> mother is hiding at the top of a tree with a number of evil spirits lying in wait to set about the party and retrieve her son. Bandhudatta again gained mastery over the evil woman and bound her to the spot where she remains until this day.

The question arises of why the temple of Karunāmaya should be situated in Lalitpur when the king and his preceptor were from elsewhere. This also is dealt with in the accounts:

> A dispute then arose as to where the deity should be kept. Narendra Deva would have preferred to build a temple in his capital of Bhaktapur, Bandhudatta insisted that it should be built in his city of Kāntipur [Kathmandu] but the farmer Rathācakra wanted it to be built in Lalitpur. So they summoned an old man of Lalitpur to decide the issue. The king of Lalitpur tricks the man into choosing his city even though he would have preferred it to be built in Bhaktapur. On pronouncing his judgement the old man dropped dead because of his dishonesty but the judgement had been made and could not be changed.
>
> The flask was taken to a monastery in Lalitpur where an image was made for the deity. The image was then installed in its purpose-built temple in the middle of a monastery and the king inaugurated an annual chariot festival. There were already seven other such festivals in Lalitpur, however, so they summoned all the other deities who agreed to suspend their festivals in favour of Lokeshvara's. One deity however, Jātadhari Lokeshvara (Cākwāḥdyaḥ), disagreed and appeared to Bandhudatta in a dream ordering him to keep his festival as it was. This they did and the festival of Cākwāḥdyaḥ was kept alongside the new one.

In another account, a *yaksha* demanded a human sacrifice from a priest. Behind him his son happened to be standing because he had just become old enough to join his father. The demon demanded his blood so the young man was sacrificed.

Any resident of Lalitpur can recount the legend of the *bhoto* (a vest or waistcoat-type article of clothing). One version of this is recorded in the *Mardāryavalokiteshvara Avādana kathā* (Locke 1980: 295-6; also recounted in Khatry 1996: 98):

> The *bhoto* once belonged to Karkotaka, the king of the *nāga*s who lives at Taudāha pond to the south of Cobhār. Once a Jyāpu *vaidya* cured the sore eye of Karkotaka's wife. In return Karkotaka gave the farmer his precious *bhoto.* One day, while the Jyāpu was working in his field, a demon came and stole the *bhoto* that the farmer had taken off. At the time of the Jawalakhel Jātrā, however, the farmer saw a tall, strange figure wearing the vest. The farmer accosted the stranger and tried to retrieve the *bhoto* from him. But the demon was big and a tough fight ensued. The case was taken before the king who ruled that, as there was insufficient evidence that the *bhoto* belonged to either party, it must be kept in the custody of Matsyendranāth himself until reliable evidence was forthcoming.

10.3. History of the Jātrā

10.3.1. Origins

There has been some dispute as to the origin of the Jātrā. Anne Vergati reports that certain chronicles place the introduction of Karunāmaya as 523 CE (1995: 91). Sylvan Lévi showed that this date is impossible and that it should be corrected to 657 CE to coincide with Narendra Deva's reign (1905: I, 378-9, in Vergati 1995: 91). The chronicles contain several references to the origin of the Jātrā. The text of the *Gopālarāja Vamshāvali*, however, is at odds with the assessment of the later chronicles. The *Gopālarāja Vamshāvali* is straightforward and reliable for the most part. Wars, droughts, famines and epidemics are all recorded and here it is written that the Jātrā was initiated during Narendra Deva's reign (Vajracarya and Malla 1985: 126, Folio 23). There seems to be no reason to dispute this. Locke and Slusser agree that the origin of the festival should be placed around 644–80 CE during the reign of Narendra Deva (Locke 1980: 297). The association of the three protagonists in the Karunāmaya legend with the three royal centres, however, may have only come about in the fifteenth century once the three cities had become distinct kingdoms (Owens 1989: 89, n.24).

Some authors have conjectured that Bũgadyaḥ may have been a very old deity that later became Karunāmaya. One piece of evidence cited in this regard is the ambiguity of the god's gender. It may have been one of the local goddesses that were paraded around the city in the same way as Vishnu Devi, Bāl Kumāri, and Mahālakshmi are still today. Iconographic representations of Karunāmaya also attest to the antiquity of the cult. Vergati reports that the first known iconographical document representing 'Rāto Lokeshvara' is an eleventh century (1015 CE) manuscript (1995: 202).

The tradition of a drought as the immediate precursor to the Jātrā is certainly old. A version of the *Svayambhu Purāna*, dated to around the reign of Yaksha Malla (1428–1482), attributes the bringing of the deity to a severe drought (Locke 1980: 281). Vergati notes, however, that in a scroll (dated 1617 CE, Plate I-IV) of the legend of Red Avalokiteshvara the drought was reported to be the result of war between the kings and not the entrapment of the *nāgas* (ibid.: 222).

10.3.2. Transformation—the Jātrā under the Mallas

Under the patronage of the Mallas the Jātrā underwent a considerable transformation. It is clear from the historical evidence that the Mallas selected from and reshaped the existing Jātrā so that it would serve the purpose of consolidating their hegemony over the people of the city.

The early Malla kings inherited a city that was overwhelmingly Buddhist though they themselves were decidedly Brahmanical with little enthusiasm for promoting Buddhist ideology or custom. They took Taleju Bhavani as their chosen deity (*ishtadevatā*) and were strongly influenced by the Maithil Jhā Brahmans who had come up from the court of Simraun Gadh and introduced

Maithili as the court written language. Malla art, literature and religion were strongly influenced by the Hindu Tantric tradition.

The timing of the Jātrā is an issue of some discussion. Dharmasvarmin's account, written in the mid-thirteenth century, places the Jātrā in the 'middle autumn month'. But Ripu Malla, in 1313, is reported to have attended the bathing ceremony in the spring. Locke interprets this as a change in the timing of the festival in the intervening period. Popular folklore from the late Malla period associates the festival with the bringing of rain. Locke conjectures that a prolonged drought had occurred at this time and that its end was attributed to Karunāmaya (1980: 330).[2]

During the early Malla period the *de facto* rulership of Lalitpur was in the hands of strong feudal lords (the Pradhānangas or Pramānas). It was only in 1597 that the Mallas, in the person of Shiva Simha of Kathmandu, managed to conquer the Pramāna barons and impose a strong monarchy on the city. Even after this the Pramānas continued to wield considerable influence being the chief landowners and controllers of trade. Shiva Simha's grandson Siddhi Narasimha (reigned 1619–1660 CE) and *his* son Sri Nivas (reigned 1660–1684) had an uphill task trying to control the disparate elements and bring a certain kind of order.

One major strategy the later Mallas employed to impose a centralized order to the city was to co-opt the Jātrā. This entailed adopting Bũgadyaḥ as their *ishtadevatā*, installing him for half the year in a newly built temple at Ta Bāhāḥ, taking personal control and patronage of the cult, and proclaiming the Jātrā the national festival of the city state (ibid.: 334, 339-40).

In 1673 (Phagun 793 NS) Sri Nivas had a large stele placed in the newly built temple of Karunāmaya at Ta Bāhāḥ. Locke gives a synopsis of the inscription: the king of Manigala (Lalitpur) must take personal responsibility for the arrangements for the bathing ceremony, the chariot Jātrā and the bringing of Sri 3 Trailokyanāth Bũga Ishtadevatā to Ta Bāhāḥ (ibid.: 309). It goes on to detail certain obligations that the king lays on the people. In order to ensure the perpetuity of the Jātrā, Sri Nivas donated considerable amounts of personal land in *guthi* trust (ibid.: 310).

It is clear that throughout much of Malla times at least the Bhoto Jātrā had no place in the festivities. A *thyasaphu* (biographical entry on a legal document) of 1664 records the order of the king in prescribing the schedule of events of the Jātrā but, though it prescribes three nights of rites at Jawalakhel, it makes no mention of the *bhoto* (ibid.: 306).[3] Vergati notes, moreover, that in the 1617 scroll, mentioned above, the last episode of the Jātrā was Dropping the Coconut (1995: 221). As Slusser points out, western observers provide the first notice of the *bhoto* (1998: I, 375).[4] The Bhoto Jātrā, then, is clearly a later addition to the Jātrā.

The so-called Golden Age of Lalitpur came to an end in 1705 with the death of Sri Nivas's son Yog Narendra. That year the breaking of the main forward beam of the chariot was considered as an ill omen indeed. Yog Narendra died before the chariot could be pulled to Jawalakhel so they got Bhaskar Malla of Kathmandu to come in his place (D.R. Regmi 1965/66: III, 52, thyasaphu B).

10.3.3. Eighteenth century decline

The eighteenth century witnessed a steady decline in the fortunes of Lalitpur as it did of the other cities of the Valley. Inter-state skirmishes and intrigue, and, in Lalitpur, the reemergence of the Pramānas, led to a rapid turnover of monarchs. Furthermore stronger kings in Kathmandu and Bhaktapur gained control of the Valley exits causing the deterioration of Lalitpur's trade (Slusser: 1998: I, 338). The ascendancy of the house of Gorkha in the west finally toppled the Mallas from their thrones in 1768/69.

The eighteenth century Mallas continued to patronize the cult of Karunāmaya however. A copper plate still attached to the chariot relates that Rajya Prakash Malla donated gilt plating to it (Burleigh 1976: 65). But there was a change in attitude towards the Jātrā. Vira Mahindra Malla assumed the throne in 1710 (829 NS) in the month of Caitra immediately after Lok Prakash died, 'because of the necessity of performing the proper rituals for the Macchindranath cart festival' (ibid.: 56-57). But by 1712 Mahindra Malla could not be bothered to come from Kathmandu (where he was on a visit) in order to be present at the bathing ceremony (Locke 1980: 317). The festival, it seems, was no longer important to the king to legitimize his authority.

For their part the Shah kings, ruling over a much wider kingdom than any of the Malla kings had, could not hope to patronize all the festivals of the lands that they had conquered. The Jātrā in Lalitpur, however, was one festival that they did consider of sufficient importance to warrant their patronage. Sylvain Lévi, who visited Nepal in 1898, notes that the most important part of the procession was the section from Nugaḥ to Lagā̃ (Lagankhel), when the king, the prime minister, and the eminent people of the state took part mounted on elephants (ibid.: 325). This custom was over by the time Percival Landon attended in 1924 (Landon 1976).

10.4. The cast

The cast of the Jātrā comprises a complex array of individuals and groups from every stratum of Lalitpur society including gods and evil spirits, and kings and Untouchables. Here I list only the major players; those that have only a minor role will be introduced as they enter the stage. First I will introduce the immortals, then the mortals.

10.4.1. The immortals

a. Bũgadyaḥ

Various names are used for Bũgadyaḥ depending on who is doing the talking and to whom they are talking. Those who speak Nepali will usually call the deity Matsyendranāth. In Newar it is nearly always either Karunāmaya or Bũgadyaḥ. Buddhists nearly always refer to him as Karunāmaya. Children speak of him as Bābādyaḥ. Hindus usually think of him as Shiva, though the Brahmans of Lalitpur relate a story that illustrates his identity with Krishna (Gellner 1992: 81; Owens 1989: 171, 2000: 720-721). In Newar Buddhism, Bũgadyaḥ is the most important of a number of manifestations of Avalokiteshvara, the *bodhisattva* Padmapāni Lokeshvara.

b. Cākwāḥdyaḥ

As with Bũgadyaḥ, Cākwāḥdyaḥ is identified as Avalokiteshvara and Karunāmaya. Nepali speakers usually refer to Cākwāḥdyaḥ as Minnāth. The image of Cākwāḥdyaḥ is kept at Tangaḥ Bāhāḥ where it stays until it is time for the chariots to move. Its chariot is a good deal smaller than that of Bũgadyaḥ. It is taken down at the end of Bhoto Jātrā and replaced in its temple.

c. Bhairava

The dangerous deity, Bhairava, is manifested in a number of ways in the festival.[5] The four wheels of the chariots are considered to be the four Bhairavas from different places in the Valley: Harisiddhi Bhairava, Hayagriva Bhairava (of Bũga), Lubtanasanhara Bhairava (of Lutu Bāhāḥ in Bũga), Nandakunda Bhairava (also called Lhonde Konde). These four are considered to be the same four who carried Matsyendranāth into the Valley (Locke 1980: 265). The mask on the front of the main beam of the chariot (*daḥmā*) is also considered to be Hayagriva Bhairava (ibid.: 266).

d. Nāgas

The main beam of the chariot, joined to the axles to make a strong wooden frame, is considered to be Karkotaka Nagarāja, the king of the snake gods (ibid.). The streamers that hang down from the top also represent *nāga*s, as do the pulling ropes.[6] This demonstrates a clear association with the need for rain.

10.4.2. The mortals

a. Pānjus

In relation to Bũgadyaḥ the Pānjus are the group of thirty-two members of the inner circle of the Monastic Community (Samgha) of Bũga Bāhāḥ (Amaravatinama Vihārā) whose role it is to officiate in the worship of Bũgadyaḥ. This group comprises seven Vajrācāryas and twenty-four Shākyas, the other member considered to be Bũgadyaḥ himself. In relation to Cākwāḥdyaḥ, any member of the Tangaḥ Bāhāḥ who has taken the Consecration of the Vajra-Master (*ācāḥ luyegu*) is called Pānju (Locke 1980.: 254). The wives of the Pānjus also have a role to play during the festival.

b. Bārāhi

The Bārāhi by now need no introduction (§2.6.4). The Bārāhi Daḥ Guthi, as we have seen, comprises, ideally, twenty-four members, one of whom is considered to be Bũgadyaḥ himself. The Bārāhi have the most extensive ritual and feasting responsibilities of any of those involved in the Jātrā other than the Pānjus (Owens 2000: 713).

c. Yāngwa

The Yāngwa are a group of Maharjan Farmers who receive a special initiation (*dekha*) of Mahākāla which is said to prevent them from falling off the chariots (Gellner and Pradhan 1995: 168). Their work in the construction is to bind the wooden frame of the chariots with cane that they have soaked in the ponds that are adjacent to the construction sites. During the movement of the chariots they also have the responsibility to man the ropes that help to keep the chariot upright. They are the only ones allowed to climb the chariot at this time always removing footwear before they do so.

d. Yala Juju

The king of Lalitpur, the Yala Juju, participates in every significant episode of the Jātrā.[7] Today his presence is symbolized by the sacred sword (*khwā̃*) that is brought to the site of the festival with great show and pomp on all the high events of the Jātrā. These include those of the bathing ceremony, the installation of the image on the chariot, and each time the chariot is pulled.[8]

The Guthi Corporation pays a group of five men to fulfil a number of ritual functions during the festival. They accompany the image of Bũgadyaḥ at every move from its removal to Lalitpur in the winter, to its return to Bũga at the end of the Jātrā. The chief carries the sword, the Yala Juju, another wields the cane (*kathi*) of Siddhi Narasimha Malla, and another holds the oil lamp (*cilakha*), another carries the parasol over the sword and another the mat for the sword. Other men help on an *ad hoc* basis carrying the large ceremonial parasol over the palanquin of Bũgadyaḥ. They are also responsible for swishing the yak-tail fans in front of the deity. Older men say that in the past these roles were the responsibility of a group called the Mā̃ta.[9] Some years ago, however, they left the role and the Guthi Corporation now contracts it out each year. For the past several years a group of Dā̃gols has performed this role. At the moving of the Bũgadyaḥ image on its palanquin the chief Mā̃ta carries the feet of Bũgadyaḥ in a richly decorated box tied onto the crown of his head by a white cloth. The Mā̃ta always ride on the platform of the chariot when it is pulled. This group also accompanies the Kumāri at each of her outings through the year, escorts the *phulpāti* to Mul Cok (§8.8.2), and attends the exhibition of King Siddhi Narasimha Malla's throne on Jyesth Punhi (§9.26).[10]

e. Rope haulers

Several hundred young men are needed to pull the Bũgadyaḥ chariot through the city. The thick hemp ropes (*jangala*) are attached to the chariot's chassis. The men are directed by one of their number called the Haḥphā Biyemha

(Encouragement Giver) who stands precariously on the front of the *daḥmā*, the main forward beam of the chariot.[11] The Haḥphā Biyemha is chosen for his strength from among the men of the sector of the city into which the chariot is to be pulled on that leg of its journey. Boys, many around ten years of age, pull the Cākwāḥdyaḥ chariot which is a lot lighter directed by a somewhat older, teenage boy of their number.

f. Ghaḥku

The Ghaku are another lineage of Maharjans whose role is to act as brake men for the larger chariot as it is moving along to stop the chariot moving too fast or to turn the chariot as it is moving.[12] A Ghaḥku also sits on the front of the smaller chariot to turn it by placing his feet against one front wheel or the other, as it is moving. The Ghaḥku perform a number of sacrifices to the wheels, as manifestations of Bhairava, during the course of the festival.

g. Sese Brahmans

Two Rājopādhyāya Brahmans, descendants of the priests to the Malla kings, are appointed to ride at the front of the larger chariot (Locke 1980: 268). Dressed in white turbans and sashes they stand behind the director of the rope haulers and give the go ahead for the chariot to move. Modern chronicles attribute King Siddhi Narasimha Malla with placing the two Brahmans on the chariot (ibid.: 303).

h. Shah King

The present king (the descendant of Prithvi Narayan Shah, §1.2) participates in the festival on only one occasion: that of 'Showing the Vest', or Bhoto Jātrā. It is clear that his presence is intended to a continuation of the presence of the Malla kings who preceded them.

10.5. The stage

Throughout the Jātrā, the city space of old Lalitpur is made use of to represent the city itself, as we have seen (§5.1). The route of the chariot Jātrā is unique among all the processions of Lalitpur. Niels Gutschow points out that the procession route taken by the Jātrā is a linear one (1982: 193, Fig. 233). Linear processions, as I have shown (§5.6.2), take place when a deity from outside the city visits the city and progresses through it. The presence of a second temple of Bũgadyaḥ at Ta Bārāhi, within the boundaries of old Lalitpur, modifies the journey of Bũgadyaḥ during the preparations for the Jātrā. The image must be brought into the city for a time and then removed at its installation in the chariot.

Cākwāḥdyaḥ, though a resident of the city, is also pulled through city space on what is a modification of Bũgadyaḥ's route. Cākwāḥdyaḥ, as the lesser deity, is pulled to welcome the greater and from then on follows the greater in deference. It is to be surmised, therefore, that before the establishing of the Bũgadyaḥ festival, the Jātrā of Cākwāḥdyaḥ took place on a different route.

Map 16 shows the route of the Jātrā through city space. Gutschow's map (196) shows the delineation of the boundaries of the three areas of the city according to the day on which the residents do *bhujyaḥ* (ibid.: 174). It is perhaps significant that the three areas correspond roughly with the three main areas of the city in relation to their cremation grounds (ibid.: 163, Map 177). It is clear from other evidence that the city of Lalitpur did not exist in anything like its present form at the time that the Jātrā was instituted. Could it be that here we have in ritual form what was, at the establishing of the Jātrā, three separate settlements? Each settlement would have been centred at the point where today that area of the city has its special worship, with the exception of the central area that presumably, at one time, celebrated its

Map 16. The Jātrā.

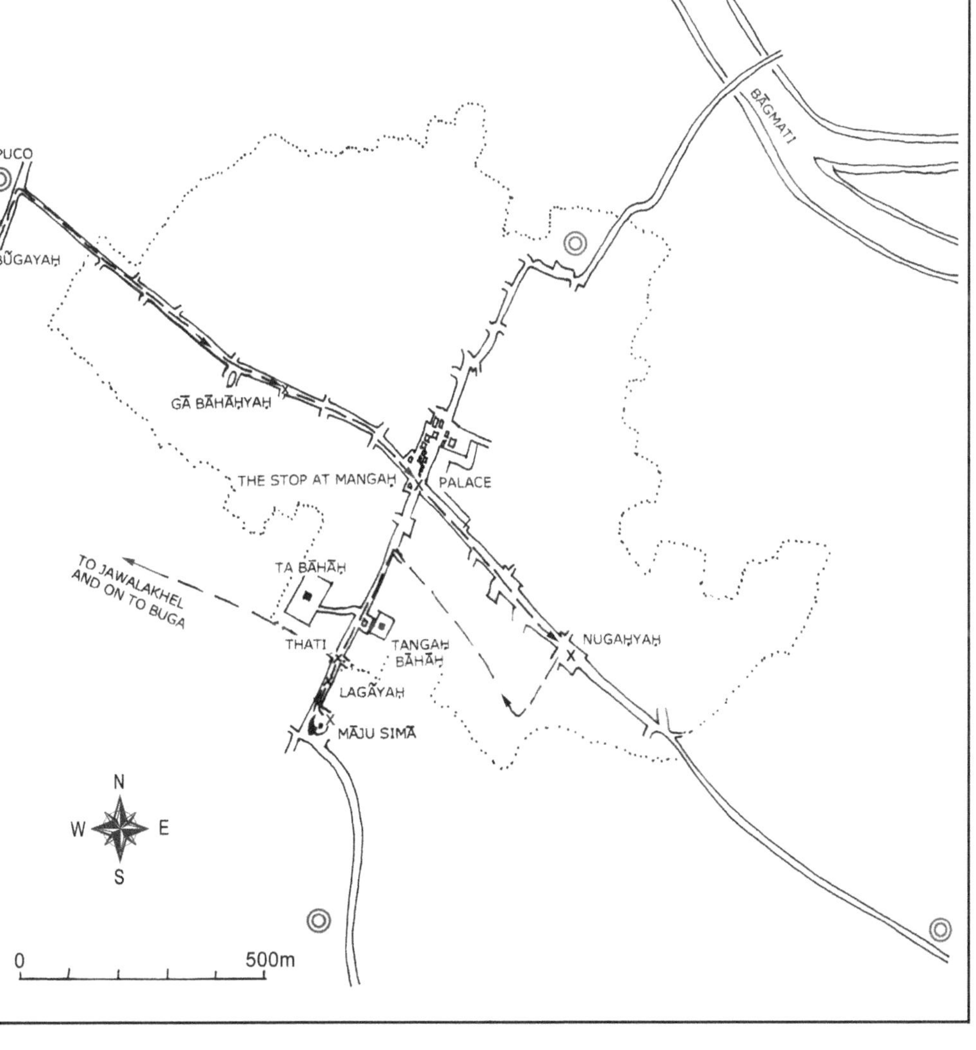

special day when the chariot reached Mangaḥ. The reason the central sector now defers its own celebration until the chariots reach Lagankhel must somehow be bound up with the exit of the chariot from the city and the ritual of 'Dropping the Coconut'.

10.6. The props

The chariots of Bũgadyaḥ and Cākwāḥdyaḥ are, as we have seen, built by two lineages of craftsmen—the Bārāhi Carpenters who construct the frame and the Yāngwa Farmers who lash the structure together with vines. Five different kinds of wood are employed in the construction of the chariots (Appendix 4, p. 294).[13]

Since Rana times the *guthi* lands from which the timber has been harvested have been in control of the government Guthi Corporation which has been very reluctant in recent years to provide wood for the chariot. In 1997 one of the main beams needed replacing but local people who now manage the forest would not let them fell a tree. A long dispute ensued with a tree eventually being made available. In 1998 the problem was again acute. The king's own preceptor (Rāj Guru), a Parbatiyā Brahman, told the Bārāhi to make a palanquin (*khaḥ*) instead of a chariot which caused no little offence to the people of Lalitpur. Again this politically tricky impasse was resolved with the allocation of a limited amount of new wood.

The chariots are virtual replicas of each other. Though the Cākwāḥdyaḥ chariot is not a great deal shorter than that of Bũgadyaḥ (around two-thirds the height), it *is* a great deal easier to build and move. The chariots are effectively constructed of four main elements: the chassis, the platform with the shrine, the 'tower' and the wheels. In assembling the chassis the axles (made of cast brass or *dhalot*) at first rest on the four posts that give the chariot enough height to enable the placement of the wheels at the end. Integral with the chassis is the main, curved beam that projects out at the front and rear—the *daḥmā.* The chassis of the smaller chariot is exactly the same as the larger one in construction but each part is correspondingly smaller.

The square wooden platform that supports the shrine rests on this chassis. The shrine, which is assembled on the platform and bears no load, stands two metres high. The platform is such that a side deck is left on all sides for the attendants to move about on. Above the shrine looms the tower that is built of a wooden frame tied together with vines and ropes. This frame is assembled from seven overlapping units, each of which on the larger chariot is about two metres high and on the smaller about one metre. The tower of the larger chariot is furthermore supported by sixteen tall poles fitted into and on top of the infrastructure and extending the full height of the tower, which tops around twenty metres above the ground. Juniper branches (Locke 1980: 265) are tied around the tower as a decoration. At the top of the tower rests a copper disk representing a lotus. Above this is the one and a half metre diameter *baymwa*—a network of rope lashed around a saucer shaped frame. The chariot runs on four wheels, each two metres in diameter, constructed from twenty-five separate elements (Plate 20). The threat of crushing by wheels is no hollow threat. Bhairava, therefore, manifested in the wheels, must be propitiated with blood.

Plate 20. Assembling new wheels for Būgadyaḥ's chariot.

Legend has it that it was King Bala Deva (Narendra Deva's son) who decided that the chariot should be drawn from Bũga only once every twelve years because of the difficulty it gave. On that occasion, every twelve years, the chariot is built completely new. The wheels are built at I Bahi and taken to Bũga where the chariot is built. The chariot is pulled to Lalitpur and then after the Jātrā is pulled back to Bũga. Parts of the chariot are also replaced whenever they are needed.

10.7. The play

Nepali (1965: 369), and Locke following him (1980: 261), divides the Jātrā into three acts: Bathing and consecration; chariot Jātrā; and Bhoto Jātrā. It will be seen from the discussion below that, at least from the perspective of this observer, the play may be analysed somewhat differently:

Preparation
Act 1. Bũga Festival
Act 2. Ga Bāhāḥ Festival
Act 3. Nugaḥ Festival

Act 4. Finale: Lagã Festival and Dropping the Coconut
Farewell to Bũgadyaḥ

The four acts of the play are framed, then, first by a series of preparatory rituals and then by a series of leave-taking rituals.[14]

10.7.1. Preparation

a. Seeing the day (*dī Swayegu*)

In the autumn month of mārga, four Lalitpur Joshi astrologers—the 'astrologers of the four pillars (*pengu tãye joshipi*)'—meet at the larger of the two shelters (*jhinkhunututidu phalcā* or Mani Mandap) at Mangaḥhiti to determine the auspicious time for bringing Karunāmaya from Bũga to Lalitpur.[15] Ideally Bũgadyaḥ should reside in Lalitpur from the time that the sun crosses over the Southern Hemisphere, i.e. from the autumnal equinox. As Paush (December/ January) is considered an inauspicious month Bũgadyaḥ is always brought from Bũga before the end of the previous month of Mārga.

b. Preparatory rituals

The trip from Bũga to Lalitpur is preceded by three days of rituals and other preparations (Owens 1989: 104). This includes the bathing and repainting of the image by the Nyeku lineage of Shresthas.[16] The morning before the image is carried to Lalitpur the Yala Juju visits Bũga in procession (ibid.: 207).

c. Bringing of Bũgadyaḥ (Bũgadyaḥ *halegu*)

On the morning of the day for the bringing of Karunāmaya from Bũga, the Nasantya Dāphā Guthi visits the village in the morning where they do a special, *dyaḥ laswa pujā* to Bũgadyaḥ and sing *bhajan*s.

The Yala Juju arrives at Bũga in procession during the morning and acts as *jajmān* while a Suwaḥ sacrifices a goat to Bhairava.[17] In the afternoon, the image is brought from Bũga to Lalitpur carried on a palanquin by eight Pānjus with great celebration.[18] The Yala Juju and his entourage accompany the procession.[19] On arrival at Ekāntakuna a pair of long horns (*kā*) are sounded to greet the deity.[20] Here, a mile to the southwest of the city, the palanquin is placed for a moment on the Bhani Mandap, a large stone mandala, where a welcome (*laskus*) ritual is performed. From here the image is carried straight to Ta Bāhāḥ where the principal Pānju's wife, the Pānjuni Thākāli, performs a *laskus* ceremony to Bũgadyaḥ. With this ritual completed, the image is installed in its winter temple. The Nasantya Dāphā Guthi eats a feast at *guthiyār*'s home in evening organized by *wala pa.*

d. Siddhi Narasimha hymn singing (Siddhi Narasimha *mẽ halyu*)

From the next day, every morning for a month, the Nasantya Dāphā Guthi sings thirty-two hymns, attributed to Siddhi Narasimha Malla, to Karunāmaya at Ta Bāhāḥ. On the last day the *guthi* does a special *pujā* to Nāsadyaḥ which includes the sacrifice of a pure, black goat and the eight-fold ritual division of the head (*sikāḥ bhu*) between the eight elders.[21]

e. Bārāhi Sisā Pāru Guthi

On the first day of the dark half of Paush (Thilāgā 1) the Bārāhi select trees for building the chariot. *Pujā* is done to the tree and to forest animals. The Bārāhi describe the process like this:

> Once we have completed the *pujā* we leave, and when we return to bring the wood, the tree has fallen by itself. Even the bend that is required for the *daḥmā* is already there in the wood.

That evening they eat the first of ten feasts of the annual cycle.[22]

f. Sasu Pujā (Sri Pancami, Māgh-*shukla*/Sillāthwa 5) (§9.9)

On this special day for the worship of Sarasvati (Sasu—Sillāthwa 5) the Nasantya Dāphā Guthi does a special *pujā* to this goddess of learning at Kwāchẽ Bāl Kumāri. This is followed by *pujā* and singing to Bāl Kumāri herself. In this the *guthi* expresses its desire for help in acquiring the needed skills to memorize the *bhajan*s they sing during the year.[23]

g. Bathing of Karunāmaya (Bũgadyaḥ Nhawã or Karunāmayaya Snāna) (Vaishākh-*krishna*/Caulāgā 1)

On the first day of the dark lunar fortnight of Caitra (Caulāgā 1), the Jātrā, proper, begins. The first in a series of major Jātrā events is celebrated with the bathing of Bũgadyaḥ (Bũgadyaḥ Nhawã or Karunāmayaya Snāna). Four days before this the Pānjus come to Lalitpur to collect offerings for the ceremonies (Locke 1980: 262). On the morning of the bathing the Nasantya Dāphā Guthi sings hymns to Karunāmaya at Ta Bāhāḥ. Later, also at Ta Bāhāḥ, the currently officiating Pānju performs a Flask Worship (*kalasha pujā*), at the conclusion of which he removes the spirit of the deity and invokes it into a large silver *kalasha* (ibid.). The image of Bũgadyaḥ is then handed over to the Nyekus for the bathing and repainting.

As evening approaches, large crowds gather to watch the colourful procession of Bũgadyaḥ on his palanquin from Ta Bāhāḥ to Lagankhel and his subsequent ritual bath (*snāna*). This is the first of several grand events that punctuate the Jātrā and marks the festival's beginning. Towards dusk, the Yala Juju arrives at Ta Bāhāḥ with the 'Juju Palton' armed escort in their traditional fatigues.[24] The Taleju God-Guardian, who has just completed a special *pujā* to Degutale, carries in procession the *pujā* dish with four pots (*kalasha*), a loincloth (*doti*), towel (*rumāl*), blanket (*panga*), to Ta Bāhāḥ to present to the Nyekus.[25] The four silver pots are set in front of Bũgadyaḥ's temple ready to be brought to Lagankhel for the bathing. Bũgadyaḥ is carried out by four Nyekus, placed on the palanquin, and brought in procession out of the west gate of Ta Bāhāḥ, up to Iti, along to Thati and up past the seated Kumāri to Lagankhel where the image is installed on a ritual platform (mandala).[26] The sword of the Yala Juju is placed on its mat on the ground, point forward, around ten metres from the front of the mandala and the Mãta wielding Siddhi Narasimha's cane, makes sure that the king has a clear view of the proceedings.

Two of the Nyekus then return to Ta Bāhāḥ to bring the pots to the mandala in preparation for the bathing. The chief Pānju wearing his ceremonial head-dress does a ritual dance (*lasya*) with chants, bell, *vajra* and *mudra*s to the eight guardians of the four cardinal and four intercardinal directions (ibid.: 263). At the auspicious moment (*sāit*), the two Nyekus bathe the image by pouring over the base. Owens remarks that with the bathing of the image comes the acknowledgement that the image is dead and must be brought to life (1989: 119). The image is returned on its palanquin to Ta Bāhāḥ where it will now be prepared for its Jātrā. As soon as Bũgadyaḥ leaves Lagankhel, the crowd moves, en masse, down the road to Tangaḥ Bāhāḥ where Cākwāḥdya is bathed in the same way at his own mandala. It is instructive that Bũgadyaḥ, and not Cākwāḥdyaḥ, is bathed outside the old city boundary. Cākwāḥdyaḥ, the older of the two, is normally resident in the city. Bũgadyaḥ, however, though he resides in the city for some months each year, belongs, in fact, to the village of Bũga and, for that reason, is bathed outside the City of Lalitpur.

That evening, the Bārāhi and Yāngwa do *pujā* to four stakes (*hamaki*) at each of the sites in Puco and Tangaḥ where they will assemble the chariots. Afterwards the Bārāhi retire to eat a feast.

h. Assembling of chariots

Over the next two weeks (Vaishākh-*krishna*/Caulāgā 2-15) images and chariots are prepared for the Jātrā itself. The image of Bũgadyaḥ is repainted by the Nyekus. From the second day of the lunar fortnight until the Jātrā is successfully completed, Bārāhi men must remain ritually pure: they must bathe every day, eat no garlic, chicken meat or chicken eggs, only eat what is prepared in their own homes, and abstain from sexual intercourse. These ritual stipulations are followed strictly. 'Otherwise,' say the Bārāhi, 'we will fall off when we are up [the tower]'. The chariots are constructed on top of the stakes (*hamaki*) which are driven into the ground to form a temporary jack. Once the chassis is completed the Yāngwa then complete that element by twisting bunches of soaked and supple vines together and tying them around the wooden beams to keep them together. The Bārāhi then assemble the tower of the chariot on top of the chassis. On the tenth day they complete their part of the assembling of Bũgadyaḥ's chariot. All the Bārāhi men gather for the emplacement of the wheels. Finally the top cross-frame of the topmost unit of the tower, the *yaka khaḥ*, is fitted. The chariot is completed by the Yāngwa over the following days.

i. Sacrifice to Bhairava

From the twelfth of the fortnight up to the new moon (Vaishākh-*krishna*/Caulāgā 12-15) a total of eight buffaloes is sacrificed to the image of Bhairava at Bũga, by the Butchers of that settlement. In the past a total of fourteen buffaloes was sacrificed but costs have led this to be reduced in recent years.

j. Reconsecration of the images (*pratistha vidhi*)

On the thirteenth day of the fortnight (Vaishākh-*krishna*/Caulāgā 13) the newly repainted image of Bũgadyaḥ is taken through a series of life-cycle rituals. This is the occasion for the first of three visits by the Khwapa Juju who is summoned to perform the role of opening the eyes of the image as soon as the life has been restored to it.[27] He touches his sword to the paintbrush of the Nyekus, which they then use to paint the pupils of the eyes (Owens 1989: 123). The sword, in its red and gold brocade cloth cover, is then placed point-up on a chair in front of the Guthi Corporation office directly in front of, but at some distance from, the main door of Bũgadyaḥ's temple. That night the Nyekus perform the first of two series of Ten Life-Cycle Rituals (*dasa karma*) and Tantric Initiations. In addition to this they also perform the Confinement ritual (Bārhā Tayegu) which, Locke says, is, in fact, an eleventh rite (1980: 264f).[28] As part of this *pujā*, seventy-five copper pots, all (except two large ones representing Ganesh and Brahma) about a foot high are worshipped and placed in a square around the area directly in front of the temple.

k. Receiving of the 'tax' (Kar Kaya)

That same day, at Ta Bāhāḥ, the 'tax' (*kar*) is distributed to a number of different groups that work on the festival, as payment for services rendered. Two buffaloes are sacrificed and the meat distributed. The food is distributed to the Bārāhi, Yāngwa, Bwãsi, the Butchers of Bũga and the Suwaḥ.

l. Completion of Cākwāḥdyaḥ's chariot

On the fourteenth day of the fortnight (Vaishākh-*krishna*/Caulāgā 14) the Bārāhi men gather at Tangaḥ to complete the construction of the Cākwāḥdyaḥ chariot. The four wheels are rolled out of a storeroom and hoisted onto the axles. Next, young single men assemble the top four frame sections of the tower. Just one single man must place the last cross frame, the *yaka khaḥ*, on top. It is harder to do this on Cākwāḥdyaḥ's chariot than it is on Karunāmaya's, because it is too narrow for one man to climb up into the space at the top inside the spire. Tradition has it that whoever does this will receive a son when he marries so it is considered an auspicious role.

That evening, at Ta Bāhāḥ, the Mock Marriage feast (*ihi bhu*) takes place, participated in by all those who work on the chariots.

m. The visit to Kotwāl

On the final day of preparation, the new moon day (Vaishākh-*krishna*/Caulāgā 15; the day for Seeing the Mother's Face, §9.20), a group processes to the village of Kotwāl to the south of Bũga (Owens 1989: 127). The group includes the Mālini (representing the Jyāpu Rathācakra) who accompanies the Jhal Pānju (who will sit on the right of Bũgadyaḥ in the Jātrā and represents Narendra Deva) and the principal Vajrācārya *pujāri* (who represents Bandhudatta).[29] They spend the night at the shelter there with various other assistants including a Suwaḥ who will later do a sacrifice of a goat. On this day also, the final two buffaloes are sacrificed at Bũga.

n. The bringing of Diladyaḥ (Diladyaḥ *hayegu*)

The next day is the first day of the waxing lunar fortnight (Vaishākh-*shukla*/ Bachalāthwa 1). The Nasantya Dāphā Guthi comes early in the morning to the village to sing *bhajan*s. The first *pujā* of the day is offered to Bũgadyaḥ's mother represented by a bas relief image of her hand carved in a rock on the eastern wall of the gorge (ibid.). After summoning the *nāga*s the priest goes down to the water and sprinkles jasmine flower petals on the river. The Mālini and other Pānju then retrieve these downstream in silver flasks (*kalasha*). This is considered to be a reenactment of the event in which Karunāmaya, in the form of a bee, entered a *kalasha.* A Flask Worship (*kalasha pujā*) is then performed in honour of the demons (*rākshas*) from Kāmarup. This is followed by a secret sacrifice of a goat, by the Suwaḥ, to a group of aniconic stones referred to as Diladyaḥ. The *kalasha* is then brought to Ta Bāhāḥ where the deity is then invoked into the newly painted and prepared image of Bũgadyaḥ. As on the last day for Siddhi Narasimha hymn singing the Nasantya Dāphā Guthi feast is organised on an informal (*pharmās*) basis. In the past this used to be the responsibility of a *wala pā.*

o. Final preparation of the chariot

Later the same day, the Lusā Guthi brings the panels, windows, and doorframes, which together form the shrine of the chariot, from Uku Bāhāḥ.[30] These are affixed to the chariot platform and shrine by the Bārāhi. The mask of the *daḥmā* is fitted to the front of the main forward beam. Later the Yāngwa adds the *baymwa* and green juniper branches. A lineage of Citrakārs paints the wheels and *daḥmā* of the chariot. Today they must 'open the eyes of Bhairava' before Bũgadyaḥ is placed on the chariot (Plate 21 (p. 236); cf. Toffin 1995b: 241).

That evening, the Ghaḥkus offer the first in a series of sacrifices to the chariot wheels (Owens 1989: 129). They sacrifice a ram and direct the spurt of blood over each of the four wheels in turn.

10.7.2. Act 1. The festival of Bũga (Bũgayaḥ)[31]

a. The procession to 'Bũga'

We have now arrived at the festival itself. Preparations are now complete. The Jātrā now begins. At dusk crowds gather again at Ta Bāhāḥ. This is the second occasion that the Khwapa Juju visits the festival. It is the Khwapa Juju, carried by the Bhaktapur Shrestha, who opens the event by proceeding behind a Paḥmā̃ta *muhāli* player to the temple to do *pujā* to Bũgadyaḥ.[32] He exits and showers the crowd with *prasād* (the deity's blessed substance). The Yala Juju follows him, and the image is carried out of the temple and placed on his palanquin for the procession to Puco. This event clearly shows the precedence of the king of Bhaktapur over the king of Lalitpur in this festival and harks back to the establishing of the Jātrā by Narendra Deva. Bũgadyaḥ

Plate 21. Opening the eyes of Bhairava on the wheels of Būgadyaḥ's chariot.

is then carried on his palanquin by the Pānjus, in grand procession and accompanied by the Yala Juju, from Ta Bāhāḥ to Puco where he is installed in his shrine on the chariot before a vast crowd of worshippers and onlookers (cf. Gellner 1992: 131; Locke 1980: 265). The Mā̃ta, adorned with fresh, new white sashes and *dhākā*-weave caps, faces smeared with vermilion, climb up onto the chariot platform.[33] The chief Mā̃ta places the Yala Juju sword in front of the entrance to the shrine and the others stand around the chariot to give out *prasād* to the thronging crowds.[34]

b. Phaila Bhu

The following evening, the Bārāhi elders eat a special feast called Phaila Bhu at the *thākāli*'s house. This feast includes the sharing of the head of the sacrificial ram as the *sikāḥ bhu*.

c. The gift of a cow (*Sā dān*) (Vaishākh-*shukla*/Bachalāthwa 3)

The following day, *Akshaya tritiya*—an important day in the ancient Hindu calendar—the Yala Juju offers the gift of a cow to a Rājopādhyāya Brahman at the Mani Mandap.

10.7.3. Act 2. The festival of Ga Bāhāḥ (Ga Bāhāḥyaḥ)

a. The procession to Ga Bāhāḥ (*Ga Bāhāḥ salegu*)

On the fourth day of the waxing lunar fortnight (Vaishākh-*shukla*/Bachalāthwa 4) the actual procession of the chariots begins with the pulling of Bũgadyaḥ's chariot to Ga Bāhāḥ (cf. Locke 1980: 269).[35]

In the afternoon Cākwāḥdyaḥ is installed on his chariot at Tangaḥ Bāhāḥ and pulled from there to Puco *stupa* (*thur*) to await Bũgadyaḥ's chariot. Late afternoon a crowd of several thousand participants and onlookers gathers in Puco for the main attraction of the day. *Dhimay bājã* groups arrive from various localities of the city bringing a rising sense of excitement with their military-style drumming and clashing of cymbals.[36] Men begin to dance. The horn blowers arrive and position themselves a little down the road to be at the head of the procession. After them the Yala Juju arrives with the guard and band of fifes and drums. The chief Mãta and his assistants climb onto the platform and place the sword in its seat of honour in front of Bũgadyaḥ. The two Sese Brahmans climb aboard, station themselves in front of the platform and behind a richly brocaded cloth positioned at the rear of the forward beam and don their new white turbans. Thick hawser ropes are dragged across the road and the young men take up the strain. Finally, amid much celebration, the director (the Haḥphā Biyemha) climbs onto the front of the forward beam immediately behind the mask of Hayagriva Bhairava, and the pulling of the chariot begins.

It is impossible to convey the tremendous atmosphere of anticipation and excitement of this moment. The haulers make a few trial attempts by which the leader and the rope-haulers get a feel for the weight of the chariot and for the rhythm of yanking (for at first the chariot has to be jerked off its posts). Then the chariot starts to move with a deafening salute by the muskets of the Palton and great celebration by the crowds (Plate 24, p. 241). After turning the chariot ninety degrees, the procession takes off down the road with this massive vehicle lumbering precariously through the vast company of devotees. The *dhimay bājã* groups precede it, drumming energetically and clashing the cymbals vibrantly. The chariot stops and the drums and cymbals lower the tempo and volume playing a more measured march-like rhythm. They switch once again to the ecstatic high-energy rhythm as the great vehicle jolts once again into action and hurtles towards the Puco *thur* where Cākwāḥdyaḥ's chariot has been awaiting it—a scene described so memorably by Percy Brown in the epigraph.

On the larger chariot's arrival at the mound, Cākwāḥdyaḥ precedes Bũgadyaḥ into the old city and to Ga Bāhāḥ for the festival's first major stop (Plate 22, p. 238). On arrival, the Palton, which has marched ahead of the chariot, fires another deafening volley in the air and the day's work comes to completion. This is the occasion for the residents of the western sector of the city to eat a ritual pre-purification feast that includes buffalo pieces (*chwaylā bhu*). Married-out daughters and their families (*mhyay macā*) and sisters' children and *their* families (*bhincā macā*) are invited to share this in the home. On this day also Rājopādhyāya Brahmans and local Maharjans worship the Jyāpu Kumāri of Mikha Bāhāḥ (Allen 1987: 58-60).

Plate 22. Būgadyaḥ's chariot negotiating its way through the city.

b. Ga Bāhāḥ festival (*bhujyaḥ*)

The next day is the main *pujā* day (*bhujyaḥ*) for the residents of the western part of the city (the area extending from Kumāripāti in the south to Patan Dhokā in the north and from Na Bāhāḥ in the west to Mahāpā towards the centre). Groups of men visit the deity to sing *bhajan*s (Plate 23). Relatives are invited, *pujā* is offered and a feast is eaten. There is some debate among residents as to whether this event constitutes a *nakhaḥ* or not. In a sense it is not, as it is a *jātrā* and normally a *jātrā* does not entail have such an important feel to it. Shops would normally stay open, for instance. But for those residents for whom this is their *bhujyaḥ* it is one of the most important days of the year rivalled only in the breadth of invitations to Mohani (§8.8.5). So in that sense it is a *nakhaḥ*.

10.7.4. Act 3. The festival of Nugaḥ (Nugaḥyaḥ)

a. The procession to Nugaḥ (*Nugaḥ salegu*)

The following evening the Yala Juju returns to the chariot for the onward movement of the deities through the city. As before, at dusk, the chariots are pulled, again with much fanfare, this time from Ga Bāhāḥ through the centre of the city to Nugaḥ where it comes to rest for its second main stop. Būgadyaḥ, having been welcomed into the city by Cākwāḥdyaḥ, precedes the lesser deity throughout the rest of the city. As the chariots lurch through the city they pass the Lalitpur Kumāri who sits on her throne in front of Haḥ Bāhāḥ in the second of her outings to watch the Jātrā.

Plate 23. Singing hymns to Karunāmaya. .

Immediately after the chariots cross the Mangaḥ crossroads, they stop for a few minutes as the Taleju god guardian offers a towel to Karunāmaya. This is then divided up and given as white neck cloth (*tuyu kwakhu*) to all the functionaries—Pānjus, Bārāhi, Yāngwa and Ghaḥku as the deity's blessed substance (*prasād*). This ritual seems to be a remnant of a more material custom that was necessary it is said, in the distant past, when a stream (the Haḥkā Khusi) ran down through this spot. It was needful, goes the legend, for everyone to 'change his loincloth'.[37]

On arrival at Nugaḥ, muskets fire, the people cheer and throng around to receive *prasād*. The residents of the eastern sector of the city now retire to their homes to eat their pre-purification feast (*chwaylā bhu*).

b. Nugaḥ festival (*bhujyaḥ*)

The following day is another important event in which residents of the eastern sector of the city do the special *pujā* (*bhujyaḥ*) to Karunāmaya and eat a feast in their homes. The Bārāhi, as residents of this sector, also do a special *pujā*. In this, the Pānju *pujāri* does a Fire Offering (*yajña pujā*) to Karunāmaya for the Bārāhi. This *pujā* includes the sacrifice of a pure black goat to Bhairava. In the evening the Bārāhi share a feast at the *thākāli*'s house with two Pānju *pujāri*s and their Jyāpu assistants (Owens 1989: 217). This feast includes the eight-fold ritual division of the head (*sikāḥ bhu*).

10.7.5. Act 4. Finale: the festival of Lagã (Lagãyaḥ) and Dropping the Coconut

a. The procession to Lagã (*Lagã salegu*)

The following evening the chariots, again with the Yala Juju aboard, begin their long journey to Lagankhel (Nw. Lagã). Before this, in the morning, the Bārāhi do another special *pujā* to Bũgadyaḥ and Cākwāḥdyaḥ. This is followed by a unique *pujā* to 'Twāydyaḥ' (the fictive kin of Karunāmaya) in his temple, which is situated in a small courtyard immediately to the north of the golden waterspout (Lũhiti).[38]

In the evening the chariots are hauled up to Uku Bāhāḥ where they usually stay the night. From Uku Bāhāḥ the procession meanders along to Cāka Bahi and thence up and out of the city to Lagankhel.[39] The journey to Lagankhel usually takes two or three days. On arrival the chariots are brought to a stop to the south-west of the shrine to Mā̃ju Simā (Karunāmaya's mother), next to the mandala on which Bũgadyaḥ was bathed. Here they will stay for three days.[40]

b. The five sacrifices (*panca bali*)

Two days later, in the middle of the night, five animals (*panca bali*) are sacrificed to Bhairava: one male each of buffalo, ram, goat, duck and fish (Owens 1989: 133-5). The *jajmān* at this ceremony is the Yala Juju himself though the sacrifices are actually performed by the Suwaḥ and Butchers of Bũga. Two reasons are given for this sacrifice: on the one hand Bhairava is a dangerous god and needs to be propitiated to prevent danger to the people. On the other these sacrifices are intended to ward off a different kind of evil—the *yaksha*s—the demons and ghosts that have attached themselves to the chariots and need to be propitiated before the festival can come to a successful conclusion. Later in the day the Pānjus do an elaborate *pujā* at the same location. This is the final event at which the Khwapa Juju is present.

c. Lagã procession (*Lagãyaḥ*)

On the fourth day of their arrival at Lagankhel the chariots continue their journey. The mask of Harkā̃ndyaḥ (Bhairava) that was displayed by a Rājkarnikār *guthi* at Yẽnyaḥ (§8.5.1) is again displayed at the side of the road at Haugaḥ. Men journeying up the road to pull the chariot are fortified by generous quaffs of *thon* poured through a pipe in the mask. Upon the arrival of the Yala Juju at Lagã, the chariots, with Bũgadyaḥ in the lead and under the watchful gaze of the Kumāri seated for the second time in the Lagankhel shelter, are pulled around Mā̃ju Simā, an image of Karunāmaya's mother.[41] Once Cākwāḥdyaḥ has done one complete circuit it is pulled straight down the road towards the city. This leaves Bũgadyaḥ to do one more circumambulation after which it ends up following the smaller chariot again. When Bũgadyaḥ arrives at a particular spot, a stone's throw from the old city gate, the chariot is halted (cf. Gutschow 1982: 174). This locality is the neighbourhood of a number of households of the Dyaḥlā caste who are traditionally considered untouchable.

The arrival at Lagã is the signal for residents of the middle sector of the city to eat the pre-purification meal (*chwaylā bhu*) together.[42]

d. Sacrifice to Karunāmaya's mother (Mãju Simā *bali*)
That night sheep are sacrificed to Karunāmaya's mother at Mãju Simā with the Yala Juju acting as *jajmān*.

e. Lagã festival (*bhujyaḥ*)
The day after the chariot's arrival at lower Lagã, residents of the middle sector of the city eat a ritual feast together (*bhujyaḥ*). This is the day that some lineages (e.g. one of the Tamvaḥ lineages) get together to decide when they will celebrate Lineage Deity Worship (*digu dyaḥ pujā*). Rājkarnikār lineages also take this as the beginning of their Dewāli period.

f. Dropping the Coconut (Nekya Kukyu)
That same evening, the ritual of 'Dropping the Coconut' (Nekya Kukyu) is performed. As before, at each of the grand events of the Jātrā a great crowd gathers at Lagankhel. The Kumāri is escorted on her fourth outing from Haḥ Bāhāḥ to take her throne in the shelter at the Thati crossroads. Some time later, the Yala Juju arrives with Palton escort (Plate 24). As always the chief Mãta takes his place on the platform and lays the sword in front of the deity.

After a long wait, a Yāngwa climbs up into the lotus at the top of the tower. A great cheer rises as he begins to climb. Once at the top he begins throwing *yaḥ mari* (a traditional Newar sweet made from rice and molasses) into the

Plate 24. Yala Juju's 'Palton' escort.

crowd and at people on surrounding houses unfurling a white banner as he does so. Anticipation mounts as the man stands as if to throw the coconut. He throws more *yaḥ mari* instead. Then suddenly he launches the coconut into the crowd. A tangle of young men then wrestles to try to snatch the coconut away. Victory belongs to the man who manages to present the coconut, Bũgadyaḥ's *prasād*, and a symbol of fertility, to the Yala Juju on the chariot (Slusser 1998: 336). Being thus blessed he is now free to re-enter the city as its ruler for another year. The one who presents the *prasād* to the king, it is said, is ensured of a son.

A carnival atmosphere prevails throughout the festival. There is, however, a very real possibility of serious violence breaking out. The young men, many intoxicated with liberal doses of beer (*thon*), fight spiritedly for the coconut and police have great difficulty preventing this break of normal order from degenerating into an all out brawl. This again expresses in a material way, the cosmic chaos and disorder from which the deity must save the city—the chaos is cosmic but it can break out on the ground too.[43]

Later all those who have done *bhujyaḥ* will eat a feast. The Bārāhi too eat a feast together. On this occasion the Bārāhi also feed two Guthi Corporation officials. After eating, the calendar is consulted, other considerations of ritual purity of the *guthi* members are weighed, and the date for Karunāmaya's Lineage Deity Worship is selected.[44] The link between the Jātrā and Lineage Deity Worship is further expressed among certain lineages by the conflation of the *bhujyaḥ* feast with a Lineage Deity Guthi feast.[45]

Pujā has been offered now by the entire city. The deity will soon be returning to his own home, but before he leaves will give the people a token of his blessing; a sort of first-fruits of what is to come with the ensuing rice season.[46] This structural linking of the Jātrā with Lineage Deity Worship is also echoed in a parallel symbolism. The broadcasting of the rice cake *yaḥ mari* is repeated by each lineage as they do their Lineage Deity Worship together over the subsequent weeks. This is clearly a giving of *prasād* to the worshippers in return for having worshipped the deity. The Jātrā, proper, is now over. All that is left is for the deity to await his departure.

10.7.6. Farewell to Bũgadyaḥ

a. Lone women's pulling (*Yākamisa Salegu*)[47]

The departure of Bũgadyaḥ to his home begins the next day. Early in the morning the Yala Juju, accompanied as usual by his honour guard, takes his place, once again, on the platform of the chariot for a most unique event. The chariots are pulled a few yards down the road to the Thati *twaḥ* crossroads immediately outside the old boundary of the city. The thing that makes this day's procession unique is not just the short distance that the chariots are pulled but the fact that (assisted, admittedly, by men) the chariots are pulled by 'lone women' (i.e. unmarried women who have lost their parents).[48] This is the only occasion, in fact, in which the chariots are pulled in the morning and is the occasion for the Lone Women's Festival (*yākamisā bhujyaḥ*). It seems that this event is a concession to the *yākamisā* who would not otherwise have any part to play in the festival. It does not form an essential part of the festival, which is why it takes place after Dropping the Coconut. It does, nevertheless, give the *yākamisā* an opportunity for involvement. That evening, the Bārāhi Daḥ Guthi eats another feast.

b. Crowning of Karunāmaya (*Kiki Swā̃*)
On the chariots' arrival at Thati the Nasantya Dāphā Guthi pays a visit to an image called Dulāngadyaḥ at Lagankhel.[49] The *guthi* offers *pujā* to the deity, eats a meal (*samay*) together, and then proceeds down the road to Bũgadyaḥ. Here they do a special *pujā* (*kiki swā̃*) to the central leaf (*kikipā*) of Bũgadyaḥ's headdress. If there is a long delay in the process of the Jātrā due to breakdown then the ceremony will be completed wherever the chariot has reached. In the evening the *guthi* eats a feast organized by the particular *wala pa*.[50]

c. Karunāmaya's Lineage Deity Worship (*digu dyaḥ pujā*)
On the day of 'Dropping the Coconut' the Bārāhi Guthi selects the day for theirs and Karunāmaya's Lineage Deity Worship (§9.23.7). The Bārāhi consider themselves to be the agnatic relatives of Bũgadyaḥ, although the Pānjus deny this, affirming that Bũgadyaḥ is *their* agnate.[51] The main (second) day always falls on a Thursday and may be the first or second Thursday after the chariot's arrival at Thati. Rarely is it later. With the completion of Karunāmaya's Lineage Deity Worship, the chariot may move on to Jawalakhel.

d. Seeing the day (*dī swayegu*)
At dawn on the main day of the Bārāhi Lineage Deity Worship a small crowd gathers, as they did months before, at the shelter in front of Mangaḥhiti. *Pujā* is offered to the stone throne in the shelter.[52] Two Pānjus, one each representing Bũgadyaḥ and Cākwāḥdyaḥ, offer a silver plate each of *prasād* wrapped in a red cloth which is unwrapped and placed on the throne. The four Joshi astrologers arrive, sit on mats together in the shelter and, searching their astrological almanacs, determine the auspicious day (*dī*) for the pulling of the chariot from Thati. In Malla times, local people report the kings of each of the three cities would be present at this important occasion.

e. Worship of the 'clothes' of Karunāmaya
Early in the morning on each day that the chariot is at Thati, people go to do *pujā* to Karunāmaya. During this time an informal group of friends gets together to do *pujā* to the red banners and flags that hang down from the top of the chariot. This is followed by a feast at a temple of Bhairava just south of Lagankhel.

f. The stay at Thati

Locke reports some interesting folklore surrounding the deities' stay, which can often be several weeks, at the Thati crossroads (1980: 272). It is said that Bũgadyaḥ leaves his chariot at night to sleep with the Dyaḥlā women of that place. Towards the end of this time a procession of Pānjus goes to Kirtipur carrying flowers as *prasād* from Bũgadyaḥ to present to the unmarried women of a certain locality of that city, especially to one referred to as the Kipu Jyāpuni. The tradition has it that at one time Bũgadyaḥ had visited this place during his sojourn at Thati and this is a gift to the women for having slept with him (Owens 1989: 193). Are there echoes here of Tantric sexual initiation?

g. First *bhuja pujā*

The night before the chariots are pulled to Jawalakhel, two rice sculptures are constructed at the Mulcok and carried in procession with the Yala Juju to the chariots where they are offered to the *daḥmā*s.[53] Rice fights ensue as the sculptures are destroyed in the process (Owens 1989: 221).

h. Pulling the chariot to Jawalakhel

Tradition has it that, if Bũgadyaḥ is not moved from Thati by the festival of Mohani (§8.8), that then the image should be carried to Bhaktapur for the winter. Opinion is divided over whether this has actually ever happened.

On the day that the chariots are due to be pulled to Jawalakhel, the astrologers go to Thati and determine the exact auspicious moment with their water clock. At that moment a five-coloured string representing the five Transcendent Buddhas is attached to the chariot and pulled signifying the formal, if not actual, beginning of Bũgadyaḥ's journey back to his own home temple.

That evening, a great crowd gathers and the deities are pulled with full ceremony as they have been throughout their journey. The Kumāri is brought, as usual in her own procession, to take her place at her shelter on the way to get her last *darshan* of Karunāmaya (ibid.: 273).[54] As before, the chariots are only pulled once the Yala Juju is installed in his place. The directors of the chariot-haulers on this leg of the Jātrā may be drawn from anywhere in the Valley but are normally from Puco, the residents of which will be celebrating their festival (*bhujyaḥ*) once the chariots reach Jawalakhel which is typically after two or three days.

i. Jawala Jātrā

The day after the chariots' arrival at Jawalakhel the residents of Puco have their festival (*bhujyāḥ*). The residents other outlying 'villages' follow them.[55]

j. Second *bhuja pujā*

Four rice sculptures are carried in procession. The Yala Juju and his entourage accompany them from Puco to Jawalakhel where they are presented as offerings to the *daḥmā*s. As with the previous *bhuja pujā* rice is snatched by onlookers and thrown about.

k. Preparation for Bhoto Jātrā

On the third day of the chariots' arrival at Jawalakhel two ceremonies are done to propitiate the *yaksha*s, ghosts and goblins (*bhut/pret*) who are supposed to have come with Matsyendranāth's mother and are waiting for an opportune moment to take him back to Kāmarup (ibid.: 274). The first is the scattering of a mandala made of rice to the four winds as a *bali* offering. This is followed by another ceremony involving fifteen or sixteen wives of the Pānjus. The ceremony, Locke notes, is a remnant of a Tantric Initiation (*dekha*) 'by which these women were initiated as *yogini*s and given the power to bind or frighten away the evil spirits' (ibid.: 275).

l. Ajimā Pujā

The following morning a special *pujā* is offered to the goddess Ajimā who is said to reside under the chariot.

m. First Sacrifice to Hayagriva Bhairava

The Yala Juju acts as the *jajmān* for a further sacrifice to Hayagriva Bhairava at Bũga on the same morning (Owens 1989: 223).

n. A final leave-taking: Showing the Vest (Bhoto Jātrā)

That evening, the final grand event of the festival is held with the showing of the vest (Bhoto Jātrā). For many this is the most important event of the entire festival. Indeed, for non-Newars this *is* the festival. Many thousands of people, both Newars and non-Newars, come from all over the Valley to get a *darshan* of Bũgadyaḥ's vest. The entire area around what is now the Jawalakhel roundabout is chock-a-block with onlookers. Police on horseback and members of uniformed youth organisations try to keep the crowds from blocking the roads. In the shelter on the south side of the chariot the Mridanga Bhajan Khalaḥ sings *bhajan*s playing traditional Newar instruments. A large contingent of army guards stands facing the chariot on the eastern side opposite the royal shelter. Behind them stands the silver band of the guards, equipped with cornets and sousaphones.

As dusk approaches, the Yala Juju arrives with the Palton escort and the sword is set, as before, on the chariot platform. Soon afterwards government ministers arrive and take their places in the shelter in front of the chariot. Sirens scream and the Prime Minister and finally the king arrive. The Shah king and all his ministers do *pujā* to Bũgadyaḥ and Cākwāḥdyaḥ and received *prasād* from the deities' attendants. As they do this a curious mixture of sounds echoes over the crowd as the military band belts out the national anthem and Mangal Dhun in four-part harmony, on one side, while the Mridanga Bhajan Khalaḥ sings traditional hymns on the other.

The Shah king takes his seat and the focal event of the day takes place. An official of the Guthi Corporation brings out the vest from the deity's keeping and holds it aloft from each corner of the platform for all the people to receive a view.[56] This doing he circumambulates the deity three times. Local people say that if one sees the *bhoto* he can have one year of sin expiated. With this the Bhoto Jātrā is brought to completion and the king and his ministers, and the crowds, return to their homes.[57]

o. The return to Bũga

Upon departure of the king and his ministers, Bũgadyaḥ is immediately prepared for removal from the chariot and carriage to Bũga.[58] The palanquin is brought to the front of the chariot in readiness to receive its cargo. The chief Mãta removes the Yala Juju sword. The silver box containing the 'feet' of Bũgadyaḥ is then tied onto the top of his head using a white cotton cloth. It is now dark and the Mãta light oil torches. The ceremonial umbrellas (large for the image, small for the sword) are set up. The image is then carefully taken down by the Pānjus, positioned on the palanquin and whisked off in exactly the same processional order as it did when the image was brought from Bũga some months before.

When the procession reaches the top of the bluff above Nakhu, the residents of Bũga meet it hurling 'reproaches and abuse at the deity for remaining so long away from home and for dallying with the sweeper women' (Locke 1980: 276). Shortly later, upon arrival at the deity's main temple in Bũga, the image is put to one side and shut inside his temple. He then has to undergo purification rites because, says Locke, he has slept with the Dyaḥlā women and taken food from all castes. The Mãta bid farewell to the deity and return to Lalitpur, the sword and cane being replaced in the old palace.

p. Bicā Pujā

On the fourth day of Bũgadyaḥ's return to Bũga thousands of residents of Lalitpur visit Bũgadyaḥ to offer *pujā* and to check that the deity is happily ensconced in his village temple. Among the visitors to Bũga on this day is the Nasantya Dāphā Guthi which goes early in the morning to sings *bhajan*s.[59]

q. Second Sacrifice to Hayagriva Bhairava

The same day, the final sacrifice to Hayagriva Bhairava is performed, again sponsored by the Yala Juju (Owens 1989: 224).

r. Division of the banners

Some days after Bũgadyaḥ is taken back to Bũga the Pānjus return to Lalitpur to retrieve the *nāga* banners (*patāḥ*). These are first taken down by the Yāngwa and presented to the Bārāhi *thākāli*. The Pānjus and Bārāhis are each entitled to one half of all the banners, which are valued for their curative powers (ibid.: 164).

s. Kwenā Pujā

The following Tuesday, the Pānjus and Bārāhi celebrate the completion of their responsibilities by doing a *pujā* to Kwenādyaḥ, Puco.[60] This brings the period of the Bārāhis' ritual purity to an end. For the Bārāhi this *pujā* is also a penance (*prayascitta*) for having eaten garlic at their Lineage Deity Worship, performed during their period of abstinence from such foods.

10.8. Interpreting the Jātrā

The Jātrā can be analysed on a number of levels: on the surface, the Jātrā is all about the worship of a powerful and merciful deity who, it is hoped, will repay his devotees by bringing the monsoon rains and blessing the people with a good rice crop. But on other levels, the festival can be understood as conveying a message of conflict resolution and urban renewal and of the importance of the king in making this happen.

10.8.1. The bringing of rain

The Jātrā is fraught with anxiety. Rice being the staple of the Newar people it is vital that sufficient rain falls during the monsoon for the rice to grow and give a decent yield. Droughts and famines figure prominently in the chronicles (e.g. the *Gopālarāja Vamshāvali*) and exist to the present in the collective memory of the Newars (Vajracarya and Malla 1985). So the main anxiety is the constant worry of survival against the ravages of uncontrolled nature with her uncertainties. The myth of the coming of Matsyendranāth, repeated every spring in homes across the city, expresses this very real difficulty. This is also conveyed in the Sanskrit poem *Matsyendrapadyasatakam* (Locke 1980: 282).

The Jātrā itself is fraught with difficulties that seem to express, in a tangible way, the more abstract anxieties of the cosmos. The chariot is huge. It needs hundreds of young men to pull it. The wheels are also considerable—more than two metres across—and would crush a person in an instant if they happened to get in the way while it was moving; as has occasionally happened. Animals are sacrificed to the wheels to prevent that from happening. The tower of the chariot is also very tall. The Yāngwa have the job of riding high on the tower of the chariot as it is pulled and it is not surprising to hear of one and another being killed by a fall. In the 2002 Jātrā, there was a surge in the crowd resulting in a devotee being pushed under the chariot and having both legs crushed.

The chariot itself topples over completely from time to time, one year doing so three times. There are parallels here with other major festivals of the Valley. One year, at the celebration of the festival of Biskaḥ in Bhaktapur, I witnessed the raising of the tall pole (the *yaḥsī*) from the steps of the small temple next to the pole. The danger inherent in such operations was brought home forcefully to me the next morning when I learnt that, after I had left, the *yaḥsī* had in fact crashed onto the very steps on which I had been sitting, killing two onlookers. The following year I was watching the placement of the *baymwa* onto the top of Bũgadyaḥ's chariot. Suddenly a gasp went up from the crowd as, breaking its coupling, the half-ton construction plummeted twenty-five metres to the ground.

The analogy with Bhaktapur's Biskaḥ Jātrā is not superficial. Biskaḥ Jātrā, as it is celebrated in Bhaktapur, carries a similar message as Bũgadyaḥ's does in Lalitpur.

For Biskaḥ this seems to be something like this: admire and celebrate the civic order. That order may momentarily and frighteningly sway and lurch, but when the city works together—or refrains, really, from not working together, for the task is not difficult—and accepts the traditional directives of the mesocosmic order, it will all hold together.... (Levy 1990: 500)

Parish takes it a step further. The 'message' of Biskaḥ, he asserts in mild criticism of his mentor, is not only 'admire and celebrate the civic order' but also, in a dialogical rhetoric, a message of limitation or, if I may paraphrase him, 'thus far and no further' (1997a: 157).

So there are many difficulties that the Jātrā brings. But these, it could be said, are self-imposed. The chariot does not need to be so big if it is simply to carry the image. One the size of Cākwāḥdyaḥ's, or Janmadyaḥ's would be more than adequate.[61] To carry the king and his attendants as well, however, it does have to have a large base. Owens makes the point that the chariot festivals in India (Jagannāth, Subhadra and Bālarām) make use of much more stable chariots (1989: 181). Although they are huge (giving us the word 'juggernaut') they also have much wider bases than that of Bũgadyaḥ. Furthermore, the Indian chariots are pulled in a stately fashion, in stark contrast to the headlong dash that often characterizes the pulling of Bũgadyaḥ's chariot.

It would help us at this point to remember Levy's astute observation: symbolic forms must be *engaging*. It is this engagement that gives the chariot festival its significance above any other festival in Lalitpur. The structure of the chariot *must* be precarious to engage the whole city in its construction and movement. It is not so much an invitation to disaster as an invitation to intense involvement. It is this engagement that binds the city together to ensure the festival's success.

The Jātrā is not the only festival of the Valley that is connected to the need for rain. The Trisul Jātrā of Deopātan parallels the Jātrā in certain ways: the same king (Narendra Deva) and priest (Bandhudatta) are said to have instituted it; the children carry a particular kind of shirt on cross-sticks reminiscent of the *bhoto* that is shown at Jawalakhel Jātrā. 'The Trisulyātrā', however, contends Axel Michaels, 'is basically a festival for warding off an inimical demon...' (1987: 185). Again, '... the rituals ... are very much concerned with the threat of demons and the means to ward them off on the one hand, and the agricultural cycle, mainly the evocation of rain, on the other' (ibid.: 192). Is there, in fact, a connection between the two? The threat of the demonic, those forces that are usually outside the urban order both spatially and cosmically, increases dramatically during the season of rice transplantation. The people have to go outside, beyond the Pale, so to speak, in order to raise from the ground, where the demons lurk, a harvest of sustaining food. So the festival is about both gods and demons: a worship of the one and a binding of the other.

The worship of Ajimā during the final leave-taking event of the Jātrā takes this one step further. The height of the monsoon season—the months of Ashādh and Srāvan (mid-June to mid-August)—was always the time of the greatest threat of smallpox. As Ajimā was the goddess of smallpox it was to her that citizens of the Valley would do *pujā* to ward of the deadly peril. Gods, as well as demons, then, needed to be propitiated in order to ensure the blessings of the monsoon without its attendant evils.[62]

10.8.2. The resolution of conflict

There is a curious mixture of old and new at the Bhoto Jātrā. On the one hand there is the traditional hymn singing of the Mridanga Bhajan Khalaḥ, the role of the Pānjus and the keeping of the sword on the chariot. On the other there is the modern and, in some ways, ill-fitting additions of the military band, the Guthi Corporation officials, and even the Shah king himself. Is there an echo of such conflict in the legend of the *bhoto*? The vest was given, goes the legend, to a farmer of Lalitpur from whom it was later stolen by a devious goblin. The subsequent fight over possession was never decisively won but ended in a stalemate with the *bhoto* being taken into the care of the deity until irrefutable evidence on one side or the other was brought forward. Both the Yala Juju and the Shah king return year after year to witness that the *bhoto* is still in the deity's possession. The present order, though in a way unacceptable to the citizens of Lalitpur, is here to stay at least for the time being. The accoutrements of modernity manifested at the Bhoto Jātrā are clearly demonstrations of the Shah regime's intent to expropriate the Jātrā and use it to consolidate its role as the new hegemony. But this hegemony is contested. The Yala Juju remains on the chariot while the 'real' king stands beneath offering his *pujā* from below. The irony, even subversion, of such a phenomenon cannot be entirely lost on thoughtful Lalitpurians.

The fight between the farmer and the demon can be also seen as a reflection of the ongoing conflict between the farmer and evil forces to produce fruit from the soil. The *nāga*s can give or withhold rain and so must be placated and treated well. But apart from that they are powerless. This is plain in the origin myth when Gorakhnāth sits on them to prevent rain. It takes a greater deity to release them and restore order to a context of disintegration. And it takes that same deity to safeguard the existing order until such a time as the present conflict between man and nature, good and evil, is finally decided. It was necessary also for the king, as maintainer of order within his realm, to make that preliminary judgement. The king, however, is too human to bring such a cosmic dispute to an ultimate resolution. He must give it to the deity for safekeeping.

The conventional wisdom about such festivals in South Asia is that they function simply to confirm the legitimacy of the statuses of ruler and ruled

(Owens 2000: 706, Toffin 1986). Owens is surely right, however, in pointing out that the Jātrā illustrates how ritual can be 'at once a product of extensive co-operation and an arena of contestation and conflict…' (2000: 707). This is well illustrated by the conflict between the Bārāhi and Yāngwa. Lineages contest their respective positions in the city's hierarchy and the Jātrā is an opportunity to express that contestation.

The Jātrā, then, functions as a didactic of Newar theodicy. There is a battle between good and evil. That is played out in the ordinary lives of people even as they go about their daily lives as farmers and artisans. The Jātrā gives an opportunity to express that ritually. But why is there evil? Why is it that suffering, as famine, is allowed? There is a cosmic struggle going on which is not yet played out. The king cannot bring victory to the forces of good. He can only impose a certain degree of order onto the situation by calling a great deity to aid him. Karunāmaya, then, ensures that disorder will not break out and wreck this unstable equilibrium. It is not a final answer but in this present evil age, the *kāli yuga*, one cannot expect too much.

10.8.3. The renewal of the city

The Jātrā is deeply connected with the founding of Lalitpur as a city. In this, it is parallel to the great festivals of the other cities, such as that of Biskaḥ in Bhaktapur.

> *Bisket Jātrā* is a mythical evocation of the founding of a town, the ancient capital of a kingdom, which, in a certain way, is the microcosm of the entire territory of that kingdom. This foundation is 're-played' each year at the festival; the town is thus 'renewed' at each New Year and the forces re-generated which condition the fertility and prosperity of the kingdom. (Vergati 1995: 184)

Vergati discerns a common thread to all three great local festivals of Valley—those of Biskaḥ in Bhaktapur, Indra Jātrā in Kathmandu, and the Jātrā in Lalitpur (ibid.: 25).

> From a structural perspective all three Newar festivals of the Valley aim at ensuring the prosperity of the kingdom. All take place over a period of nine days, as does the greatest festival of North India. The similarity in the conception of time, which they manifest, is important. All include processions of divinities taking place inside town-limits, displaying in this manner the hierarchy of the gods among themselves and also the relationship between the gods and the inhabitants of the territory. These processions celebrate the foundation of the king's capital and the regeneration of the social and religious order….[63]

Local tradition links the origins of the Indra Jātrā in Kathmandu to the creation of the city (Toffin 1992a). It is not surprising therefore, that Indra Jātrā is the major annual festival of that city. In Lalitpur, however, Indra Jātrā (or Yẽnyaḥ as it is usually called by Lalitpurians) does not have anywhere near the importance that it has in Kathmandu. It is the Jātrā of Karunāmaya that forms Lalitpur's focal annual celebration. And, not surprisingly, it is the Jātrā that is associated with the genesis of that city. Gellner points out that there is, in the popular mind, an assimilation of the two peasant figures, Rathãcakra and Lalita, the former responsible for bringing Karunāmaya to the city, the latter for founding the city itself (1996: 129; cf. Locke 1980: 248, 252). The founding of the city and the establishment of its most important god are thereby assimilated. Gellner goes on (ibid.):

> As Toffin (1993: 119-222) has pointed out in a recent analysis, Newar, and indeed Asian, cities frequently begin, in myths at least, with the establishment of a presiding deity: in the mythical, Hindu version, this is Kumbheshvara whose importance in the daily lives of most of the city's inhabitants is certainly less than that of Karunāmaya. In fact, as mentioned already, during the Licchavi period when Narendra Deva probably inaugurated Karunāmaya's festival, Lalitpur as such did not yet exist. But it is certainly possible that the establishment of the festival was part of the process by which the older settlements grew into an important city.

Levy explains that much of what is centred on Indra Jātrā in Kathmandu (autumnal equinox) is arranged around Biskaḥ in Bhaktapur (vernal equinox) (1990: 457). In Lalitpur, though, neither Indra Jātrā (Yẽnyaḥ) nor Biskaḥ are particularly important festivals. The opening of the Jātrā, however, like Bhaktapur's Biskaḥ, is arranged around the vernal equinox.[64] Thus it is possible to see the renewal of the city as taking place at the renewal of the year.

The exit of the deities from the city during the Jātrā presents a significant phenomenon. The chariots leave the ordered world of the city for the disordered world of the country. It is here that the people who have come to embody that notion of disorder, the Dyaḥlā, live. The exit of the deities, with the king and his retinue, from the city represents the, albeit temporary, breakdown of the spatial and moral order. While the chariots are outside the city, in the field of Lagã, the boundary is not clear. Notions of order and disorder threaten to collapse into one another. Another way of looking at this is to see it as a sort of rite of passage in the classic Van Gennepian sense. The king, identified here with the deity, is first of all separated from the city, remains in a liminal state for a period, and is finally reincorporated into the city in his renewed status by the mercy of the deity.

This is then another representation of the threat to the city's survival which the festival was instituted to avert. Unlike the case of Bhaktapur's parallel yearly festival of Biskaḥ, however, the Dyaḥlā have no part to play in the Jātrā (ibid.: 486).

10.8.4. The legitimation of kingship

Many observers have commented on the presence of the king at the showing of the *bhoto*. But, as we have seen, the notion of kingship if not its embodiment, has a much more central place than this. The Shah king's presence at the Jawalakhel Jātrā is a mere appendage to the centrality of the Malla king throughout the chariot's course through the city. It is my contention that the Malla king, the Yala Juju, as symbolized by his sword, is the most significant social phenomenon of the entire festival.[410] It is the king, as much as the deity, who is the rainmaker. As Michaels puts it (1987: 192):

> ...[The pre-monsoon] festivities of the Newars do not only deal with superhuman powers, such as the evocation of rain, but also with the benefits of the expected rain, such as the distribution of land, irrigation, claims on the best soil, etc. - in other words: they also deal with human power and, for example, as Anne Vergati has phrased it: with the king as rain-maker.

Toffin's (1992a) analysis of Kathmandu's Indra Jātrā shows a number of important parallels to Lalitpur's Bũgadyaḥ Jātrā. Indra is venerated as a warrior king but also as a god of vegetation associated with the general welfare of the kingdom. These two aspects correspond to the dual nature of Hindu kingship: protecting his subjects and mediating between man and nature. Toffin explains that the position of the king is ambiguous: in a sense he is a god, and yet he is also subject to the gods, dependent on them for legitimacy (ibid.: 87).

> Where there is no king, assert the classical texts, rain will not fall. Generative power was expressly listed among the various manifestations of sovereignty. The ruler was a producer of wealth (ibid.).

It will be remembered that the figure of King Narendra Deva is key in the story of how Bũgadyaḥ came to the Valley in the first place. Sri Nivas took this association further. For the king to be seen as the rainmaker there had to be an identification of the king with the deity. Sri Nivas manifestly adapted the Jātrā so that there would be a clear identification of the monarch with Karunāmaya.[411] This is how he did it:

1. He adopted Bũgadyaḥ as his patron deity (*ishtadevatā*).
2. He personally rode on the chariot at every stage of its journey through the city. In this way every citizen of his kingdom could get a view of the king at the same time as a *darshan* of the deity. The identification of king and deity was plain.
3. He built a temple for the deity in the city and reordered the cult of Bũgadyaḥ so that half the year the deity would be rightly worshipped within the city itself.
4. He regulated the festival to ensure the widest possible participation by the people (Locke 1980: 309).
5. He ensured that the purity of the deity (and thence of himself) would not be compromised by the entrance to the temple of those who were considered untouchable (Burleigh 1976: 40).

6. Finally, he underwrote the entire cost of the Jātrā by granting land to be used in its upkeep (ibid.).

This strategy paid off. During the 26 years of his reign 'there was more peace and, apparently, more prosperity than before or after' (ibid.: 37).

But there is one further ritual episode in the Jātrā in which kingship takes centre stage. In common with many other royal festivals throughout India, the Lalitpur Jātrā includes a phase in which the procession moves outside the city in a classic ceremony of 'crossing the limit' (Fuller 1992: 124). We have already seen how this seems to be bound up with ideas of renewal but here we can go further. In other such festivals there are clear hints that in doing so the king is asserting his sovereignty over a wider area, ultimately all of India. In Lalitpur's Jātrā, then, the king moves out of the city not only in a ritual separation as part of a rite of passage but also to demonstrate his sovereignty over the very world that would threaten it.

In what seems to be a Tantric twist, the Jātrā can also be seen as the marriage between the king of Lalitpur (Yala Juju) and the deity of Bũga. Bũga is called the deity's *thaḥ chẽ* ('own home', the natal home of a married woman); Lalitpur its marital home. The people of Lalitpur are its kinsmen and the Yala Juju is its husband. The ambiguous nature of the god's gender leads to this possibility. Locke points out that the *bodhisattva* Padmapāni Lokeshvara is neither male nor female and hence may be incarnate as a man or woman. Avalokiteshvara is always portrayed as a male in Nepal but the four Lokeshvaras are often referred to as the four sisters and Minnāth is often called the daughter of Matsyendranāth. So it is perfectly reasonable that Bũgadyaḥ should be regarded, for some purposes, as a royal bride, as indeed goddesses are often portrayed in Hindu mythology and sculpture. This would seem to fit with the probable origin of the deity as a powerful female deity of Bũga.

The symbolism of the sword retains its power today in spite of the loss of real power to the Shah dynasty. Discussing the analogous Rām Lila festival in India, Lutgendorf (1989: 41) reports that, by the time that the festival had reached its full month-long pageant in the early nineteenth century, real political power had passed to the British. The festival had not lost its appeal however; 'the symbols used to legitimate authority can serve equally well to compensate for its loss' (quoted by Fuller 1992.: 42). In Lalitpur, over two hundred years after his death, when the sword arrives at the Jātrā, people can still be heard to say, 'Sri Nivas has come!'

10.9. Conclusion

The Jātrā, the great festival of Lalitpur, is a window on a former era when the kings of the city were at the centre of national life. It was this centrality of kingship that was emphasised annually as the chariots were pulled through the settlement. This celebration and reenactment of the creation of the city placed the monarch firmly in the hub of the city's ritual life. By careful use of city space and the involvement of all the people of the city the identification of the king with the greatest of deities produced a deep respect for his kingship. The people were reminded, whenever they received a *darshan* of the deity, that their salvation was in the hands of their king every bit as much as it was in the hands of god.

11. KINSHIP AND KINGSHIP IN CREATIVE TENSION

> Castes are merely families to whom various offices in the ritual are assigned by heredity.
>
> Arthur Maurice Hocart (1950 [1938], quoted in D. Quigley (1993: 116)

> ...caste solidarity is often a check against abuses which the despotic rulers of the country are too apt to indulge in.
>
> Abbé J.A. Dubois (1897: 33), quoted in L. Dumont (1980: 398n., 84g)

The main aim of this work has been to describe and analyse caste as it has been experienced in the Newar City of Lalitpur. I have attempted, in the foregoing discussion to build a case for the centrality of kingship in Newar life. This is seen, not only in the structure of the caste system but also in the arrangement and use of urban space, and in the annual cycle of festivals. At this point it will be helpful to recap the salient features of the argument as I have presented it.

1. As in other societies in South Asia, kinship is the primary criterion of Newar identity. It is only as a member of a particular lineage that an individual or family can prove his caste credentials and therefore have any acceptable place in society.
2. Many castes have neither economic nor ritual relations with each other. Analysis of a caste system, therefore, is not helped by recourse to a ladder-like hierarchical diagram. Hierarchy is contested. The ladder as it is perceived by one caste is different from that perceived by another. Each caste, however, has relations with the centre—that is, with the king and his court.
3. There is a distinction between a 'carpenter' and a 'Carpenter'. A carpenter is one who plies his trade as a woodworker irrespective of his lineage but a Carpenter is one who belongs to such a lineage irrespective of his trade. Though at some time occupation must have been a significant factor in the development of caste, this seems to have changed so that the mere adoption of a trade now plays no part in an individual's caste identity.
4. The king was at the centre of city life. This was expressed spatially by the location and expansion of the royal palace at the settlement's geographical core. Moreover, the Malla kings of medieval Lalitpur adopted and extended the symbolism of the sacred mandala diagram in order to express this ideal ritually as well as spatially.

5. Traditionally, membership of locally based *guthi*s has been a very important factor in the social life of Newars. By cutting across caste boundaries and bringing together members of different castes within the *guthi*, the locality reduced the power of caste to define loyalties. This division of loyalties gave the royal centre the instrument it desperately needed to increase its control over the disparate groups that made up the city as a whole. The demise of the city as the capital of an independent kingdom, however, has redefined local space and loosened the significance that the locality has on its residents.
6. The civic order of Lalitpur, like that of the other Newar settlements, is under constant threat. Nowhere is this seen more clearly than in the annual collapse of that order during the monsoon season. Sickness and death stalk the *galli*s and courtyards. The untamed wilderness outside the walls threatens to overturn all that is sacred in the city. Many of the annual ritual events, then, are for the reestablishing of that sacred order.
7. The civic order is centred on the royal function. The centrality of the king, therefore, must be reestablished on a regular basis. The king must command the sacrifice. He must enact the ritual repeatedly in order to secure the kingdom from the forces of anarchy and conflict.
8. The centrality of the monarchy was legitimized by the conflation of the identity of the king with that of the gods, particularly Vishnu. This was further accomplished by the cooption of the greatest of all the festivals of Lalitpur, the Jātrā, and the consequent conflation of the identities of the *bodhisattva* Karunāmaya with that of the king.

Newar society has emerged out of a particular ecological context. The Newar view of the raw outside is instructive to us in understanding the construction of the city. As I have demonstrated (§7.5 and §7.25), the people have traditionally been entirely dependent on the annual cycle of seasons and in particular on the monsoon rains. The rains flood the paddy fields and bring the harvest of rice on which the Newar economy is founded. But the world around is anarchic, chaotic, and threatening. The wild outside was traditionally viewed as the abode of malicious spirits and vengeful demigods. There was no protection against violent marauders. Today, with the demise of Lalitpur as an independent political unit and the imposition upon it of the institutions of the modern nation state, the old realities have all but disappeared (even with a Maoist insurgency). Nevertheless, the rituals that came out of that milieu live on expressing those old realities *as if* they were the stuff of the present. It seems likely that much of that ritual will slowly disappear along with those realities even as they have been over the last couple of decades. The value of a study of that ritual, then, is more in what it teaches us about a former time. As Dil Mohan Tamrakar said, 'It seems that before we had electric lights people used to see evil spirits much more often. Nowadays hardly anyone sees them.' It is no surprise therefore, that rituals of expulsion should be dropped as in fact they have been by many at Gathã Mugaḥ.

The Newar settlement is a safe space created out of that wild environment as a stronghold against the forces of evil. It is a confined space with physical walls and ritual boundaries that repel both invader and ghost. It is, moreover, a sacred space from which all impurity must be removed, a mandala described by protective and empowering deities. This is the world of the Newar—a world infused with ritual. At the centre of this world and at the centre of this ritual is the king. It is the task of the king to impose order and dispense justice. As order is sacred, that order can only be imposed by the enactment of ritual. It is as the grand patron of the sacrifice that the king most poignantly expresses his royalty.

The king wields the sword. But there is a brake on the king's power. The lineage competes for the loyalty of the individual. Lineage solidarity is vital for normal family life. It is as a lineage that the great monsoon-bounding festivals of Lineage Deity Worship and Mohani are enacted. The dissolution of the lineage, therefore, is a threat to the very identity of the individual. There are, therefore, two great loyalty-demanding institutions in Newar society—kinship and kingship. As Quigley points out, these two institutions are the key ingredients in Arthur Maurice Hocart's 'Royalist' theory of caste (1993: 127). The position of the king is ambiguous because, though a man from a particular kinship group, he must transcend the ordinary rules of kinship in order to be a valid representative of all kinship groups in his realm. Kingship, therefore, is a fundamental denial of kinship. It is an assertion that not all men are brothers, that the institution of kinship is not powerful enough to uphold the social order.

This delicate political tension is expressed in the ritual. Hocart's position can be summarized as follows: 'There are two kinds of families: those who rule and those who are ruled. It is the ritual task of the ruled to keep their rulers free from pollution and the ritual task of the rulers to ensure that they do' (Quigley 1993: 122).

This is further reduced to the 'simple' principle: '*Those who rule must be pure*' (ibid. emphasis his). This is the rationale behind the repetition of the sacrificial ritual. Death and destruction invade not only the city but also the palace on a regular basis. The king must reestablish his credentials by resuming his role as the grand patron of the sacrifice, which is precisely what we observe in the annual cycle of festivals. 'Through ritual the illusion is given that actual kings and their actual Brahmans embody the ideal.... But effectively the illusion lasts only as long as the ritual does, and this is why rituals must be repeated again and again' (Quigley 1997: 570).

The king is at the apex of this sacrificial system. The key to Hocart's theory, therefore, is the centrality of the king.[1] The caste system of Lalitpur may now be diagrammed in a satisfactory way (Figure 5).

It might be objected that, if this is the case and Kshatriyas are actually 'higher' than Brahmans, then why does it often seem to be the exact opposite? Quigley demonstrates that there was a shuffling of the categories during colonial rule in India. The colonials took the part of the Kshatriya rulers *except* in the matter of adjudicating caste (1993: 123-6). Assuming that this was the territory of the Brahmans, the colonial rulers left it to them. This had the effect of elevating the position of the Brahman and demoting the Kshatriya. The irony is that the disjunction of status and power, that is central to Dumont's theory, was not a traditional phenomenon but a post-traditional one.

Dirks (1987: 59) comes to the same conclusion: 'In pre-colonial Hindu India, the king—both as historical figure and as a trope for the complex political dynamics underlying the Indian social order—was a central ordering factor in the social organization of caste.'

Dumont wants to explain caste as the outworking of the notion of hierarchy, a product of Hindu culture. But Hindu and Brahmanical society has always

Figure 5. The caste structure of Lalitpur

Castes are portrayed in a rough proportion to distance from the centre and size (though many of the smaller castes are proportionately smaller still).

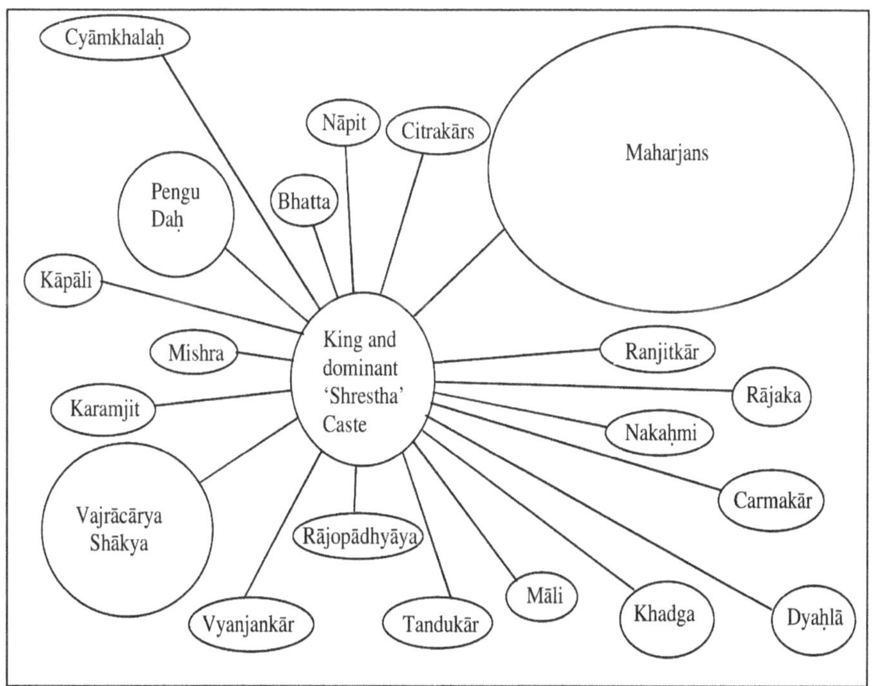

been characterized by ideological pluralism (§1.3). Caste, on the other hand, is pervasive even in places where such values are not at all emphasized (Raheja 1988b: 504). Caste, therefore, is a structural phenomenon not a cultural one. The institution is not dependent on cultural values.[2]

Caste structures, then, emerge out of the interplay between the two antagonistic forces of kingship and kinship. Kingship is centripetal whereas kinship is centrifugal. 'Caste results when kingship attempts to assert itself against kinship but ultimately fails because the conditions do not allow for stable kingdoms' (Quigley 1993: 129) as the Abbé Dubois also observed in the nineteenth century (see epigraph above). Kinship boundaries need to be markedly unambiguous as a way of creating stability in this political climate. Notions of pollution and separation, therefore, are not the building blocks of the system but the derivatives of it.

Social order was to be maintained by the regulation of social distinctions. A change in occupation was no longer sufficient to make a person a member of a *thar.* Why else would it have been necessary for the Malla kings to import Stonemasons and Carpenters from other cities? Surely a group of local Maharjans could have been given the contract? After all, someone was building the houses in Lalitpur. But the artisans with the necessary ritual and lineal qualifications were only available in neighbouring towns.

The most elementary social distinction is that between those who belong to the society and those who do not. Untouchables live on the outside: they inhabit the wild exterior. They are the quintessential barbarians whose existence affirms in the starkest terms the value of remaining as an insider. Their ritual exclusion, however, may not have been an ancient phenomenon. The inscription at the temple in Bũga erected by Sri Nivas in 1673 gives the first written mention, to my knowledge, of certain castes being denied access to a local holy site. The Mallas may not have created untouchability but it is apparent that they regularized it. It was a convenient concept to bolster the system.

The caste system is ultimately not about hierarchy but about *order.* The order, that is the civic order by which society functions, is under constant threat. Through the sacrifice, which he commands, the king continually regenerates the order of the universe. Order and ritual are inextricably linked. 'Ritual is essentially a question of order; order is essentially a question of ritual. He who controls the order controls the ritual; he who controls the ritual controls the order' (Quigley 1993: 139).

The ritual then enacts and demonstrates that order. Without it the order would collapse, not just temporarily as it does at various times in the annual cycle, but permanently and irrevocably. This approach to caste treads a middle path between the extremes of the materialist and idealist theories. Dumont's notion that caste stems from the ultimate value of hierarchy is mistaken. The demand for purity is all about making boundaries to include and exclude. The materialist stance is also mistaken because its insistence that caste is all about wealth and power does not adequately explain the ritual. Central to that ritual is the king.

> Kings are not only legitimate; they define the realm of the legitimate... The fundamental duty of these members of the elite is to subdue disorder, destroy lawlessness, and enforce law and order.... [And] as kings, by virtue of defining what is orderly, they define disorder too. (Dirks 1987: 70)

At the heart of Newar life, then, is the desire for order. Caste is a particular kind of order that, like any order, negates a certain degree of freedom. Furthermore, there is a higher price to be paid by those who are at a greater distance from the centre. There may not be equal justice for all. But if one is to have order, then that is a phenomenon one has to live with. There can be order without justice but there cannot be justice without order. Order, then, must take priority. Caste is the result.

Of all the cultural phenomena I have described in this work, this high value of order is nowhere more starkly modelled than in the traditional Newar leaf-plate feast *(laptyā bhway*; Plate 25, §8.8.7). The traditional feast, as served on special occasions of the household, lineage or *guthi*, has a number of significant features that both reflect and mould Newar values. As Geertz would put it, the Newar feast serves as both a model *of* and a model *for* Newar culture (1973: 93-94).

> Unlike genes, and other nonsymbolic information sources, which are only models *for*, not models *of*, culture patterns have an intrinsic double aspect: they give meaning, that is, objective conceptual form, to social

Plate 25. Maharjan men at a leaf-plate feast (*laptyā bhway*).

> and psychological reality both by shaping themselves to it and by shaping it to themselves. (Ibid.)

As a model *of* Newar culture, the feast describes the ideal order of the universe. This order reflects and interacts with the cosmic order—the order of the gods. Moreover, order is constructed out of raw ingredients. The fruits of the field are domesticated, transformed by cooking into a form that is healthful and sustaining. But even in such a state these dishes cannot be consumed willy-nilly. A strict sequence must be adhered to, if one is to avoid negative consequences. Furthermore, the feasters eat together, demonstrating a strong element of equality and solidarity. Again, there is an order to their seating that, while not contradicting the value of equality within the group, affirms an order to interpersonal relations that is equally significant.

As a model *for* Newar culture, the feast demonstrates what the culture needs to look like in order to maintain its integrity. Feasters return to their daily lives reminded of their place in the overall scheme of things. They have participated in a demonstration, an enactment of the ideal order.

Newars act out their lives in a particular kind of order. The traditional order emerged out of the interplay, the creative tension of kinship and kingship. It was expressed in the annual march of the festivals as they were played out in the sacred space of Lalitpur's mandalic stage. Kinship vied with kingship for the affections and loyalties of the citizen. So long as neither got the upper hand, that order was not upset. For centuries, in fact, it continued to provide fertile soil for its further development. Today, however, that traditional order is undergoing a major overhaul.

The rapidly changing political context both from within the modern nation state and from the world as a whole has challenged the caste system in a way that it has never been challenged before. The ongoing transformation of hierarchically related castes into competing quasi-ethnic groups within the larger context of a developing Newar ethnic consciousness has loosened the hold that the old institutions and values had on Newar society. Though that transformation is well under way it remains to be seen how it will play out. Will the old principles of kinship and kingship reassert themselves or will they be forever compromised by principles of individuality, freedom, and the like. Newars never were the hapless victims of their circumstances. They will continue to create and recreate their society from within even as outside forces act upon them.

Endnotes

Chapter 1: Introduction

1. Though I use the term 'Untouchable' throughout the book, I do not consider the members of such communities untouchable to myself. I merely use the term because it is the traditional term as used by the majority community. Since in this work I am trying to explicate a tradition, I want to retain the traditional designation to better facilitate understanding. I trust that I do not cause offence by doing this and I sincerely hope that such a view of underprivileged communities is not thus perpetuated.

2. Some of these articles have recently been reprinted along with new chapters in D.N. Gellner, *The Anthropology of Buddhism and Hinduism* (2001).

3. The single exception was that of the time that a girl actually stays in her darkened room during the Confinement (Bārhā Tayegu) rite, in which no men are welcome (Annex 9).

4. Throughout this study I use the masculine to refer to both genders, as has traditionally been the case in English. To write he/she and his/hers is cumbersome and unnecessary. By adopting this policy I do not intend to denigrate women.

5. Levy quotes approvingly Kierkegaard's interpretation of Abraham's imminent sacrifice of Isaac (1990: 725, n. 44). According to Kierkegaard (1954[1843]: 41), Abraham doubted the meaning of his act and suspected that it was actually an especially reprehensible act of murder. Kierkegaard argues from this that he had to make a 'leap of faith'—a commitment to counterintuitive propositions—in order to do that act against his own reasonable judgment. Kierkegaard's interpretation, however, flies in the face of the Bible's own witness to that event. We are told there that 'Abraham reasoned that God could raise the dead' (Hebrews 11: 19). Abraham, then, did not prepare to sacrifice his own son believing that he may be committing a heinous act, but believing that he was doing something right and good though he could not fully understand its significance. That is not, however, to argue against Levy's use of Kierkegaard but simply of Kierkegaard's use of Abraham.

6. Levy replies to Gellner's question of coherence by asserting that he is really not disagreeing with Parish but that the coherent order of the city is generated out of the plurality of differences (1997: 589). In this he seems to be dissembling, using a dialectic approach again to bring seeming contradictions into a new synthesis.

7. Unless otherwise indicated all dates are Common Era (CE, or Anno Domini, AD). There is some controversy over the starting date of the Licchavi Era, hence whether the Jaya Varma statue should be considered Licchavi or pre-Licchavi in origin.

8. The figure is closer to 30 per cent when one deducts the Dalits from this group.

9. *Kāshyap* is the name of a mythical *rishi. Kāshyap-gotra* is widely corrupted to *kāshi-gotra.*

10. Some politically motivated Maharjans, however, would assert their credentials by positing a pre-Hindu egalitarian past with the view to inclusion in such a list.

11. The Newar language revival movement has some following among young people. Dharma Krishna Sikaḥmi, an instructor in the Newar script, *Pracalit Lipi*, informed me that many young people learn the script so they can send secret love letters to their sweethearts!

12. For my part the initial, and later official version of events is most credible.

13. It is important, however, not to exaggerate the city's density by isolating it from its hinterland which, though not so relevant for ritual purposes, is an important part of the city's traditional economy (Mikesell 1993: 249).

14. The Tāmrakār Sukuḥ lineage tree gives a vivid picture of the change in demographics: three generations ago two mothers had eighteen births between them; of these six died in infancy (Tamrakar with Tamot 1994: 16). One of these sons had three children that all died in infancy. One is led to believe that, though this case is extreme, it is not untypical.
15. Very few of these actually board their pupils and many in fact employ a mixed medium of English and Nepali for instruction. School Leaving Certificate results in 2002, with fully two-thirds of entrants failing the basic qualification, occasioned many outbursts of anger in the press. This failure of the state education sector and the contrasting very high pass-rates of the private schools has led the Maoists to target private education for extortion and violent attack dubbing the schools 'education shops'.
16. David Gellner, personal communication.
17. Given the present political climate, however, I recognise that this will not be acceptable to many but beg the reader's patience.
18. This meal is sometimes referred to as a 'snack'. It is true that Newars do not view it as a meal in the same way as one based on boiled rice meal but large quantities may be eaten washed down by equally generous quaffs of home brew (*thon*).

Chapter 2: Newar Kinship

1. This even though Levy does take great pains to demonstrate repeatedly that in many respects Bhaktapur *is* typical of the rest of South Asia at an earlier period of its history.
2. Fürer-Haimendorf (1956), Levy (1990: 138), Gellner (1995b: 225), Lewis (1995: 50), Vergati (1995: 37-38), and Löwdin (1998: 125) all use the term *phuki* to refer to the patrilineal *group* rather than individual members.
3. Vergati's (1979: 119) statement that 'The founder of the lineage is a human being whose identity and name can be verified' may be true for smaller lineages such as these *kawaḥ* but is not true for those lineages which may have an older origin.
4. Gellner uses the term 'clan' when the lineage is large enough to have sections (*kawaḥ*) the size of ordinary lineages (1992: 24) but Ishii prefers 'Maximal Lineage' because the former term has been used in a different social context by other scholars (Fürer-Haimendorf 1956: 21-25; Nepali 1965: 159-61).
5. Gellner refers to the Pengu Daḥ as the 'Tāmrakār *et al.*' and distinguishes five sub-groups (1992). Joy Shepard based her research on what she calls the 'Panchthare' of Patan. She explains the name as meaning the 'five-clan intermarrying group' (1985: 59). She also, rightly, insists on a distinction between the 'Panchthare' and the Urāy (ibid.: 131f.).
6. This issue surfaces in the discussions of earlier observers (e.g., see the discussion in Chattopadhyay 1980, Appendix C).
7. The Bārāhi claim that they used to be 'higher caste' but that, because their marriage options were so limited ('the men used to go back to Kāmarup to get a wife and not return'), they were forced to intermarry with the Pengu Daḥ. This would seem to be a tradition dating back only to the nineteenth century when many lineages, in a trend set by the Rana rulers, constructed genealogies that posited an Indian, and therefore prestigious, pedigree.
8. These issues are almost entirely lost on earlier generations of observers (e.g., Fürer-Haimendorf 1965). Many modern writers, also, such as Nepali (1965), Rosser (1966), Bista (1996 [1966]) and Toffin (1984: 235, n.20), do not differentiate between the Pengu Daḥ and Urāy.
9. Levy's assertion (1990: 312) that all the groups that worship a common Lineage Deity are assumed to be descended from a common ancestor and that they therefore cannot intermarry is imprecise. The issue is whether they worship a common Lineage Deity *together.*

10. This is not such an unusual phenomenon: Quigley reports that in Dhulikhel one Shrestha Lineage Deity is worshipped by eight separate lineages (1985b: 24).

11. Agnates, in Roman law, were all those descended from a common male ancestor. In modern anthropological usage they are those persons that are related to one another through links with males alone.

12. Tantric ritual (from that body of scriptures called the Tantras), of which there are several different kinds, includes actions that would be considered taboo in the non-Tantric context, such as the offering and consumption of spirits and meat and among some groups ritual copulation (Bharati 1965). Access is gained by initiation (*dikshā*, Skt.) from an adept. Tantrism has heavily influenced religion in Nepal, having been adopted by Brahmans (Levy 1990: 300-319) and Vajrācārya priests (Gellner 1992: 324-6) alike.

13. Gajurel and Vaidya call all the workers of copper, brass and bronze, Kasa (1985: 41). The title Kasa actually belongs only to the Kamsakārs of Kathmandu, some lineages of Shākya in Lalitpur (D. Gellner, personal communication) and, previously, some Mulmi/Nyāchyā Shresthas of Lalitpur who used to make and sell bronze.

14. The Coppersmiths of Kathmandu (Tavaḥ) do not belong to the marriage circle of the Pengu Daḥ. Their relationship to the Tamvaḥ of Lalitpur is dealt with later (§4.4.2).

15. Kashinath Tamot traces the etymology of Tavaḥ, Tamvaḥ and Tamot from Tāmrakuttaka, via Tāmvata and Tamvata.

16. Nepali states that the Lalitpur 'Tamots' claim to have come from Mathurā (1965: 163). On that basis Gellner (1992: 350, n. 16) wonders if that is why they are so strongly *shivamārgi*. Nepali's informant (a Kathmanduite probably) seems to have mixed up the Tāmrakārs with the Rājkarnikārs as none of the Tāmrakārs of Lalitpur have such a tradition.

17. A copper plate inscription at the Lokeshvara temple at Co Bāhāḥ dated 782 NS (1662 CE) apparently includes the name of a Tāmrakār of Chasapakha Bāhāḥ (Locke 1980: 358). I have not been able to locate this *bāhāḥ* and wonder whether the coppersmith might not have been a member of another *thar* such as a Shākya.

18. Dil Mohan Tamrakar pointed out that all the Lalitpur Tamvaḥ invoke the ancestry of Kāshyap Gotra when they do Ancestor Worship. Such mythical ancestry, however, extends well beyond the boundaries of the Tamvaḥ.

19. Naḥ Bāhāḥ is an 'Independent Branch Monastery' (Gellner 1987b: 373, 399). Monastic Initiation (*Bare chuyegu*) is performed by members of the Monastic Community (Samgha) that is made up of the men of two Shākya families (cf. Locke 1985).

20. They also point to the different customs of the Panauti and Bhaktapur Tamvaḥ, especially the fact that, until recently they did not practice *macā jākwa* but instead elaborately celebrated the second birthday. It must be said, however, that some lineages that *are* accepted for membership of the Ugracandimai Sewā Samiti have equally unusual customs such as that of 'Sending the Goat' (*dugucā choegu*) practised by the wider Naḥ Bāhāḥ lineage (Appendix 1, p. 288).

21. The *digu dyaḥ* was transferred to Taksār by invoking the deity into a brick that was incorporated into a house in Bhojpur. The house itself is now seen as the *digu dyaḥ* and worshipped with the sacrifice of a goat during Dewāli and Mohani.

22. Toffin (1984: 263) posits the initial migration at around 1880 CE which is later than locals would put it. Panauti Tamvaḥ reckon the migration took place around ten generations ago.

23. Gutschow and Kölver reported 19 families of Tamvaḥ in Bhaktapur in 1975.

24. A Bhojpur inscription dated 1930 VS (1877 CE) bears his name.

25. One of Lewis and Shakya's transcriptions deserves a comment at this point. Tax 11 (1988: 40) records the contribution of Newars who had migrated from 'Daugal Tole' in Lalitpur. There is no neighbourhood with that name in Lalitpur and many of the personal names sound like they could easily be Tamvaḥ so it would seem that it should read 'Haugal' and that the 'H' was mistaken as a 'D'.

26. Rana Bahadur Shah, the grandson of Pritvi Narayan, ruled 1777–1799.

27. This is attested by the *Buddhist Vamshāvali* (Wright 1972: 263) and by other writings (see also Lienhard 1992: 99-101).

28. Gellner (personal communication), has pointed out that this sort of situation is not uncommon in South Asia. There are well-known examples of castes from Gujarat, for example, some of whose members are Hindu and others Jain; and others from Punjab and Haryana where, at least in the past, some were Hindu and others Sikh.

29. On the other hand, as the lineage *bāhāḥ*, such as Naḥ Bāhāḥ were founded largely by laymen, it is just as possible that such lineages originated from laymen and not former monks.

30. The Rājkarnikār Samāj records differ from my own somewhat. There is a large percentage of overlap but the differences are from the Samāj's looser method of determining a household and the fact that neither their nor my records are complete.

31. A number, whose family has lived in east Nepal for a few generations, go by Halawāi and one, until recently, by Pradhan (Halawai 2001: 87-88).

32. Ghana Shyam Rajkarnikar devotes a chapter of his memoirs to the origin and meaning of his *thar* (1995: 53-61). The etymology of the name, he asserts, is *rāj-kar-kār* (i.e., one who works with his hands for the king) (ibid.: 60). This is highly unlikely. The name is more likely to be derived from the flower *karnnikāra* mentioned in an inscription dating from 792 NS (Tamot 2000: sv).

33. Ruled 1380–1395.

34. K. Tamot, personal communication.

35. Lévi's (1905) list, as reported by Chattopadhyay (1980), includes 'Karnika' which he describes as 'Weaver(?)'. This is most likely to refer, in fact, to the Rājkarnikārs, especially as the group is accorded the twenty-fourth rank, just three ranks higher than Tāmrakār. Hodgson records 'Madhikarmi' as directly above 'Barhi' and 'Lohangkami' (see Chattopadhyay 1980, Appendix C).

36. Locke calls the deity Yogambara (1985: 229).

37. A few Marikaḥmi migrated further afield to other bazaar towns of the hills such as Taksār where an inscription dated 1930 VS (1877 CE) mentions one family of 'Haluwai'.

38. It was not built by the Tāmrakārs, as Nepali writes (1965: 295).

39. I am indebted to Hemraj Shakya for this information.

40. I was not able to see this for myself.

41. Ultimately from Sthapati, the designer-painter-carpenter son of Vishvakarman, one of the four heavenly architects (Slusser 1998: 130).

42. Gellner (1992: 44) also mentions Hastakār as an alternative name for the Sthāpits but I have not yet come across anyone actually designating themselves as such.

43. A copper plate inscription in the Taleju temple is dated Māgh 741 (1621 CE) (Burleigh 1976: 33).

44. Locke reports the main Tantric shrine of Jom Bāhāḥ, which is shared by Vishvakarma Sikaḥmi and Lwahākaḥmi alike, was also built by the 'Sthāpits' (1985: 138).

45. Locke reports that the lineage deity was brought from Kāmi Nani, Lagan. In fact, the deity at Kāmi Nani is the Tantric Deity of the Kathmandu Sthāpits whose Lineage Deity remains at Bhadrakāli.

46. Mahila Shilpakar disputed whether these were really Tantric shrines at all.

47. The chariot of Seto Matsyendranāth in Kathmandu is built by Jyāpus from Lagan Tol and Thamel (see Locke 1980: 223), which explains why several observers have misidentified the Bārāhi as Jyāpu as well.

48. Perhaps this should be 'Khawa Pānju'.

49. Bandya is a common corruption of the colloquial Newar *Bare*, which is used as a referent for Shākyas and Vajrācāryas.

50. According to Owens some Bārāhi go through a shorter 'initiation' called the 'Gift of the areca nut' (*gway dān*) (2000: 165). This ritual, however, is a special invitation ritual *not* an initiation.

51. Shepard reports that this is the reason for the Pengu Daḥ sometimes being called *charthare* (1985: 226).

52. Tulsi Lal Singh informed me (personal communication) that the epithet used in the inscription is 'Balahi' (lines 8-9).

53. Though the final prohibition seems to apply only if that grandparent is still alive (Quigley 1987: 164).

54. It was made apparent to me, however, by the embarrassment I sensed in my informant, that this is not considered quite normal.

55. Toffin (1995a: 200) attempts to build a case for an opposition between Rājopādhyāya Brahmans and Newars on the dissociation between the Rājopādhyāyas' Lineage Deity (*digu dyaḥ*) and Tantric Deity (*āgã dyaḥ*). As we can see here in the case of the Tamvaḥ and Lwahākaḥmi, however, it is clear that such a dissociation is not unique to Rājopādhyāyas. The attempted dissociation of the Rājopādhyāya Brahmans from other Newars cannot be built on this basis.

56. Tantrism has had a great impact on both religious paths in the Valley since its introduction in medieval times. Tantric religion is extremely popular, having close contacts with the worship of goddesses and blood sacrifice.

Chapter 3: Intercaste Relations

1. Chattopadhyay (1980 [1927]) helpfully summarizes all the early attempts by Earle (no bibliographic data given), Hamilton (1971 [1819], 1838), Hodgson (1972 [1874], 1880), Oldfield (1981 [1880]), and Lévi (1894, 1905). Nepali (1965, 1987) and Rosser (1966) follow in this tradition. Allen (1973: 5), Greenwold (1978: 486-7), Gutschow and Kölver (1975: 56-58), Barré *et al.* (1981: 26, 28), Gutschow (1982: 45), and Toffin (1984: 231, 261, 279) also give tables of Newar castes.

2. There seems to have been a relaxing of attitudes towards intercaste marriage even during the period of my fieldwork. Many intercaste marriages are now celebrated with full ritual, though whether this reflects changing attitudes towards caste or ritual or both is not clear to this researcher.

3. Höfer points out that in the Civil Code of 1854 (Muluki Ain) 'limits to consexuality are assessed more widely than those set to commensality' (1979: 81).

4. Fürer-Haimendorf's conclusion (1960: 31) was based on scanty field evidence. It would seem that he misapprehended *thar*s that intermarry (such as the Pengu Daḥ and Urāy, as I have shown) as distinct castes.

5. Shepard reports that a Shākya ranked the 'Panchthare' (as she calls the Pengu Daḥ) as higher than Maharjan because 'the Jyāpu touch dung' (1985: 155).

6. Albeit in attenuated form (Gellner 1992: 268).

7. The price that an aggrieved husband may claim from the man who has stolen his wife.

8. He said his remarks were based on the Muluki Ain (MA) of 1854. This is actually not true of the 1854 MA, which has the following payments: Among 'Non-enslavable Alcohol-Drinkers' (usually Rs. 60) is mentioned 'other *srest*', 'Bada' and 'Udas' at Rs. 60; Jyāpu 'and their equals (*jyāpu saraha*)' at Rs. 40; and 'Salmi', 'Nakarmi', 'Mali', etc., at Rs. 35 (Höfer 1979: 137). Perhaps he was referring to a later edition. The stipulations of the 1854 MA still beg the question at which level the Pengu Daḥ were included. As the Ranas were probably not too concerned to distinguish between artisan castes of various Valley cities it seems likely that they intended the Pengu Daḥ to be classed with the Udās (Urāy) on the basis that most of the *thar* appellations are identical.

9. My informant who actually witnessed the event explained that the Maharjan women were 'Dhāgu Jyāpu'. I have not been able to find a meaning for this except that they take some kind of Tantric Initiation.

10. Shepard reports a dispute was between a 'Jyāpuni and a Marikaḥmi' and says that it was decided in favour of the Marikaḥmi because Buddhist 'Panchthare' (Pengu Daḥ) sometimes take Tantric Initiation, 'something which no Jyāpu is ever allowed to do' (1985: 155).

11. In Levy's ranking of Bhaktapur's Newar Hindu *thar*s the Tamvaḥ are ranked sixth out of twenty (1990: 625ff.). He argues that the Tamvaḥ of Bhaktapur are a special case (with the Tini) in which there is only one *thar* in the status level and that this seems to be 'an historical residue of some problem in categorization' (ibid.: 89). As will be seen in the ongoing discussion it is not a problem of Bhaktapur's categorization but rather of Levy's.

12. It seems to me that Gellner and Pradhan's assertion that 'Recently the Tulādhar *et al.* (Urāy) of Kathmandu have begun to agree to marriages with the Tāmrakār *et al.* of Lalitpur' (1995: 167) is something of an overstatement. Lienhard's (1995: 44) statement that the Tāmrakārs can 'without further ado' intermarry with the Urāy of Kathmandu is clearly unfounded.

13. The settlement of Panauti, however, does not fit the pattern of town endogamy. According to Toffin the percentage of Tāmrakārs marrying within Panauti in the 1970s was 16.3, which is much lower than expected of a society that is normally town-endogamous. The size of Tamvaḥ he settlement, however, explains this anomaly. The proportion of all castes marrying endogamously within Panauti is low because the population is not big enough to find partners outside of the exogamous categories. Toffin, working with a bipartite model of Newar settlements, hypothesized a principle of town exogamy from this (1984: 407). Ishii (1995: 151-5) modifies Toffin's proposal by constructing a tripartite typology of Newar settlements: (1) Fringe endogamous uni-caste settlements (a) with simple marriage and less formality between affines (e.g., Pyangaon), (b) with formal marriage and affinal relations characterized by reservation (e.g., Dhulikhel); (2) Intermediate multi-caste non-endogamous settlements (e.g., Satungal and Panauti); and (3) Large Urban settlements with complex intercaste relationships and tendency to territorial endogamy. The principle of town endogamy is strikingly expressed among the Pengu Daḥ in Lalitpur—most married women live less than five minutes' walk from their natal home (*thaḥ chẽ*).

14. Lewis states that the Rājkarnikārs and Tāmrakārs of Kathmandu are 'subcastes (that) have been incorporated from lineages in Patan…' (1996: 111). It is true that Rājkarnikārs have gained some acceptance among the Urāy of Kathmandu but this is not universally acknowledged. Wealthy Rājkarnikārs living in Kathmandu and even some in Lalitpur have begun to intermarry with Tulādhars, Baniyas and others, but this is still a small number and cannot be taken as the inclusion of the Rājkarnikārs in the Urāy group.

15. They did not, however, keep the patronymic, as Nepali has reported that others do in this situation (1987: 325).

16. Nem Krishna Tamrakar, the compiler of the Sukuḥ lineage genealogy—*Tāmrakārya sukuḥ khalaḥya kacamaca*—is of the opinion that there is more laxity about intercaste marriage outside the Valley. In Bhojpur, for example, several Tāmrakār women (most of whom are Nem Krishna's patrilineal relatives, *phukipi*), have married *bona fide* Shresthas (Tamrakar with Tamot 1994).

17. I know of one Bārāhi girl whose marriage was arranged with a Kathmandu Shākya. Shepard reports at least one acceptable marriage between a Lwahākaḥmi with a 'Bare' (1985: 223). Gellner (personal communication) also reports the case of a Nāg Bāhāḥ Shākya who married a Tamvaḥ girl with full ritual but without full public celebration.

18. See Appendix 2, p. 292, for complete list of life-cycle rites.

19. In the literature this woman is often referred to as *didi aji*. My informants insisted, however, that she should be named simply *aji*, as the qualifier *didi* would only be used if she was of a certain age relative to the speaker, other qualifiers being used by those of a different relative age.

20. In Malla times rates for such services were fixed by the king.

21. M.M. Mishra, personal communication.

22. According to Locke (1985) the Rājkarnikārs claim that until last century they continued to follow strict Brahman traditions; e.g., strict vegetarianism. But, he says, 'since settling in Patan have always been Buddhist'. No Rājkarnikār has reported such a scenario to me.

23. *Satya Yuga* is the mythical previous age when all was right, before the present *Kali Yuja*.

24. Owens' assertion that the Bārāhi describe themselves as *shivamārgi* (2000: 713) is over-simplified. One suspects he received his information from Surya Lal Barahi, the late *thākāli*, who was also quite insistent to me about the Bārāhi being *shivamārgi* and of *'kāshi gotra'*. His household does indeed employ solely a Rājopādhyāya *purohit*.

25. Pandit Madan Mohan Mishra's opinion (personal communication) that they are traditionally *shivamārgi* and that they may have switched to calling the Vajrācārya because of some conflict or insult seems to me less likely.

26. This is a tradition going back to Srinivas (1952) and Mayer (1966) in India.

27. In Gellner's table, area is a very approximate representation of numerical strength, the broken line indicates the existence of formalized hierarchy within the caste, and the relative status of castes depicted side by side is debated.

Chapter 4: The Economy of the Pengu Daḥ

1. It is in fact problematic to assert, as Quigley does, that the Newar household is both an economic and a ritual unit. These units are often not coterminous as I try to demonstrate in the discussion below.

2. I do not have precise data on the total population of the Pengu Daḥ, but I estimate it to be around 3,500.

3. This compares very closely with the average number of 6.9 persons per household in Bhaktapur in the early 1970s (Gutschow and Kölver 1975: 13).

4. In this very useful scheme the two basic types of household—nuclear, consisting of a husband and wife with or without children, and joint, consisting of two or more such units—are broken down into categories that show the precise nature of the parts. So a sub-nuclear household is a single-parent family and a supplemented household is one in which a fragment of a nuclear family is present in addition to a complete family. A joint family may be one in which the nuclear units are of the same (collateral) or different (lineal) generation. The change from joint household to nuclear household can happen by the death of only one person. It only takes the death of one parent, for instance, to change a household from category 8 to category 2.

5. Quigley (1985a) writes as if household divisions occur entirely at a single moment in time.

6. In a variation of this the families of two brothers I am familiar with live together but act as separate economic entities taking turns week by week to buy food and cook for the entire household. In this case even the stove and cooking vessels are not shared but each family has their own which they use when it is their turn.

7. For further discussion of the origins of metal work in Nepal see Slusser 1976.

8. For detailed descriptions of the lost-wax or cire-perdue method of brass- or bronze casting see Alsop and Charlton 1973, Gajurel and Vaidya 1984: 41 and Tamot 1995.

9. The Japanese scholar Minami (1998), drawing on his fieldwork in Dhading district, suggests a typology of water pots (Ishii 2001: 177). Ishii reports that Minami says that the techniques and economy of the Kāmi smiths there has been changing under the influence of the Tāmrakārs.

10. Brass sheets are also imported from Singapore.

11. The production of the brass water pot is also described in detail by Gajurel and Vaidya (1984).

12. Le Port lists these as claw hammer, mallet, pair of pliers, adze, hand saw, plane, 'galere', two-part 10mm rabbet plane, 18mm rabbet plane, 10mm and 30mm chisels, 5mm and 10mm heading chisel, one or two gauges, a 30mm auger, a brace and bits, gimlet and its bow, triangular file, T-square, marking gauge, string and bubble level and folding foot (1991: 109).

13. Shepard reports that when the Tāmrakārs began hiring untouchable metal workers this led to an immediate outcry (1985: 63-64). No sign of this controversy remains today.

14. Asaoka (1998) reports a parallel development between Kāmis (Parbatiyā Blacksmiths) and Nakaḥmis (Newar Blacksmiths) in the car repair and steel industry of the Valley (Ishii 2001: 177).

15. Levy reports that some Bhaktapur Tamvaḥ also farm (1990: 81) but I have not come across any either in Bhaktapur or Lalitpur, though some do indeed own fields that are farmed by Jyāpus.

16. In 1977 copper was Rs. 80 per kg (Toffin 1984: 336).

17. The makers of Nepal's first English-style bread, Krishna Pauroti, are Rājkarnikār. Ravi Rājkarnikār remembers visiting the factory when he was a boy (late 1950s) and watching the workers kneed the dough with their feet, a practice that many believe led to the name (> *pau*, Np., 'foot' + *roti*, Np., 'bread'). In fact, however, the word comes from usage in India and ultimately from Portuguese.

Chapter 5: Ordered Space

1. Mikesell (1993) asserts that it is misleading to state (as Levy does) the population density of Bhaktapur without including the fields all around as the majority of the people are cultivators.

2. D. Gellner, personal communication.

3. I have benefited much from the work of Niels Gutschow whose maps of the city (especially in his 1982 *Stadtraum und Ritual der Newarischen Städte im Kathmandu-Tal*) have provided me with much stimulus in the writing of this chapter.

4. The Bāgmati is, in fact, not the only river that has run through the city since ancient times. Another river, the Haḥkā Khusi once flowed west through Haḥkā to join, at Mangaḥ, with another river that flowed north from Lagankhel and thence down to the Bāgmati. The presence of large river-worn boulders in the sub-soil at Lagankhel bears this out. Furthermore, the courtyard at the erstwhile confluence is called Mulsi whose name seems to derive from its former use as a cremation ground. The ritual of the changing of Bũgadyaḥ's vest at Mangaḥ (§10.7.4) is also said to hark back to a time when the chariot was literally hauled through this river.

5. Alternatively the *pujā* materials are deposited at the ritual entrance to the house, the *pikhā lakhu.* They are not thrown at the *chwāsā*, as an umbilical cord would be, because they are considered clean. It is interesting here to note that the *pikhā lakhu* provides a boundary for the house to the wider city outside it, in much the same way as the river provides a boundary for the city to the wider world outside it.

6. cf. Dhanavajra Vajracarya (1964).

7. The fact that some Khadgis also lived *outside* the old wall indicates that perhaps the distinction between Untouchable and merely Water-Unacceptable was at times hazy.

8. The data for this map are partially gleaned from Gutschow (1982: 162, Map 176) and from the map prepared by Nutan Sharma and published in Gellner and Pradhan (1995: 275, Fig. 9.2). I have interpolated the position of the wall a little differently. See also Gutschow and Kölver (1975: 49) and Gutschow's maps in Levy (1990: 164,179) for a similar mapping of Bhaktapur.

9. Crossroads are usually considered inauspicious in South Asia. They are the abode of evil spirits such as the reverse-footed *kicikini.*

10. This list came out of a hard won consensus after a long discussion involving Nem Krishna Tamrakar and a group of elderly Maharjan men at Haugaḥ.

11. Gutschow (1982: 163, Map 177) shows the locations of Lalitpur's Eight Mother Goddesses.

12. Some of the names and positions of the Dashmahāvidya in Gutschow's map are different (1982: 165, Map 183).

13. The proximity of these two deities leads to the common but mistaken belief that the Mahāvidya is Bāl Kumāri.

14. This also fits with the existence of the Lineage Deity of the Paḥmā Sikaḥmi (and Paḥmā Shrestha) at Thāpahiti just along the road east of Cāka Bahi, which must have been outside the city at the time it as established (§2.6.4).

15. I am grateful to Nutan Sharma, Dil Mohan Tamrakar, and Nem Krishna Tamrakar for helping me prepare this list.

16. A fourth cremation ground is used exclusively by the Dyaḥlā of Thati and is located about 400m south-west of their settlement.

17. Oldfield's report that the majority of Lalitpur's cremations took place at Bāl Kumāri seems unlikely (1981 [1880]: 125).

18. Gutschow's map is inaccurate (1982: 163, Fig. 177). He draws strict boundaries so that the inhabitants of Kuti Saugaḥ, for instance, go to Bāl Kumāri. In fact, though Maharjans of that locality cremate their dead at Bāl Kumāri, the Sikaḥmi go to Shankamul via Cyāsaḥ on a circuitous route (Map 14). Likewise, the Bārāhi of Yānamugaḥ.

19. This devotion was clearly demonstrated after the palace massacre of 2001 when thousands of men shaved their heads as if in mourning for their father.

20. Gutschow (1982) was apparently unaware of the Vishnu Devi Jātrā. The two *jātrās* of Mahālakshmi (Gutschow's map only shows one) have, since Gutschow wrote, become defunct. Gutschow suggests that each of these *jātrās* traces a route around the territory corresponding to that *ashtamātrika.* An analysis of the corresponding localities in terms of the cult, however, reveals that this is, in fact, not the case. I am not aware of an analogous procession for any of the other of the Eight Mother Goddesses.

21. Gutschow's list of stopping places on the *pradakshinapātha* is not wholly accurate (ibid.: 168, Fig. 188 caption).

22. For many residents this is the *pradakshinapātha.*

23. The term as it is used in Lalitpur, however, seems not to have the connotation of chronological precedence that Ishii reports for Satungal.

24. There is an exception to this in that small groups of men also use the route on Swãya Punhi which, being a modern festival in the Valley, does not follow traditional rules.

25. Sometimes *pitha pujā* may be more informal with no fixed number of Power-Places visited.

26. I have remarked above that some of the phenomena that Newars use to orient themselves in space are Valley-wide; i.e., not confined to any one settlement. The four mandalic hills are not the only points of Valley-wide significance. Stoddard (1979) has reported that such points are somewhat contested. It seems that there is a fairly clear recognition of four Nārāyanas—Changu, Ichangu, Visankhu and Sesha Nārāyana. Agreement on four Valley-wide significant images of Ganesh, however, is very difficult to come by. Neither is there agreement in the common mind of which of the Eight Mother Goddesses belong to the valley as a whole. It seems to me that, although there is a notion that such sets of deities, fitting in as they do with the concept of Nepal Mandala, do exist, their significance is quite limited. Clear recognition of deities arranged in space tends to follow the reality of political boundaries and centres. The Nepal Valley was rarely one entity politically before 1768/69. The Newars as a whole had very little self-concept as a single group until they became included in the new nation under the Shahs.

27. Michael Witzel (1992: 796-801) has reported a positive correlation between the high/low couple and the gender opposition of male and female in the city of Lalitpur. But, as Toffin says (1966a: 84), this Tantric exegesis by a learned priest is not so helpful as it is not shared by the laity.

28. The Bhimsen temple, at the north end of the square, is an exception to this rule (cf. Toffin 1991: 78; Barré *et al.* 1981: 51-53).

Chapter 6: Territorial Organizations

1. Gutschow's map (1982: 158, Fig. 170) seems overly positivistic in its precise demarcating of the localities. The 24 *twaḥ* of Lalitpur are surely no more than an ideal number that was never clearly delineated.

2. Quigley calls the seniormost lineage male the *nayaḥ* rather than the *thākāli* (1985b: 50), a usage I have not come across.

3. In reality there is always something of a lag between the death of one *thākāli* and the induction of another such that there were several spaces available at the time of my study. One factor contributing to this situation is that of the high cost of induction.

4. Gellner reports that the sections of large *guthi*s are termed *'kawaḥ'* (1992: 247). I have not come across such a usage in my fieldwork (but §2.3). Shepard asserts that the two words *wala pala* refer to two different groups with different responsibilities (1985: 184). This does not correspond with what I have been told.

5. The Tamvaḥ Cidhā Guthi also meets during the intercalary Purushottam month.

6. At the time of writing, on the death of a *nāyaḥ* none of his descendants wanted to become a *guthiyār* let alone accept the responsibility of *nāyaḥ*. The *guthiyār*s then appointed a member who had no known agnatic relationship with the former. It was also decided that, in keeping with the times, the position of *nāyaḥ* would no longer be forced onto the son of one who had deceased.

7. None of my informants felt able to make a judgement on this point. Ram Govinda Rajkarnikar was insistent that the number of original Rājkarnikār brothers was two. Nevertheless, at some point the descendants could have formed four clearly defined lineages.

8. Fürer-Haimendorf's (1956) assertion that 'There is today... no hereditary office which passes in unilateral succession from father to son', clearly the rule, must however be modified to take such a situation into account.

9. Quigley himself admits that other localities include artisan and agricultural *guthi*s that operate as a credit bank (1985b: 53).

10. It might be argued that some death *guthi*s are also agnatic. This is true but in principle such *guthi*s are open to those from outside the lineage. Since they are not then *essentially* agnatic I treat them as *thar guthi*s.

11. Gellner's informant Asha Kaji Vajracharya indicates that the Pengu Daḥ receive an abbreviated form of Tantric Initiation (1992: 51-52, 268).

12. Gellner (personal communication), points out that this makes the Pengu Daḥ analogous to some Shrestha lineages who have Brahmu *purohit*s but Vajrācārya *dikshā* (*dekhā*) *guru*s.

13. Contra Vergati (1995: 41), lineages which are not related never form a Lineage Deity *guthi* but may, however, form a death *guthi* that worships the Lineage Deity together as tutelary deity; e.g., Tamvaḥ Cidhā and Tadhā *guthi*s.

14. Similarly, in Dhulikhel, Quigley was often told that the *dyaḥ pujā* group was *like* a *guthi* but not actually a *guthi* (1985b: 14). One wonders here whether the group functioned as a *guthi* even though the term was not used for it. Among the Pengu Daḥ some reserve the term only for death *guthi*s.

15. Gellner, in a personal communication, reports that this situation seems to be equally true of Shākyas and Vajrācāryas.

16. Lewis organizes the music groups of Asan differently. According to his scheme, there are two types of music groups among the Asan Tulādhar community: the Gũlā, Dāphā and Panca Tāl Bājā groups are old; the *bhajan* groups started in 1950s and emulate Hindu groups using *tabala*, harmonium, sitar and violin (Lewis 1984: 183).

17. Toffin asserts that in the village of Theco the death *guthi* is a 'secret society, impregnated with sacramental values, which contributes to defining a sense of mystical community' (1996a: 76). That is likely to be more strongly felt in the village than it is in the city with its more complex system of overlapping boundaries and somewhat less multiplex roles in interpersonal relations.

18. I wonder whether Quigley may have been mistaken in reporting that *si guthis* and *dyah pujā guthis* do worship on the same day (1985b: 53). Most likely this was a death *guthi* doing *pujā* to the Lineage Deity as the *guthi*'s tutelary deity.

19. Shepard reported that in the early 1980s the 'Lhonkami' and 'Sikami' have one *sana guthi* each (1985: 182). I have not been able to establish whether this was in fact so. Today, of the Shilpakārs' two death *guthis* the Tadhã Guthi membership is drawn from both groups. The Cidhã Guthi formed as a split from the Tadhã Guthi. The normal *thar* specificity of the death *guthi* is also broken elsewhere: Toffin reports that of the three Tamrakar death *guthis* in Panauti one is shared with 'Udas' (1984: 386).

20. Some informants remember another death *guthi* called Pauca *guthi* that could no longer function as only three *guthiyars* remained. It seems that the tutelary deity of this *guthi* was also Tamkadyah.

21. *Pãcāku* is usually the first food consumed *after* the completion of a Newar Buddhist rite (Gellner 1992: 302).

22. In contrast, Lewis reports that for the Urāy of Kathmandu *many* voluntary *guthis* are multicaste associations (1995: 59).

23. Harkhā̃dyaḥ is an epithet of Bhairava.

24. It seems that Lienhard had this group in mind when he wrote about the 'Bālagopāla Mandir' music group (1995: 45).

25. No 'water-unacceptable' caste men participate.

26. Presumably the harmonium was added to *dāphā* ensembles in the nineteenth or early twentieth century.

27. Shepard reports that the Nasantya Dāphā Guthi was established by Marikaḥmi (1985: 194).

28. Shakya (1995) says that the *dhāḥ bājã* is especially played by Shākya, Vajrācārya and Tāmrakār. This may be further evidence of some of the Tāmrakārs' previous Buddhist, even monastic, background.

29. Lienhard (1995) confuses this group with the Nasantya Dāphā Guthi and also with the Kati Pyākhã *khĩ bhajan khalaḥ.*

30. Lewis (1984) specifically mentions the influence on Mahāyāna Buddhism but it is surely equally true of non-Buddhists.

31. This point is also made by Toffin (1977).

32. In a personal communication, Gellner points out that in some cases–Kamsakārs among the Urāy, Mānandhars, Citrakārs and Rājopādhyāyas–it has been possible to graft modern forms of organization on to pre-existing, pre-modern organizations. In all these examples, the caste (or thar in the case of Kamsakārs) small enough to be able to maintain a traditional caste council.

33. At the time of writing, however, an attempt was made to create such a group. The absence of any group representing the Sikaḥmi and Bārāhi, however, prevented it from being complete. It would appear that it is only a matter of time before this does become a reality.

34. In recent years this inflationary cycle has led to the number of trays exceeding a hundred—enough to bankrupt a household of modest means.

Chapter 7: The Renewal of Order I: Restoring Civic Space

1. One could also see the dynamism of Newar culture in the way that it is adapting under the influence of modernity; but that is not my purpose here.

2. Though the Narasimha Jātrā is clearly a Vaishnava festival the designation *shivamārgi* is not seen in any way incongruous.

3. An epithet of Vishnu.

4. Because of the precession of the lunar calendar the solar festivals do not always fall at the same point among the lunar festivals. I have chosen, arbitrarily, to slot the solar festivals in according to the calendar that is on my wall at the time of writing these chapters: 2003 CE (2059/60 VS).

5. Throughout Chapters 7-10, where I generalize I do so on the basis of information supplied to me by my Pengu Daḥ informants. In many cases I was not able to confirm the validity of these generalizations.

6. Eck (1993: 258-78) divides Banāras' seasons into five (hot, rainy, autumn, cold and spring) but gives no indication whether this is an emic construct or not.

7. I am grateful to Narendra Rajbhandari for furnishing this list.

8. The use of the word *yuga* for season is interesting as it is the same word used for epoch, as in Satyā Yuga or Kāli Yuga.

9. As I was completing the final editing of this chapter snow fell for the first time in sixty years in the city itself—a full three weeks after the hot season had begun!

10. Kesar Lall has translated some of these folk tales into English under the title *Tales of Three Brothers.*

11. Dil Mohan was of the opinion that most Lalitpurians continue this practice. Pressler explains in detail the significance of the sacred plant (1978: 175-215).

12. This consists of beaten rice (*baji*), puffed rice (*khay*), black soybeans (*hāku musya*), ginger (*pālu*), black-eyed beans (*bhuti*), the savoury pancake (*waḥ*), spirits (*aylāḥ*) and beer (*thon*).

13. This practice is increasingly abandoned in favour of a simple waft of incense by all but old people.

14. For the last twenty years or so this practice has been abandoned in Lalitpur continuing only in some of the more conservative villages.

15. The practice was abandoned partially because Priya Pokhari was reduced to a mere puddle.

16. In the evening, the *guthi* eats the concluding feast of the annual series, which includes the sharing of the head of the sacrificial victim (*sikāḥ bhu*) with the *guthi* sitting in the following order: first—*thākāli*, second—lead *khẽ* player, third–lead singer and thence in order of seniority.

17. Parbatiyā traditionally complete their rice transplantation by Caturmāsya Vratarambhaḥ (Ashādh-*sukla*/Dillāthwa 11) (Treu 1993: 151).

18. This is different from the Tibetan Buddhist holy month, which falls in the spring.

19. See photo of this event in Gellner 1995b: 222 (Plate 15).

20. My informants affirmed that this still happens though I did not observe it myself.

21. Toffin reports that the Citrakārs of Lalitpur are occasionally called on to repaint the masks of Dipankara for this event (1995b: 241).

22. According to my informants *shivamārgis* alone celebrate this festival.

23. Eck also reports that for the Brahmans of Banāras this is the annual 'day of atonement (*prayascitta*)' (1993: 264).

24. The items are listed as *ikapaḥka*, *datyavan*, *akhya* and *vastra*.

25. On this day in India, in a ritual reminiscent of the Nepalese Brother Worship (*kijā pujā; bhai tikā*, Np.), girls tie coloured threads round their brothers' wrists and make them their protectors receiving a small gift in return (Klostermaier 1989: 309; Eck 1993: 265). In recent years, some Newars have begun to adopt this custom.

26. Locke reports that Buddhists observe this day as that on which the Buddha attained enlightenment, overcame the *māra*s and preached his first sermon (1980: 235).

27. In Banāras, at Manikārnika Ghāt, there exists a similar tank called Manikārnika Kund. Up the steps from the river a wide landing houses the tank with its steps leading down to the water at the bottom. The *kund*, surrounded by an iron railing at the top is some sixty feet square at the top narrowing to twenty at the water's edge. The well is said to spring from a source independent of the Ganges, an underground river that flows directly from Gaumukha, the 'Cow's Mouth', in the Himalayas where the Ganges itself emerges from a glacier (Eck 1993: 239).

28. Rājopādhyāya Brahmans eat no *kwāti* until the following day. Anderson reports this to be the custom of all high-caste, thread-wearers (1988: 93).

29. Before 1990 these newspapers were the only medium for criticizing the government.

30. As far as I am aware, Sā Paru is observed only by *shivamārgi* Newars (*contra* P.H. Bajracharya 1959: 5).

31. The whole event, in fact, is organized by the Krishna Mandir committee.

32. A Brahman always plays the part of Krishna. The others may be played by any other ('clean'?) caste in 2001 Tāmrakārs played Rukhmani and Balabhadra, while a Shrestha played Satyabhama. The character of the devotee, Balabhadra is usually played by a child belonging to the family of the patron of the *pujā*, which this year was Dil Mohan Tamrakar.

33. The girls hold, in pairs, brooms, cow's milk for sprinkling on the path, puffed rice (*tāy*) for broadcasting, yak-tail fans (*cuvar*), peacock feather fans and maces (*dhala kaci*). Hired men carry ceremonial umbrellas over each pair and male attendants walk alongside carrying plastic chairs for the girls to sit down at each stop.

34. As with the girls at the front, the boys of the Krishna *bandhu* are attended by men carrying ceremonial umbrellas above them and carrying chairs for the boys to sit on at intervals. In front of the Krishna *bandhu* on some years a man pulls a brass drum (*dhunguri*) containing stones that make a great noise as it is rolled along. At the very rear a Maharjan *dhimay bājā* group plays its repertoire.

35. Webster attributes the phenomenon of men dancing as bullocks pulling a plough in the Sā Paru festival to a pre-Hindu ritual (1981: 125). To my mind, this is better explained in keeping with the satirical nature of the procession as it is celebrated in Bhaktapur: Jyāpu who do not plough mock those who do. In this case the phenomenon is not an anomaly to his argument.

36. Each year a different monastery has the responsibility of organizing the *pujā* and it is at that monastery that the procession begins. I followed the event in 1999, when it was run by Haugaḥ *twaḥ*.

37. The festival is organized by a succession of ten localities, each of which is situated astride the contripetal *pradakshinapātha* (§5.6.3).

38. The order in which the *nava bājā* ensembles process is: *dhāḥ bājā* (4 *dhāḥ*, 2 pairs *bhusyāḥ;* 1 *naykhĩ*, 1 pair *cusyāḥ*); 2 Kāpālis playing *muhāli* (cf. Plate 12); 4 or 5 *nyaku* horns (some high-pitched, others low-pitched); *bay bājā* ensemble (2 or 3 *khĩ* or *magaḥ khĩ*, a dozen or so wooden *bay* flutes, *cinta jhyāli*, and *cusyāḥ* played entirely by Maharjans); *damokhĩ*

bājā (3 *damokhī*) with 3 Damai (1 clarinet and 2 trumpets); finally, bringing up the rear as usual, is the Maharjan *dhimay bājā* (1 *dhimay*, 1 *bhusyāḥ*). Except for the castes already mentioned, the instruments are played by any clean castes of the locality. Gyanu Raj Shakya (1995) says that the *dhāḥ bājā* is played especially by Shākyas, Vajrācāryas, and Tāmrakārs. Perhaps this is another indication that some of the Tāmrakārs are descended from *buddhamārgi* Shākya or Vajrācārya lineages.

39. This may be yet another indication that many of the Tamvaḥ are descended from *buddhamārgi* lineages.

40. The Nyaku Jātrā procession does not, however, include the Jyāpu *bay bajā* as this ensemble is playing along the Matayā route itself.

41. The Nava Bājā repertoire includes performances on the following instruments: *dhāḥ, dhimay, naykhī, kacakhī, khāmjari* (*julijulipa*), *vyā, dholak, mridanga* (*pacimā*), *nagara, jor nagara, dhwā dhwā, magaḥ khī, dāha, damaru* (*dabu dabu*) and *damokhī.* Wegner (1987) reports that, ideally four Kāpāli *muhāli* players are required to keep proper balance, though today only one performs.

42. The Nava Bājā completes two more performances. The day after Matayā the ensemble plays in the village of Būga (Būgamati) before Būgadyaḥ (Karunāmaya/Matsyendranātha). The following day (Gūlāgā 4) the Nava Bājā performs at Svayambhu. On the way to Svayambhu the group plays three or four tunes at Hanumān Dhokā, Kathmandu. The ensemble used also to perform in front of the Krishna temple in Mangaḥ on Krishnashtami (Gūlāgā 8) but in recent years this has been discontinued because of the crowds.

43. No image is carried through the streets so, contra Shrestha and Shrestha (1995: 40), this procession does not fit the criteria for a *jātrā.*

44. Towards the rear of the procession the Maharjan *bay bājā* ensemble plays their flutes, *khī, magaḥ khī* and *cusyāḥ.* Finally, as ever, the *dhi may bājā* take up the rear. Notably the *damokhī* are absent: 'Their work finished yesterday'.

45. I was not able to witness these events myself.

46. Organization of the *jātrā* rotates among the seven Rājopādhyāya lineages of the city.

47. From the story in the *Srimad Bhagavata Purāna* (Lienhard 1995: 170, n.336).

48. All are flanked by attendants and followed by hired men carried ceremonial umbrellas. A Maharjan conveying a carrying pole with baskets of *pujā* materials and the Brahman lineage *thākāli* follows the boys. The procession is completed by the *dhimay bājā* played by two Maharjans from the same *twaḥ.*

49. Kane reports that Krishna Janmashtami is 'probably the most important *vrata* and *utsāva* celebrated throughout the whole of India' (1968-1977: V, 128, quoted in Levy 1990: 452).

50. Modelled on the celebration of Matayā, the event is organized on a rotating basis by eight different localities of Lalitpur: Nugaḥ, Cāka Bahi, Purnacandi, Puco, Pim Bāhāḥ, Ikhāchẽ, Kwā Bāhāḥ and Mangaḥ.

51. Levy reports that Krishna Janmashtami is minor in Bhaktapur and seems to have been introduced by Krishna devotees during the 1960s (Levy 1990: 452).

52. The one based at the Kūḥchẽ (Corner House) being run by the Krishna Jātrā Guthi, an organization belonging entirely to the Kūḥchẽ lineage of Tāmrakārs.

53. In Bhaktapur the Bhimsen Jātrā (Sukhū Bhisīdyaḥ Jātrā) is on Kachalāgā 15 (November) (Levy 1990: 648).

54. In 1999 the following sites were visited during the course of the procession: Vishvakarma temple, Ikhā; Tū Cuka; Iku Bāhāḥ Nani; Ita Puku; Talachẽ; Naikwā Bahi; Purnacandi;

Chaya Bāhāḥ; Pim Bāhāḥ; Mikha Bāhāḥ; Yala Dhwaka, Balipha; Kumbheshvara, Konti; Belāchẽ; Cyāsaḥ; Walkhu; Bhimsen temple, Mangaḥ; Sundari cok, Mangaḥ; 'House', Mangaḥ; Kot, Mangaḥ; Nugaḥ; Binchẽ Bāhāḥ; Kone Bāhāḥ; Naḥ Bāhāḥ; Itāchẽ, Haugaḥ; Haugaḥ Cok—a total of 25.

55. Burleigh notes that the Bhindyaḥ temple in Mangaḥ was built in Mārga 801 (1681 CE), during the reign of Sri Nivas, by Bhagi Ratna Bhaiya (1976: 42). I was informed by the local Shrestha *guthiyār*s who control the temple and *jātrā* that the Bhimsen Jātrā was instituted in 1484. As this is before the founding of the present temple it suggests that an older temple stood at the same site.

56. These include *khĩ bājã*, *nagara bājã*, *magaḥ khĩ*, *bay bājã*, *dhimay bājã* and *dāphā* groups.

57. In Kathmandu this event is marked by a *melā* at Svayambhu.

58. According to Locke, Buddhists do not visit Gokarna but do a *pujā* at Jana Bāhāḥ (1980: 237).

59. During the first year of marriage a prestation must be given by wife-takers to wife-givers on this day.

60. I am indebted to the Medical Director of Patan Hospital, Dr Mark Zimmerman, for making these data available.

61. The graph shows the monthly sum total of all six clinics.

62. With a waiting time of hours many are put off from visiting the hospital. The likely impact on the data is to flatten the graph as greater numbers on any particular day would cause others to seek different options.

63. Nepali's assertion that 'Excessive eating, especially during the festival period, has been the principle cause for the outbreak of epidemics in the Newar community,' is not supported by the evidence adduced here (1965: 74).

64. Other health facilities report similar patterns. In recent years, at the Travel Medicine Center (CIWEC Clinic) in Kathmandu, a previously unknown parasite was discovered and dubbed 'cyclospora'. The pattern, the clinic reports, is that the greatest number of cases of infection with cyclospora is seen in June and July with a rapid decrease in numbers thereafter (CIWEC newsletter of September 2001).

65. In describing the pre-monsoon period of 1924 Landon (1976 [1928]) reports, 'One by one the wells had dried up, and, though this was in a sense a relief, as there was cholera in the Valley and some of the lost wells had been condemned, the consequent rush to the remaining water supplies carried with it no little danger of spreading the infection still farther' (quoted in Locke 1980: 212).

Chapter 8: The Renewal of Order II: Restoring Civic Society

1. Klostermaier reports that, in India, business people and students bring their books before the image and artisans their tools to be blessed (1990: 311).

2. The *saptarshi* are a group of seven principal saints (*hrishi*).

3. On this day also, in two unrelated events, the Tamvaḥ Mahālakshmi Guthi returns to Mahālakshmistān to do *pujā* to the important Mother Goddess and the Bārāhi celebrate their Cathaḥ Guthi by sacrificing a black goat to the image of Ganesh at Tyāgaḥ. They eat a feast, which includes the ritual division of the goat's head (*sikāḥ bhu*). This ends the annual cycle of rituals and feasts of the Bārāhi. There seems to be no direct connection between this day and the Bũgadyaḥ Jātrā.

4. Nutan Sharma informed me (2004) that this procession had been dormant for some time before being revived in 1992 by the residents of Purnacandi. The procession follows the

centripetal *pradakshinapātha* along much of its route, taking detours to visit those shrines that are off of it.

5. Gutschow includes a photo of a group of 81 people returning to Mangaḥ from Vārāhi-*ghāt* where they have just done Power-Place worship (1982: 173, Fig.194).

6. My informants in Lalitpur spoke of an elephant effigy of clay (formerly of wood) that is also established on this day though I cannot confirm this.

7. It would seem that this festival has less importance in Bhaktapur than it has even in Lalitpur (Levy 1990: 456-62).

8. The word *yaḥsī̃* (which Toffin reports to derive from *yaḥ*, 'beloved', and *sī̃*, 'wood') itself could be from the Newar *yalasī̃* which designates the sacrificial stake of cosmological significance (Toffin 1992a: 81; see R.P. Pradhan 1988: 392).

9. Wright's chronicle reports that as Sri Nivas 'was sitting one night at a window on the eastern side of the durbar, he saw that the Ashta-matrika-ganas entered the durbar and, after dancing, vanished again. The Raja was pleased, and calling into his presence the Bauddhacharyas of Buya Bihar, Nakabahil Tol, and Onkuli Bihar, he ordered them by turns to worship the Ashta-matrikas in their houses during the Aswin Navaratri, and to bring them to dance at the durbar' (1972: 245).

10. The thirteen deities comprise the Eight Mother Goddesses plus Bhairava, Ganesh, Kumār, and the guardian deities Singini and Vyangrini (cf. D.R. Sharma 1996: 280; Vergati 1995: 148).

11. Unlike the masks of the Nine Durgas, which are destroyed at the end of each annual cycle, those of the Gan Pyākhã are kept from year to year.

12. The responsibility to put on this dance for a long time rotated between the three localities of Bu Bāhāḥ, Uku Bāhāḥ and Nakaḥ Bahi (compare spelling with Wright above [1972: 245, n. 1]). Some time ago it was left to the men of Nakaḥ Bahi to continue alone, a situation made easier in recent years as it has come under the patronage of the municipality, for whose officials the troupe does a special programme on the first day.

13. Also in stark contrast to the Nine Durgas of Bhaktapur and to the Gathu Pyākhã of Theco the Gan Pyākhã do not accept blood sacrifice—a phenomenon that is clearly the result of the Buddhist character of the city and especially of the dancers.

14. *Khī̃* drum, seven pairs of bells (*tāḥ*), and five *pwanga* horns.

15. See photo of this event in Gellner and Quigley 1995: 190.

16. My informants named these four characters 'Guruju' (i.e., Bandhudatta the *purohit*), Guruman (Bandhudatta's wife), Jyami (Jyāpu), and Jaymā (*jajmān*). These are clearly the principal characters in the myth underpinning the founding of the Bũgadyaḥ chariot festival (§10.2).

17. The dances are based on the Tantric Vidhi scriptures.

18. Day five, the first day of the *hemanta* season is theoretically one of only two days during Caturmāsa on which marriage and other movable life-cycle rituals may be observed (the other being five days later on Vijāya Dasami, Kaulāthwa 10). This day is also one of only three or four days in the year that such life-cycle rituals may be performed without the necessity of determining the appropriate auspicious time (*sāit*).

19. These temples are the large, multi-roofed structures on the north-west and north-east corners of the courtyard respectively.

20. In a parallel ritual the Nāyaḥ lineage also carries the Tantric image down from the Vishvakarma temple where it normally resides and establishes it in the house of the lineage *thākāli* for the remainder of the festival.

21. This escort includes two Maharjan horn (*kẽ*) players and three Kāpāli *muhāli* players as well as the cane of King Siddhi Narasimha Malla. We will encounter this group again especially in relation to the Bũgadyaḥ chariot festival (§10.4.2).

22. After a short *pujā* to the *ghata* and *dholi* by a Parbatiyā priest, a Chetri man sacrifices a goat to the Devi that resides in the Flask. The flask, the flowers, and the severed head of the goat are then taken into the Chetri Dashaĩ room. Apart from a further goat sacrifice on each of the next three mornings there is little activity connected with this material. It is noteworthy that no Newar priests are involved in any part of this ritual and the vast majority of the local population ignores the whole thing.

23. Mohani is the only festival in which they do this. The Cyāsaḥ Butchers are entitled to the heads of the slaughtered animals, which they will collect on Day 10.

24. Some substitute *karathon*, a fortified beer that looks like thin yoghurt.

25. The essential items for this particular meal, which are all on the plate from the start, are beaten rice, black soybeans, ginger, potato pickle, boiled white soybeans (*bhuti*), spinach (*tukāca*), and boiled buffalo meat (*hwangu cwayla*).

26. In a departure from the norm that reflects their former status under the Ranas, the Nāyaḥ lineage of Tāmrakārs does Kumāri *pujā* on the previous day, in imitation of the Shah kings.

27. About a litre. Some understand the etymology of *kũchẽ* to be from *kuchi*—the two *mana* measure.

28. The same group that escorted the Phulpāti into the city (§10.4.2).

29. It is clear from the chronicles that, as on all occasions that the Guthi Corporation group acts, the Malla king himself would have made this trip (Wright 1972: 238).

30. In 2000 there were ten girls aged between eighteen months and three years.

31. As an alternative some Newars cut a sugar cane (*tu*) and/or a ginger stem instead (Gellner 1992: 219).

32. The Gan Pyākhã do, in fact, perform one more time, on the following night, at the platform of Nakaḥ Bahi. For the most part, this is attended by the people of the locality. The performance includes several comedy acts by, among others, the four human characters that we met on Day 7 and others that are very similar to those that are performed by the Kati Pyākhã troupe later. This final performance is much longer than those of the previous days, extending well into the wee hours.

33. It is not known whether there is any connection between this group and the Nine Durgas dance troupe of Bhaktapur, which is also drawn from the Gathu.

34. In larger feasts served in more confined spaces this is accomplished by serving multiple sittings.

35. In the past this may have been universally strictly observed from oldest to youngest as it still is in *guthi* feasts.

36. The images were not brought down to the Mohani Dega and no buffaloes were sacrificed.

37. In Mewar, according to Tod (1914), a buffalo sacrifice was performed each morning of the festival, except the sixth, up to the eighth morning (the day of Mahishasura's death.) Since then the scale of animal sacrifice has become considerably less but the festival retains much of its importance (Fuller 1992: 112ff.).

38. In Mysore the state sword was worshipped inside the palace on all nine days of the festival (Fuller 1992: 116).

39. This ceremony is repeated throughout north India also. In Banáras, at the Panchaganga Ghāt, hundreds of 'sky lamps' are hung each evening in little wicker baskets at the tops of tall bamboo poles and a great conical stone lamp holder which rises above the *ghāt* and holds hundreds of wicks is lighted. These lamps, people say, brighten the way for the dead as they return to the world of the ancestors after their yearly visit to earth (Eck 1983: 273).

40. Not all see the pole as a *yaḥsī.* They are now only about ten cubits (*hātha*) high but used to be 32 cubits high, the same as the chariot of Būgadyaḥ and the *yaḥsī* of Bhaktapur's Biskaḥ Jātrā.

41. The *Buddhist Vamshāvali* reports that as Siddhi Narasimha's queen, Bhanumati, died the day after Kati Punhi, no one was allowed to perform 'Aragmata-dipa-dan' (Alāmātā Cyākyu) until the mourning was completed after three fortnights. Musical instruments were played but no singing. Mohani was not celebrated the following year (Wright 1972: 238-9).

42. As unlikely as this may sound, I know a woman who actually experienced this. Needless to say it caused great anxiety.

43. Kwaḥ Pujā seems to be a ritual that has survived from Vedic times. Witzel interprets it, however, in accordance with the belief that a departed soul flies around as a bird and needs to be fed (1997: 504).

44. Tulasi Ram Vaidya pointed out to me that this harks back to the days when a man's wealth was measured in the number of cows he possessed (*Godhan*).

45. High-caste Hindus also observe Govārdāna Pujā to Krishna on this day (Gellner 1992: 61).

46. Most non-Newars know the festival as 'Bhintunā' because of this.

47. One informant suggested these represented Brahma and Shiva.

48. On the first Mha Pujā after the marriage of a daughter, her parents will send a gift (Mha Pujā ku) to the in-laws (*samdhi*). If, for some reason (such as the death of a *phuki*) Mha Puj Pujā is not observed, the gift will not be sent until the following year. The Mha Pujā ku is brought by members of bride's family and the bride herself who will go back to her natal home to help bring it.

49. Whether or not the Nepal Sambat relates to the harvest of rice and that of Vikram Sambat (the official calendar of the Kingdom of Nepal) to that of wheat is worthy of further study. Gutschow marks the rice season as ending on Lakshmi Caturdasi (Kaulāgā 14) (1982: 10).

50. Kashinath Tamot, personal communication.

51. Note, however, that Shākya and Vajrācārya men, anomalously, have to go to the home of their married out sister to receive the *pujā* (Gellner 1995b: 228).

52. On the first Kijā Pujā after marriage the wife-takers, in a reverse of the previous day send a 'load' of gifts (also called Kijā Pujā *ku*) to the wife-givers' house. Usually much that had been given by the wife-givers the previous day will be returned along with some more personal gifts.

53. If a brother cannot be present a *mandala* is made, anyway, and *pujā* performed. The next day the gifts are sent to the brother by express delivery if possible.

54. As with other *thay bhu* the contents consist at least nominally of *'chaurasi byanjan'* or the '84 varieties of delicious food'.

55. Alternatively some Newars throw it at the *pikhā lakhu.*

56. Fuller (1992) reports that, according to the most widely told story, Lakshmi Pujā is linked to the return of Rām to Ayodhyā from Lanka with his bride Sitā, having slain the demon

king Ravana. He is welcomed with lamps that signify Lakshmi. Rām is again on his throne and order has finally been established. This significance seems to have been entirely lost in Lalitpur and other Newar communities where the festival has been radically transformed to communicate a different message.

57. *Nakhaḥtyā* literally means 'end of the festival'. The festival is not considered complete until one's married-out family have been properly feasted.

58. Hemraj Shakya reckons that this is the reason why Buddhists regard the worship of Sadaksarilokeshvara in Kārtik as the first of these monthly Observances (which take place at Ta Bāhāḥ and Bũga) of the year (1089 NS: 53-54). Locke, however, suggests that it is equally possible that this is simply because the New Year begins during Kārtik (1980: 259-60).

59. See Lienhard 1995: 170, n. 336.

60. Pressler recounts the myth on which this play is based (1978: 242-4).

61. Lalitpurians insist that, in the past, the young Citrakār man playing the demon-king would indeed die and not be revived. It was only as a newer, less potent, mask of the deity was created that the actor was able to survive the ordeal at all.

62. The water must be drawn from the left-hand spout of the nearby Mangaḥhiti.

63. A particular mixture of popped corn, roasted wheat, peas, soybean, beans, and other items.

64. On this day also, some *guthi*s, such as the Shilpakār Tadhã Guthi, meet for a feast.

Chapter 9: The Approaches of Disorder I: The Season of Anxiety

1. This is especially so at the temple of Dhanesvara Mahādyaḥ, Panauti, which is particularly related to wealth and rice.

2. If they could not come on the full moon day itself married out daughters and their families (*mhyay maca*) are invited to a feast (*nakhaḥtyā*) soon afterwards.

3. Also called Hāmwa Sãlhu or Cikã Buyegu (Np.: Māgh Samkrānti).

4. According to Slusser the cult of Agni practiced at Lalitpur is not purely Vedic but permeated with Tantrism and Shiva-Shakti worship (1998: 266).

5. The *thākāli* may be engaged to do a *hom pujā* to the flame at any time during the year.

6. In the village of Bũga a festival for Bũgadya is also held on this day (Locke 1980: 278).

7. Levy reports that Ghyaḥcaku Sãnhu was celebrated in late December 1974 (1990: 463). As far as I know, however, it is invariably in mid-January.

8. Levy reports that in Bhaktapur this full-moon celebration is distinguished from others by the fact that on this day no-longer-usable clay pots are discarded at the *chwāsā* (1990: 423). It is not observed in this way in Lalitpur perhaps because the Potter community in Lalitpur is not as large as it is in Bhaktapur.

9. This day is also observed as the beginning of the two-month *vasanta* season.

10. In Banāras the festival begins with the lighting of fires on the night before full moon but no such fires are lit in Lalitpur (Eck 1993: 277).

11. Anderson reports that this has been going on for days already (1988: 251). On a low-level this may be true but it seems that it has never been very serious.

12. In Kathmandu, instead of discarding the tree they burn it (*cir dāhāḥ*).

13. Indeed Klostermaier (1990: 311) asserts that Holi constitutes the New Year celebration for most Hindus.

14. There is an image of Luku Mahādya now located inside the house of a Tāmrakār in Ikhā. Like others this image was once also located in a courtyard. Now that it is enclosed within the house, however, the image must not be covered over the top, so a small space is kept open throughout the entire height of the house to the roof where a narrow gap is open to the sky. The house, then, incongruously includes a centrally placed atrium.

15. Anderson's (1988: 264) remark, quoted approvingly by Levy (1990: 431), that Pāhā Cahre falls at a time (March) 'when typhoid, dysentery, cholera and smallpox flourish with the advent of hot weather, prior to the cleansing monsoon rains' is not accurate. As we can see in the graph (Figure 4), the incidence of illness rises steadily from this time but does not drop until the completion of monsoon, not its arrival.

16. Levy (1990: 433, 649) places it in Caulāgā rather than Caulāthwa.

17. In 1999 I was told that the procession took three hours visiting a total of nineteen *pithas* including all Dashmahāvidya but not all Ashtamātrika.

18. At least four Tāmrakār *guthi*s are included in this celebration.

19. Apart from this and in deference to Vaishnavite sensitivities, as on Krishnashtami (§7.9) no animals are to be slaughtered on this day.

20. This route corresponds to that found in Gutschow's map (1982: 173, map 195).

21. One suspects that the Bisket Jātrā Gutschow refers to as falling on Rām Navami is the major one that happened to be going on in Bhaktapur at that time (1982: 11).

22. It seems that Caitra Dashaĩ may have been celebrated more in Malla times. Wright's chronicle tells us that Jaya Prakash Malla 'assigned lands for the expenses of the daily *ārati pujā*, and for keeping a lamp constantly burning during the two Navarātris every year' (1972: 225-6).

23. I was not able to observe this event myself.

24. During the first year of marriage a prestation is given by wife-takers to wife-givers as at Mha Pujā.

25. A small Tamvaḥ *guthi*-Akshaya Tritiya Guthi-does *pujā* and eats a feast together at the Tamvaḥ lineage deity at Jawalakhel but regular Tamvaḥ Lineage Deity Worship does not begin for another couple of weeks.

26. In 2001 King Gyanendra himself visited Nāg Bāhāḥ on this occasion, as it was the 50th anniversary since celebrations had been held there. One wonders whether the visit gave more legitimacy to the movement or to the king's reign, which had begun less than a year before in very dubious circumstances (§1.8).

27. Stahl (1979: 120) states that they should always be near both the ghāt and the pitha. In Dhulikhel few are near the *ghāt* and the *pitha* (Quigley 1987b: 19). In Lalitpur, however, the Lineage Deities of the Pengu Daḥ are neither. With the urbanization of the land surrounding the old cities many of these sites are now enclosed within private property. Others are situated in degraded, rubbish-strewn spaces adjacent to busy roads, such as those of some Maharjan lineages at Puco, opposite the Narayani Hotel (now the Namaste Supermarket).

28. But see Gellner (1992: 82).

29. Some large Maharjan lineages, for instance, do *pujā* to aniconic stones on Thilā Punhi (§9.4). This would seem to be the act of a death *guthi* to its tutelary deity rather than that of a Lineage Deity *guthi*. If indeed these are Lineage Deity *guthi*s perhaps this phenomenon points to the antiquity of such lineages.

30. With the death of Ganesh Lal Tamrakar in 2001 *thākāli pujā* has been dropped altogether.

31. The Tamvaḥ of Bhaktapur, however, do Lineage Deity Worship on a Thursday or a Sunday, on or as close as possible to Swãya Punhi (Buddha Jayanti).

32. Lineage Deity Worship cannot be performed collectively if the lineage is in a state of pollution, such as after a member has died and the mourning period is not complete, or in the time immediately after a birth (Quigley 1985b: 16).

33. Krishna Das Tamrakar explained the five faces of Mahādyaḥ represent different 'moods'. Those to north and south can receive meat, spirits and beer. Those on the east and west cannot. Therefore, since the entrance to this shrine is facing east only vegetarian offerings are made.

34. Some informants suggested that a pure white goat is also acceptable. The important thing seems to be that it must be without blemish, or be mixed in colour.

35. The *prasād* includes beaten rice (*baji*), meat (*lā*), black-eyed beans (*bhuti*), fish (*nyā*), black soybean (*hāku musya*), ginger (*pālu*), duck eggs (*haẽ khẽy*), *khay* (whey with oil and salt mixed in), homebrew beer (*thon*), and spirits (*aylaḥ*).

36. Dharma Krishna Pwahsyah interpreted this to me as follows: 'When we cut a goat we incur sin. That is why we eat the *sikāḥ bhu*. Then we collect up the bones of the head, put them in one bowl and take them to the *chwāsā*. In this way atonement (*prayascitta*) is made for our sin.'

37. Until a few years ago at least one lineage of Marikaḥmi also used to the full Lineage Deity Worship. There were 300 individuals in this large lineage. After the lineage broke up into several units ('because of fighting') they now do a much-attenuated version.

38. Contra Nepali (1965: 194-6) and Witzel (1997: 507), the worship is not directed at the ancestors themselves. 'More accurately it is the worship of a particular god or gods, whose identity is more often unknown than known but who somehow symbolize the ancestors' (Quigley 1985b: 12).

39. With the single exception of those of the Nasantya Dāphā Guthi (§6.2.5, §7.10).

Chapter 10: The Approaches of Disorder II: Sri Nivas has Come

1. From William Shakespeare, *As You Like It*, 2/7.

2. But William Douglas (personal communication) reports from textual sources that there were originally three *jātrā*s of Bũgadyaḥ throughout the year and that Sthiti Malla chose to emphasize the spring festival.

3. Many commentators have discussed the folklore that has arisen around the status of the *bhoto*. It is commonly thought of as a fake, the 'real' one being held at the British Museum in London. A search through the records of that institution, however, reveals no reference to the artefact (cf. Locke 1980: 279, fn.48).

4. The earliest mention of the *bhoto* is in the Hodgson papers at the India Office Library in London (Vol. 20, Folio 269).

5. Nepali states that animal sacrifice is offered to 'figures of Bhairava seated in the cars' (1965: 372). As far as I know there are no images of Bhairava seated in the chariot itself.

6. There are also a number of lesser images of deities manifested in the chariot. Behind Bũgadyaḥ an image of a red *bodhisattva*—Bhimeshvara Tathagata, a future incarnation of Mahādyaḥ—faces out. Images of a horse (*vahāna*, the vehicle of Surya), a bull (the vehicle of Shiva), a Garuda (the vehicle of Vishnu) and a swan (the vehicle of Brahma) are also placed on the chariot (Locke 1980: 266). At the top of Bũgadyaḥ's chariot is placed an image of Amitābha, the Transcendent Buddha of Avalokiteshvara, an image of Vajrāsattva brought from Kwā Bāhāḥ, and an image of Svayambhu.

7. The Capuchin monk Father Giuseppe observing the festival in the eighteenth century records that at that time both the king and the 'Baryesus' rode on the chariot (Giuseppe 1801). This was also witnessed by other foreign observers in the following decades.

8. The sword, asserts Owens, is representative not only of the king's presence but also of his power (1989: 179, n. 19). This is attested to by the keeping of the sword, under Taleju's watchful eye, at the Mul Cok in Lalitpur's old palace.

9. For convenience I will use the now anachronistic, but less cumbersome 'Mãta' from here on.

10. Locke reports that the original Mãta, (which he calls Bisats), were court officials of the Malla kings who were given charge of the *guthi* lands belonging to Bũgadyaḥ (1980: 267). This group was also entrusted with the task of organizing all the arrangements for the festival and overseeing the various groups of workers. The *guthi* land they were in charge of was taken away from them in the time of King Girvan Yuddha because of misappropriation of funds.

11. It is said that the role of the Haḥphā Biyemha goes back to Nepal's first 'experiment with democracy' in the late 1950s (Owens 1989: 188). In recent decades it has been the Jyāpus who have asserted their rights as the tillers of the soil and as those who have been oppressed over the centuries by 'landlordism'. The position of the encouragement giver is precarious in more ways than one as Owens points out (2000: 721). They are chosen, and only remain in their position, by popular consent; if they are not effective in their leadership they can be compelled to give their place to another at the will of the mass of chariot pullers.

12. The brake shoes are cut from *mahelsĩ*, which is hard enough to withstand compression of the wheels, and the brake handles are cut from the elastic *baḥsĩ* enabling the handles to spring in the hands of the brakemen without fracturing them.

13. Interestingly, *dhũsĩ* (wood of the sal tree, *Shorea robusta*, L.), being very hard and rot-proof and while being the highest quality of wood used in house construction, is not used on the chariot as it is not flexible.

14. Other festivals of Bũgadyaḥ take place throughout the year (Locke 1980: 278f). These festivals, however, are not related to the Jātrā itself. The daily worship (*nitya pujā*) and monthly Observances (*vrata*) of Bũgadyaḥ are not a direct concern of the city.

15. According to the *Buddhist Vamshāvali*, this tradition goes back at least to the reign of Yog Narendra Malla (1684-1705) (Wright 1972: 247). Owens suggests that the number of astrologers reflect the number of principle stopping places during the procession (1989: 104). This is based on a misunderstanding of their title, however, which is not *pengu ta* but *pengu thã*.

16. The Nyekus live in Tangaḥ and are *shivamārgi* (Locke 1980: 262, note 23). The chronicles assert that the Nyeku Shresthas originally came from Bhaktapur but it is not known when or why they were given this office (cf. Wright 1972: 240).

17. The Suwaḥ are a group of Jyāpu Farmers who act as assistants to the Pānjus whenever a sacrifice is to be conducted. It is their role to do the actual sacrificing. They also have the responsibility to cook the rice for the rice sculptures to be offered to the *daḥmās* on the chariots.

18. The eight Pānjus whose job it is to carry the image in the palanquin to Lalitpur must be in a state of ritual purity (Owens 1989: 112).

19. Owens reports that the actual descendant of Malla kings carries the sword at this point (1989: 114). In 2002 this was certainly not the case. Gellner reports, in a personal communication, however, that a Vaidya man claiming to be a descendent of early Lalitpur kings does have a role in Mohani.

20. The two *kā* players precede Bũgadyaḥ whenever it moves from this time on throughout the Jātrā.

21. There used to be a *guthi wala pā* in charge but this no longer functions. It is considered *pharmās*—which is to say that the *guthiyār*s organize the feasting informally, one making the meat, another making a vegetable dish, yet another bringing the beaten rice and then settling the cost together.

22. A lineage of Maharjans from Bũga has the job of felling the trees for the chariots. Wood for the chariots has traditionally been available from dedicated *guthi* lands. One historical account reports that the king assigned the provision of the wood to one 'Moti Maharjan from Magala Desa' (Locke 1980: 293). Locke identifies this locality as Mangal Bazaar. If 'Magala Desa' is indeed the neighbourhood (*twaḥ*) of Mangaḥ it is not known how the present lumberjacks of Bũga came to play this role.

23. That evening, the *guthi* eats a feast prepared by the turn-holder.

24. The Juju Palton is the armed escort for the king. The group is not always the same but typically includes a band of eight flutes, two drums and two cymbals with twenty men-at-arms. They march with the Yala Juju and stand guard nearby when the sword is taken on board the chariot. At the auspicious moment of bathing and at each stage of its journey at the moment the image is moved or installed a deafening volley of musket fire is released into the air. As the Bũgadyaḥ chariot moves the Palton marches ahead and stands by the road until the chariot gets near again. The group is also variously called the 'Guruju Palton', 'Gurujuya Palton', or simply 'Palton' (cf. Owens 1989: 114).

25. The god guardian (*dyaḥ pāla*) of Degutale Taleju whose temple lies within the old palace compound is a man of the Rāghubamsi lineage of Shresthas, said to be a descendant of the Malla kings.

26. The Lalitpur Kumāri, who is considered a living incarnation of Taleju, does not have an active part in the Jātrā. Rather, she is brought, in her own procession, carried by her attendants, flanked by the Mã̄ta, and led by the Paḥmã̄ta, to sit on her throne in certain specific locations. There she watches the passing of the chariots and receives a view (*darshan*) of the deities. The fact that she receives a *darshan* of Karunāmaya clearly demonstrates the superiority of the latter.

27. The king of Bhaktapur, the Khwapa Juju, is now represented by his sword, and has an important role to play on three occasions of the Jātrā. The sword is carried by a member of the 'Chathariya' Shrestha caste of Bhaktapur and is accompanied by three other men. This group is also called the Representative of King Narendra Deva (Narendra Deva Jujupratinidhi). When this sword is present Lalitpurians say that 'the king of Bhaktapur is visiting' and, indeed, in earlier times he would have done so in person.

28. Locke elaborates on all these rituals in his description of the cult of Seto Matsyendranāth (ibid.: 208-21). Giving a particular deity rituals that belong to both sexes is not unique to Karunāmaya. The Navadurga of Bhaktapur also go through the full range of rituals that a woman must go through before becoming a full member of society (Gutschow and Basukala p.146).

29. Or, 'Lalita Jyāpu' (ibid.).

30. While the Jātrā is not in progress the Lusā Guthi of Uku Bāhāḥ keeps the gilded brass side panels, windows, doorframes, *toranas* etc. that belong to the chariots at their monastery.

31. The name of this event is a clear demonstration that it used, at one time, to take place in the village of Bũga itself, as it still does every twelve years at the Mahājātrā.

32. The Paḥmāta comprise a group of four Kāpāli musicians—two *muhāli* players, one drummer (playing the *dholak*), and one cymbal player (playing the *jhyāli*). Apart from their role in leading the Kumāri's own processions during the Jātrā, the Paḥmāta take part in at least one other event of the Jātrā, that of Bũgayaḥ, in which they lead the Khwapa Juju to initiate the procession from Ta Bāhāḥ. A Vādyakār, whose lineage is considered a sub-group of the Kāpāli, plays the *dholak*. Today, few are able or willing to play this role such that, in private processions, such as those for a wedding, Lalitpurians invariably invite non-Newar Damai musicians to play Indian film music on Western-style brass instruments.

33. Owens reports that the 'descendant of Narendradeva from Bhaktapur' carries the silver foot cover of Bũgadyaḥ to the chariot at the image's installation (1989: 129). At least on the three occasions I witnessed the event (1999, 2000, 2001), it was the chief Matã who carried the foot cover.

34. Lienhard states that the musicians and singers of the Bālagopāla temple have a feast fifteen days after Karunāmaya has been installed into his chariot (1995: 45). This seems unlikely to be a regular feast associated with the Jātrā, as this is not a particularly special day in the Jātrā sequence.

35. From this point on the onward movement of the chariots is no longer subject to the progress of the lunar calendar as it is dependent on their ongoing roadworthiness. From time to time the chariots get stuck due to mechanical problems delaying the onward procession by days or even weeks.

36. Pairs of Maharjan men take part in the festival on each day of the chariots' moving by processing from their neighbourhoods (*twaḥ*) to where the chariots are stationed playing the *dhimay* drum and *bhusyāḥ* cymbals as they go.

37. Locke connects the stop at Mangaḥ with folklore about a 'small stream' that used to run there (1980: 269, note 32). Other evidence indicates, however, that the stream was once quite large (viz. boulders at Lagankhel). This must have been before the water fountains at Mangaḥ and Tangaḥ were built which would make it before the Jātrā, at least as we know it, ever existed. This contradictory ethnographic and archaeological evidence needs somehow to be resolved.

38. 'Twāy' is the Newar equivalent of the Nepali 'mit' or fictive brother/sister (Messerschmidt 1982). Sometimes Newars will form a fictive relationship with a friend or acquaintance, usually of a different caste, and sometimes even of entirely different community. Such relations have ritual responsibilities to each other.

39. Gutschow's fourth stop at Mahābuddha and fifth stop at Cāka Bahi (1982: 174) are not formal stops but merely breaks between Nugaḥ and Lagã because it is inconvenient to pull the chariot so far in one day.

40. The prescribed locations for the stopping of the chariot are called *lagã* and it is this that gives Lagã, and the open area around the Maju Sima (Lagankhel), its name.

41. According to the legend, Karunāmaya's mother followed him to Lalitpur in order to steal him away. Today she is worshipped as a tree in the Bus Park (formerly an open field) at Lagankhel.

42. Locke asserts that the women of the Dyaḥlā caste sleep under the chariot at night while it is here. Although one can imagine people giving such a report, this practice seems highly unlikely to be anything more than folklore.

43. In the *hom pujā* a coconut is frequently among the offerings consigned to the fire (Locke 1980: 112). This is widely recognised to represent the *jajmān*'s head (Owens 1989: 109). Could there be a hint here of substitutionary propitiation?

44. No astrologer is consulted on this occasion.

45. One lineage of Rājkarnikārs has a *bhujyaḥ guthi* feast on this day. Each *guthiyār* takes a turn to do both *bhujyaḥ* and *digu dyaḥ pujā*.

46. Locke interprets this event as part of an *ashta mangala* ceremony conducted in thanksgiving for the progress of the festival so far (1980: 271).

47. I was not able to observe this event myself.

48. I was offered no explanation of this phenomenon. It remains to be seen whether there is any relation to the stories Locke (1980: 272-3) describes of Bũgadyaḥ's promiscuity (see below). The Yākamisā Salegu is said to be in celebration of an occasion in which a poor untouchable woman is said to have pulled the chariot by herself to Thati where she lived in a rest house (Owens 1989: 131).

49. Dulāngadyaḥ seems to be a manifestation of Bhairava.

50. This is perhaps what Lienhard had in mind when he reported a feast on the fifteenth day after the placing of the image on the chariot (1995: 45).

51. The Pānjus deny that Purnacandi is Bũgadyaḥ's lineage deity (Owens 1989: 163). The Pānjus' aniconic Lineage Deity lies in a field east of Jawalakhel in Bũga (ibid.: 111).

52. The throne is interpreted by some as another manifestation of Karunāmaya itself.

53. Five Shākyas have the responsibility to construct these rice sculptures. One man of the Tandukār caste has the responsibility to fetch water for this.

54. The shelter she sits in gives the area its name—Kumāripāti.

55. Jawalakhel has only become a settlement in recent times, before being simply an open field or common (*khyaḥ*). Locke enumerates the other 'villages' as 'Pulchowk, Kirtipur, Panga, Baubahal. Bhaktapur, Thimi and Naro Bhare near Thimi' but Pulchowk is also listed for day one (1980: 273).

56. The Guthi Corporation is the government agency responsible for the running of the festival today and, as such, is the sponsor of the event. It is the GC that pays the various functionaries employed during the course of the Jātrā. Many of those employed as officers and office workers of the GC are not Newars at all but very often Parbatiyā Brahmans with no knowledge of Newar.

57. Foreign observers have often made much of the sentiment that this event is meant to bring the first of the monsoon rains. Landon reports that, when the *bhoto* was shown in 1924, a spot of rain hit him that instant and the prolonged dry period ended straight away (1976: 212; cf. also Slusser 1998: 375).

58. Nepali reports a ceremony that takes place immediately after the display of the *bhoto* in which a copper disk is dropped from the tower of the chariot (Nepali 1965: 374). I did not observe this on either of the occasions that I witnessed the event.

59. In the evening the *guthi* eats a feast organized by the particular *wala pa*. This occasionally falls after their concluding feast on Dillā Pujā. This is because the return of Bũgadyaḥ to his home temple in Bũga is determined by the progress of the procession (or lack of progress due to breakdowns) and subsequently by astrological factors taken into account by the Joshis when they meet at the shelter in Mangaḥ.

60. Kwenādyaḥ, it will be remembered, is the image of Ganesh that is considered a form of the important Ganesh at Cobhār, also known as Jal Vināyak.

61. Janmadyaḥ of Kathmandu, often called Seto Matsyendranāth, is pulled through the streets of that city in a much smaller chariot.

62. Locke records that the Seto Matsyendranāth festival in Kathmandu has no connection with rain but that it is considered to be a protection against disease (1980: 222).

63. The Jātrā, in actually fact, always lasts longer than nine days, and often much longer.

64. Unlike Biskaḥ, the Jātrā is scheduled according to the lunar calendar and not, that of the sun, as would be supposed. The bathing of the deity, the event that marks the beginning of the Jātrā, though at times taking place very close to the vernal equinox, may at times be two or more weeks after the event.

65. Owens argues that prior to the Rana period the actual participation of the king in the Jātrā was exceptional, limited to particularly problematic processions or the twelve-yearly processions from Bũga (1989: 182). This argument, being based on the lack of historical references quoted in Locke (1980), is in my mind not very sound. Arguing from silence is surely, at best, of dubious value. There is a telling reference in the *Gopālarāja Vamshāvali* (folio 63) to Sthiti Malla's participation in the Jātrā of 1387 CE (507 NS) (Vajracarya and Malla 1985: 164). We are informed that Sthiti Malla and his sons arrived on the fourth day of the lunar fortnight (i.e. the day in the present Jātrā in which the chariot is pulled to Ga Bāhāḥ) and stayed 14 days (presumably until the ceremony of 'Dropping the Coconut' had been completed and the Jātrā was finished). Again we must not make too much of this but it does at least suggest that he was setting a precedent in doing so. Whether this became a regular participation is not known but the importance attached to the presence of Sri Nivas Malla's sword and his father Siddhi Narasimha Malla's cane in today's Jātrā is surely telling of royal participation in the seventeenth century.

66. Douglas, in a personal communication, reports that Sri Nivas is the last example, together with his son, of a widespread Asian pattern of Lokeshvara-identified Buddhist kingship.

Chapter 11: Kinship and Kingship in Creative Tension

1. Dumont's ally, Pocock, acknowledged this phenomenon: 'At the ideal level the city is the centre of caste as at the political level it is the centre of the king whose prime duty, one need scarcely stress, was the maintenance of the caste order' (1960: 66).

2. Toffin believes that Newar cities are more centralized because of the influence of Buddhism (1991b: 75). Such a view, however, is entirely unnecessary in the light of my argument. Newar society is not built around the centrality of the king because of its Buddhism but because it is paradigmatically Hindu in the structural, not the ideological sense (Quigley 1995b: 319-20).

Appendix 1

Tamvaḥ Lineages

There are thirteen maximal lineages, arranged here alphabetically in English. No precedence or hierarchy is implied. Sub-lineages are indicated by indentation. Maximal lineages bold and underlined. Sub-lineages underlined only. Not all lineage categories are recognized as such by the members. Lineages that have been deduced purely from ethnographic evidence are shown with a name given by me for analytical purposes in square brackets.

Lalitpur lineages
Lineage Deity: Tamkadyaḥ/Chwaskamini/Ugracandimai, Jawalakhel, Lalitpur.

<u>Bhyā (Ram)</u>
One of the four original Ikhā lineages. 8 households. No distinct Tantric Deity.

<u>Hãchu</u>
One of the four original Ikhā lineages. 7 households. Tantric Deity: Hãchu Galli.

<u>Haugaḥ</u>
Haugaḥ *twaḥ*. 37 households. No distinct Tantric Deity.

<u>*Dhasi Hãe (Gutter duck)*</u>
Haugaḥ and Cāka Bahi. 14 households.

<u>*Kwakhā (Necklace of holy cloth)*</u>
1 household.

<u>*Manaḥ (Who does not eat)*</u>
5 households.

<u>*Mulasi (Main head piece)*</u>
1 household.

<u>Itāchẽ (The house on the southern side)</u>
Haugaḥ. 40 households. Tantric Deity: I Bāhāḥ Bahi. There is no longer any initiated member so this deity is no longer worshipped, except perhaps by Shākyas and Vajrācāryas. Itāchẽ lineage now views Vishvakarma Tantric Deity as their own, though they are denied access into the innermost shrine. Itāchẽ lineage is divided into four *kawaḥ*, which today have little significance. The following named lineages have recently grown out of three of these *kawaḥ* and look set to be more significant in future.

<u>*Bāgaḥ (Dwarf)*</u>
1 household.

<u>*Dhusi (Hunch-back)*</u>

8 households.

Dhyākwa (Corner)

8 households.

Jyoti (Light)

One of the four original Ikhā lineages. 9 households. This lineage continues to perform Lineage Deity Worship together but not as a *guthi.* No distinct Tantric Deity.

Gwārā (Round one)

5 households.

Kothujhvaḥchẽ (Lower row house)

Haugaḥ. 14 households. Image of Tantric Deity at Kothujhvaḥchẽ was stolen so now this lineage does Tantric Deity *pujā* to stone in remembrance of the deity. The Lineage Deity *guthi* is now defunct.

Kũḥchẽ (Corner house)

Cāka Bahi. 18 households. Tantric Deity: at temple of Vishvakarma behind original corner house.

Talachẽ (Big house)

6 households.

Kwaḥ (Crow)

Cāka Bahi. 15 households. Lineage Deity *guthi* continues to function. The Tantric Deity is located at Kwā Bāhāḥ and visited for special *pujā* on Panca Dān.

Lā Manaḥ (Who doesn't eat meat)

3 households.

Lachica

Ikhā. 5 households. No distinct Tantric Deity.

[Naḥ Bāhāḥ *et al.*]

Cāka Bahi. 57 households. The Tantric Deity of this lineage at Naḥ Bāhāḥ is worshipped by all of these lineages. This then is the main criterion I have used to refer to all as being part of this maximal lineage even though some would not recognize themselves as such. Moreover, this maximal lineage is united by the performance of 'Sending the goat' (*dugucā choegu*) in which a goat is led out from the house at the exact moment a new bride is welcomed.[1] The goat is then taken out of the city to the Mahālakshmisthān *pitha* where it is sacrificed.

Naḥ Bāhāḥ

31 households.

[Greater Jhvaḥchẽ *et al.*]

26 households. It is said that the three sub-lineages that make up this lineage (Jhvaḥchẽ, Cabāchẽ and Pwāḥsyāḥ) are agnatically related

and, therefore, should not intermarry. Some say, however, that theoretically it would be acceptable if the prospective couple were at least the prescribed seven generations apart. This never seems to have happened, however. In one case the daughter of a woman of Jhvaḥchẽ lineage married a man of Pwāḥsyāḥ lineage.

This lineage shares common brass movable crowns of Tamkadyaḥ and Mahādyaḥ that are placed over the two stones at Lineage Deity Worship. These images are kept by the *thākāli* of the entire group. Cabāchẽ lineage is known to be a branch of Jhvaḥchẽ whereas Pwāḥsyāḥ lineage has no such memory. At present the *thākāli* of the full lineage does the full Lineage Deity Worship. A gilded brass crown (*dyaḥyā matuḥ*) is kept for this purpose at the *thākāli*'s house from whence it is carried in procession to Tamkadyaḥ for Lineage Deity Worship. Upon completion of the *thākāli pujā* all other households follow. Members of the three sub-lineages also constitute a *pāthyāye guthi* together.

[Lesser Jhvaḥchẽ *et al.*]
17 households.

Jhvaḥchẽ (Row house)
4 households.

Cabāchẽ (Cāka Bahi house)
13 households.

Twānāḥ (Shin)
2 households.

Pwāḥsyāḥ (Stomach ache)
9 households. Lineage Deity *guthi.*

Nāyaḥ (Leader)

One of the four original Ikhā lineages. Before 19th century called Nhutun lineage. 14 households. Tantric Deity: Vishvakarma temple, Ikhā.

Nwa Mawāḥ (Dumb [lit. 'who does not speak'])
1 household.

Sukuḥ (Lean and thin)

Tangaḥ. 30 households.

Dune (Inside) Sukuḥ
4 households.

Pine (Outside) Sukuḥ
26 households.

Panauti lineage

43 households living mainly in Panauti and Bhaktapur. Tantric Deity and Lineage Deity located at both Panauti and Bhaktapur.

All the Tamvaḥ of Panauti and Bhaktapur belong to what seems to be one maximal lineage though there is no name for this. Informants reckon their ancestors migrated from Lalitpur to Panauti at least ten generations ago though evidence for this is scant and not considered firm enough for membership by the Ugracandimai Seva Samiti. In 1995 the first marriage took place between two apparently branch lineages of Panauti Tamvaḥ that have been called informally Man Bahadur lineage and Sankha lineage after their respective patriarchs. All the Panauti Tamvaí retain the same Rājopādhyāya domestic priest (*purohit*). Few marriages have taken place among the Bhaktapur Tamvaḥ. But there are two *sanā guthi*s that could correspond to two different branch lineages. Bhaktapur Tamvaḥ tell of the migration of their ancestors from Panauti five generations ago. Some intermarriage of Tamvaḥ of Panauti and Bhaktapur has taken place.

1. The goat must be pure black, with no defect, equal length horns, perfect teeth and black tongue as at Lineage Deity Worship. In the past the bride would touch her head to the goat. Now she touches with her hand. In so doing her impurity is transferred to the goat. The custom was explained to me in this way: "A long time ago the bride was being welcomed into the house. As soon as she entered she died suddenly. So the Joshi said they need to do *dugucā choegu*." An older woman told me, "We do *dugucā choegu* because the bride might bring ghosts (*bhut/pret*) with her." I have not been able to find any other community that practises this custom, Newar or non-Newar.

Appendix 2

Lwahãkaḥmi Lineages

Seven exogamous lineages. Maximal lineages bold and underlined. No sub-lineages discovered.

Four original lineages

The original four Lwahãkaḥmi lineages have exclusive access to the Tantric Deity located behind Cibhāḥ Nani, Jom Bāhāḥ.

These lineages are alphabetically arranged in English.

Hukā Bāgaḥ (Short hookah)

Ikhā Lakhu and Bũga Nani. 13 households.

Katilāḥ (Selfish)

Tulsi Nani. 19 households.

Khica (Dog)

Bijāpu Nani. 9 households.

Yākami (Alone) or Pāyā

Tu Nani and Bijāpu Nani. 4 households.

Three Additional Lineages

None of these lineages have access to the above Tantric Deity.

Gãyrāsimga (Rhino horn) or Sukuḥ (Lean and thin)

Tichu Galli. 5 households.

Khwapa (Bhaktapur)

Ikhā Lakhu. 1 household.

Kāji (Manager)

Bega Nani. 3 households.

Appendix 3

Hollow Metal Craft Products

Products of the Coppersmith

āsi	middle vessel of copper for distilling spirits (*aylaḥ*)
arga	copper water pourer for offering pure water (*ganga jal*) to Surya (form of Vishnu) or Linga (form of Shiva)
chapri/panca pala	copper plate with five large and four small indentations for Brother Worship (Kijā Pujā)
chapri/sapta pala	copper plate with seven equal sized indentations also used for Kijā Pujā
cwāmu bātā	top copper vessel for *aylaḥ* production
ghaḥ	the characteristic water pot in its two forms *Newaḥ ghaḥ* and *Magaḥ ghaḥ*
jal dhāra	copper vessel that stands on tripod
kalasha	copper flask used at wedding; combination brass and copper used for *pujā* at First Rice-Feeding ([Macā] Jãkwa)
kamandalu	copper water pot for giving water to soul of the dead
karma pātra	dish for *pujā;* when used for the Mock Marriage rite (*ihi*) this must have sacred designs (mandalas) written on it
kolla	copper dish for making *pinda*s
kot	similar to *kolla* but with lip
maka	large decorated copper censor
nilaḥ thalaḥ	small copper water pot with spout
panca patra	small copper water vessel for use in worship
phosi	bottom copper vessel for *aylaḥ* production; also used for boiling rice
tahãpa	like *nilaḥ thalaḥ*
tepaḥ	copper barrel for storage of husked rice etc
trikuti	tripod; also made of iron by blacksmiths

Products of the Bronzesmith

kasaũri	thick bronze vessel for cooking lentils or rice
kẽy bhu	bronze plate for daily use
thay bhu	larger bronze plate ritual purposes particularly Marriage and Mock Marriage.

Appendix 4

Types of Timber in Use in the Kathmandu Valley

Timber in general use

dhũsĩ (*sāl* or *agratha,* Np.; *Shorea robusta,* L.). Found on the Tarai, the highest quality of wood in use. Being very hard and rot-proof *dhũsĩ* is used for external woodwork such as the exposed parts of door and a window frames. Its lack of flexibility, however, makes it unsuitable for use on the chariots. Woodcarvers find it an acceptable wood to carve their intricate designs in.

gwaisasĩ (*Schima wallichii,* L.). Another hard wood, but not as strong as *dhũsĩ.* It is used for the joist and rafters of traditional houses. Now scarce in vicinity of the Valley.

salla (chir pine; *Pinus roxburghii,* L.). Used for furniture, joists and staircases. Now scarce in vicinity of the Valley.

utis (alder; *Alnus nepalensis*, L.). Another wood used for joists. Now scarce in vicinity of the Valley.

Chapasĩ (*Mechelia champaca,* L.). Traditionally used for good quality carving alongside *dhũsĩ.*

Halusĩ (*Adina cardifolia,* L.). A high quality, lighter, blond hardwood that, though not carved traditionally, is used for carving today.

sisau (*Dalbergia sissoo,* L.). A rich, brown hardwood with a distinctive grain used for carving and furniture.

Timber used in construction of Bũgadyaḥ's chariot[1]

swasĩ [for frame]

Traditionally obtained from Godavari but has become difficult to procure in recent years as the local forest managers have banned felling.

naḥsĩ [for wheels]

Obtained from Chitwan; *naḥsĩ* is a very strong wood.

tirbasĩ (*nāgbasĩ*) [main forward beam (*daḥmā*)]

Obtained from Bālāju, the tree that provides this wood needs to have the peculiar crook at the base in order to form the upward curving 'prow'.

tũsĩ [for platform]

Obtained from Lagankhel, four boards are used to construct the platform.

laḥsĩ [for longitudinal poles]

Sixteen poles of this flexible wood are tied around the tower of the chariot to give it overall strength. In recent years, as this is no longer available, the Bārāhi have been forced to use an inferior variety of this wood leading, as they see it, to more frequent breaking of the chariot.

mahelsĩ [for brake shoes]

Harvested at Godavari, this wood is extremely hard, giving the brakes sufficient strength to withstand the compression of the wheels.

baḥsĩ [for brake handles]

This wood, obtained locally, has an elastic quality enabling it to spring in the hands of the brakeman without breaking.

1. I am indebted to Dil Kumar Barahi for helping me to compile this list. Note that Shepard's list is inaccurate (1985: 273).

Appendix 5

Types of Carved Windows

Traditional carved windows can be classified in a number of ways. One way is according to which floor they are situated. Another is according to the number of openings. So *sopā jhyāḥ*, for instance, is the appellation for a composite window made up of three *sa jhyāḥ*. These can be of any odd number, hence *nyāpā jhyāḥ*, etc. A further typology is according to the window's position in the building, hence the unusual *kũ jhyāḥ* (corner window).

Below are the names of the different types of windows according to the design of the main element. Most of these can be combined into multiple forms:

sa jhyāḥ	ordinary window usually with arched opening.
tiki jhyāḥ	latticed window
suryā jhyāḥ	has a small circular opening in middle with criss-cross lattice in style of sun's rays.
maykā jhyāḥ	peacock window
desaymaru jhyāḥ	unique window, free design, fits no particular category.

Appendix 6

Traditional Newar Confectionery

The following inventory of confectionery includes all that are understood to be the traditional product of the Marikaḥmi of Lalitpur.[1] Other sweets sold in the shops are all thought to be recent introductions from India.[2]

aĩta — White wheat flour, sugar and clarified butter are kneaded together with baking soda. The strands are then tightly platted into a fist-like bundle symbolic of the tightness of the *samdhi* (in-law) bond and deep-fried in clarified butter or oil. On removal from the pot the pieces are dipped in a thick sugar solution and left to cool. This sweet is an important ingredient in the contracting of Marriage (§4.2.4).

anarsā — This small, ball-shaped sweet made from a mixture of rice flour and sugar with a coating of poppy seeds. The balls are then deep-fried in clarified butter or oil.

barphi — To manufacture the popular *barphi* condensed milk is mixed with sugar in the ratio of five-to-one. Various spices such as cardamom are added according to taste and the mixture allowed to set in a tray. A variation of *barphi* is *perā,* which is made by working the dough into balls, shaping in the palm of the hand to the required shape, such as a small disc or bowl, and then decorated with spices.

cāku mari — Although the name of this sweet is a general term for a sweet it has also acquired a specific identity of its own. White wheat flour is kneaded with a little clarified butter and after cutting into two-inch long pieces is deep-fried in clarified butter. As in the preparation of *aĩta* the cooked sweets are dipped in a thick sugar solution and left to cool.

catā̃ mari — This rice-flour *mari* is prepared as a paper-thin crepe by griddling the batter on a covered hot iron plate with clarified butter. The item is usually served with a meat or egg topping.

guli mari — In the preparation of this sweet chickpea flour is mixed with whole-wheat flour and a little clarified butter and kneaded. The dough is cut into smaller pieces than those of *cāku mari* are. After deep-frying they are dipped in thick sugar solution.

hali mari — This sweet is identical to *guli mari* but is made in a variety of colours.

lākha mari To prepare the pretzel-like *lākha mari* baking soda is added to a mixture of two parts rice flour to one part black gram flour. The resulting dough is drawn or piped into strips and braided into a ring. The ring of dough is then deep fried in clarified butter and dipped in thick sugar solution. *Lākha mari* comes in a variety of shapes. The shape of the sweet is highly symbolic expressing the tightness of the relationship between the giver and the recipient (§4.2.4).

lāl mohan The *lāl mohan* is fabricated by mixing two parts condensed milk with one part of wheat flour and some baking soda. The dough is deep fried in clarified butter or oil and dipped in sugar solution.

panjābi The sweet pastry *panjābi* is prepared from wheat flour. The dough is cut into long strips, which are then divided into smaller pieces, dipped in sugar solution and for deep-fried in clarified butter or oil.

phini Like the *panjābi*, this sweet pastry is made of wheat flour dough. It is then formed into circles, coated in sugar solution, decorated with a yellow centre and deep-fried in clarified butter or oil. A tray full of this sweet is essential as part of the presentation during the ceremony of the Giving of the Areca Nut (*gway biyegu*).

yaḥ mari This steamed pastry is prepared from rice flour and usually filled with sesame seed and molasses. The shape is variously interpreted as that of a *stupa* or a fig. *Yaḥ mari* is not normally available at sweetshops because it has a short shelf life. From time to time, and especially at Thila Punhi it is made in the home and eaten hot and fresh. On the occasion of the first four or five birthdays of a child a number of *yaḥ mari* are strung on a lace and given as a garland.

---

1. I am indebted to Ravi Rajkarnikar of 'House' for helping me to compile this inventory.

2. There is some reluctance in the literature to refer to all these items, collectively known as *mari*, as sweets. Levy refers to them as 'sweetcakes' (1990: 422, 673). My Marikaḥmi informants, however, feel this to be a misnomer as the word 'cake' connotes both a different cooking process (baking), and a different ingredient: egg (the eating of which is taboo to many Newars).

Appendix 7

Pengu Daḥ Households in the Modern Economy

I have here in summary form described the present economic activity of a few somewhat representative households of the Pengu Daḥ.

Bārāhi

In this household, apart from their annual duty in preparing the chariots for the Jātrā, father and both sons operate a workshop making picture frames employing six salaried workers. Both the house *thākāli*'s wife and that of his elder son are employed in the home doing the housework.

Lwahākaḥmi

Master carver making temple, and other traditional shelter and house pieces such as windows, doors and struts. Wife does housework. Younger brother shares the workshop but is mostly involved in turning of piecework for contractor.

Rājkarnikār

1. Rājkarnikār householder No. 1 is a retired sweetmaker. The family shop in Mangaḥ is now leased as a small cafe. Although the inheritance is not yet ḍivided, the two younger brothers have built their own house in nearby suburbs. Each younger brother has two children in school.

Wife - housework.
Son - engineer.
Son's wife - housework.
Younger brother 1 - alcohol distribution business.
Younger brother 1's wife - housework.
Younger brother 2 - food distribution business. Small plastic-ware shop.
Younger brother 2's wife - teacher of Nepali language to foreigners.

2. Rājkarnikār householder No. 2 runs food business and is the elected ward representative.

Wife - manages household servants.
Younger brother 1 and mother jointly run family sweet business.
Younger brother 1's wife - beautician.
Younger brother 2 - alcohol distribution business.

Sikaḥmi

Our single Sikaḥmi case study is of an elderly householder who runs a furniture workshop at the house with his eldest and youngest sons. The second son has a salaried job in charge of maintenance at the office of a development agency. The youngest son also runs a plumbing business making such items as solar water heating systems. The wives of both elder brothers do the housework.

Tamvaḥ

1. Tāmrakār householder No.1 is a retired coppersmith. He lives in a joint family with his three sons and their wives and children. The family lives, for most purposes, as two separate units, between the old house in Tichu Galli and their new cement house outside the ring road. The eldest son exercises a high degree of leadership in the family. The household includes five school-age minors.

Income and division of labour:

Son 1 - bank manager
Wife - kitchenware shop in Haugaḥ
Daughter - air stewardess
Son 2 - copperware shop in Haugaḥ
Wife - household duties
Son 3 - separate copperware shop in Haugaḥ
Wife - household duties

The household also has income in the form of cash from a bank that is renting a third house in Haugaḥ.

2. Tāmrakār householder No. 2 lives with his younger brother in a single house as a supplemented joint family. As the *thākāli* he runs the main retail shop on one side of the house front. He is also a partner in a copper importing business and a copperware factory at nearby Patan industrial estate.

Son 1 - manager of above factory
Son 2 - retail of copper and brass raw materials and unfinished pieces including those that have come out of the above factory in house-front shop on other side of front door from father's shop.
Younger brother - manages and works in the workshop at back of house producing traditional copper and brass pots. Sometimes up to eight Kāmi labourers employed.
Mother, wife and younger brother's wife do the housework. Daughter is a schoolteacher.

3. This Tāmrakār householder and his wife are childless and middle-aged. Their only income is in the form of cash in exchange for the craft of traditional copper water pot (*ghaḥ*). Wife does the housework.

Appendix 8

Catalogue of Annual Events

Introduction

The Newars follow two ritual calendars according to the procession of the sun and moon. In the catalogue that follows I have attempted to summarize all the main festivals of Lalitpur as well as the minor ones that I am aware of. Several of these minor feasts are relevant for the Pengu Daḥ alone. Other castes will have their own particular special days.

The Solar Calendar

The solar calendar according to the official Vikram Sambat, as used by the Nepalese government, has twelve months each beginning and ending midway through the months of the Gregorian calendar. The New Year begins half way through April. The year 2000 CE, then, was year 2056/7 VS.

Vaishākh (April-May)	Biskaḥ. *Nakhaḥ.*
Jyesth (May-June)	
Ashādh (June-July)	
Shrāvan (July-August)	
Bhādra (August-September)	
Ashvin (September-October)	
Kārttik (October-November)	
Mārga (November-December)	
Paush (December-January)	
Māgh (January-February).	Ghyaḥcāku Sãnhu (Māgh Samkrānti). *Nakhaḥ.*
Phāgun (February-March)	
Caitra (March-April)	

The Lunar Calendar

Each lunar month is divided into two fortnights—*shukla* and *krishna:* the waxing and waning halves respectively—each having a distinct name in Newar. Lalitpurians, as other Newars, however, also refer to the lunar fortnight by the name of the solar month it normally falls in followed by the suffix *-shukla* or *-krishna.* Every two months the fifth day of the waxing fortnight (*shukla pancami*) heralds the formal beginning of a new season.

For ease of comparison, in the list below I follow the pattern laid out by Levy (1990: Appendix 5) although I begin the inventory at a different point (§7.3). In addition, I have added the Nepali/Sanskrit name of each fortnight for ease of comparison across South Asia. It must be remembered, however, that the lunar month of Vaishākh, for instance, never actually coincides exactly with the solar month of that name.[1] I have not attempted, as Levy did, to put a level of importance on each festival. Instead, I have noted which are considered *nakhaḥ* by a general consensus among knowledgeable Tāmrakār men in Lalitpur. It proved impossible in fact, to get a complete consensus even among a smallish group, which demonstrates how difficult it would be if one attempted to do so for the whole city. Generally, the more important a festival is, the broader the scope of invitations to the feast (*nakhaḥtyā*), which is usually held on the evening following the *nakhaḥ.* All events that are connected to the Bũgadyaḥ Jātrā are marked 'Jātrā'.

Minor festivals, such as Ghyahcāku Sãnhu, are sometimes called *macā nakhaḥ.* There is no compulsion to invite one's married out daughters and their children (*mhyay macā*). A moderately important *nakhaḥ,* such as Yaḥmari Punhi and Gathḥ Mugaḥ Cahre, is one on which it is thought necessary to call *mhyay macā.* On major feasts, such as Mohani and the Jātrā, as well as *mhyay macā,* one's daughter's husband and one's married-out sisters' children and their families (*bhincā maca*) are also invited.

Dillāthwa (Ashādh-*shukla*; June/July)

Dillā is Bhimsen's month. Dillā Pujā throughout month.

1.
2.
3.
4.
5.
6.
7.
8.
9.
10.
11. Caturmāsya Vratarambhaḥ. Beginning of Caturmāsa season. Vishnu/Nārāyana begins his four month long sleep.
12. Tulasi Piye. Sacred basil seedlings are planted in pots at the home to be worshipped as Vishnu over the coming four months.
13.
14.
15. Dillā Punhi/Guru Punhi. Guru Pujā. Not a *nakhaḥ.*

Dillāgā (Shrāvan-*krishna*; July)

1.
2.
3.
4.
5.
6
7.
8.
9.
10.
11.
12.
13.

14. Dillā Cahre. Gathā̃ Mugaḥ. Seen as the first festival in the year. Tamvaḥ Cahre Guthi day. *Nakhaḥ.* Nasantya Dāphā Guthi sings *bhajans* to Nāsadyaḥ, Haugaḥ. Concluding annual feast of *guthi.*
15.

Gũlāthwa (Shrāvan-*shukla*; July/August)

This month is especially important for the worship of Buddha.

1. Gũlā Dharma. First day of the important Buddhist month. Gũlā Pāru Guthi begins intensive daily worship of Buddha. Beginning of nightly processions (Bagi Wanegu) of *bājā̃ khalaḥ.* Begin fasting and text reading.
2.
3.
4.
5. Nāg Pancami. Worship of holy serpents. Beginning of cold half of year. Beginning of *sharad* season (until Kaulāthwa 4).
6.
7.
8. Yala Pancadān. Buddhists give alms to Shākyas and Vajrācāryas. Tamvaḥ Kwaḥ lineage goes to Kwā Bāhāḥ to worship Tantric deity.
9.
10.
11.
12. Bahidyaḥ Bwayegu. Displaying deities in monasteries. Until Gũlāgā 5.
13.
14. In evening Nava Bājā̃ Khalaḥ plays in Kumbheshvara temple Precincts.
15. Gũ Punhi. Tying of protective threads. Festival at Kumbheshvara. Important.

Gũlāgā (Bhādra-*krishna*; August)

1. Sā Pāru. *Shivamārgis* such as the Tamvaḥ take part in procession with cows for dead around *pradakshinapātha.* Groups of musicians and singers sing Newar *bhakti bhajans* as they process. Especially important for those who have lost a relative during the past year. Important.

   Bāhāḥ Pujā. Worship at each of eighteen major monasteries (*bāhāḥ*) and four mounds (*stupas*) in and around Lalitpur. Procession visits each site in turn. Completely separate from Sā Pāru. Seems to have an element of preparation for the next day's Matayā procession.
2. Nyaku Jātrā/Matayā. *Buddhamārgis* especially process around Lalitpur visiting all votive *caityas* for dead. Major festival for Lalitpur's *buddhamārgis*. All who have lost a relative during past year participate. Nyaku Jātrā *bājā̃ khalaḥ* processes around main *pradakshinapātha* including performance of Nava Bājā̃ Khalaḥ in front of *lũjhyāḥ.* Important.
3.
4.

5. Narasimha Jātrā.
   Matayā Ganesh Pujā (day varies).
6.
7. Krishna Janmashtami. Worship at Krishna temple in Mangaḥ. Important.
8. Krishna Pujā. Morning. Procession to all public images of Krishna in Lalitpur.
   Krishna Jātrā. Evening. Procession of two Krishna images in palanquins around city.
9. Bhimsen Pujā. Morning. Procession of devotees around Bhimsen (Bhindyaḥ) shrines of the city.
   Bhimsen Jātrā. Evening. Procession of Bhimsen around city.
10.
11.
12.
13. Yẽ Pancadān. Minor. Some people go to Kathmandu to give dān to Vajrācāryas and Shākyas.
14. Jugaḥ Cahre. Mahālakshmi Pujā.
15. Bāya Khwā Swayegu ('Seeing the Father's Face'). *Nakhaḥ.*

Yālāthwa (Bhādra-*shukla*; August/September)

Yālā Pujā. This month is especially important for the worship of the Devi.

1. Gũlā Pāru. Feasts to mark the end of Gũlā month. Especially important for Gũlā Pāru Guthi.
2.
3.
4. Cathaḥ. Worship of Ganesh and moon. *Nakhaḥ.*
5. Bārāhi *cathaḥ guthi*
   Kwakha Jā Biye. Special *saptarshi pujā* followed by feeding of crows.
   Mahālakshmi Guthi *pujā* and feast.
6.
7.
8. Kayashtami. Beginning of observances for Mohani.
   Dashmahāvidya Pujā: pilgrimage to the Ten Great Knowledges.
   Yalasiba: pilgrimage to the Twelve Power-Places all located outside the city begins today and continues throughout following lunar month.
9.
10.
11. Yẽnyaḥ: Day 1. Raising of Yamadyaḥ.
12. Yẽnyaḥ: Day 2.
13. Yẽnyaḥ: Day 3. *Pujā* and *samay*: Kwalku-Cyāsaḥ.
14. Yẽnyaḥ: Day 4. *Pujā* and *samay*: Tangaḥ-Guita.
15. Yẽnyaḥ Punhi: Day 5. *Pujā* and *samay*: Haugaḥ-Mangaḥ, Bhimsensthān. Worship of Indra, Ganesh, Mahākāla, Bāl Kumāri and other Mother Goddesses. *Nakhaḥ.*

Yālāgā (Ashvin-*krishna*; September)

1. Yẽnyaḥ: Day 6. *Pujā* and *samay:* Ikhā-Patan Dhokā.
   Sixteen [Day] Ancestor Worship (*sohra shrāddha*) may be done

between this day and new moon (Yãlāgā 15). All *phuki* get together to do *shrāddha* for all ancestors of lineage.

2. Yẽnyaḥ: Day 7.
3. Yẽnyaḥ: Day 8. Yamadyaḥ taken down.
   Gatilā. Observance of Vasundharā. Celebrates rice harvest.
4.
5.
6.
7.
8.
9.
10.
11.
12.
13.
14.
15.

Kaulāthwa (Ashvin-*shukla*; September/October)

This month is devoted to worship of Nārāyana.

1. Mohani: Naílā swãne. Beginning of Mohani (Np. Dashaĩ).
   Seeds of barley and corn are planted in Tantric god house.
   Each night until ninth performance of Gan Pyākhã dance-drama group.
2. Mohani.
3. Mohani.
4. Mohani.
5. Mohani. Beginning of *hemanta* season (until Thilāthwa 4).
   According to some this is the only day during Caturmāsa on which Marriage and other movable life-cycle rituals may be observed (although see Kaulāthwa 10).
6. Mohani.
7. Mohani: Swã swãne (Phulpāti). Purification of house.
8. Mohani: Tāpã. Worship of tools etc. Worship of 5 liquids. *Samay baji.*
   Kuchẽ Bhway.
9. Mohani: Syāko tyāko. Killing of goat as sacrifice to Durga.
   Buffaloes are sacrificed in Mul Cok to Taleju.
10. Mohani: Cālã (Vijāya Dasami). Main day of Mohani. Seniors give *prasād* to juniors. *Nakhaḥ.*
    Final performance, during day, of Gan Pyākhã group.
    Welcome of Gathu Pyākhã and first performance.
    Some say this day also is appropriate for Marriage and other movable life-cycle rituals.
11. From now until Kati Punhi (Kojagrat Purnimā) relatives will visit each other's homes, be fed and receive *prasād* from host
    Performance of Gathu Pyākhã group each night till Kati Punhi.
12.
13.

14.
15. Kati Punhi. Last day for visiting relatives. Last performance of Gathu Pyākhã.
Reconsecration of *caityas*.

Kaulāgā (Kārttik-*krishna*; October)

1. First day of traditional Kati Pyākhã performance. Kārttik Vrata at Bũga and Cobhār. Alāmātā Cyākyu: lights are offered to Nārāyana in the Himalaya from rooftops and tall poles till Sakimilā Punhi.
2.
3.
4.
5.
6.
7.
8.
9.
10.
11.
12.
13. Beginning of Swanti (Np. Tihār). Khwā Pujā. Worship of crows.
14. Khica Pujā. Worship of dogs. End of the rice season.
15. Sā Pujā. Worship of cows in morning.
Lakshmi Pujā. Worship of goddess of wealth in evening. *Nakhaḥ.*

Kachalāthwa (Kārttik-*shukla*; October/November)

1. Mha Pujā. Worship of self. Nhugu Dã (Newar New Year).
2. Kijā Pujā. Worship of brothers. Last day of Swanti.
3. Lakshmidyaḥ khwakau. Final *pujā* to Lakshmi and receiving of *prasād.*
4.
5.
6.
7.
8. Mukhaḥ Ashtami. Main Eighth Day observance of year. Buddhists fast.
9.
10.
11. Haribodhini Ekadasi. Nārāyana awakes. End of Caturmāsa. Kārttiksnāna Caturmāsya Vrata Samapti. Hundreds of red sari-clad women line up in front of the Cār Nārāyana temple, Mangaḥ, to do *pujā.*
Melā at Buddhanilkantha and other Vaishnavite shrines from today until full moon.
12.
13.
14.

15. Sakimilā Punhi. Feasting. Display grain drawings for end of Kārttik seva. Harvest festival.
    Kwenādyaḥ Jātrā (minor).
    Traditional final night of Kati Pyākhā performance.

Kachalāgā (Mārga-*krishna*; November)

1.
2.
3.
4.
5.
6.
7.
8.
9. Significant day for *guthi* feasts; e.g., Tamvaḥ Cidhā Guthi. Many *guthi*s can be seen feasting together at Jawalakhel and elsewhere.
10.
11.
12.
13.
14. Bālā Cahre. *Shivamārgi*s especially, but not solely, go on pilgrimage out of the city to do *pujā* at Pashupatināth if they have lost a family member during the past year.
    Feast of Shilpakār Tadhā Guthi.
15.

Thilāthwa (Mārga-*shukla;* November/December)

1.
2.
3.
4.
5. Vivāhā Pancami. Wedding anniversary of Rām and Sita. Marriage possible without consulting astrologer.
    Beginning of *shishir* season (until Sillāthwa 4).
6.
7.
8.
9.
10.
11.
12.
13.
14.
15. Yaḥmari Punhi (Thila Punhi). Winter solstice. Eating rice-flour pastries. *Nakhaḥ.*
    Vishnu Devi Jātrā (minor). Jyāpu and Shākya *guthi* feasts.

Thilāgā (Paush-*krishna*; December)

1. Mahālakshmi Pujā. Tamvaḥ Pwāḥsyāḥ lineage does *pujā* at Mahālakshmi. Feast together.
   Bārāhi Sisā Pāru Guthi. The Bārāhi select trees for building the chariot. This is the first feast of the annual cycle for the Bārāhi.
2.
3.
4.
5.
6.
7.
8.
9.
10. Disi Pujā. Worship of Cakrasamvara. Winter solstice.
11.
12.
13.
14.
15.

Pohelāthwa (Paush-*shukla*; December/January)

1.
2.
3.
4.
5.
6.
7.
8.
9.
10.
11.
12.
13.
14.
15. Milā Punhi. Beginning of Svasthāni Observance.

Pohelāgā (Māgh-*krishna;* January)

1.
2.
3.
4.
5.
6.
7.
8.
9.

10.
11.
12.
13.
14.
15.

Sillāthwa (Māgh-*shukla*; January/February)

1.
2.
3.
4.
5. Sri Pancami. *Pujā* to Sarasvati (Sasu Pujā). Singing of *bhajan*s to Sarasvati at Kwachḥ Bāl Kumāri by Nasantya Dāphā Guthi. Sasu Pujā continues until Cillāgā 15.
   Beginning of hot season.
   Beginning of *vasanta* season (until Caulāthwa 4).
   At this time also inviting of guests (until Cillāgā 15).
6.
7.
8.
9.
10.
11.
12.
13.
14.
15. Sri Pancami. *Pujā* to Sarasvati (Sasu Pujā). Singing of *bhajan*s to Sarasvati at Kwachḥ Bāl Kumāri by Nasantya Dāphā Guthi. Sasu Pujā continues until Cillāgā 15.
    Beginning of hot season.
    Beginning of *vasanta* season (until Caulāthwa 4).
    At this time also inviting of guests (until Cillāgā 15).

Sillāgā (Phāgun-*krishna*; February)

1.
2.
3.
4.
5.
6.
7.
8.
9.
10.
11.
12.
13.

14. Sillā Cahre. Mahā Shivarātri. Big festival at Pashupati. Men light bonfires in roads and sit around them all night. *Nakhaḥ.*
15.

Cillāthwa (Phāgun-*shukla*; February/March)

1.
2.
3.
4.
5.
6.
7.
8. Cir Swayegu. Beginning of Holi celebrations. Tree is set up in front of Krishna Mandir.
9.
10. Varsabandhana. Anniversary of Krishna temple.
11.
12.
13.
14.
15. Holi Punhi. Throwing of red colour and water. Cir Wāchwaygu. Tree (set up on Cillāthwa 8) is cast into Bāgmati.
    Cakandyaḥ Haigu.

Cillāgā (Caitra-*krishna*; March)

1.
2.
3.
4.
5.
6.
7.
8.
9. Tamvaḥ Daru Guthi *pujā* and feast.
10.
11.
12.
13.
14. Pahā̃ (Pāsā) Cahre (Pisāca Caturdasi, Np.). Shiva worshipped as Luku ('hiding') Mahādyaḥ. *Nakhaḥ.*
15. Sala Yaḥ (Sala Bwāki). Ghode Jātrā. Festival of Kwachẽ Bāl Kumāri. Afternoon drunken horse made to gallop with eyes covered. Evening Bāl Kumāri Jātrā.

Caulāthwa (Caitra-*shukla*; March/April)

1.
2.
3.
4.

5. Beginning of *grishma* season (until Tachalāthwa 4).
6.
7.
8. Caitra Dasami (Dashaĩ). Power-Place Worship (Pitha Pujā).
9. Rām Navami. Worship of Rām. Beginning of two-day Rām festival (Minor Dashaĩ of Rām).
   Two Tamvaḥ death *guthi*s have feast.
10.
11.
11.
12.
13.
14.
15. Lhuti Punhi. Pilgrimage to Jāmācwa.
    Feast of Shilpakār Tadhã Guthi.

Caulāgā (Vaishākh-*krishna*; April)

1. Nhawã. Bathing (*snāna*) of Karunāmaya and Cākwāḥdyaḥ. Jātrā.
2. Beginning of construction of chariot by Bārāhi. Jātrā.
3.
4.
5. Shilpakār Tadhã Guthi feast.
6.
7.
8.
9. Tamvaḥ Cidhã Guthi *pujā* and feast.
10. Tamvaḥ Tadhã Guthi *pujā* and feast.
11.
12. Bhairava Pujā. Sacrifice of two buffaloes at Bũga. Jātrā.
13. Nandi Dev Pratinidhi. Khwāpa Juju visits Karunāmaya. Jātrā.
    Kar Kaya. Two buffaloes sacrificed at Ta Bāhāḥ. All male Bārāhi are feasted at *thākāli*s house. Jātrā.
14. Sacrifice of two more buffaloes at Ta Bāhāḥ. Jātrā.
15. Maya Khwā Swayegu. Married out daughters visit natal home to give sweets to mother. *Nakhaḥ.*
    Sacrifice of last two buffaloes and a pure black goat at Ta Bāhāḥ. Jātrā.

Bachalāthwa (Vaishākh-*shukla*; April/May)

1. Bũgayaḥ. Preparation for and placing of Bũgadyaḥ on chariot. Jātrā.
2. Phaila Bhu. Bārāhi feast. Jātrā.
3. Akshaya Tritiya. Dewāli begins for most Lalitpur *thar*s.
   Gift of the cow (*sā dān*) to Brahman. Jātrā.
   Tamvaḥ Akshaya Tritiya Guthi *pujā* and feast.
4. Chariot pulled to Ga Bāhāḥ. Jātrā. (From this time on all Jātrā dates are dependent on the vicissitudes of the chariot on its journey through the city; the following are ideal only.)
   Jyāpu Kumāri worshipped.
5. Ga Bāhāḥyaḥ. *Bhujyaḥ* for western sector of the city. Jātrā.

6. Chariot pulled to Nugaḥ. Jātrā.
7. Nugaḥyaḥ. *Bhujyaḥ* for eastern sector of the city. Jātrā. From the next day some Pengu Daḥ begin to observe Lineage Deity Worship.
8. Chariot pulled to Lagankhel to visit mother. Jātrā.
9.
10.
11.
12. Lagãyaḥ. Chariot pulled around Mẽju Simā shrine and down the road a little. Jātrā.
    Start of Tamvaḥ Lineage Deity Worship.
13. *Bhujyaḥ* for remaining, central sector of the city. Jātrā.
    'Nekya Luigu' ('Dropping the Coconut') in evening. Jātrā.
14. Chariot is pulled by women to Thati. Jātrā. Yākamisā Bhujyaḥ.
    Kiki Swã. Crowning of Karunāmaya. Jātrā. Chariot remains at Thati until an auspicious moment determined by the astrologers. Remainder of Jātrā is dependent on this.
15. Swãya Punhi. Buddha Jayanti.

Bachalãgā (Jyesth-*krishna*; May)

1.
1.
2.
3.
4.
5.
6.
7.
8.
9.
10.
11.
12.
13.
14.
15.

Tachalāthwa (Jyesth-*shukla*; May/June)

1.
2.
3.
4.
5. Beginning of *varsha* season (until Gũlāthwa 4) corresponding to heaviest period of monsoon.
6. Sithi Nakhaḥ. Beginning of rice-transplantation. Final day for Lineage Deity Worship. Last festival (*nakhaḥ*) of year. No music from Sithi Nakhaḥ to Gathā̃ Mugaḥ except the Nasantya Dāphā Guthi.
7.

8.
9.
10. Dasa Harā. Mid-summer festival. Bathing in river. First day of green leaf vegetable season
11.
12.
13.
14.
15. Jyesth (Jya) Punhi. Summer solstice. Krishna painting and Siddhi Narasimha Malla's throne are displayed.

Tachalāgā (Ashādh-*krishna*; June)

1.
2.
3.
4.
5.
6.
7.
8.
9.
10.
11.
12.
13.
14.
15.

Endnote

1. I was caught out by this when, near the beginning of my fieldwork, I went to observe 'Jyesth Punhi' at Mangaḥ only to discover that I was a month early—'Jyesth Punhi' that year was to be observed in Ashādh!

Appendix 9

Life-Cycle and Death Rites of the Pengu Daḥ

Introduction

Newar life-cycle rites can be divided firstly into those observed during the life of the individual (*samskāras*) and those that follow death. In this appendix I will summarize the rites performed for or by a member of the Pengu Daḥ, as they constitute the group I am most familiar with. Readers will find it most helpful to compare this with those of Toffin (1984), Gellner (1992: 199, Table 7.2), and Levy (1990: Appendix 6). Finally, I analyse the rites by means of a flow chart (Figure 6).

Life-cycle rites (*samskāra*)

The Pengu Daḥ observe a total of eight life-cycle rites (*samskāras*).[1]

Birth Purification (Macābu Bẽkegu)[2]

Upon the birth of a new baby, assuming that the mother is of the same caste as the father, all close patrilineal relatives (*syāḥ phuki*) are impure until the ceremony of Birth Purification (Macābu Bẽkegu) is performed. This ritual is enacted on the fourth, sixth, eighth, or tenth day after birth.[3] This is the only life-cycle ritual that does not require the presence of a Brahman or Vajrācārya priest. Instead, for this the Aji is called (§3.4.3). In the past the Aji also acted as the midwife. All mothers gave birth in the home but few do so today. The heart of the purification ritual is the *pujā* by the Aji to the dangerous goddess Ajimā or Hāritimai. After the ritual all members of the lineage are considered pure.[4] The mother and child leave for her natal home (*thaḥ chẽ*) after the purification.[5]

First Rice-Feeding ([Macā] Jākwa)

For the next life-cycle ritual an auspicious day is selected, which for a girl must be in the fifth, seventh, or ninth month, and for a boy in the sixth, eighth, or tenth month.

On this day, a *pujā* is performed by the domestic priest. Then all agnatic relatives in order of seniority feed the baby from a ritual plate (*thay bhu*) piled high with (ideally) eighty different dishes.[6] The naked baby is then dressed in a suit of red cloth with gold brocade. Various items of jewellery are placed on his ankles and wrists and on his ears. The baby is then presented with a tray of various objects such as a pen, and various items that are associated with the family trade, and must include a small piece of brick and a dish of unhusked rice. Everyone gathers round to see which item the baby should touch or take as a portent for his future. Now the baby's maternal relatives feed the baby in their turn. The maternal uncle has not been allowed to pick up the baby until now. Now he picks up the baby and carries him in procession to nearby temples.[7]

First Head-Shaving (Busā Khāyegu, Busakha)

The First Head-Saving ritual usually takes place almost as a preparatory element of Loincloth Worship. When boys are roughly between the ages of four and twelve they undergo this ceremony which effects their partial transition to adulthood and membership of the lineage.

An Ancestor Worship is performed by the domestic priest. At the auspicious time, the boy's mother's brother shaves a small lock of hair from the boy's head. Following this, the full head is shaved by the Nāpit Barber, leaving only the topknot. The boy is then prepared to go through the next and more elaborate *samskāra.*

Loincloth Worship (Kaytā Pujā)

As with Mock Marriage this ritual is preceded by the full Fire-Offering ritual performed by the domestic priest. After the First Head-Shaving the boy is completely undressed, bathed, and then dressed in the loincloth signifying his coming of age—he can no longer run about naked as a child. He then acts as an ascetic receiving alms from relatives who pour rice in a bowl at his feet (*bhicu dān*). He is then dressed in the garb of the *sannyasin* given a bow and arrow and deerskin mat and led to a prepared ground where a he performs the ritual of the Seven Steps. This fun and dramatic event is watched by all the relatives and friends. The boy must step on each of seven leaves that have been placed on the ground. But before he steps on the seventh he must make as if to run away. Then follows a comic scene in which the boy's mother's brother has to run to catch the boy before he 'crosses the Bāgmati'. If he were to cross the River he would be considered to have chosen to be a lifelong ascetic. So it is imperative that he be caught. Other relatives snatch the boy away so he won't be caught and only bring him back on payment of protection money. It is all done in jest and eventually the boy is brought back to take the seventh step, complete his life as an ascetic, and join the ranks of the lineage as a full adult householder (*grihasti*). He must now follow caste rules and can only marry within prescribed caste boundaries. That evening relatives and friends are feasted.

The transition of status is expressed in the funeral rites, both those of the boy and his involvement in those of his parents. If a boy dies who has not undergone Kaytā Pujā then his body is carried to the cremation ground by four *guthiyār*s. If after Kaytā Pujā then eight *guthiyār*s carry it. Only after Kaytā Pujā can he light the funeral pyre of his father.

Mock Marriage (Ihi)

The Mock Marriage ritual is unique among the peoples of South Asia[8] and is practised by all Newars.[9] Premenarche rites are discussed extensively by Allen (1987).[10]

The ritual takes place over a period of three days.[11]The first day is devoted to ritual purification of the bodies of the girls and those of their parents. The *Nauni* comes to the ground floor of their homes for this ritual. The girls then visit their mother's brother and receive presents of new clothes (Vergati 1995: 66). On this day they may only eat *dhau sagã.*

On the second day (*doso khunu*) the girls again go through a purification ritual early in the morning. For this the domestic priest must supervise. Before the sun rises the priest must arrange the *duso mandala* and fix the seat (*svastika āsāna*) of each girl. These preparatory rituals take several hours.

Early on the domestic priest performs an Ancestor Worship at the local Ganesh temple. Here Mahādyaḥ is worshipped in the form of *alindyaḥ* (§3.4.3). Before the *shrāddha* traditionally the Karmācārya sacrifices a goat at the *pitha*. The most important moment of the second day (which is the first main day) is the *sat brindika* when the girls are measured. In a later ritual, the girls crush[12] black gram seeds between a small roller and board with the left foot representing the purification of past sinful actions (Allen 1987: 84). After several hours of ritual the exhausted girls eat from a *thay bhu*, their first meal of the day.

The third day (*kanyadān khunu*) the domestic priest is up early preparing for a Fire Offering (*yajña*) that is performed later that morning. The climax of the ritual is the giving in Marriage of the girl by her father. At this ritual the girl holds in the palms of her hands the *bel* fruit. This is variously interpreted by participants. Some say that the girl is marrying the fruit who is the embodiment of Kumar, Shiva's son. Others say that she is marrying Vishnu and that the fruit is Shiva acting as witness to the fact. This seems to reflect differences of emphasis between Vaishnavites and Shaivites. The performance of the Mock Marriage ritual transforms the girl's status one step toward womanhood and full membership of her caste and lineage. She must now refrain from eating food that may have been polluted by lower castes and must be more careful of her behaviour in public. At the next Lineage Deity Worship the girls of the lineage who have performed *ihi* during the past year present a *bel* fruit to the domestic priest as to the deity signifying full membership in the lineage of their fathers (Vergati 1995: 72).[12]

Confinement (Bārhā, Bārāy Tayegu/Cwanegu)

The Confinement ritual was originally performed on the occurrence of the first menstrual period of a girl. These days it is almost always completed before the onset, as a pre-menarche ritual. In this ritual the girl is sequestered in a blacked-out room in the house where she may not emerged until the full eleven days has been completed.[13] During this period she may not set eyes on any male.[14] After the first four days of seclusion relatives and friends visit the girl. They bring presents and keep her company to wile away the dark days. They also make a small cotton effigy, which is identified as the *khya*, and hang it on the wall where it stays for the remaining eight days (Allen 1987: 90). On the Twelfth Day the women of the house purify the house with the usual mixture of red clay and cow dung. They then bathe and dress the girl in a gold brocaded red sari, bring her out with veiled face, and lead her to the roof terrace (*kaḥshi*).[15] Here her face is revealed to the sun reflected in water before any male can view her.[16] That evening close relatives and friends are feasted. In keeping with the impure nature of the ritual the feast is not a grand affair as it is at Mock Marriage or First Rice-Feeding.

Confinement is the second of a three-phase sequence of rites whose effect is to transform a pre-menstrual virgin into a married non-virgin (Allen 1987: 92).

Marriage (Ihipāḥ, Bihā Yāyegu)

Marriage is regarded as a sacrament. Consequently, a widow experiences a loss of status. She cannot, for example, fill the role of the *thākāli nakī*. Divorce among the Pengu Daḥ is very rare indeed. If it does happen it is very difficult for the woman.[17]

The rituals surrounding the giving and taking of a wife are numerous and well documented by Bajracharya (1959). Among the Pengu Daḥ who, like many Newars, aspire to high caste status, elopement is not at all common.18 Moreover, these days it is common practice to add a *swayamvara* ceremony to a traditional Newar wedding.

Old-Age Initiation ([Burā/Buri] Jākwa)

Old-Age Initiation may be observed a total of four times at the following ages:

1st	77 years, 7 months, 7 days, 7 *ghau*, 7 *pala*
2nd	1,008th full moon since birth (roughly 82 years, 9 months)[19]
3rd	88 years, 8 months, 8 days, 8 *ghau*, 8 *pala*
4th	99 years, 9 months, 9 days, 9 *ghau*, 9 *pala*[20]

The heart of this ritual, which requires the ministrations of two or three domestic priests, is the divinizing rite. At the auspicious moment the initiate is anointed with milk from conch shells poured by the priests and their wives and the initiate's sons. He is then dressed in fine clothes as for a wedding and receives *pujā* from the relatives. When both a husband and wife are both alive the wife goes through the ritual along with her husband. Then, according to which initiation has been conducted, there may be a procession through the locality.[21] A great feast is held that evening.

At the fourth initiation, called First Rice-Feeding (*maca jākwa*), the initiate is lowered into a large clay pot (*tepaḥ*). A hole is then broken in the side of the pot near the bottom and he is pulled out as if he is being born again. He is then fed rice in a rerun of the First Rice-Feeding (*maca jākwa*) ritual.[22]

Death Rites

I list here the funeral rites as Lalitpur Tamvaḥ typically observe them.[23] *Buddhamārgi* members of the Pengu Daḥ, such as the Marikaḥmi, differ somewhat from this pattern.

Day 1. Cremation (Shi Uyegu)

The body is cremated by the *guthi*.[24] All *guthiyār*s and other close friends (*malāmi*) accompany family.

Days 1 to 10. Mourning (Du)

No shaving, combing of hair, looking in mirror. Restricting of diet (salt, tomatoes, meat, egg, fish, turmeric, and garlic).

Day 2-7. To Come to Start Eating (Cipã Thika Wayegu).

Kāpāli comes to receive food (including beaten rice, sweets, and spirits) offered in name of deceased by married-out daughters (or married-out sister or mother's brother's daughter). He must come only to the *pikhā lakhu* and not inside 'god's place' ('*dyaḥya tāy*').

Day 7. Seventh Day Plate (Nhaynhu Bhu)

Main day for feeding of spirit of dead (*pret*) by married-out daughters. Kāpāli comes to receive food.

Day 10. Mourning Purification (Du Bẽkegu)

All close patrilineal male relatives have their head shaved and all male and female of same group have toenails cut. After this, they take a ritual bath without soap and don white clothes.[25] The Brahman domestic priest conducts an Ancestor Worship at Bāgmati near Shankamul *ghāt*.

Day 11. House Purification (Ghaḥsu)[26]

Fire Offering (*yajña.*) performed by Ghaḥsu Kārmacārya. Inauspicious gift (*dān*) is presented to the Karamjit death specialist.[27] In the morning, Ancestor Worship is conducted at Bāgmati as the day before. The deceased is now said to have left this world and no longer be a ghost (*pret*). He has now become an ancestor (*pitri*).

Day 12. 'Forty-fifth-day' ('month and a half') Feast ('Latyā' Bhway)

This feast traditionally is on 45th day but now it is considered more convenient to complete it on the Twelfth Day.[28] An inauspicious gift (*dān*) is presented to the Brahman domestic priest.[29]

Day 13. Self Decoration (Samāh Payegu)

Ancestor Worship is performed. Mourning for the most part is complete. Lineage members may tidy their hair, put on make-up, wear jewellery etc. Normal work, business, etc resumes.[30]

Ancestor Worship is performed a total of four times in the first month then on or soon after the 45th day. Thereafter on the following months: 3, 4, 5, 5.5, 6, 7, 8, 9, 10, 11, 11.5, and 12, and after that on each anniversary.

Typology of Life-Cycle Rituals

Pradhan (1986: 60-70), after Das (1982), offers a local Hindu typology of rituals, which Gellner reports is also valid for Buddhists (1992: 144-6). Pradhan divides rituals into cosmic rituals (or public festivals) and life-cycle rituals. Newar lifecycle rites can be divided in terms of two oppositions: pure/impure and auspicious/inauspicious. First Rice-Feeding, Loincloth Worship, Mock Marriage and Marriage and Old-Age Initiation are both auspicious and pure. Birth Purification and Confinement are auspicious but impure. Ancestor Worship is pure and inauspicious. Death rituals are both impure and inauspicious. Pure rites begin with a rite of purification (*nisi yayegu*) and, when auspicious, end with consumption of *sagã.* Impure rites begin with the event incurring impurity and end with purifications called *bẽkegu.*

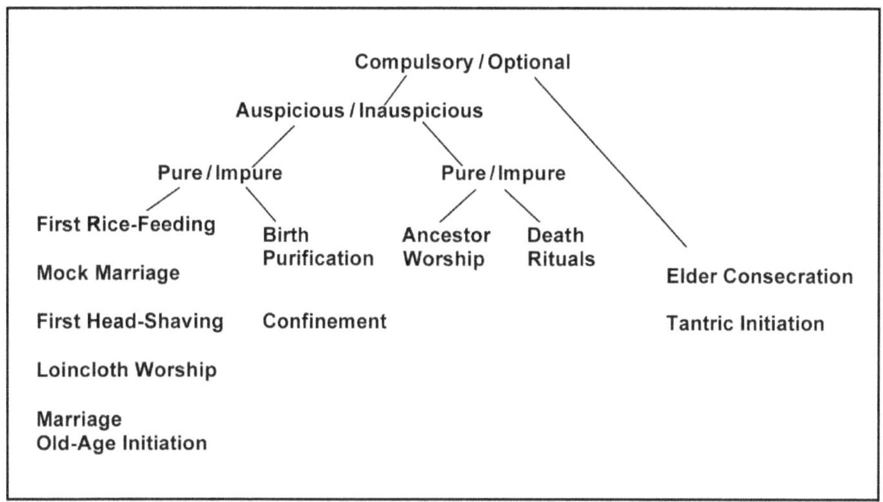

Figure 6. Typology of life-cycle rituals.

Many life-cycle rituals are movable. That is, they can be observed at a convenient date. Others, such as Birth Purification and Old-Age Initiation are more or less restricted to particular dates. Some rituals are semi-restricted such as Confinement, which cannot be delayed if menstruation starts. First Rice-Feeding also can only be observed on certain months.

We can tease out a cascade of binary oppositions:

Compulsory/Optional - Auspicious/Inauspicious - Pure/Impure (Figure 6).[31]

Compulsory rituals can be auspicious or inauspicious and either pure or impure. They occur throughout the course of a normal life, death and after-death. Optional Rituals are not completely optional in that, after the initial, truly optional event, they become compulsory. They are always pure and auspicious.

Endnotes

1. Since First Head-Shaving and Loincloth Worship are for boys only, and Mock Marriage and Confinement are only for girls, each person experiences six Life-Cycle Rites throughout life, assuming they live long enough. As I described in relation to Bũgadyaḥ, the 'ten sacraments' (*dasakarma*) are also used to consecrate or re-consecrate a holy image (§10.7.1). They are also repeated at the third and fourth Old-Age Initiation thus rendering the person divine (Gellner 1992: 198).

2. The Pengu Daḥ also used to observe Cutting the Umbilical Cord (*pi dhyenegu*). A Pisaki Nay (woman of the Khadgi Butcher caste) performed this on the fourth day after birth. With the advent of modern medicine and the widespread adoption of hospital birthing this practice has fallen into disuse.

3. Nepali (1965: 92) states that Birth Purification is generally observed on the sixth day of the birth in the case of the first child and on the fourth day for subsequent children, but I found no such pattern.

4. Nepali describes the various taboos and customs surrounding birth and post-partum recovery (1965: 84ff.). My impression is that many of these customs have somewhat relaxed since he observed them.

5. Naming does not usually involve a ceremony, which contrasts the Newars with the Parbatiyās. The Joshi gives a horoscope name before Birth Purification. The familiar name is given any time before the second birthday. But according to Nepali, some high-caste Newars use the First Rice-Feeding ceremony as the occasion in emulation of the Parbatiyās (1965: 98).

6. The *thay bhu* is served on four occasions throughout a person's life: First Rice-Feeding, Mock Marriage, Marriage, and Old-Age Initiation.

7. Toffin's (1975b) description of a First Rice-Feeding in Pyangaon demonstrates just how different that community is from the core Newar community in the cities.

8. Although, see the description of the Munda tribe's Tree Marriage ritual by Pressler (1978: 112)

9. Until recently, when child-marriage was made illegal, Rājopādhyāya Brahmans practised child marriage. Since then they have taken to practising Ihi along with the rest of the Newar population (Allen 1987: 89).

10. See also Vergati (1995: 62-84) and Levy (1990: 665-70).

11. Vergati states that Ihi is staged between Māgh and Vaishākh (1995: 65). Other months such as Mārga, however, are also acceptable.

12. Nepali reports that Newars living in Birganj had ceased observing Ihi but when they found that marriage with Newars in the Valley was difficult they resumed (1965: 107). This practice continues today in Birganj.

13. Bārhā Tayegu means 'placing the barrier' (Gellner 1991: 113).

14. If girl dies during Confinement she is called 'Bāhrāsi' and buried in the ground under the house. One such house in Tichu Galli is regarded as haunted for this reason.

15. Allen (1987: 91) says this is done by the Nāpit Barber and his wife but I have not seen this.

16. This seems to be because the girl is now considered to be in the full power of her sexuality so that only the sun, as Kumar, can withstand it and not as Allen suggests (1987: 91) because of fear of the sun's power.

17. This is in marked contrast to the writings of several authors including Nepali (1965: 223) and(Toffin 1984: 120).

18. Nepali's assertion (1965: 230) that 'elopement is the most common method of obtaining a wife' is certainly not recognized by the Pengu Daḥ.

19. Swami Dayanand Bharati, a Tamil Brahman, informed me that this is also practised in South India.

20. The otherwise comprehensive list of the Rājkarnikār Samāj does not include the fourth *jãkwa* (Rajkarnikar, Narayana Govinda 2001).

21. Levy (1990: 677-8) refers to all as *rathārohan* (chariot ride). However, only on the third and fourth is the initiate pulled on a chariot around the locality in much the same way as he was taken on procession at his First Rice-Feeding (§3.4.4). On the first he is carried on a palanquin and on the second he is not taken on procession at all.

22. I regret that I have not had the privilege of observing this ritual. A Maharjan woman of Saugaḥ underwent this initiation in March 2003 but I only found out about it after the fact. The nature of it means that very few Newars have observed it either. There is a marked

lacuna of ethnographic writing on any of these initiations.

23. Bhaktapur Tamvaḥ differ slightly according to their context. At rites when *yajña* is performed (*ihi, bura jãkwa,* and *ghaḥsu*) seven specialists are needed: Brahman, Karmācārya, Prajāpati, Joshi, Citrakār, Shivācārya, and Karamjit.

24. Tāmrakārs no longer use Gwã cremation specialists as they used to because it was considered that they did not do a good job.

25. Sons must wear white for a full year. This is still compulsory for all Newars but is not so for many Parbatiyā Brahmans and Chetris who observe food restrictions the same as Newars but are not so concerned about the wearing of white after the 45th Day rite.

26. Nowadays performed by Vajrācārya priest, as the Ghaḥsu Kārmacārya no longer perform this (§3.4.4).

27. Nowadays the *gift* is 'given' to the Bāgmati River, as the Karamjit are no longer fulfilling this role. *Buddhamārgis* do not employ the Karamjit death specialist.

28. Kashinath Tamot, in a personal communication, informed me that during the Rana Era the period for mourning was reduced from 45 days to 13 days for all castes except Brahmans. This expedient was brought in because it was found that the bureaucracy was severely hampered by the longer period.

29. At the 45th day rite (which is more likely to actually be on the 45th day) the close patrilineal male relatives of a deceased Marikaḥmi cease to wear the white cap. One informant saw this as a defining difference between *shivamārgi* Tāmrakārs and *buddhamārgi* Rājkarnikārs.

30. A number of factors determine the length of the mourning period. Among these are gender, marital status, status vis-à-vis adulthood, and distance (§2.3). In this regard, though he is correct for all other relationships, Toffin (1984:389) erroneously states that Panauti Tamvaḥ observe 21 days mourning for brothers. In fact they observe '45' days as Tamvaḥ of other cities do.

31. It could just as well be in the reverse order. A three-dimensional diagram with universally perpendicular axes would present the data better but would be very difficult to reproduce on paper.

Bibliography

Works in South Asian Languages

Deep, D.K., 1995, 'Mataya: the Buddhist festival of lights', in D.R Shrestha and S.P. Lal Shrestha (eds.), *Nyaku Jātrā Matayāḥ*, Lalitpur: Manga Matayāḥ Vyavastha Samiti. (2052 vs) (Nepali)

Halawai, Lakshmi Bahadur, 2001, *Thukhe Nã Swaya Māli Ki?*, in N.G. Rajkarnikar (ed.), *Rājkarnikār Smārikā 2058*, Yala [Lalitpur]: Rājkarnikār Samāj. (Newar)

Pokharel, B., *et al.* (eds.), 1983, *Nepāli Brihat Shabdakosh*, Kathmandu: Royal Nepal Academy. (Nepali)

Paudel, Nayanath and Devi Prasad Lamshal (eds.), 1963, *Bhāshā Vamshāvali*, 2 vols., Kathmandu: Rāshtriya Pustakālaya. (2020 and 2023 vs) (Nepali)

Rajkarnikar, Ghana Shyam, 1995, *Samjhanāko Laharamā Laharindai Jā̃ndā (Reminiscences)*, Kathmandu: Shristi Rajkarnikar. (2052 vs) (Nepali)

Rajkarnikar, Narayana Govinda (ed.), 2001, *Rājkarnikār Smārikā 2058*, Yala [Lalitpur]: Rājkarnikār Samāj. (Newar, Nepali, and English)

Shakya, Hemraj, 1970, *Nepal Sanskritiya Mulukha*, Lalitpur: Candralakshmi Devi Shakya. (1089 ns) (Newar)

Shakya, Gyanu Raj, 1995, 'Matayāḥ Jātrā Ra Dha Bājā', in D.R. Shrestha and S.P. Lal Shrestha (eds.), *Nyaku Jātrā Matayāḥ*. Lalitpur: Manga Matayāḥ Vyavastha Samiti. (Nepali)

Sharma, Kunu 1961, *Kirtipatākā*, Yogi Naraharinath (trans.), Lalitpur: Jagadambhā Prakāshan. (2018 vs) (Sanskrit, Nepali)

Shrestha, Dilendra Raj and S.P. Lal Shrestha (eds.), 1995, *Nyaku Jātrā Matayāḥ*, Lalitpur: Manga Matayāḥ Vyavastha Samiti. (2052 vs) (Nepali)

Tamot, K., 1981, *Bhojpurāy Lugu Pulisa*, Yala [Lalitpur]: Sahityayā Mulukha. (1101 ns) (Newar)

_____ 1992, *Bhojpuryā Abhilekha*, Yala [Lalitpur]: Ram Bahadur Tulādhar Parivār. (1112 ns) (Newar)

_____ 2000, *A Dictionary of Classical Newari, Compiled from Manuscript Sources*, K.P. Malla (ed.), Cwasā Pāsā, Kathmandu: Nepal Bhasa Dictionary Committee. (Newar)

_____ n.d., Newari Lexicon (I. Alsop, ed.), in progress; URL: http://www2.pair.com/webart.musqllex (Newar).

Tamrakar, Nem Krishna with Kashinath Tamot, 1994, *Tāmrakārtay Sukuḥ Khalayā Kacāmacā*, Lalitpur: Nem Krishna Tamrakar. (1115 ns) (Newar)

Tuladhar, K. (ed.), 1996, *English–Nepalbhasa Wordbook*, Kathmandu: Bhulukha Publications. (1116 ns) (Newar)

Vajracarya, Dhanavajra, 1964, 'Mallakālamā desharakshako vyavasthā ra tyasaprati prajāko kartavya', *Purnima* 1(2):20-33. (2021 vs) (Nepali)

_____ 1973, *Licchavikālka Abhilekh*, Kirtipur, Nepal: Center for Nepal and Asian Studies, Tribhuvan University. (Sanskrit and Nepali)

Vajracarya, Dhanavajra and K.P. Malla (eds.), 1985, *The Gopalarajavamsavali*, Nepal Research Centre Publication 9, Wiesbaden: Franz Stiener Verlag. (Sanskrit, Nepali and English)

Vajracarya, Dhanavajra and Tek Bahadur Shrestha, 1980, *Pancalisana-Paddhatiko Aitihāsika Vivecana*, Kathmandu: Tribhuvan Visvavidyālāya. (2036 VS) (Nepali)

Works in other languages (English unless otherwise indicated)

Alexander, W. and A. Street, 1951 (1944), *Metals in the Service of Man*, Middlesex: Penguin Books.

Allen, M.R., 1973, 'Buddhism without Monks: The Vajrayana Religion of the Newars of the Kathmandu Valley', *South Asia* 2:1-14.

_____ 1987 (1975), *The Cult of Kumari: Virgin Worship in Nepal*, Kathmandu: Madhab Lal Maharjan.

Alsop, I. and J. Charlton, 1973, 'Image Casting in Oku Bahal', *Contributions to Nepalese Studies* 1:22-49.

Anderson, M.M., 1988 (1971), *The Festivals of Nepal*, Calcutta: Rupa.

Appadurai, A., 1986, 'Is Homo Hierarchicus?', *American Ethnologist* 13:745-61.

Asaoka, Koji, 1998, 'Nepaaru ni okeru Tekkiseisan to sono Gijutsu no Hen'you' (Changes of iron production and its techniques in Nepal), *Aija no Kinzoku-Shokunin-Bunka to Kindaika* (*Modernization and the Culture of Metalworkers in Asia*), Ajia Bunka Kenkyuu Bessatsu 8 (Asian Cultural Studies Special Issue 8):1-17. (Japanese)

Bajracharya, P.H., 1959, 'Newar marriage customs and festivals', *Southwestern Journal of Anthropology* 15:418-28.

Barré, V., P. Berger, L. Feveile and G. Toffin, 1981, *Panauti: une ville au Népal*, Collection Architectures, Paris: Berger-Levrault. (French)

Bernier, R.M., 1977, 'Wooden windows of Nepal: An illustrated analysis', *Artibus Asiae*, 39 (3/4):251-67.

Berreman, G.D., 1960, 'Caste in India and the United States', *American Journal of Sociology* 66:120-127.

_____ 1971, 'The Brahmanical view of caste', *Contributions to Indian Sociology* (NS) 5:16-23.

_____ 1972 (1963), *Hindus of the Himalayas*, 2nd. ed., revised and enlarged, Berkeley: University of California Press.

Béteille, A., 1964, 'A Note on the referents of caste', *European Journal of Sociology* 5:130-4.

Bharati, A., 1965, *The Tantric Tradition*, New Delhi: B. Publications.

Biardeau, M., 1989, *Histoires de Poteaux: Variations Védiques autour de la Déesse Hindoue*, Paris: École Française d'Extrême Orient. (French)

Bista, D.B., 1991, *Fatalism and Development: Nepal's Struggle for Modernisation*, New Delhi: Orient Longman.

_____ 1996 (1966), *People of Nepal*, 6th ed., Kathmandu: Ratna Pustak Bhandar.

Bista, K.B., 1972, *Le Culte du Kuldevata au Nepal en particulier chez certains Ksatri de la vallée de Kathmandu*, Paris: CNRS (National Centre for Scientific Research). (French)

Bouglé, C., 1971 (1908), *Essays on the Caste System* (*Essais sur le régime des castes*), translated with an introduction by D.F. Pocock, Cambridge, UK: Cambridge University Press.

Bouillier, V. and G. Toffin (eds.), 1989, *Prêtrise, pouvoirs et autorité en Himalaya, Purushārtha* 12, Paris: Editions de l'EHESS. (French)

Brown, P., 1997 (1912), *Picturesque Nepal*, Delhi: Pilgrims Books Pvt. Ltd.

Burkert, C., 1997, 'Defining Maithil identity: Who is in charge?', in D.N. Gellner, J. Pfaff-Czarnecka and J. Whelpton (eds.), *Nationalism and Ethnicity in a Hindu Kingdom.* Amsterdam: Harwood Academic Publishers.

Burleigh, P., 1976, 'A chronology of the later kings of Patan', *Kailash–Journal of Himalayan Studies* 4(1):21-71.

CBS, 2002, *Population Census, 2001 National Report*, Kathmandu: Central Bureau of Statistics.

Chattopadhyay, K.P., 1980, *An Essay on the History of Newar Culture*, Kathmandu: Educational Enterprises (reprints from *Journal of the Asiatic Society of Bengal* 19 [10] [1923]:465-560).

Coon, E., 1989, 'Possessing power: Ajima and her medium', *Himalayan Research Bulletin* 9(1):1-9.

Dahal, D.R., 1979, 'Tribalism as an incongruous concept in modern Nepal', in M. Gaborieau and A. Thorner (eds.), *Asie du Sud: Traditions et Changements*, Paris: Centre d'Études de l'Inde et de l'Asie du Sud.

_____ 2003, 'Social composition of the Population: Caste/ethnicity and religion in Nepal', in *Population Monograph of Nepal*, Kathmandu: Central Bureau of Statistics.

Deep, D.K., 1999, *The Nepal Festivals*, Kathmandu: Ratna Pustak Bhandar.

Dirks, N.B., 1987, *The Hollow Crown: Ethnohistory of an Indian Kingdom*, Cambridge: Cambridge University Press.

Doherty, V.S., 1978, 'Notes on the origins of the Newars of the Kathmandu Valley of Nepal', in Fisher (ed.), *Himalayan Anthropology: The Indo-Tibetan Interface*, The Hague and Paris: Mouton.

Dougherty, L.M., 1986, 'Sita and the goddess: A case study of a woman healer in Nepal', *Contributions to Nepalese Studies* 14(1):25-36.

Dubois, Abbé J.A., 1897, *Hindu Manners, Customs and Ceremonies*, H.K. Beauchamp (trans.), Oxford: Oxford University Press.

Dumont, L., 1964, 'Marriage in India: The present state of the question: Postscript to Part I: Nayar and Newar', *Contributions to Indian Sociology* 7:77-98.

_____ 1980 (1972), *Homo Hierarchicus: The Caste System and Its Implications* (translated by M. Sainsbury, L. Dumont and B. Gulati), Chicago and London: University of Chicago Press.

Dumont, L. and D. Pocock, 1957, 'For a sociology of India', *Contributions to Indian Sociology* 1:7-22.

_____ 1959, 'Pure and impure', *Contributions to Indian Sociology* 3:9-39.

Dutt, B.B., 1977 (1925), *Town Planning in Ancient India*, New Delhi: New Asian Publishers.

Eck, D., 1993 (1983), *Banāras: City of Light*, New Delhi: Penguin Books India.

Evans-Pritchard, E.E., 1940, *The Nuer: A Description of the Modes of Livelihood and Political Institutions of a Nilotic People*, Oxford: Clarendon Press.

_____ 1951, *Social Anthropology*, London: Cohen and West.

Fisher, J.F. (ed.), 1978, *Himalayan Anthropology: The Indo-Tibetan Interface*, The Hague and Paris: Mouton.

Fuller, C.J., 1989, 'Misconceiving the grain heap: A critique of the concept of the Indian jajmāni system', in J. Parry and M. Bloch (eds), *Money and the Morality of Exchange*, Cambridge: Cambridge University Press.

_____ 1992, *The Camphor Flame: Popular Hinduism and Society in India*, Princeton, NJ: University Press.

_____ 1996, *Caste Today*, Delhi: Oxford University Press.

Fürer-Haimendorf, C. von, 1956, 'Elements of Newar social structure', *Journal of the Royal Anthropological Institute* 86(2):15-38.

_____ 1957, 'The inter-relations of castes and ethnic groups in Nepal', *Bulletin of the School of Oriental and African Studies* 20:243-53.

_____ 1962, 'Caste in the multi-ethnic society of Nepal', *Contributions to Indian Sociology* 6:12-32.

_____ (ed.), 1966, *Caste and Kin in Nepal, India and Ceylon*, Bombay: Asia Publishing House.

Gaborieau, M., 1982, 'Les Fêtes, le temps et l'éspace: structure du calendrier hindou dans sa version indo-népalais', *L'Homme* 22(3):11-30. (French)

Gajurel, C.L. and K.K. Vaidya, 1984, *Traditional Arts and Crafts of Nepal*, New Delhi: S. Chand.

Geertz, C., 1973, *The Interpretation of Cultures*, New York: Basic Books.

Gellner, D.N., 1982, 'Max Weber, capitalism and the religion of India', *Sociology* 16(4):526-43.

_____ 1984, 'Cities and mandalas (review of Barré *et al.*)', *Contributions to Nepalese Studies* 12:115-26.

_____ 1986, 'Language, caste, religion and territory: Newar identity ancient and modern', *European Journal of Sociology* 27: 102-48.

_____ 1987a, *Monk, Householder and Priest: Newar Buddhism and Its Hierarchy of Ritual*', D.Phil, University of Oxford.

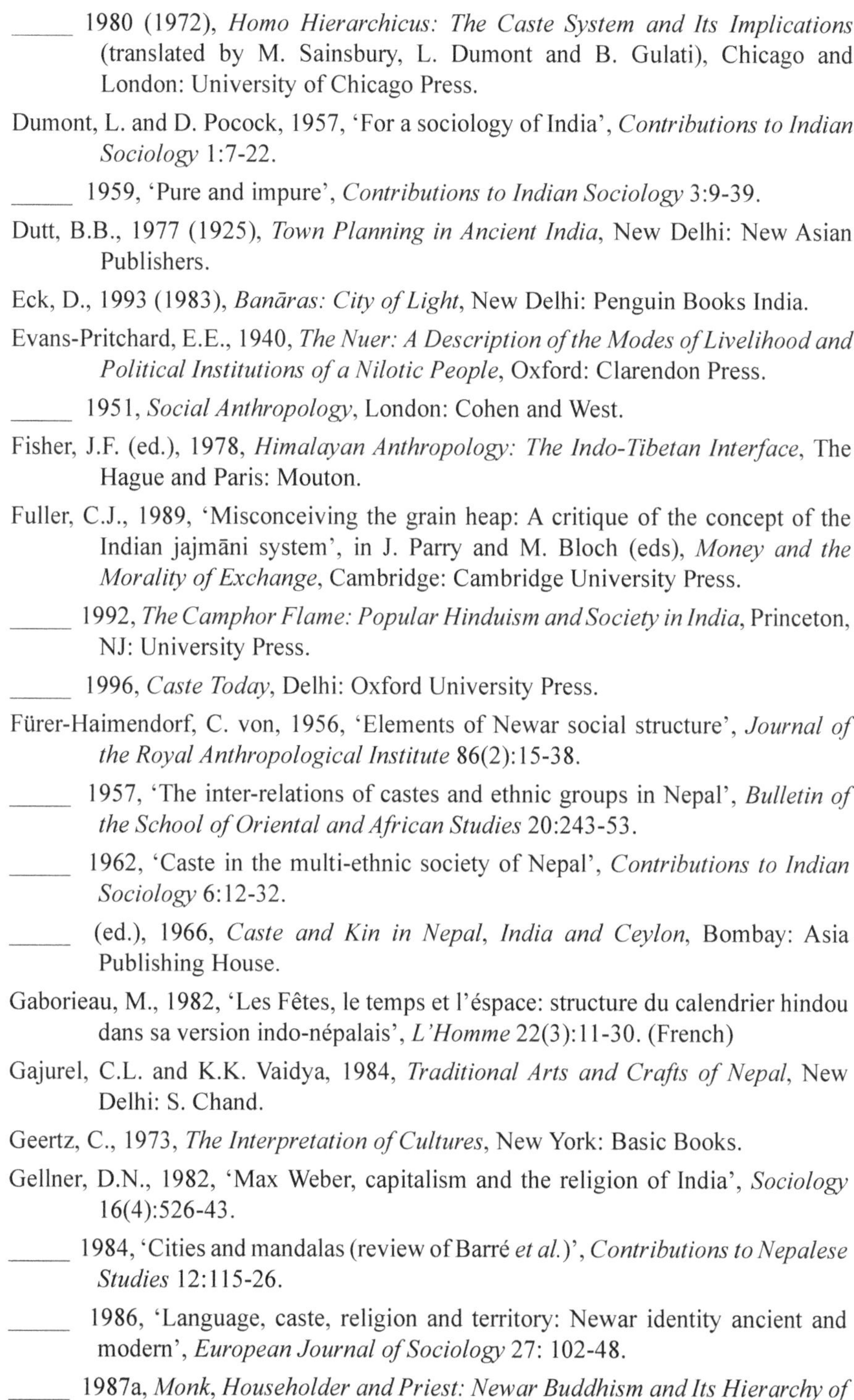

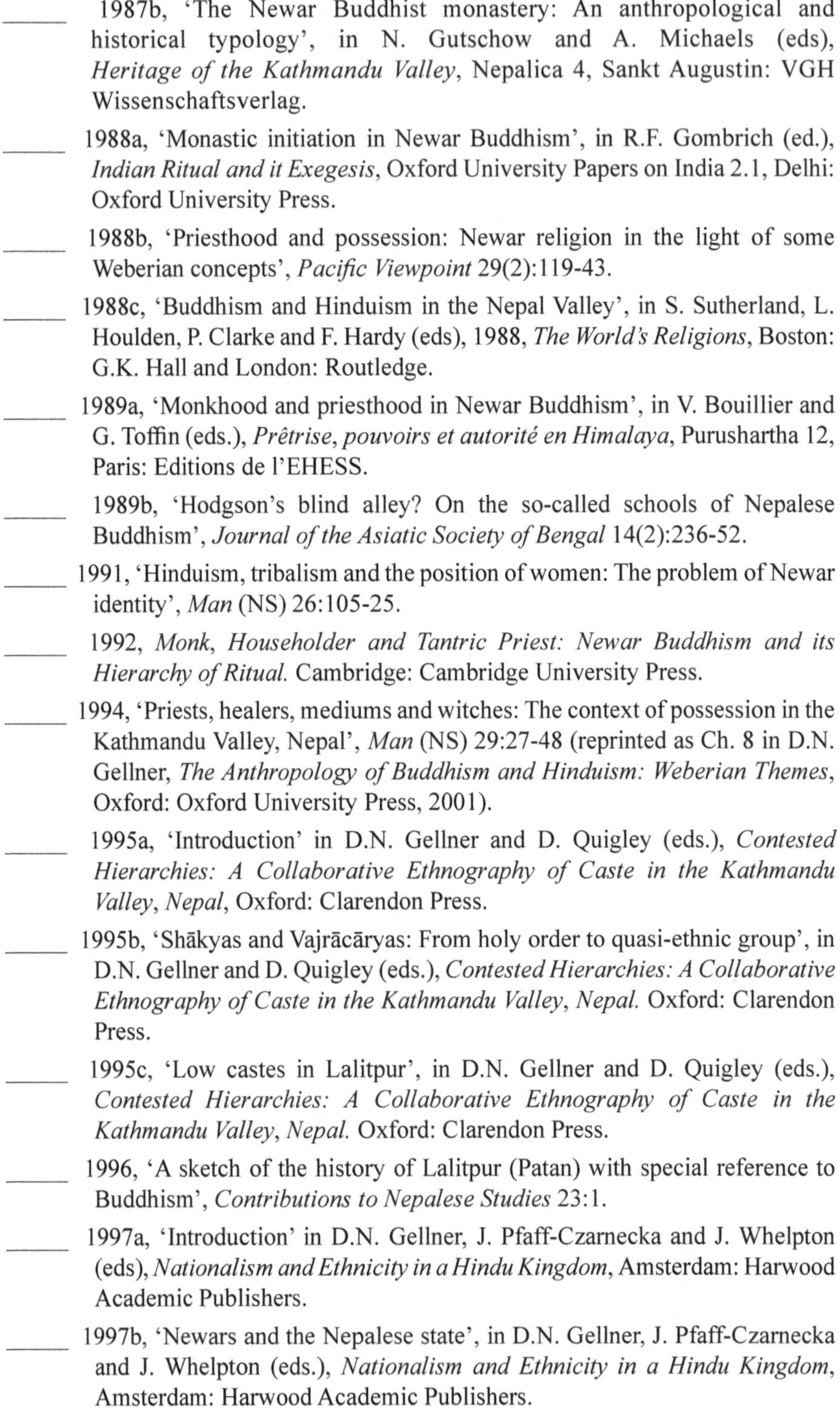

——— 1987b, 'The Newar Buddhist monastery: An anthropological and historical typology', in N. Gutschow and A. Michaels (eds), *Heritage of the Kathmandu Valley*, Nepalica 4, Sankt Augustin: VGH Wissenschaftsverlag.

——— 1988a, 'Monastic initiation in Newar Buddhism', in R.F. Gombrich (ed.), *Indian Ritual and it Exegesis*, Oxford University Papers on India 2.1, Delhi: Oxford University Press.

——— 1988b, 'Priesthood and possession: Newar religion in the light of some Weberian concepts', *Pacific Viewpoint* 29(2):119-43.

——— 1988c, 'Buddhism and Hinduism in the Nepal Valley', in S. Sutherland, L. Houlden, P. Clarke and F. Hardy (eds), 1988, *The World's Religions*, Boston: G.K. Hall and London: Routledge.

——— 1989a, 'Monkhood and priesthood in Newar Buddhism', in V. Bouillier and G. Toffin (eds.), *Prêtrise, pouvoirs et autorité en Himalaya*, Purushartha 12, Paris: Editions de l'EHESS.

——— 1989b, 'Hodgson's blind alley? On the so-called schools of Nepalese Buddhism', *Journal of the Asiatic Society of Bengal* 14(2):236-52.

——— 1991, 'Hinduism, tribalism and the position of women: The problem of Newar identity', *Man* (NS) 26:105-25.

——— 1992, *Monk, Householder and Tantric Priest: Newar Buddhism and its Hierarchy of Ritual.* Cambridge: Cambridge University Press.

——— 1994, 'Priests, healers, mediums and witches: The context of possession in the Kathmandu Valley, Nepal', *Man* (NS) 29:27-48 (reprinted as Ch. 8 in D.N. Gellner, *The Anthropology of Buddhism and Hinduism: Weberian Themes*, Oxford: Oxford University Press, 2001).

——— 1995a, 'Introduction' in D.N. Gellner and D. Quigley (eds.), *Contested Hierarchies: A Collaborative Ethnography of Caste in the Kathmandu Valley, Nepal*, Oxford: Clarendon Press.

——— 1995b, 'Shākyas and Vajrācāryas: From holy order to quasi-ethnic group', in D.N. Gellner and D. Quigley (eds.), *Contested Hierarchies: A Collaborative Ethnography of Caste in the Kathmandu Valley, Nepal.* Oxford: Clarendon Press.

——— 1995c, 'Low castes in Lalitpur', in D.N. Gellner and D. Quigley (eds.), *Contested Hierarchies: A Collaborative Ethnography of Caste in the Kathmandu Valley, Nepal.* Oxford: Clarendon Press.

——— 1996, 'A sketch of the history of Lalitpur (Patan) with special reference to Buddhism', *Contributions to Nepalese Studies* 23:1.

——— 1997a, 'Introduction' in D.N. Gellner, J. Pfaff-Czarnecka and J. Whelpton (eds), *Nationalism and Ethnicity in a Hindu Kingdom*, Amsterdam: Harwood Academic Publishers.

——— 1997b, 'Newars and the Nepalese state', in D.N. Gellner, J. Pfaff-Czarnecka and J. Whelpton (eds.), *Nationalism and Ethnicity in a Hindu Kingdom*, Amsterdam: Harwood Academic Publishers.

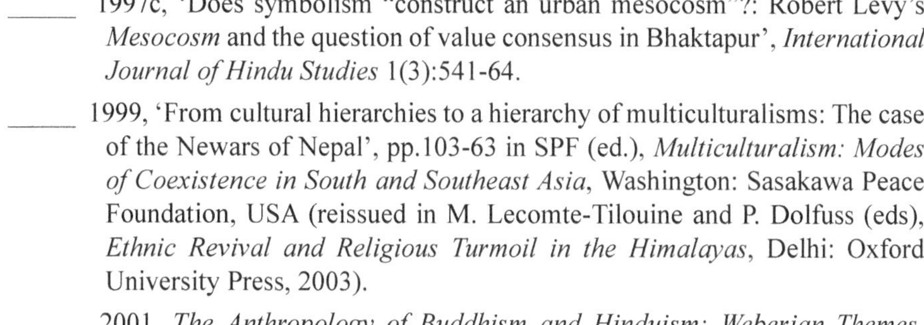

_____ 1997c, 'Does symbolism "construct an urban mesocosm"?: Robert Levy's *Mesocosm* and the question of value consensus in Bhaktapur', *International Journal of Hindu Studies* 1(3):541-64.

_____ 1999, 'From cultural hierarchies to a hierarchy of multiculturalisms: The case of the Newars of Nepal', pp.103-63 in SPF (ed.), *Multiculturalism: Modes of Coexistence in South and Southeast Asia*, Washington: Sasakawa Peace Foundation, USA (reissued in M. Lecomte-Tilouine and P. Dolfuss (eds), *Ethnic Revival and Religious Turmoil in the Himalayas*, Delhi: Oxford University Press, 2003).

_____ 2001, *The Anthropology of Buddhism and Hinduism: Weberian Themes*, Oxford: Oxford University Press.

Gellner, D.N., J. Pfaff-Czarnecka and J. Whelpton (eds), 1997, *Nationalism and Ethnicity in a Hindu Kingdom*, Amsterdam: Harwood Academic Publishers.

Gellner, D.N. and R.P. Pradhan, 1995, 'Urban peasants: The Maharjans (Jyāpu) of Kathmandu and Lalitpur', in D.N. Gellner and D. Quigley (eds.), *Contested Hierarchies: A Collaborative Ethnography of Caste in the Kathmandu Valley, Nepal.* Oxford: Clarendon Press.

Gellner, D.N. and D. Quigley (eds.), 1995, *Contested Hierarchies: A Collaborative Ethnography of Caste in the Kathmandu Valley, Nepal*, Oxford: Clarendon Press.

Gellner, D.N. and U.S. Shrestha, 1993, 'Portrait of a Tantric healer: A preliminary report on research into ritual curing in the Kathmandu Valley', in G. Toffin (ed.), *Nepal, Past and Present*, Delhi: Sterling Publishers Pvt. Ltd. (reprinted as Ch.9 in D.N. Gellner, *The Anthropology of Buddhism and Hinduism: Weberian Themes.* Oxford: Oxford University Press, 2001).

Giuseppe, Father, 1801, 'An account of the kingdom of Nepal 1768-71', *Asiatick Researches* 2:307-22.

Gutschow, N., and M.V. Bajracharya, 1977, 'Ritual as mediator of space in Kathmandu, *Journal of the Nepal Research Center* 1:1-10.

Good, A., 1982, 'The actor and the act: Categories of prestation in South India', *Man* (NS) 17:23-41.

Gould, H.A., 1964, 'A Jajmāni system of North India: Its structure, magnitude and meaning', *Ethnology* 3:12-41.

Grandin, I., 1989, *Music and Media in Local Life: Music Practice in a Newar Neighbourhood in Nepal*, Linköping Studies in Arts and Sciences 41, Linköping, Sweden: Linköping University, Department of Communications Studies.

Greenwold, S.M., 1975, 'Kingship and caste', *European Journal of Sociology* 16(1):49-75.

_____ 1978 (1974), 'The role of the priest in Newar society', in J.F. Fisher (ed.), *Himalayan Anthropology: The Indo-Tibetan Interface*, The Hague and Paris: Mouton (previously published as 'Buddhist Brahmans', *European Journal of Sociology* 15:101-23, 1974).

Gurung, H., 1997, 'State and society in Nepal', in D.N. Gellner, J. Pfaff-Czarnecka and J. Whelpton (eds), *Nationalism and Ethnicity in a Hindu Kingdom*, Amsterdam: Harwood Academic Publishers.

Gutschow, N., 1982, *Stadtraum und Ritual der Newarischen Städte im Kathmandu-Tal: Eine Architektur-Anthropologische Untersuchung*, Stuttgart: Kohlhammer. (German)

Gutschow, N. and G.M. Basukala, 1987, 'The Navadurga of Bhaktapur–Spatial Implications of an Urban Ritual', in N. Gutschow and A. Michaels (eds.), *Heritage of the Kathmandu Valley*, Nepalica 4, Sankt Augustin: VGH Wissenschaftsverlag.

Gutschow, N. and B. Kölver, 1975, *Ordered Space, Concepts and Functions in a Town in Nepal*, Wiesbaden: Franz Steiner.

Gutschow, N. and A. Michaels (eds), 1987, *Heritage of the Kathmandu Valley*, Nepalica 4, Sankt Augustin: VGH Wissenschaftsverlag.

Hale, A., 1986, 'User's guide to the Newari dictionary', in T.L. Manandhar, *Newari-English Dictionary* (edited by A. Vergati), Delhi: École Francaise d'Extrême Orient and Agam Kala Prakashan.

Hamilton (Buchanan), Francis, 1838, *Eastern India*, 3 vols., London: Wm. H. Allen.

_____ 1971 (1819), *An Account of the Kingdom of Nepal*, Bibliotheca Himalayica 10, New Delhi: Manjushri Publishing House (first published by Constable, Edinburgh, 1819).

Harper, E.B., 1959, 'A Hindu village pantheon', *Southwestern Journal of Anthropology* 15:227-34.

Hasrat, B.J., 1970, *History of Nepal, As Told by Its Own and Contemporary Chroniclers*, Hoshiarpur, Punjab: V.V. Research Institute Book Agency.

Heesterman, J.C. 1993. *The Broken World of Sacrifice: An Essay in Ancient Indian Ritual*, Chicago & London: The University of Chicago Press.

Hocart, A. M., 1950 (1938), *Caste: A Comparative Study*, London: Methuen.

Hodgson, B.H., 1880, *Miscellaneous Essays Relating to Indian Subjects*, 2 vols, London: Trübner and Co.

_____ 1972 (1874), *Essays on the Languages, Literature and Religion of Nepal and Tibet*, Bibliotheca Himalayica 2.7, Delhi: Manjushri Publishing House.

Hoek, B. van den, 1993, 'Kathmandu as a sacrificial arena', pp. 360-77 in Peter J.M. Nas (ed.), *Urban Symposium*, Leiden, New York and Köln: E.J. Brill.

Hoek, B. van den, D. Kolff and M. Oort (eds), 1992, *Ritual, State and History in South Asia*, Leiden: E.J. Brill.

Hoek, B. van den and B.G. Shrestha, 1992, 'Guardians of the royal goddess: Daitya and Kumar as the protectors of Taleju Bhavani of Kathmandu', *Contributions to Nepalese Studies* 19(2):191-222.

Höfer, A., 1979, *The Caste Hierarchy and the State in Nepal: A Study of the Muluki Ain of 1854*, Khumbu Himal Series 13(2):25-240, Innsbruck: Universitätsverlag Wagner (reprinted by Himal Books, Kathmandu, 2004).

Ibbetson, D.C.J., 1883, *Report on the Punjab Census of 1881*, Calcutta: Superintendent of Government Printing.

Inden, R.B., 1986, 'Orientalist constructions of India', *Modern Asian Studies* 20:401-46.

Ishii, H., 1978, 'Structure and change of a Newari festival organisation', in J. F. Fisher (ed.), *Himalayan Anthropology: The Indo-Tibetan Interface*, The Hague and Paris: Mouton.

_____ 1980, 'Recent economic changes in a Newar village', *Contributions to Nepalese Studies* 8:157-80.

_____ 1987, 'Social change in a Newar village', in N. Gutschow and A. Michaels (eds), *Heritage of the Kathmandu Valley*, Nepalica 4, Sankt Augustin: VGH Wissenschaftsverlag.

_____ 1995, 'Caste and kinship in a Newar village', in D.N. Gellner and D. Quigley (eds), *Contested Hierarchies: A Collaborative Ethnography of Caste in the Kathmandu Valley, Nepal*, Oxford: Clarendon Press.

_____ 2001, 'Japanese studies on the Himalayas and Nepal (Social Sciences and Humanities, 1900-2000)', *European Bulletin of Himalayan Research* 20(1):165-208.

Jameson, M.H., 1997, 'Sacred space and the city: Greece and Bhaktapur', *International Journal of Hindu Studies* 1(3):485-99.

Kane, P.V., 1968-77 (1941), *History of Dharmashāstra*, 2nd ed., 5 vols, Poona: Bhandarkar Oriental Research Institute.

Ketkar, S.V., 1909, *The History of Caste in India*, vol. 1, Ithaca, NY: Taylor and Carpenter.

Khatry, P.K., 1996, 'Rain for the drought: An anthropological inquiry into the structure of a Buddhist festival in Kathmandu', *Contributions to Nepalese Studies* 23(1):89-108.

Kierkegaard, S., 1954 (1843), *Fear and Trembling*, rev. ed., New York: Doubleday.

Klostermaier, K.K., 1990 (1989), *A Survey of Hinduism*, New Delhi: Munshiram Manoharlal (first published by the State University of New York Press, Albany, 1989).

Kooij, K.R., van, 1977, 'The iconography of the Buddhist wood-carvings in a Newar Buddhist monastery in Kathmandu (Chushya-Bāhā)', *Journal of the Nepal Research Center* 1:39-82.

Kolenda, P.M., 1968, 'Religion, caste, and family structure: A comparative study of the Indian joint family', in M.B. Singer and B.S. Cohn (eds), *Structure and Change in Indian Society*, Chicago: Aldine.

Kölver, B., 1976, 'A ritual map from Nepal', *Folia Rara* 65:68-80.

Lall, Kesar, 1994, *Tales of Three Brothers*, Kathmandu: Ratna Pustak Bhandar.

Landon, P., 1976 (1928), *Nepal*, Bibliotheca Himalayica 16, Kathmandu: Ratna Pustak Bhandar.

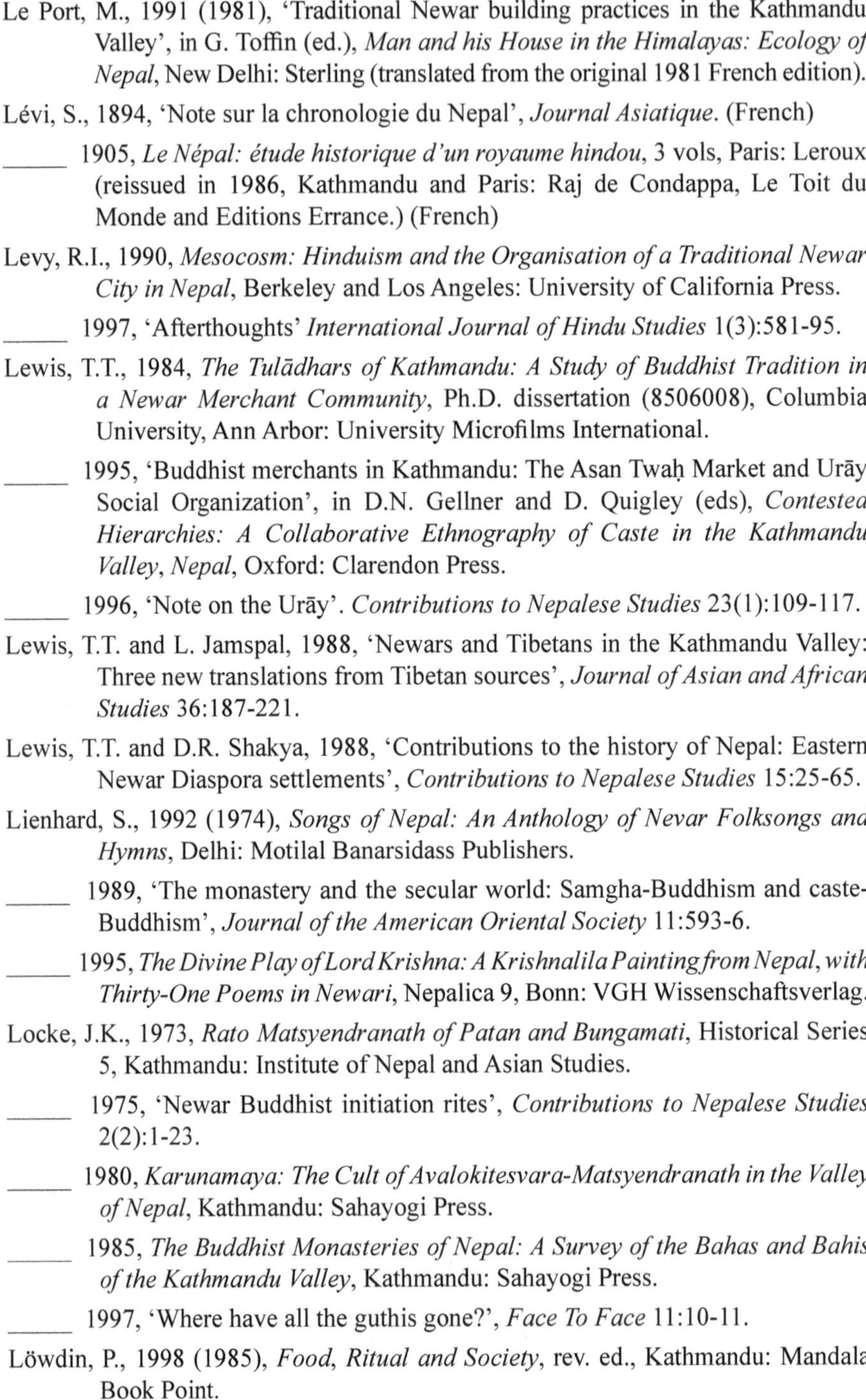

Le Port, M., 1991 (1981), 'Traditional Newar building practices in the Kathmandu Valley', in G. Toffin (ed.), *Man and his House in the Himalayas: Ecology of Nepal*, New Delhi: Sterling (translated from the original 1981 French edition).

Lévi, S., 1894, 'Note sur la chronologie du Nepal', *Journal Asiatique*. (French)

_____ 1905, *Le Népal: étude historique d'un royaume hindou*, 3 vols, Paris: Leroux (reissued in 1986, Kathmandu and Paris: Raj de Condappa, Le Toit du Monde and Editions Errance.) (French)

Levy, R.I., 1990, *Mesocosm: Hinduism and the Organisation of a Traditional Newar City in Nepal*, Berkeley and Los Angeles: University of California Press.

_____ 1997, 'Afterthoughts' *International Journal of Hindu Studies* 1(3):581-95.

Lewis, T.T., 1984, *The Tulādhars of Kathmandu: A Study of Buddhist Tradition in a Newar Merchant Community*, Ph.D. dissertation (8506008), Columbia University, Ann Arbor: University Microfilms International.

_____ 1995, 'Buddhist merchants in Kathmandu: The Asan Twaḥ Market and Urāy Social Organization', in D.N. Gellner and D. Quigley (eds), *Contested Hierarchies: A Collaborative Ethnography of Caste in the Kathmandu Valley, Nepal*, Oxford: Clarendon Press.

_____ 1996, 'Note on the Urāy'. *Contributions to Nepalese Studies* 23(1):109-117.

Lewis, T.T. and L. Jamspal, 1988, 'Newars and Tibetans in the Kathmandu Valley: Three new translations from Tibetan sources', *Journal of Asian and African Studies* 36:187-221.

Lewis, T.T. and D.R. Shakya, 1988, 'Contributions to the history of Nepal: Eastern Newar Diaspora settlements', *Contributions to Nepalese Studies* 15:25-65.

Lienhard, S., 1992 (1974), *Songs of Nepal: An Anthology of Nevar Folksongs and Hymns*, Delhi: Motilal Banarsidass Publishers.

_____ 1989, 'The monastery and the secular world: Samgha-Buddhism and caste-Buddhism', *Journal of the American Oriental Society* 11:593-6.

_____ 1995, *The Divine Play of Lord Krishna: A Krishnalila Painting from Nepal, with Thirty-One Poems in Newari*, Nepalica 9, Bonn: VGH Wissenschaftsverlag.

Locke, J.K., 1973, *Rato Matsyendranath of Patan and Bungamati*, Historical Series 5, Kathmandu: Institute of Nepal and Asian Studies.

_____ 1975, 'Newar Buddhist initiation rites', *Contributions to Nepalese Studies* 2(2):1-23.

_____ 1980, *Karunamaya: The Cult of Avalokitesvara-Matsyendranath in the Valley of Nepal*, Kathmandu: Sahayogi Press.

_____ 1985, *The Buddhist Monasteries of Nepal: A Survey of the Bahas and Bahis of the Kathmandu Valley*, Kathmandu: Sahayogi Press.

_____ 1997, 'Where have all the guthis gone?', *Face To Face* 11:10-11.

Löwdin, P., 1998 (1985), *Food, Ritual and Society*, rev. ed., Kathmandu: Mandala Book Point.

Lutgendorf, P., 1989, 'Rām's story in Shiva's city: Public arenas and private patronage', in Sandria B. Frietag (ed.), *Culture and Power in Banāras:*

Community, Performance, and Environment, 1800-1980, Berkeley: University of California Press.

Malla, K.P., 1983, 'River-names of the Nepal Valley: A study in cultural annexation', *Contributions to Nepalese Studies* 10(1-2):57-68.

_____ 1985, 'Introduction', in D. Vajracarya and K.P. Malla (eds) *The Gopalarajavamsavali*, Nepal Research Centre Publication 9, Wiesbaden: Franz Stiener Verlag.

_____ (ed.) 1989, *Nepal: Perspectives on Continuity and Change*, Kathmandu: Center for Nepal and Asian Studies, Tribhuvan University.

_____ 1996, 'The profane names of the sacred hillocks', *Contributions to Nepalese Studies* 23(1):1-9.

_____ 1997, 'I am helpless against the modern trends', *Face to Face* 11:12-15.

Manandhar, T.L., 1986, *Newari-English Dictionary* (edited by A. Vergati), Delhi: École Francaise d'Extrême Orient and Agam Kala Prakashan.

Marriott, M. and R.B. Inden, 1985, 'Social stratification: Caste', *Encyclopaedia Britannica*, 15th ed., 27:348-56 (first published in 1974).

Mayer, A.C., 1960, *Caste and Kinship in Central India: A Village and Its Region*, London: Routledge and Kegan Paul.

Messerschmidt, D.A., 1982, '*Miteri*: Ficture kin ties that bind', *Kailash* 9:5-44.

Michaels, A., 1987, 'The Trisulyātrā in Deopātan and its legends', in N. Gutschow and A. Michaels (eds), *Heritage of the Kathmandu Valley*, Nepalica 4, Sankt Augustin: VGH Wissenschaftsverlag.

Mikesell, S.L., 1993, 'A critique of Levy's theory of the urban mesocosm', review article, *Contributions to Nepalese Studies* 20 (2): 23 1-54.

Minami, Makito, 1998, 'Nepaaru ni okeru Shokugyou Kaasuto no Bunpu to Doukaji-gyou no Tenkai' (The spread of the service caste population and the development of coppersmithing in Nepal), *Aija no Kinzoku-Shokunin-Bunka to Kindaika (Modernization and the Culture of Metalworkers in Asia)*, Ajia Bunka Kenkyuu Bessatsu 8 (Asian Cultural Studies Special Issue 8):43-70. (Japanese)

Nepali, G.S., 1965, *The Newars: An Ethno-Sociological Study of a Himalayan Community*, Bombay: United Asia Publications.

_____ 1987, 'Changes in rigidity and flexibility of caste in the Kathmandu Valley', in N. Gutschow and A. Michaels (eds), *Heritage of the Kathmandu Valley*, Nepalica 4, Sankt Augustin: VGH Wissenschaftsverlag.

Oldenberg H., 1919, *Die Weltanschaung der Brahmana-Texte*, Göttingen: Bandenhoeck and Ruprecht. (German)

Oldfield, H.A., 1981 (1880), *Sketches from Nepal*, 2 vols, Delhi: Cosmo Publications.

Ortner, S.B., 1978, *Sherpas through their Rituals*, Cambridge: Cambridge University Press.

OUP, 1997, *School Atlas for Nepal*, New Delhi: Oxford University Press.

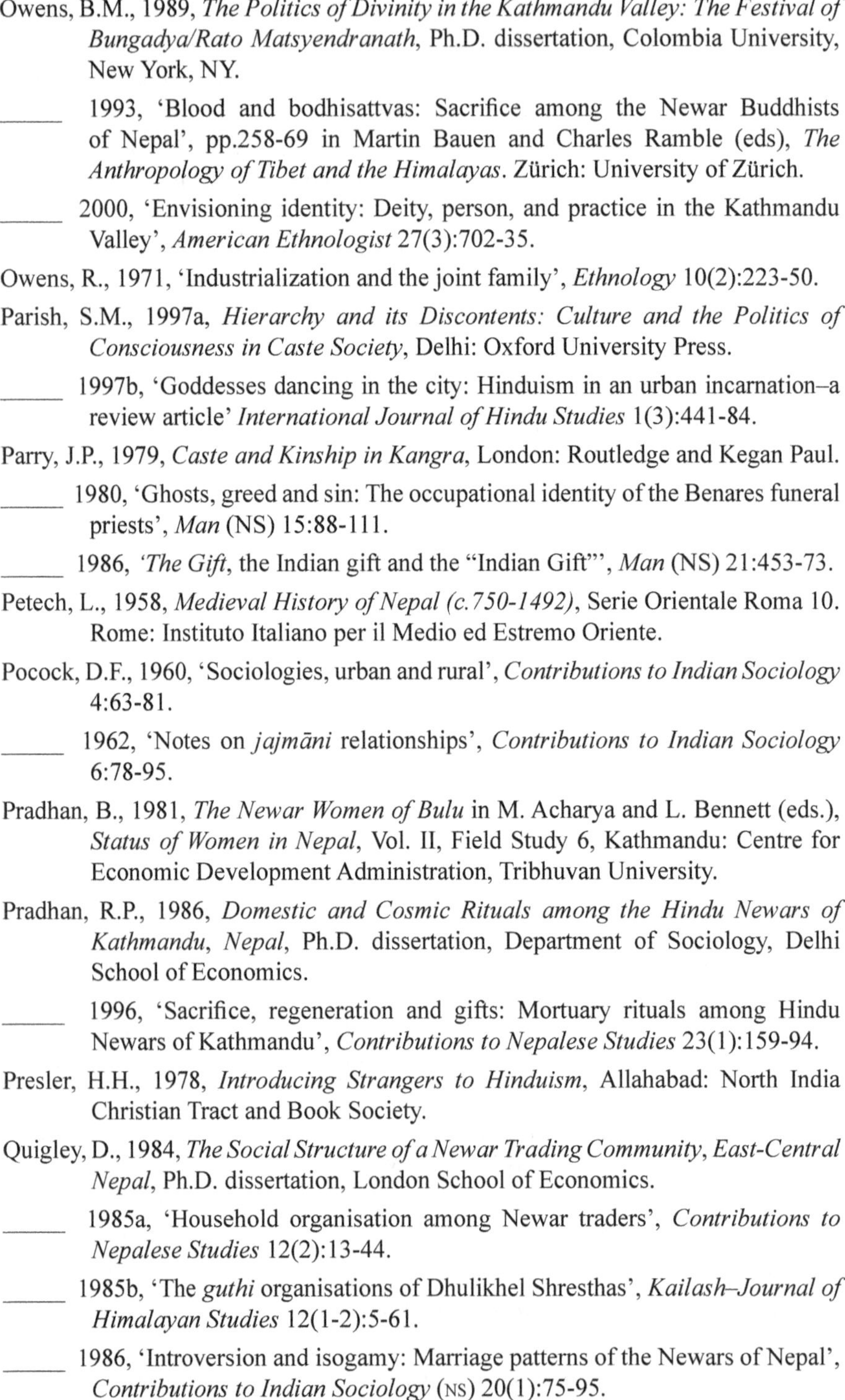

Owens, B.M., 1989, *The Politics of Divinity in the Kathmandu Valley: The Festival of Bungadya/Rato Matsyendranath*, Ph.D. dissertation, Colombia University, New York, NY.

_____ 1993, 'Blood and bodhisattvas: Sacrifice among the Newar Buddhists of Nepal', pp.258-69 in Martin Bauen and Charles Ramble (eds), *The Anthropology of Tibet and the Himalayas*. Zürich: University of Zürich.

_____ 2000, 'Envisioning identity: Deity, person, and practice in the Kathmandu Valley', *American Ethnologist* 27(3):702-35.

Owens, R., 1971, 'Industrialization and the joint family', *Ethnology* 10(2):223-50.

Parish, S.M., 1997a, *Hierarchy and its Discontents: Culture and the Politics of Consciousness in Caste Society*, Delhi: Oxford University Press.

_____ 1997b, 'Goddesses dancing in the city: Hinduism in an urban incarnation–a review article' *International Journal of Hindu Studies* 1(3):441-84.

Parry, J.P., 1979, *Caste and Kinship in Kangra*, London: Routledge and Kegan Paul.

_____ 1980, 'Ghosts, greed and sin: The occupational identity of the Benares funeral priests', *Man* (NS) 15:88-111.

_____ 1986, '*The Gift*, the Indian gift and the "Indian Gift"', *Man* (NS) 21:453-73.

Petech, L., 1958, *Medieval History of Nepal (c.750-1492)*, Serie Orientale Roma 10. Rome: Instituto Italiano per il Medio ed Estremo Oriente.

Pocock, D.F., 1960, 'Sociologies, urban and rural', *Contributions to Indian Sociology* 4:63-81.

_____ 1962, 'Notes on *jajmāni* relationships', *Contributions to Indian Sociology* 6:78-95.

Pradhan, B., 1981, *The Newar Women of Bulu* in M. Acharya and L. Bennett (eds.), *Status of Women in Nepal*, Vol. II, Field Study 6, Kathmandu: Centre for Economic Development Administration, Tribhuvan University.

Pradhan, R.P., 1986, *Domestic and Cosmic Rituals among the Hindu Newars of Kathmandu, Nepal*, Ph.D. dissertation, Department of Sociology, Delhi School of Economics.

_____ 1996, 'Sacrifice, regeneration and gifts: Mortuary rituals among Hindu Newars of Kathmandu', *Contributions to Nepalese Studies* 23(1):159-94.

Presler, H.H., 1978, *Introducing Strangers to Hinduism*, Allahabad: North India Christian Tract and Book Society.

Quigley, D., 1984, *The Social Structure of a Newar Trading Community, East-Central Nepal*, Ph.D. dissertation, London School of Economics.

_____ 1985a, 'Household organisation among Newar traders', *Contributions to Nepalese Studies* 12(2):13-44.

_____ 1985b, 'The *guthi* organisations of Dhulikhel Shresthas', *Kailash–Journal of Himalayan Studies* 12(1-2):5-61.

_____ 1986, 'Introversion and isogamy: Marriage patterns of the Newars of Nepal', *Contributions to Indian Sociology* (NS) 20(1):75-95.

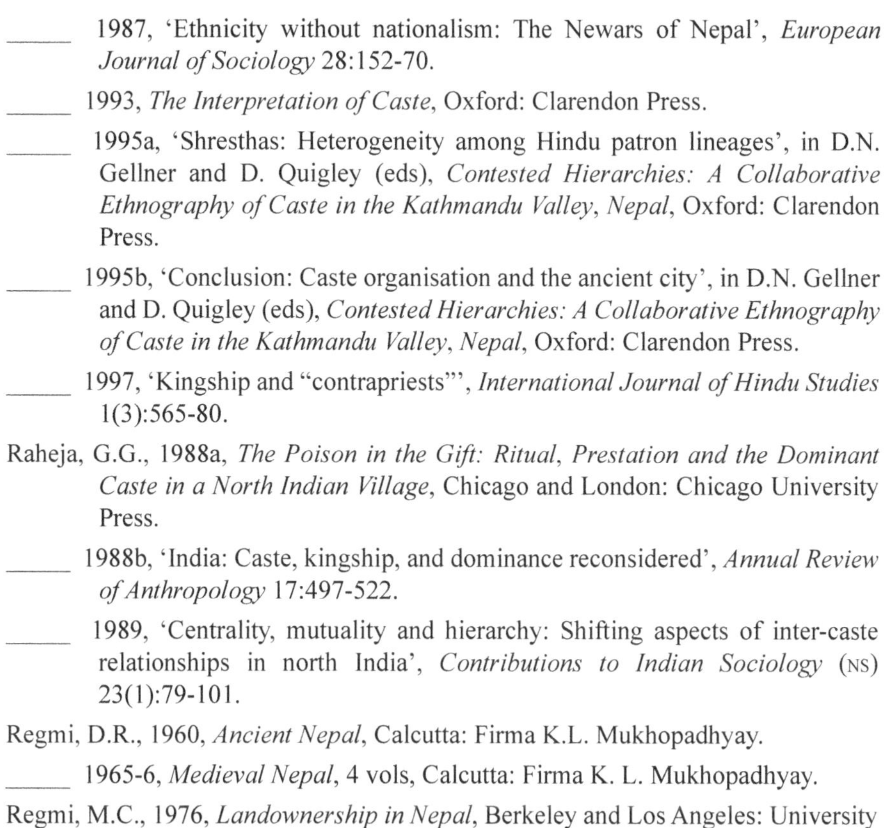

_____ 1987, 'Ethnicity without nationalism: The Newars of Nepal', *European Journal of Sociology* 28:152-70.

_____ 1993, *The Interpretation of Caste*, Oxford: Clarendon Press.

_____ 1995a, 'Shresthas: Heterogeneity among Hindu patron lineages', in D.N. Gellner and D. Quigley (eds), *Contested Hierarchies: A Collaborative Ethnography of Caste in the Kathmandu Valley, Nepal*, Oxford: Clarendon Press.

_____ 1995b, 'Conclusion: Caste organisation and the ancient city', in D.N. Gellner and D. Quigley (eds), *Contested Hierarchies: A Collaborative Ethnography of Caste in the Kathmandu Valley, Nepal*, Oxford: Clarendon Press.

_____ 1997, 'Kingship and "contrapriests"', *International Journal of Hindu Studies* 1(3):565-80.

Raheja, G.G., 1988a, *The Poison in the Gift: Ritual, Prestation and the Dominant Caste in a North Indian Village*, Chicago and London: Chicago University Press.

_____ 1988b, 'India: Caste, kingship, and dominance reconsidered', *Annual Review of Anthropology* 17:497-522.

_____ 1989, 'Centrality, mutuality and hierarchy: Shifting aspects of inter-caste relationships in north India', *Contributions to Indian Sociology* (NS) 23(1):79-101.

Regmi, D.R., 1960, *Ancient Nepal*, Calcutta: Firma K.L. Mukhopadhyay.

_____ 1965-6, *Medieval Nepal*, 4 vols, Calcutta: Firma K. L. Mukhopadhyay.

Regmi, M.C., 1976, *Landownership in Nepal*, Berkeley and Los Angeles: University of California Press.

Rosser, C., 1966, 'Social mobility in the Newar caste system', in C. von Fürer-Haimendorf (ed.), *Caste and Kin in Nepal, India and Ceylon*, Bombay: Asia Publishing House.

Said, E.W., 1994, *Orientalism*, New York: Vintage Books (first published in 1979; revised, updated and reprinted in the OUP, *School Atlas for Nepal*, New Delhi: Oxford University Press, 1997).

Sekler, E.F., 1987, 'Urban design at Patan Durbar Square: A preliminary inquiry', in N. Gutschow and A. Michaels (eds), *Heritage of the Kathmandu Valley*, Nepalica 4, Sankt Augustin: VGH Wissenschaftsverlag.

Shakespeare, Wm, 1994, *As You Like It*, London: Penguin Popular Classics.

Sharma, B.K., 1999, *The Origin of Caste System in Hinduism and its Relevance in the Present Context*, Delhi: Indian Society for the Propagation of Christian Knowledge.

Sharma, D.R., 1996, 'A note of the historical and cultural significance of Vajrayogini of Sãkhu', Contributions to Nepalese Studies 23(1):271-83.

Sharma, P.R., 1978, 'Nepal: Hindu-tribal interface', *Contributions to Nepalese Studies* 6:1-14.

_____ 1983, 'The land system of the Licchavis of Nepal', *Kailash–Journal of Himalayan Studies* 10:11-62.

Shepard, J.W., 1985, *Symbolic Space in Newar Culture*, Ph.D. dissertation, University of Michigan.

Shrestha, C.B. and U.M. Malla, 1971, 'Urban centres of the Kathmandu Valley', *The Himalayan Review* 4:33-39.

Singer, M. and B. S. Cohn (eds), 1968, *Structure and Change in Indian Society*, Chicago: Aldine.

Slusser, M.S., 1976, 'On the antiquity of Nepalese metal-craft', *Archives Asian Art* 39:80-95.

_____ 1998 (1982), *Nepal Mandala: A Cultural Study of the Kathmandu Valley*, 2 vols, reprint edition, Kathmandu: Mandala Book Point (originally published Princeton, NJ: Princeton University Press).

Sresthacarya, I., 1977, 'Newari kinship terms in the light of kinship typology', *Contributions to Nepalese Studies* 4:111-28.

Srinivas, M.N., 1952, *Religion and Society among the Coorgs of South India*, Oxford: Clarendon Press.

_____ 1956, 'Industrialization and urbanization of Rural Areas', in 'Symposium on Rural-Urban Relations', *Sociological Bulletin* 5:2.

_____ 1998 (1996), *Village, Caste, Gender and Method: Essays in Indian Social Anthropology*, Delhi: Oxford University Press.

Stoddard, R.H., 1979, 'Perceptions about the geography of religious sites in the Kathmandu Valley', *Contributions to Nepalese Studies* 7(1-2):97-118.

Tamot, K. and I. Alsop, 1996, 'A Kushan-period sculpture from the reign of Jaya Varma–AD 185, Kathmandu, Nepal', *Asian Arts* (July 10, 1996) [http://webart.com/asianart/article/jaya/index.html].

Tamot, R., 1995, *The Indigenous Craftsmen Subjected to the Domination of Industrial Capitalism: An Anthropological Case Study of the Craftsmen of Taksar*, Masters Thesis, Tribhuvan University, Nepal.

Thapa, S., 1995, 'Human development and the ethnic population sub-groups in the 75 districts in Nepal', *Contributions to Nepalese Studies* 22(2):181-92.

Tod, J., 1914 (1829), *Annals and Antiquities of Rajast'han*, vol. 1, London: Routledge.

Toffin, G., 1975a, 'Etudes sur les Newar de la Vallée de Kathmandou: Guthi, funérailles et castes', *L'Ethnographie* 70:206-25. (French)

_____ 1975b, 'Jãko: A Newar family ceremony', *Contributions to Nepalese Studies* 2(1):47-56.

_____ 1976, 'La *Si Ka Bheay*, "Festin de la Tête", chez les Newar', *Kailash–Journal of Himalayan Studies* 4:329-38. (French)

_____ 1977, *Pyangaon: une communauté néwar de la vallée de Kathmandou: la vie matérielle*, Paris: CNRS (National Centre for Scientific Research). (French)

_____ 1978, 'L 'Organisation socialle et religieuse d'une communauté néwar (Népal)', *L'Homme* 18(1-2):109-34. (French)

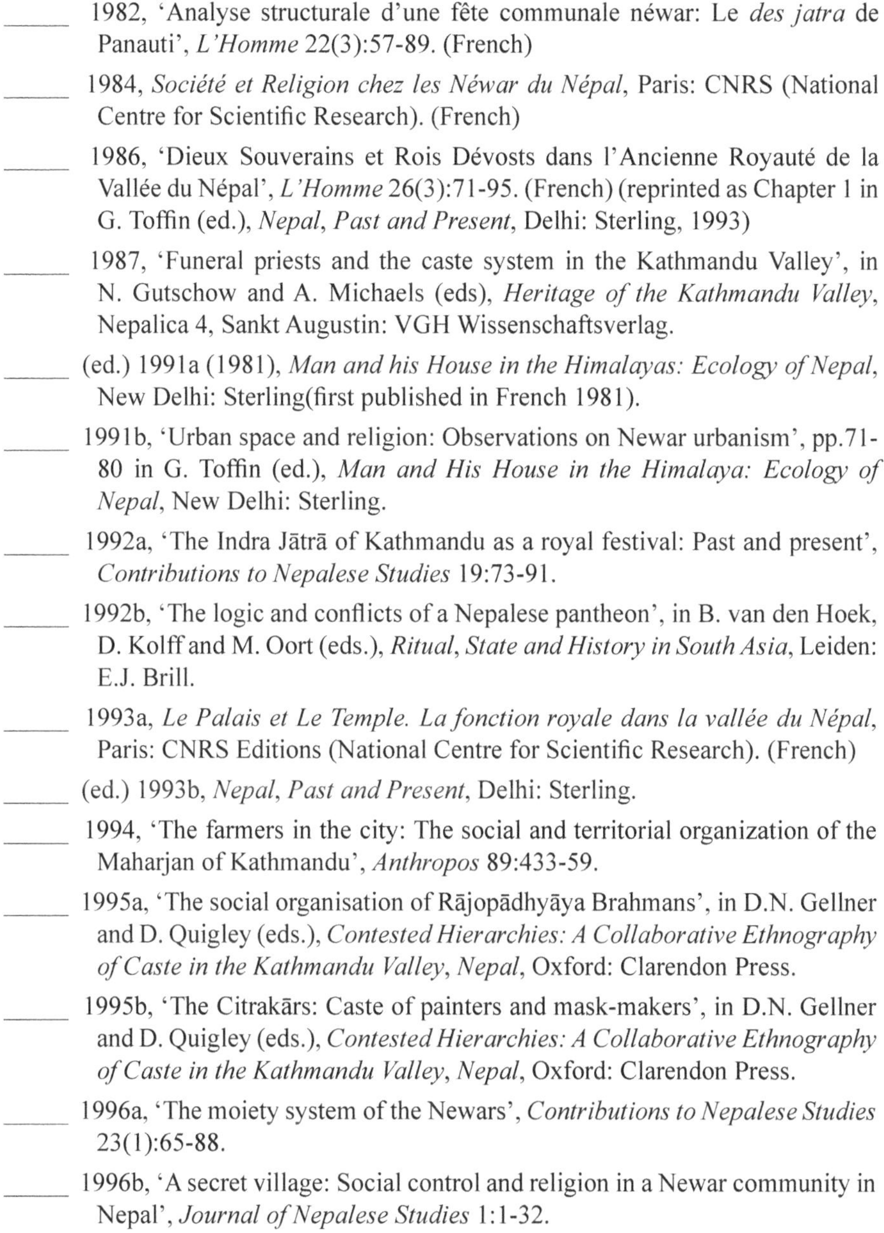

_____ 1982, 'Analyse structurale d'une fête communale néwar: Le *des jatra* de Panauti', *L'Homme* 22(3):57-89. (French)

_____ 1984, *Société et Religion chez les Néwar du Népal*, Paris: CNRS (National Centre for Scientific Research). (French)

_____ 1986, 'Dieux Souverains et Rois Dévosts dans l'Ancienne Royauté de la Vallée du Népal', *L'Homme* 26(3):71-95. (French) (reprinted as Chapter 1 in G. Toffin (ed.), *Nepal, Past and Present*, Delhi: Sterling, 1993)

_____ 1987, 'Funeral priests and the caste system in the Kathmandu Valley', in N. Gutschow and A. Michaels (eds), *Heritage of the Kathmandu Valley*, Nepalica 4, Sankt Augustin: VGH Wissenschaftsverlag.

_____ (ed.) 1991a (1981), *Man and his House in the Himalayas: Ecology of Nepal*, New Delhi: Sterling(first published in French 1981).

_____ 1991b, 'Urban space and religion: Observations on Newar urbanism', pp.71-80 in G. Toffin (ed.), *Man and His House in the Himalaya: Ecology of Nepal*, New Delhi: Sterling.

_____ 1992a, 'The Indra Jātrā of Kathmandu as a royal festival: Past and present', *Contributions to Nepalese Studies* 19:73-91.

_____ 1992b, 'The logic and conflicts of a Nepalese pantheon', in B. van den Hoek, D. Kolff and M. Oort (eds.), *Ritual, State and History in South Asia*, Leiden: E.J. Brill.

_____ 1993a, *Le Palais et Le Temple. La fonction royale dans la vallée du Népal*, Paris: CNRS Editions (National Centre for Scientific Research). (French)

_____ (ed.) 1993b, *Nepal, Past and Present*, Delhi: Sterling.

_____ 1994, 'The farmers in the city: The social and territorial organization of the Maharjan of Kathmandu', *Anthropos* 89:433-59.

_____ 1995a, 'The social organisation of Rājopādhyāya Brahmans', in D.N. Gellner and D. Quigley (eds.), *Contested Hierarchies: A Collaborative Ethnography of Caste in the Kathmandu Valley, Nepal*, Oxford: Clarendon Press.

_____ 1995b, 'The Citrakārs: Caste of painters and mask-makers', in D.N. Gellner and D. Quigley (eds.), *Contested Hierarchies: A Collaborative Ethnography of Caste in the Kathmandu Valley, Nepal*, Oxford: Clarendon Press.

_____ 1996a, 'The moiety system of the Newars', *Contributions to Nepalese Studies* 23(1):65-88.

_____ 1996b, 'A secret village: Social control and religion in a Newar community in Nepal', *Journal of Nepalese Studies* 1:1-32.

Toffin, G., V. Barré, L. Berger and P. Berger, 1991, 'The Pode house: A caste of Newar fishermen', in G. Toffin (ed.), *Man and His House in the Himalaya: Ecology of Nepal*, New Delhi: Sterling.

Treu, M.G., 1993, 'A translation of Lakshmi Prasad Devakota's "The fifteenth of the month of Asadha"', *Contributions to Nepalese Studies* 20:2.

Vaidya, Karunakar, 1986, *Buddhist Traditions and Culture of the Kathmandu Valley (Nepal)*, Kathmandu: Sajha.

Vajracarya, Dhanavajra, 1987, 'The development of early and medieval settlements in the Kathmandu Valley: A review of the inscriptional evidence', in N. Gutschow and A. Michaels (eds), *Heritage of the Kathmandu Valley*, Nepalica 4, Sankt Augustin: VGH Wissenschaftsverlag.

Veer, P. van der, 1988, *Gods on Earth: The Management of Religious Experience and Identity in a North Indian Pilgrimage Centre*, London: Athlone.

Vergati, A., 1979, 'Une Divinité lignagère des Néwar: Digu-dyo' *BEFEO* 66: 115-27 (reprinted as Ch. 2 in A. Vergati, *Gods, Men and Territory : Society and Culture in Kathmandu Valley*, New Delhi: Manohar, 1995).

_____ 1995, *Gods, Men and Territory: Society and Culture in Kathmandu Valley*, New Delhi: Manohar.

Weber, M., 1958, *The Religion of India* (translated and edited by H.H. Gerth and D. Martindale), New York: Free Press.

Webster, P., 1981, 'To plough or not to plough? A Newar dilemma: taboo and technology in the Kathmandu Valley, Nepal', *Pacific Viewpoint* 22(2):99-135.

_____ 1983, 'Peasants and landlords: Land tenure in the Kathmandu Valley, Nepal', *Pacific Viewpoint* 24(2):140-66.

_____ 1987, 'Bolajya–The social organisation of labour amongst the Newars of the Kathmandu Valley', in N. Gutschow and A. Michaels (eds), *Heritage of the Kathmandu Valley*, Nepalica 4, Sankt Augustin: VGH Wissenschaftsverlag.

Wiser, W.H., 1936, *The Hindu Jajmāni System*, Lucknow: Lucknow Publishing House.

Witzel, M., 1992, 'Meaningful ritual: Structure, development and interpretation of the Tantric Agnihotra ritual of Nepal', in B. van den Hoek, D. Kolff and M. Oort (eds), *Ritual, State and History in South Asia*, Leiden: E.J. Brill.

_____ 1997, 'Macrocosm, mesocosm, and microcosm: The persistent nature of 'Hindu' beliefs and symbolic forms', *International Journal of Hindu Studies* 1(3):501-39.

Wright, D. (ed.), 1993 (1877), *History of Nepal* (translation of the Nepali *Buddhist Vamshāvali* Munshi Shew Shanker Singh and Pandit Shri Gunanand), New Delhi and Madras: Asian Educational Services.

Zanen, S.M., 1986, 'The goddess Vajrayogini and the kingdom of Sankhu (Nepal)', *Purusartha* 10:125-66.

Index[1]

[1] Page numbers in italics indicate location of primary references or definitions of key terms.

M

About the Author

After studying Geology at Aberystwyth, Mark Pickett journeyed to South Asia, where for twenty years he was involved in evangelism, Bible teaching, leadership training, research, writing, and publishing, principally in Nepal and India. Nepal's Tribhuvan University awarded him the PhD for his study of the Newar people of the Kathmandu Valley, the work on which the current volume is based. Married to Becky from the USA, Mark enjoys playing with his five children, climbing mountains and listening to music, and misses buffalo curry. Dr. Pickett is currently Undergraduate Programmes Leader, Wales Evangelical School of Theology, UK.

www.ingramcontent.com/pod-product-compliance
Lightning Source LLC
Chambersburg PA
CBHW030906270326
41929CB00008B/595

* 9 7 8 9 7 4 5 2 4 1 3 6 7 *